England's Landscape

The South East

Collins

England's Landscape

The South East

BRIAN SHORT

SERIES EDITOR NEIL COSSONS

ENGLISH HERITAGE

First published in 2006 by Collins, an imprint of
HarperCollins*Publishers*
77–85 Fulham Palace Road, London W6 8JB

www.collins.co.uk

10 9 8 7 6 5 4 3 2 1
10 09 08 07 06

ISBN 10 – 0 00 715570 0
ISBN 13 – 9 78 0 00 715570 5

British Library Cataloguing in Publication Data
A CIP catalogue record for this book is available from the
British Library.

Map on previous page:
The regions: the red lines bound the general area covered by
each volume.

Author's Acknowledgements
I wish particularly to thank the following for their help and
support during the production of this book: for help and advice
with illustrations or other queries I thank Caroline Benson
(Museum of English Rural Life, Reading), Dr John Chapman
(University of Portsmouth), Julie Cochrane (Museum of
London), Howard Doble (London Metropolitan Archives),
Alasdair Grant (DEFRA), Professor Dennis Hardy (Middlesex
University), Janina Holubecki (High Weald Research Unit),
Chris Lacey (National Trust), Graham Leeson, Michael
Marshman (County Local Studies Librarian, Trowbridge,
Wiltshire), Emma O'Connor (Sussex Archaeological Society),
Tamzin Phoenix (Bridgeman Art Library), Dr Janet Waymark
(Birkbeck College) and Peter Wilkinson (West Sussex Record
Office). Colleagues at Sussex University have also helped greatly
in the production of this book: Dr Julian Murton and Dr
Danielle Schreve (Royal Holloway) commented on Table 2.1;
and Evelyn Dodds, Hazel Lintott, Geoffrey Mead, Rebecca
Powell-Tuck, Susan Rowland and Martin Wingfield, have given
great support. At English Heritage, I am deeply grateful to Adele
Campbell, Martin Cherry, Steve Cole, Damien Grady, Graham
Fairclough (who commented on the text), Val Horsler, and
Alyson Rogers. And I am grateful also to all others involved in
the production of the volume including the indefatigable picture
researchers, Julia Harris-Voss and Jo Walton; Rob Read who
constructed the maps and diagrams; and Rowan Whimster and
David Price-Goodfellow for their editorial and design work.

And not least my thanks go to Valerie, with whom I have
travelled over most of this region during the past 25 years.

ACKNOWLEDGEMENTS

SERIES EDITOR
Sir Neil Cossons OBE
Chairman, English Heritage
President, Royal Geographical Society
The series editor would like to acknowledge the contribution of
the following people:

EDITORIAL BOARD:
Professor David Cannadine
Queen Elizabeth the Queen Mother Professor of British History,
University of London

Professor Barry Cunliffe
Professor of European Archaeology, University of Oxford

Professor Richard Lawton
Professor Emeritus, Department of Geography, University of
Liverpool

Professor Brian K Roberts
Professor Emeritus, Department of Geography, University of Durham

ENGLISH HERITAGE EXECUTIVE EDITORS:
Dr Paul Barnwell, *Head of Medieval and Later Rural Research*
Dr Martin Cherry, *Former Chief Buildings Historian*
Humphrey Welfare, *Northern Territory Director*
Graham Fairclough, *Head of Characterisation*

ENGLISH HERITAGE PROJECT MANAGERS:
Val Horsler, *former Head of Publishing*
Adele Campbell, *Commercial Publishing Manager*

All new ground and air photography was taken specifically for
this series. Thanks to: Damian Grady, Senior Investigator of
English Heritage Aerial Survey and Investigation Team, and to the
photographic and dark-room teams in Swindon; Steve Cole,
Head of Photography, and the staff of the English Heritage
Photography team. Archive material from the National
Monuments Record was researched by the Enquiry and Research
Services teams led by Alyson Rogers (Buildings) and Lindsay
Jones (Archaeology/Air Photos). Graphics lists were managed by
John Vallender and Bernard Thomason. Graphics were produced
under the management of Rob Read of 3's Company
(Consultancy) Ltd, by John Hodgson and Drew Smith. All other
images were researched by Jo Walton and Julia Harris-Voss.

Publisher & Commissioning Editor Myles Archibald
Production Director Graham Cook
Edited by Rowan Whimster
Designed by D & N Publishing, Hungerford, Berkshire
Indexed by Sheila Seacroft

Printed in Italy by LEGO SpA, Vicenza

Contents

PART III: LANDSCAPES AND THE CREATIVE IMAGINATION

Foreword

The landscape of England evokes intense passion and profound emotion. This most loved of places, the inspiration for generations of writers, poets and artists, it is at once both the source of the nation's infatuation and the setting for grievous misunderstanding. For people who visit, the view of England offers some of their most lasting images. For exiles abroad the memory of the English landscape sustains their beliefs and desire for a homecoming.

But for those who live in England the obsession is double edged. On the one hand we cherish the unchanging atmosphere of a familiar place, and on the other make impossible demands of it, believing that it will always accommodate, always forgive. Only in the last half century or so have we started to recognise the extreme fragility of all that we value in the English landscape, to appreciate that it is not only the metaphor for who we are as a people but that it represents one of our most vivid contributions to a wider culture. At last we are beginning to realise that a deeper understanding of its subtle appeal and elusive character is the key to a thoughtful approach to its future.

The unique character of England's landscape derives from many things. But nowhere is the impact of human intervention absent. If geology and topography set the scene, it is the implacable persistence of generations who since the end of the Ice Age have sought to live in and off this place that has created the singular qualities of the landscape we have today. Not, of course, that the landscape before people was in any sense a static thing; on the contrary, the environment untouched by mankind was and is a dynamic and constantly changing synthesis. Every layer of that complex progression can still be found somewhere, making its own peculiar contribution to the distinctiveness of today's England. It is a compelling narrative. Through this series of regional studies our distinguished contributors – as authors and editors – have distilled something of what has created today's England, in order to decode that narrative.

Unique is an overused term. But it has a special resonance for the landscape of England, both urban and rural. What we hope readers of this series will begin to feel is the nature of the qualities that define the English landscape. Much of that landscape has of course been inherited from cultures overseas as conquest and migration brought here peoples who have progressively occupied and settled Britain. They created what might be called our shared landscapes, defined as much by what links them to the wider world as through any intrinsically native characteristics. The peoples whose common bonds stretched along the Atlantic seaboard have left a legacy in Cornwall more akin to parts of north-west France or Spain than to anywhere else in England. There are Roman roads and cities and medieval field systems that have their closest parallels in the European plains from whence they derived. Great abbeys and monasteries reflected in their art and architecture, their commerce and industry, a culture whose momentum lay outside these islands. And when disaster came it was a pan-European epidemic, the Black Death, that took away between a third and a half of the people. England's are not the only deserted medieval villages.

And yet, paradoxically, much of what today we would recognise as the quintessential England is only some two or three centuries old. Parliamentary enclosure, especially of the English lowlands, was itself a reaction to an even greater economic force – industrialisation, and the urbanisation that went with it. It has given us a rural landscape that epitomises the essence of Englishness in the minds of many. The fields and hedgerows surrounding the nucleated villages of the pre-existing medieval landscape are of course quite new when set against the timescale of human occupation. Indeed, when the first railways came through there remained, here and there, open fields where the rows of new hawthorn hedges were still feeble whips scribing lines across a thousand years of feudal landscape.

As Britain emerged to become the world's first industrial nation its astonishing transformation was at its most visible in the landscape, something new, indigenous and without precedent. It fuelled the debate on the picturesque and the sublime and was a source of wonder to those who visited from overseas. But in its urban and industrial excesses it soon came to be detested, by aesthetes, social commentators and a burgeoning class opposed to the horrors of industrial capitalism. What was perhaps the most decisive contribution of Britain to the human race provoked a powerful counteraction reflected in the writings of Ruskin, Morris, Octavia Hill and the Webbs. It was this anguish that a century ago energised the spirit of conservation in a growing band of people determined to capture what was left of the pre-industrial rural scene.

Today the landscape of England is, as ever, undergoing immense change. But, unlike the centuries just past, that change once again draws its energy and inspiration from forces overseas. A new form of global economy, North American in flavour, concept and style carries all before it. The implications for the long term future of the landscape and the people who live in it are difficult to predict. The out-of-town shopping mall, the great encampments of distribution warehouses crouching like so many armadillos across the rural shires, the growth of exurbia – that mixed-use land between city and country that owes nothing to either – are all manifestations of these new economic forces. Like the changes that have gone before they have become the subject of intense debate and the source of worrying uncertainty. But what is clear is that a deeper understanding of the landscape, in all its manifestations, offers a means of managing change in a conscious and thoughtful manner.

This was the inspiration that led to this new regional landscape series. To understand the language of landscape, to be able to interpret the way in which people make places, offers insights and enjoyment beyond the ordinary. It enables us to experience that most neglected of human emotions, a sense of place. These books set out to reveal the values that underwrite our sense of place, by offering an insight into how the landscape of England came to be the way it is. If understanding is the key to valuing and valuing is the key to caring then these books may help to ensure that we can understand and enjoy the best of what we have and that when we make our own contribution to change it will not only reinforce that essential distinctiveness but improve the quality of life of those who live there.

Neil Cossons

1

The Tapestry of Landscape and Its Threads

LANDSCAPE

This book is about the landscape of south-east England seen from the viewpoint of a landscape historian and geographer. It covers a large region of great diversity and richness whose landscape can be seen in a vast multiplicity of ways. It has also been a difficult book to write. No two people perceive any landscape, however small, in the same way and all will be influenced in their perceptions by the associated sounds and smells, the state of the weather, and their own inner state and ideology. This volume is not the place to consider such issues in depth, but they will inevitably surface from time to time as we explore the landscape of such a complex region.

Let us begin with a question. Is landscape merely a stage upon which history unfolds, influencing the twists of time through accidents of topography? Or is it something deeper, entering into the hearts of people and into their cultures to forge an unbreakable connection between themselves and the land? Landscape is certainly important in many conceptualisations of the past: it raises deeply significant issues of individual and social activity, of objective and subjective knowing, of idealist or materialist explanation. People themselves are thus part of landscape history – unless we deliberately abstract them from the view and from their material creations so as to concentrate upon the land itself.

Landscape history is deceitful. It offers the prospect of revealing the history of the landscape but may hide the fact that the landscape we see, hear, touch and smell cannot be reduced to the written word. Words can never have a one-to-one correspondence with what is 'out there', and we do not have the appropriate language or mental capacity to set down in writing, word after word and line after line, all that we sense in the landscape itself. We fall back on assumptions, clichés, and a socially constructed 'common sense' that actually may not be 'common' at all. We could use visual representations, but if so the priorities of the artist, the positioning of the photographer or the emphasis of the film-maker need to be acknowledged.

Landscape history is also difficult. Any area of land reflects the needs and desires of its inhabitants, who inherit it, change it to suit their purposes and then pass it on to the next generation. Landscape is therefore always moving on; not static but always in flux, with different aspects and areas changing faster or more slowly than others. Landscapes are also cumulative, and older landscapes may never quite die – as Gillian Tindall saw carved on a door lintel of an otherwise unremarkable Kentish Town terraced house 'The fields lie sleeping Underneath'.[1] They have sometimes changed abruptly, as in the Fire of London or the Blitz, or imperceptibly and over huge expanses of time. Furthermore, the accepted chronologies of political, cultural or social history do not necessarily offer a secure framework within which to operate.

To add to the complexity, there is the problem of what precisely we mean by 'landscape'. How does it differ from concepts such as 'scenery', 'physical surroundings', 'the view', 'environment' or 'nature'? Is it, as the art historian and critical theorist W J T Mitchell suggests, 'an appreciation of a total gestalt, a vista or scene that may be dominated by some specific feature, but is not simply reducible to that feature'?[2] Is it only a landscape if we can withdraw from it ourselves and have the leisure to see? As Raymond Williams has it, 'a working country is hardly ever a landscape. The very idea of landscape implies separation and observation.'[3] The word 'landscape' in its current normal usage emerged in the Renaissance and denoted a new consciously imagined separation between humans and their environment. At the same time came the invention of linear perspective in painting that allowed three-dimensional scenes to be rendered on canvas. Poetry, drama and garden design all shared the idea of landscape, and the place of the human spirit within it.

Landscape therefore has a problematic status that makes landscape history all the more fascinating. It follows that the attempt to offer a landscape history of south-east England must, by the nature of the enterprise, be partial, and it must be an interpretation based upon bringing selected elements of a landscape together as an ensemble that can then be investigated historically. Since every landscape is infused with centuries of human history – to quote Fay Weldon's *Letters to Alice on first reading Jane Austen* (1984) 'every acre observed, considered, valued, reckoned, pondered over, owned, bought, sold, hedged' – no pretence at total inclusivity can be offered.[4] An account of the evolution of the region's landscape structures will therefore inevitably include gaps, and perhaps it must remain sufficient to state pragmatically that 'landscape' will here consist of all the urban, suburban and rural components of the South East, whether with strong or weak human presences, as well as any significant features, such as individual buildings, that lie within them.

One way to mitigate this difficulty is to begin by developing some thematic analyses – the threads that hold together the tapestry – to help guide us through time and over the space of the South East.

LANDSCAPES OF POWER AND CONTROL

Human landscapes arise through purposeful action being exerted onto a pre-existing setting. Although contingent and serendipitous forces also modify places, we can generally demonstrate that landscapes are not just 'out there' to be seen at face value, but that they also have meaning. They are the outcome of striving, planning, war, farming and so on, comprising an ensemble of material and social practices and the symbolic representations of a society that is demonstrating its concerns, presence or power structures. Sometimes the original meaning of the landscape symbol seems to remain clear to us; sometimes, as at Stonehenge, we must hypothesise in the absence of a decipherable record.

One important thread running through this book is therefore the fact that landscapes signify something to their inhabitants and visitors and are instruments of cultural power, naturalising cultural or social relations. Landscape is ideological, both in physical creation and in perception, and it thereby acquires meaning and can be 'read' as the outcome of particular activities, such as enclosure, suburban development, reclamation or what Schumpeter referred to as the 'creative destruction' inherent within capitalism, seen clearly in the urban redevelopment process.[5] Such landscapes also contain iconographic elements that are intended to speak to larger issues, material features that symbolise non-material concepts, such as the parish church with its particular structures, or the great country house or palace with its ornamentation and surrounding controlled space.

The concept of power and control is, of course, utterly familiar to us in its historical, sociological or economic guises. But one theme that will emerge throughout this book is that many of the region's landscapes also represent power and control over people, resources and space. A large-scale landscape change requires the marshalling of resources and people, and many landscapes offer warnings of power or signs of security. Most obvious perhaps are the many military landscapes: Dover Castle's grim presence on the chalk cliffs to deter would-be invaders, Salisbury Plain's mass expropriation of land for military training, Greenham and the other Cold War landscapes. Military symbols frequently had other functions of course: Windsor Castle was also a royal residence, and many have since become 'heritage' sites or museums. Minor lords and magnates took up the theme and used battlements and moats to give fortified appearances to their residences. Indeed, the theme of power runs throughout the human chronology of settlement in the region, from prehistory to the pillboxes and half-remembered landscapes of the Second World War. The Church, too, exercised its control over thought and lives through the landscape symbolism of its great abbeys and minsters and the castellation of their gatehouses and cathedral closes, or perhaps most potently through the towers of more humble parish churches.[6] The church institutions also had the ability to plan landscapes in ways not open to villagers. The extensive systems of drainage channels on Romney Marsh, for example, illustrate the control of the cathedral community at Canterbury.

Power and status have been written into the landscape in a variety of settings within the South East. Although there were many ways in which elite power could be contested by the community, within the South East it was manifest in control over territory. Thus we have the creation of Stonehenge; Avebury and its surrounding landscape; the medieval royal hunting forests, the relict landscapes of which survive in the New Forest and Epping; the replanning of medieval villages and their fields; or the establishment and maintenance of deer parks. Enclosure landscapes show the power of individuals to take over common spaces for 'improvement', sometimes resulting in the dislocation of homes and livelihoods of poorer families. Later came even more overt displays in the landscape parks around opulent mansions, now withdrawn from the community – for example, Penshurst (Kent) with its huge hall, parks

Fig. 1.1 The entrance to the Drax estate at Charborough Park, Dorset. *The stag has five legs, because the view from the house seemed only to offer three, so another leg was inserted! The Stag Gate into the Drax estate, together with the very long wall surrounding Charborough Park (part of which is seen to the left of the gate) which resulted from the turnpike (now the A31) being diverted away from Charborough House, conveys the impression of secluded power.*

Figs 1.2–1.4 Great Chart, Kent. *The Neo-Jacobean architectural style of the Toke family's 'close' village, near Ashford, is all-pervasive, and can be seen in Fig. 1.2, Godinton House (above left); Fig. 1.3, the vernacular architecture of the village housing (below); and Fig. 1.4, the almshouses (above right). The family also dominates the memorials inside the parish church.*

surrounded by prohibitory high walls, or the use of family emblems over gateways and other exclusionist symbols (Fig. 1.1).

By the 18th century the power of the great landowners over much of the South East was considerable, many being Members of Parliament as well as serving as local JPs and holding the advowsons to their parish churches. The cultural importance of landed property was now at its height, and was displayed especially in the chalklands of the region where there had been a long history of consolidation on these more marginal chalky soils. In villages dominated by one landowner the architecture of cottages, farm buildings, almshouses and schools might involve a uniform design and colour, complete with family crest or other emblem, to be decoded appropriately by residents and visitors alike. In such 'close' communities one family might also dominate the memorials inside the parish church, demonstrating through tombs, brasses, stained-glass windows and family mortuary chapels the family's dynastic credentials (Figs 1.2–1.4).

Landscape may not belong to any one person in the South East, being a common good unlike the land itself, but nevertheless it was (and still is) assimilated into local power relations. Indeed, landscape is the very medium through which this power is projected, making all best use of the seeming naturalness of a country scene. Appeals to the past were common, and great houses were built in earlier styles, such as the fashionable 19th-century Gothic at Ashridge or Knebworth House (Hertfordshire), the latter incorporating genuine medieval remains. In addition, we might notice that the 'naturalness' of the great landscape parks of the 18th and 19th centuries, fashioned without real practical purpose but as ostentatious displays of wealth, sometimes entailed the wholesale removal of the pre-existing village with its lack of aesthetic appeal. At Stanmer, in Sussex, the village opposite the manor house was moved out of sight from the house to beyond the church and set down as a neat row of cottages. In Hampshire more than half the parks and gardens contain village earthworks or an isolated church, and the majority of these features probably result from emparking. In some cases the power of the landowner resulted in the creation of a model village, to a specified romanticised design reflecting an ideal organic community within a wider landscape, which bestowed status on the owner. Examples include the Earl of Dorchester's late 18th-century Milton Abbas (Dorset) or Angela Burdett-Coutts's Victorian-fantasy Holly Village in Highgate, with Gothic cottages for her servants built around communal green lawns. As late as 1917 Ardeley (Herts) was built with thatched cottages around a small green. Nor were churches immune from the display of power. The parish church at Stanmer was gothicised in the 1830s, and at West Wycombe (Bucks) the extraordinary building within Iron Age earthworks had classical windows, a tower surmounted with a golden ball inside which were seats, and a massive mausoleum, thanks to Sir Francis Dashwood.[7]

To the private symbolism of power can be added examples of state control, for instance within the prison or the poorhouse, whose authoritarian architectures enabled the local state to direct the lives of those powerless and unfortunate enough to be housed there. Purpose-built prisons, with or without the central 'panopticon' for surveying the site conceived by Jeremy Bentham, sprang up at the edges of country towns or within London, while the grim workhouses built after the passing of the Poor Law Amendment Act in 1834, often termed 'bastilles', had their own architectural starkness (Fig. 1.5). The use of such buildings and their very presence in the landscape were designed to elicit appropriate behaviour, which has since become cemented into our consciousness. Even the Victorian urban park had its codes of behaviour, to which most of us still conform implicitly in their mown lawns, flower beds, trees and ponds. But the Victorian park was also part of a desire for social control over public order in the cities, and so represents ideology in a physical and 'natural' shape.

THE SOUTH EAST IN NATIONAL IDENTITY

A second theme within this book arises from the fact that the historical development of Britain has unfolded through an uneven distribution of political, economic and cultural power that has in large measure been focused on the south-east of England, and particularly around London. Here the landscape has received a greater human impact, and has been more manipulated, than anywhere else in Britain. Compared with other regions, therefore, there are more landscapes of conspicuous consumption – landscape parks or large country houses – and a greater number of symbolic buildings and nationally important monuments, especially in the capital. In a suggested 'top twenty' of England's greatest houses, nine were located in the South East.[8] Power can certainly be displayed iconographically within the urban settings of the South East. The City of London is replete with historical and contemporary trophy buildings for the display of institutional wealth and prestige.

The cultural importance of the region's landscape to ideas of national identity cannot be overemphasised. The historian Martin Wiener attempted to demonstrate that a 'Southern metaphor' had triumphed over a Northern one, such that northern industrialists of the Victorian period had re-invested, not in their factories and businesses, but rather in conspicuous consumption of large southern houses and grounds – attempting in the process to gain cultural capital and social standing. The existence of a north–south divide is one that has exercised many scholars (and politicians) for some time. Although Wiener's thesis has been criticised for its over-simplistic analysis, there is support from

Fig. 1.5 The workhouse. *The ward block, built in 1898–9 to accommodate the aged and infirm, imbeciles and lunatics of St Marylebone Workhouse on Baker Street, London. The block was demolished in 1966 to make way for a new building, part of what is now the University of Westminster.*

Alun Howkins, who proposed similarly that the late-Victorian and Edwardian 'South Country' exerted a tremendous force, offering an iconic image of nationhood, for which troops would die in Flanders and, indeed, for which sacrifices were made again in 1939–45.[9]

In these images it was the landscape of the South East, and especially the village, farmland and chalk countryside of Kent and Sussex, which was promoted – often the last view that departing troops or airmen might have of England (Fig. 1.6). The recognition of the propaganda power behind these landscapes was clearly a critical factor in the success of maintaining morale and enhancing patriotic spirit during times of national crisis. During the Second World War the South East was often loosely referred to as 'the Home Counties', a term that was current by the end of the 19th century and that has entered into common usage. There is no precise geographical location for this 'home', which generally implies those counties bordering on London, and to many the term is a sign of a London-centric bias within Britain. But threats to home were real at the time, and the landscape invocation was prominent.

Fig. 1.6 'Your Britain. Fight for it Now!' – Frank Newbould's 1942 depiction of the downland. This was England – the 'South Country' – although this iconic landscape may not have held the same fascination for British fighters from the far north and west of the British Isles.

GATEWAY TO THE WORLD

The complexity of the South East is also revealed in the region's links with overseas territories. It could look both inward and outward, and this too provides a context for understanding the landscape. The connection with overseas profits has a long history, and the links between the early colonies, the later British Empire and south-east England would repay more detailed investigation. The profits from slave-based plantations underscored polite society in the region – the Bertram family in Jane Austen's *Mansfield Park* comes to mind. Certainly the profits from slave-based plantations have been recycled into country mansions: the Fullers of Brightling (Sussex) built their wealden residence on the profits – at least in part – from Jamaican sugar plantations, and the Drax family from Charborough Park (*see* Fig. 1.1) built the 17th-century Drax House on Barbados similarly on the proceeds from sugar.[10] London was the main slaving port for south-east England and from 1672 to 1698 the London-based Royal African Company was the only one allowed to trade with Africa. Up until the 1730s, when London's pre-eminence as the country's leading slave port was toppled by Bristol, merchant wealth steadily accumulated and was spent on homes and conspicuous consumption in the region around the capital. The East India and West India Docks in east London were constructed to serve such interests, while merchants and victuallers based in Deal, Portsmouth or Weymouth were also involved in the trade, and would have reinvested in their homes.

Thus London and its regional hinterland sucked in the world's resources, acting seemingly as the gateway to all corners of the Earth. By 1640 huge quantities of tobacco were reaching London from Virginia, and during the 17th century, 90 per cent of Britain's commerce passed through London, its port evolving to cope with the increasing volume of trade (*see* Chapter 7). The Thames, seen in Conrad's *Heart of Darkness* (1902), after all contained 'the dreams of men, the seed of commonwealths, the germs of empires'. For many who worked abroad in colonial offices or commercial situations, especially prior to the late 20th century, this was the landscape to which they dreamt of retiring and investing their savings, thereby reinforcing images of a conservative, middle-class region. From many possible examples, two significant landscape imports are now also part of the daily scene: the Bengali bungalow, with its one storey, thatched roof and veranda, and the rhododendron, popularised from the 18th century and thriving on the region's more acidic soils.

Is there a link between the increased appreciation of domestic landscape and the expansion of political dominance overseas? Mitchell points out that Chinese traditions of landscape flourished most strongly at the height of her imperial power before the 18th century as did those of 17th-century Holland and France and 18th- and 19th-century Britain.[11] Do perceptions of landscape therefore change as a reflection of attitudes to imperialism? In this sense landscape might act as both mirror to the glories of empire but also as an antidote, embellishing the splendours that the imperial homeland also offers. Alexander Pope's poem 'Windsor Forest' sees this south-eastern forest as an emblem of sovereignty, but with the oaks providing the materials for British commercial and naval power. It is now widely agreed that imperialism is a two-way process, whereby the cultures and exoticism of the far reaches of empire are brought home and become fashionable – the transformation of the royal residence at Brighton into the Indian-style Royal Pavilion is a case in point (*see* Fig. 6.5). Kew Gardens was designed as a microcosm of the Empire's landscapes. Such landscapes were in effect part of 'the invention of tradition' by which a sense of identity was created to facilitate the combined rule of both empire and homeland by appealing to a collective memory and implanting selective information. Memory itself was therefore neither inert nor authentic, and landscape was thus again used for political ends in appealing to a desirable past, a national narrative and sense of identity.

LONDON

It would be impossible to convey the richness of the region's landscapes without constant reference to London and its longstanding and almost overwhelming influence on its ever-expanding hinterland. John Seeley's popular *The Expansion of England* (1883) emphasised imperial unity and galvanised public opinion into enthusiasm for empire, and London claimed to be the imperial city, with the jubilee spectacles of 1887 and 1897 reinforcing this theme. The buildings and streets now had to be worthy of that role. London's monuments, grand Whitehall and City buildings for imperial government, trade and finance, and designed spaces, all spoke to a glorious history and global sense of power. Booty was brought back in triumph, such as 'Cleopatra's Needle' commemorating British successes in Egypt. The Port of London headquarters, near the Tower, was built in the early 20th century to symbolise the link between the City and the British seas by a leading imperial architect, Edwin Cooper. In 1901 St Paul's Cathedral was said to be at the centre of 'the world's capital' and

BELOW: *Fig. 1.7* **St Paul's Cathedral during the Blitz, 29 December 1940** *by* **Herbert Mason.** *The landscape impact of war was seen at this time to a far greater degree than before. The imagery of St Paul's in the Blitz was also used in* Britain under Fire *(c. 1940) and Churchill had given instructions that the iconic dome was to be protected at all costs. In June 2004 a poll of 5,000 members of the public declared this to be 'the most inspirational photograph'.*

OPPOSITE PAGE:

Fig. 1.8 **The Albert Memorial, Hyde Park.** *This monument to High Victorian ideals was subject to later criticism. An English Heritage restoration project in 1994–8 succeeded in its aim of re-establishing this as one of the most symbolic and interesting memorials in Britain.*

symbolised imperial might for many, with Lund's painting '*The Heart of the Empire*' (1904) featuring the domed building very prominently. The photograph taken in December 1940 of the dome standing amidst the chaos of the Blitz in turn became a well-known national icon of resistance (Fig. 1.7).

South Kensington was the home of the arts and sciences. Thus we have the Great Exhibition of 1851 with its global reach, in which more than 30 states or groupings of countries filled one end of the Crystal Palace and the United Kingdom and six groups of colonies and dependencies took up the other. It was opened by Victoria on 1 May and by the time it closed in October it had received 6 million visitors. Then there was the *Imperial* Institute (1888–94), later to become the redesigned *Imperial* College but with the Victorian campanile preserved, and perhaps most iconographic of all, the Albert Memorial on the site of the Crystal Palace, beside what is now Kensington Gardens (Fig. 1.8). Here Conrad's 'dark places of the Earth' are made to stand in obeisance to the gilded Prince Albert and thus to Britain. The Gothic, Eurocentric monument was designed in 1862 by George Gilbert Scott and completed in 1876. It faces the Royal Albert Hall (1865–71), another symbol of Victorian pride in this South Kensington area of Imperial 'engrained symbolism'.[12] And as a memorial to Victoria herself, the Mall was modified in 1903 as a grand processional route from Admiralty Arch to her memorial statue (1911) in front of Buckingham Palace. The list of symbolic London monuments and spaces is a long one, and includes the simple Portland Stone Cenotaph by Lutyens (1920) where fallen members of the British Empire and Commonwealth services are commemorated.

As imperial economic, political and cultural splendour declined in the 20th century and gave way to post-colonial constructions – led perhaps by the Regent's Park Mosque (1969–77) with its striking minaret – so, too, did landscape painting give way to abstraction, to the extent that landscape as a subject is now for the amateur, or is kitsch, or is there for what Mitchell calls 'prefabricated emotions'.[13] Both landscape and the empire are now diminished; the meanings of the landscape memorials are contested and have also become objects of protection or nostalgia. In the same way that the writings of Kipling or Baden Powell or the music of Elgar's *Pomp and Circumstance Marches* or *Cockaigne Overture* have been criticised as being redolent of a past imperialism, so too is the landscape redolent of such past connections. Nevertheless, as well as London, there are few townscapes in the South East which do not still prominently display their statue of Victoria or one of her predecessors.

CHANGING PERCEPTIONS

The landscape reflects deeper structures, processes and ideologies that have operated at different times in the past, or which continue to operate. It is a document full of signs to be deciphered, allowing deeper comprehension of the societies that produced the palimpsest we now see around us today. Perhaps nowhere more than in the South East is this document such a rich resource – from Stonehenge to the Swiss Re tower the symbolism is profound, sedimented from the different layers of our past, and awaiting our interpretation. And to repeat the warning, any such interpretation must be provisional and personal. Our 'readings' of the landscape remain multiple and even contested. The example of the multiple readings of Stonehenge illustrate this very clearly. Medieval church and peasant saw what the Saxons called *Stan Hencg* as imbued with magic. By the 17th century the stones were seen as a nuisance and as objects to be broken up or removed (as at Avebury), although vestigial superstitions remained. Inigo Jones was ordered by James I to make a survey and produce an explanation for the monument; John Aubrey, and later William Stukeley, proposed that Stonehenge was Celtic and Druidic; and in the 18th century John Smith of Boscombe proposed that the stones

showed the motions of the heavenly bodies. Clerics, antiquarians and landed gentry all saw the monument in different ways. The wish to appropriate it continued into the near-present when the newly created English Heritage invested in a policy of fencing and museumisation. The National Trust and Ministry of Defence own much of the surrounding land, but modern Druids claim access at the summer solstice, and as New Age Free Festival enthusiasts and travellers converge on the site a battle for the best coping strategy for traffic is waged around them (Fig. 1.9).[14] The landscape 'text' is always being added to, as archaeologists uncover more detail, and our approaches change over time with new theoretical perspectives.

Fig. 1.9 The Free Festival at Stonehenge 1985. This is just one example of the appropriation of the monument by an interest group. The first Free Festival was held during the summer solstice of 1974 and numbers continued to grow, reaching a peak in 1984, when 70,000 people attended the tenth festival on 21 June. In 1985 'the Battle of the Beanfield' followed the banning of such gatherings and the site has since been accessible only under strict supervision.

OTHER THREADS

In acknowledging the importance of representations in our understanding, it is nevertheless vital that the history of landscape also be grounded in tangible, material structures. 'Real' landscapes are thus a dialectical product of ideas and the natural environment.

In thinking about the distinctiveness of this region's landscapes, therefore, it is also helpful to point to the central contribution made by woodland and dispersed settlement over much of the region, and in contrast, the primary importance of the chalklands. We must also remember the many maritime associations of its long peninsular coastline. And finally there is the interplay between an extremely ancient landscape and an extremely modern one; indeed the modernity of the landscape over much of the region, and its continuing change, is a most important feature in the region's landscape history.

The landscapes of the South East awaiting this interpretation cover a diverse region, and a large one. It includes all that country to the south and east of the chalk escarpment running from Dorset to Hertfordshire. The area has, of course, been the subject of many excellent accounts of individual *pays*, particular counties, settlements large and small, or partial regional analyses, though none attempts the holistic historical landscape analysis of the present work. To break into this vast subject, the book is structured in three parts that deal respectively with 'Land and People', 'Ways of Life' and 'Landscapes and the Creative Imagination'. The chapters in each part develop with some regard to chronology, but the three different sections are intended to impart an analysis which first examines the inter-relationships between landscape and people, and then moves on to examine the different ways of living impacting on the region's landscapes, before returning finally to the cultural appreciation and appropriation of the land of south-east England.

Within the first part of the book, 'Land and People', Chapter 2 deals with the environmental history of the South East, its geology, land sculpture, ecological history and physical change within historical times, paying particular attention to the coast, and to anthropogenic influences. Chapter 3 develops these regional landscape patterns, using recent countryside classifications by the Countryside Agency with English Nature and English Heritage. The primary landscapes of the chalk country, the wealden woodlands, the lowland heaths, coastal marshes and developed coast are dealt with in some detail. In Chapter 4 we turn to the peopling of the region and the evolution of settlement patterns, moving chronologically from the earliest inhabitants through the development of farming settlements and later prehistory, the impact of Rome, the Saxon and medieval region, early-modern landscapes, and the modern period.

The second part, on 'Ways of Life', also contains three chapters. Chapter 5 deals with the farming landscapes of prehistory, the Saxon and medieval periods, the impact of enclosure and improvement between 1500 and 1800 and more modern farming landscapes. It also covers the region's rural industries. Chapter 6 then moves on to the contrasting urban landscapes and ways of living in the South East, primarily from the 18th century onwards. The themes dealt with most particularly are the country town, the inland spas and coastal resorts, the dockyard towns and ports, suburban growth and the development of communications. Chapter 7 deals specifically with London lives, landscapes and the reactions to London's growth and covers chronologically the development of the landscape from its earliest Roman and medieval manifestations through the early-modern centuries, the Victorian period, and the years since 1900.

The third part, 'Landscapes and the Creative Imagination', contains just one chapter. The work of painters and others dealing with visual media is discussed first, followed by literary representations of landscape, with the two giants, Dickens and Hardy, joined by the prolific nature writers. The significance of the many images thus created lies not only in the uplifting of the human spirit, but also in the huge influence that they had on middle-class opinion and the determination to protect landscapes and earlier cultural traits threatened by development, and also the desire to use landscape as a moral guide or resource for social or political purposes. The volume ends with a synthesising chapter that sets out the very particular relationship between people and their landscapes through time in this highly significant corner of England.

NOTES

1   Tindall 1977, 13.
2   Mitchell 2002, vi.
3   Williams 1973, 149.
4   Lowenthal 1994, 23.
5   Schumpeter 1942 (1975 edn), 82–5.
6   Steane 2001.
7   Williamson & Bellamy 1987, 138, 178–9.
8   Jenkins 2003, 30.
9   Wiener 1982; Baker & Billinge 2004; Howkins 1986.
10 Crossley & Saville 1991, ix–xxviii.
11 Mitchell 2002, 9.
12 Crinson 2003, 113.
13 Mitchell 2002, 10.
14 Bender 1993, 245–79; and 1998.

Environmental History
and the Landscape

Before the all-important human aspects of the South East's landscape history can be unravelled, it is appropriate to summarise the physical setting of the region as an important part of lowland England. The broad outlines of the environmental changes are set out in Table 2.1, but since this book is primarily concerned with the human cultural landscapes of the last 10,000 years, the longer-term landscape changes will be dealt with only in outline.

GEOLOGICAL STRUCTURES AND
GEOMORPHOLOGICAL PROCESSES

Topography is one of the foundations of landscape, and in the South East it results from the interaction of geological structures, complex folding and faulting, tectonic activity and many phases of erosion and deposition. The region has long been the subject of acute scientific interest in the earth and field sciences, and the names of John Farey, Gideon Mantell, Charles Lyell and William Topley are well known for work undertaken on its geology. Much of the detailed geological mapping was accomplished between the middle of the 19th century and the 1920s, to be followed by such works of synthesis in the inter-war years as the classic analysis by S W Wooldridge and D L Linton, *Structure, Surface and Drainage in South-East England* (1939). For a generation this inspired and guided much detailed research work, and established the Weald as one of the key outdoor laboratories for discerning the earth's most recent landform changes.

Chalklands are central to the South East as it is defined for this book – in other words all that land lying to the south and east of England's prime chalk escarpment running north and north-east from the Dorset coast at Chaldon Down, to the northern end of the Chilterns. In Dorset, the chalk encompasses Dorchester, the North Dorset Downs overlooking Blackmoor Vale and the Shaftesbury greensand escarpment. Further north lie Cranborne Chase, the Wiltshire Downs and Salisbury Plain and the Berkshire and Marlborough downs, the latter including a prominent escarpment on which Tan Hill reaches a height of 293m overlooking the Vale of Pewsey to the south. These constitute a formidable central mass of chalk that is continued north of the Goring Gap by the Chilterns. Gently inclined chalk lies around Savernake Forest on the Wiltshire–Berkshire border, where damp clay-with-flints yield beech-clad hills. Not far away, separated by the M4, the Lambourn or Berkshire Downs offer the least dissected open chalk countrysides. Topped by the ancient Ridgeway, 'Britain's oldest road', which runs as a modern national trail between Avebury and Ivinghoe Beacon, the downs overlook the Vale of White Horse and the broad expanse of the Thames valley beyond. The chalk, an exceptionally permeable and therefore upstanding rock formation, gives both

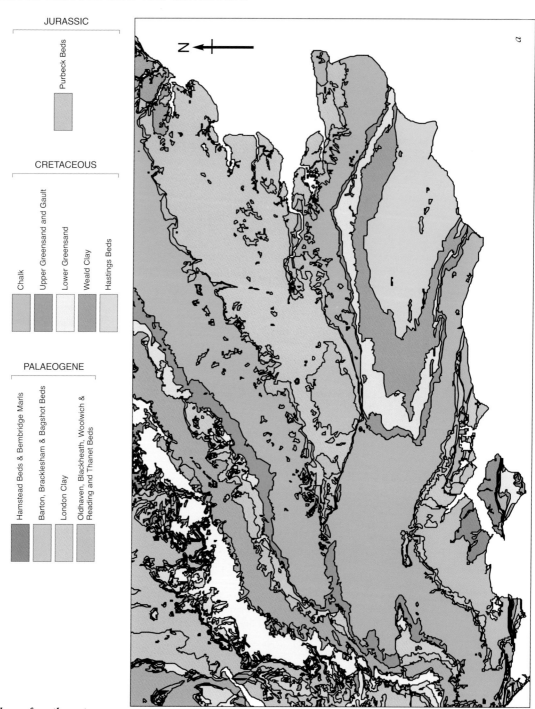

JURASSIC

Purbeck Beds

CRETACEOUS

Chalk
Upper Greensand and Gault
Lower Greensand
Weald Clay
Hastings Beds

PALAEOGENE

Hamstead Beds & Bembridge Marls
Barton, Bracklesham & Bagshot Beds
London Clay
Oldhaven, Blackheath, Woolwich & Reading and Thanet Beds

Fig. 2.1 The geology of south-east England, showing (a) solid geology, all being sedimentary and relatively soft rocks, and (b, opposite page) Quaternary deposits. The latter are particularly significant in understanding patterns of farming since the derived soils mantle or modify the underlying solid geology in many places.

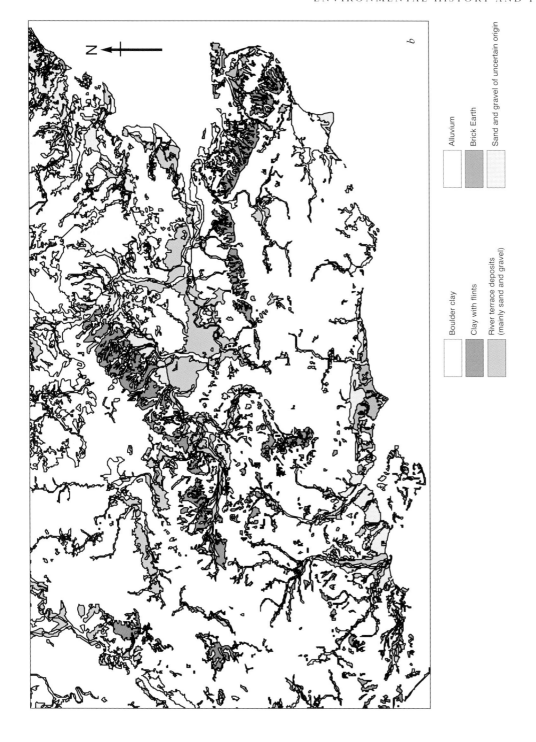

Boulder clay

Clay with flints

River terrace deposits
(mainly sand and gravel)

Alluvium

Brick Earth

Sand and gravel of uncertain origin

b

character and an upland skeleton to our region, since from Salisbury Plain it radiates eastwards in the form of the Hampshire Downs, and the North and South Downs (Fig. 2.1).

Three other important landscape structures lie within this defining chalk: the London Basin, the Weald (an anticline with its eastern end in northern France) and the Hampshire Basin. Each of these has been subject to secondary folding and faulting, which impact greatly upon the character of the landscape, especially in the Weald and across Wessex. Each has its own internal drainage system: in broad terms, a major watershed runs from Basingstoke in northern Hampshire to Romney Marsh in southern Kent, and from the centre of the region rivers drain north to the Thames and south to the English Channel.

The London Basin

Over most of the London Basin, with its margins formed by the chalk outcrops of the Chilterns and North Downs, the chalk lies buried beneath more recent river, estuarine and marine deposits such as the London Clay (Fig. 2.2). The more recent Tertiary rocks occur as sands around the edge of the basin and in outliers on the chalk dip slopes. The sandy Bagshot series are therefore to be found on the higher ground, forming prominent heathland plateaux, as around Bagshot (Berkshire) itself. The chalk on the margins dips far less in the north than in the south, so the Berkshire Downs (the most open of the region's chalk landscapes) and the Chilterns (with their 15 to 25km stretches of chalk) contrast with the North Downs, which sometimes barely exceed 400m in width, as at the Hogs Back ridge near Guildford. The chalk escarpments, with their gaps, coombes and dry valleys, and reaching as high as 260m at Aston Hill in the Chilterns, face outwards from the basin. Between Princes Risborough and Luton, for example, there are six major interruptions, including important dry gaps at Wendover, Tring and Dunstable. The chalk dip slope in the north-east gives way to the drift-covered floor of the Vale of St Albans, while east of Luton the chalk is obscured by the boulder clay which covers a large part of Essex. Solid and drift geology intermix along a line between Harlow, Brentwood and Basildon. And between here and the Thames Estuary the land is low-lying London Clay with only occasional hills, as at Langdon and Rayleigh.

The Thames, the dominant river within south-east England since the so-called Anglian cold stage more than 450,000 years ago, enters the London Basin through the wooded Goring Gap between the Berkshire Downs and the Chilterns. Part of the more recent geological history of the river was unravelled in excavations prompted by the huge amount of development in Greater London during the 1990s. A braided channel during the Late Devensian period was followed during the Late Upper Palaeolithic or Mesolithic by a meandering river bed, possibly in a floodplain nearly 5km wide, which in turn evolved by the Late Bronze Age into the present river, tidal at least up to modern Westminster. This

Fig. 2.2 Geological section across the London Basin and the Chilterns. The upfold in the chalk at Windsor has been significant in offering strong hilltop defensive properties to the castle. Note the steep upward inclination of the chalk at the Hogs Back compared with the gentler slope of the chalk in the Chilterns.

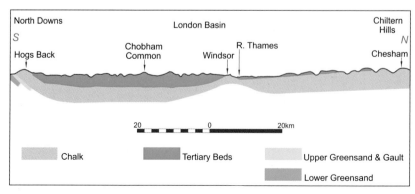

tidal inundation may have been a relatively rapid event, given that waterlain silts have been found overlying Bronze Age ard marks on sand dunes at Southwark.[1] The river is now tidal as far west as Teddington.

In the Thames floodplain the river turns north through the Henley Loop but thereafter broadly meanders eastwards along the syncline, its abandoned channels often infilled with lake sediments, as at Bermondsey, or with peat and organic debris. The sand eyots (islands) in the river started forming in the early Holocene, resulting in significant islands at places such as Thorney Island, Westminster and Southwark.[2] Downstream, the flat London Clays shade into the estuary's winding tidal creeks, characterised by somewhat isolated mudflats, saltings and islands on the Essex shore. On the Kentish shore the incline is steeper to the chalk block that lies east of the River Darent, where it gave rise to a 19th-century cement industry at Northfleet, and later Swanscombe. Among the saltings and creeks, the London Clay islands of Sheppey and Mersea (the latter with proto-Thames gravels) and the Dengie peninsula rise gently above sea level (*see* Table 2.1, overleaf).

The Thames terraces are features created by earlier courses of the proto-Thames. These expanses of water-deposited gravel have been the subject of much research, which has uncovered an earlier northern course of the river. This probably predated the first ice incursion into the London Basin, as the Thames then flowed along the Chilterns dip slope. Lower Palaeolithic artefacts have been found in the lower terraces of the sequence and include the pre-Neanderthal hominid remains that were discovered in 1935 on the Boyn Hill terrace at Swanscombe in Kent. The site has since yielded Palaeolithic artefacts, as well as environmental evidence going back 400,000 years (Table 2.1). Many of the Thames's tributaries are but shadows of their former selves, having been drained, abstracted or channelled through urban areas. Now the Colne and Lea drain into the Thames from the north but the main tributaries are from the south: the Kennet, which drains the area west of Reading, and the Lodden, Blackwater, Wey, Mole, Darent and Medway between eastern Berkshire and Kent.

On the south-western edge of the London Basin the Hampshire Downs offer an indistinct link with the Hampshire Basin near Basingstoke. In the south-west and south-central parts there are flat-topped hills and plateaux, such as the Hale Plateau near Farnham or the larger heathlands at Bagshot, Shooters Hill, Wimbledon Common and Richmond. North of the river the Hertfordshire plateau rises to 120m between the Vale of St Albans and Finchley. The latter is separated from the Thames by discontinuous low hills, as at Harrow Hill or the Bagshot Sands-capped Hampstead–Highgate Ridge (134m). Less distinctive is the continuation of the Chilterns chalk beyond Luton towards East Anglia, where it is obscured by chalky boulder clay. Further eastwards into Essex low hills at Epping, Brentwood and Billericay are again capped by Bagshot Sands and stand out above their drift-covered surroundings.

The Weald

The Weald is one of the classic landform areas of Britain, an 'unroofed anticline', uplifted in late Cretaceous or Tertiary times. Like the Thames Basin it is fringed by chalk downland to north and south, although in this case the escarpments are inward-facing (Fig. 2.3). In the London and Hampshire basins the chalk is concealed beneath younger rocks except at the margins, but in the Weald the chalk cover was uplifted and then eroded to form a large area of inverted relief. Rivers such as the Stour, Medway, Darent, Wey and Mole cut their way through the North Downs in deep valleys, while the rivers Meon, Arun, Adur, Ouse and Cuckmere similarly divide the South Downs into blocks as they flow to the sea, originally as tributaries of a 'Solent River' which once flowed parallel to the present coast and was itself a tributary of a lost 'Greater Seine' system.

TABLE 2.1 THE PLEISTOCENE AND HOLOCENE EPOCHS OF SOUTH-EAST ENGLAND.

Conventional British Stages	Marine Isotope Stage (Sub Stage)	Climate	Sites/Stratigraphic Units	Dates BC	
Flandrian	1	Temperate		500–present	
				2500–500	
				4500–2500	
				7000–4500	
				13,500–7000	
Late Devensian (Loch Lomond stadial; Windermere interstadial)	2	Periglacial	?Shepperton Gravel Formation	22,000	
Middle Devensian	3	Varying cold and temperate	Maidenhead, Canterbury, Billingshurst	57,000	
Early Devensian	4	Periglacial	Twickenham, Isleworth	69,000	
	5d–5a	Temperate	East Tilbury Marshes Gravel	113,000	
Ipswichian	5e	Temperate	Trafalgar Square, Pagham Raised Beach, Peckham	123,000	
Un-named cold stage	6	Periglacial	East Tilbury Marshes Lower Gravel	184,000	
Un-named interglacial	7	Temperate	Brighton-Norton Raised Beach, Aveley, Northfleet	243,000	
Un-named cold stage	8	Periglacial	Mucking	301,000	
Un-named interglacial	9	Temperate	Purfleet, Grays, Thurrock, Cudmore Grove	337,000	
Un-named cold stage	10	Periglacial	Little Thurrock, Orsett Heath Upper Gravel	360,000	
Hoxnian	11	Temperate	Swanscombe, Clacton	421,000	
Anglian	12	Periglacial + ice sheet in North London Basin	Orsett Heath Lower Gravel	476,000	
Late Cromerian Complex	?13	Temperate	Boxgrove (Goodwood-Slindon Raised Beach)	522,000	

Period	Cultural Period	Flora	Fauna
Sub-Atlantic (Cold and wet)	Iron Age to present	Alder, oak, birch, elm, beech	Woodland clearance completed; cereal and sheep farming etc.
Sub-Boreal (Warm and dry)	Later Neolithic and Bronze Age	Mixed alder, oak, elm and lime (elm decline)	Extensive woodland clearance for arable; extinction of auroch
Atlantic (Warm and wet)	Late Mesolithic and early Neolithic		Animal domestication
Boreal (Warm and dry)	Mesolithic	Hazel, pine, birch	Hunting and gathering clearings
Pre-Boreal (rapid warming)		Birch	
	Upper Palaeolithic	Tundra – juniper, dwarf birch, pine	No fauna known in South East
	Middle Palaeolithic (Mousterian)	Steppe-Tundra	Woolly mammoth, woolly rhinoceros, horse, spotted hyena
		Steppe-Tundra	Reindeer, bison, brown bear
			No fauna known in South East
	Humans absent from Britain	Mixed oak forest	Hippopotamus, spotted hyena, straight-tusked elephant
		Steppe-Tundra	Woolly mammoth, woolly rhinoceros
	Middle Palaeolithic (Levallois)	Open grassland with stands of mixed oak forest	Steppe-mammoth, horse, narrow-nosed rhinoceros, aurochs, red deer
		Steppe-Tundra	Woolly mammoth, woolly rhinoceros
	Lower Palaeolithic (Clactonian and Acheulean)	Mixed oak forest	Mercks' rhinoceros, fallow deer, macaque monkey, brown bear
	Humans absent	Steppe-Tundra	Woolly mammoth
	Lower Palaeolithic (Clactonian and Acheulean)	Mixed oak forest	Large fallow deer, cave bear, lion, straight-tusked elephant, Mercks' rhinoceros
	Humans absent	Steppe-Tundra, grasses and shrubs, willow	No mammals present
	Lower Palaeolithic (Acheulean)	Mixed oak forest	Hundsheim rhinoceros, Dawkins' giant deer, Savin's shrew

Fig. 2.3 Geological section across the Weald. The ancient dome of the chalk has been unroofed, leaving the older rocks towards the centre, where the rocks of the High Weald are strongly faulted, yielding a complex landscape.

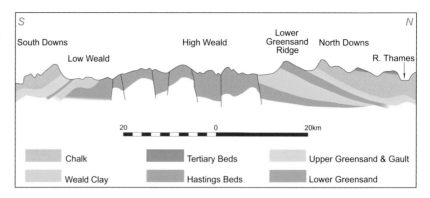

The core of this area, the High Weald, rises to 240m at Beacon Hill at Crowborough in Sussex. Created by faulting and folding, its topography is dominated by east–west ridges and valleys. It is the watershed between north- and south-flowing rivers, and so is dissected by numerous small and heavily wooded headwater valleys, known as 'ghylls'. The High Weald is surrounded by the deep, flat, well-wooded and poorly drained 'oak tree' clays of the Low Weald, which wrap around it on all sides except in the east, where the High Weald is cut by the English Channel at the cliffs at Hastings. Here it is flanked by Romney Marsh and the Pevensey Levels, two important marshland areas that have been reclaimed over the past few thousand years but which owe their original character to coastal sand or shingle barriers that allowed both natural and artificial silting to occur in their shelter.

Between the Low Weald and the surrounding chalk are the highly variable Upper and Lower Greensands and Gault Clay; the Lower Greensand, when reinforced by bands of chert, forms impressive hills such as Leith Hill (294m), Blackdown (280m) and Hindhead (273m). The distribution of landslips and mudflows is a constant reminder of continuing geomorphological processes at work, to which the Hythe Beds (part of the Lower Greensand) and Wadhurst Clays (in the Hastings Group of the High Weald) are particularly susceptible.[3]

On the outer margins of the Weald the chalk most famously meets the sea at Beachy Head and the Seven Sisters cliffs in Sussex, but elsewhere is again fringed by later Tertiary rocks, as along the Sussex Coastal Plain around Chichester, where the lower coastal plain is cut by small streams or 'rifes' which cross fertile and generally flat terrain. On the north Kent coast and the junction with the London Basin the gently undulating topography is mainly mantled by deep, rich loams. In general, the strong chalkland topography gives unity to the North Downs from its distinctive pitched Hogs Back in west Surrey through to the expanse of the White Cliffs of the 'Bulwark Shore' at Dover. Along the South Downs are the 'raised beaches' of ancient sea levels. The 40-m Goodwood–Slindon raised beach has been dated to the Hoxnian stage (400,000 to 365,000 BC), with temperate fauna found at Slindon. The 8-m beach as exposed at Black Rock, Brighton, is about 200,000 years old and was buried beneath solifluction materials and brickearth, which also underlie much of the Sussex Coastal Plain west of Worthing. At Boxgrove, where the dip slope of the South Downs is cut by the 40-m raised beach, there is the earliest evidence so far in Britain of the presence and activity of hominids. As well as a hominid tibia and two incisors, Middle Pleistocene buried surfaces yielded Lower Palaeolithic (Acheulian) flint tools and pre-Hoxnian interglacial fauna.[4] The site has been dated to the end of the Cromerian temperate stage, prior to the onset of the Anglian glaciation, about 500,000 years ago, and as such represents one of the most important sites for mid-Pleistocene archaeology in north-west Europe (Table 2.1).

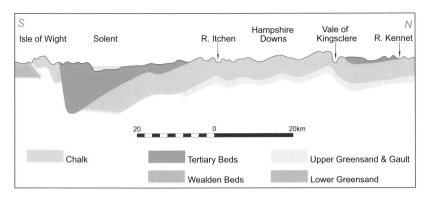

Fig. 2.4 Geological section across the Hampshire Basin, from the Isle of Wight to west Berkshire. The broad chalk expanses of the Hampshire Downs and Salisbury Plain are enhanced by the relative lack of overlying Tertiary beds.

The Hampshire Basin

The Hampshire Basin is also defined by its chalk limits, although here less steeply sloping (Fig. 2.4). To the west it is fringed by the North Dorset Downs and the deeply indented western edge of Cranborne Chase, and to the north-west by the Wiltshire Chalk, which provides the highest points of the Basin at the northern rim of the Vale of Pewsey and at Walbury Hill near Andover, which at 297m is the highest point in south-east England. The rim is then continued by the Hampshire Downs, stretching between Basingstoke, Winchester, Farnham and Andover in the north-east and then via the Vale of Kingsclere to the edge of the Weald. In common with much of the chalkland in this area, the open dry landscape of Salisbury Plain presents a country of rolling topography and hidden vales, incised here by the tributaries of the River Avon and bounded to the north by the Vale of Pewsey. Preserved from modern farming beneath a military training area covering 39,000ha, the Plain is the largest surviving tract of unimproved chalk grassland in north-west Europe and gives us an unparalleled window into the prehistory and history of southern England. The central part of the Hampshire Basin offers less interesting relief, being generally composed of Tertiary materials resting on gently sloping chalk, although flat-topped hills, topped by Bagshot Beds, reach 125m in the northern New Forest area.

The southern margins of the Hampshire Basin consist of the South Dorset Downs, the chalk escarpment of which faces south and runs parallel to the coast and overlooks Weymouth. From Chaldon Down eastwards lies the Purbeck peninsula or 'Isle of Purbeck'. Chalk defines its northern margin from Lulworth at the coast to Ballard Point and Old Harry Rocks, and it is breached at Corfe Castle and elsewhere dissected by numerous dry valleys. The chalk then continues through into the Isle of Wight, where it runs from the Needles to Culver Cliff, with older Upper and Lower Greensand to the south, except where chalk outliers form Shanklin and St Catherine's Down. Deep ravines or 'chines' are cut into the weaker rocks of the cliffs where short streams emerge to the south of the central chalk ridge. The chalk everywhere displays a steeply dipping southern component compared with the less discernible dip on the northern chalk boundaries of the Basin. South of the chalk, the Portland Limestone escarpment meets the sea at St Alban's Head and the combined Portland and Purbeck Beds broaden out south of Swanage to produce Durlston Head. The Dorset heaths extend in a shallow basin from the northern edge of the Purbeck chalk around Poole Harbour and north of Bournemouth to merge into the New Forest. Tertiary sands and gravels here yield sandy, infertile soils with heathland vegetation as a unifying feature, alongside post-Second World War conifer plantations. As in the Wealden area, the southward-oriented drainage systems are a relic of the time when the area's rivers drained into the now-submerged 'Solent River' and 'Greater Seine'.

GLACIAL MODIFICATION IN THE SOUTH EAST

The South East is thus a land of soft, relatively young rocks, nowhere reaching beyond about 300m in height, and mantled by a discontinuous cover of superficial deposits. But upon this surface modifications have been wrought through long-term climatic change, and most notably oscillations of colder and warmer phases that included full glacial, stadial, interglacial and interstadial periods. On the East Anglian coasts freshwater sediments below glacial till have yielded palaeobotanical evidence of the development of a cold tundra and polar-desert environment in the Anglian period 450,000 years ago. The most recent cold stage was that of the Devensian, which lasted from about 113,000 to 11,000 BC (Table 2.1), but at this stage no ice penetrated the South East.

Only in the north-eastern part of the London Basin was the region subjected to the direct effects of ice-sheets or glaciers. Here the Anglian period left glacial drifts as an extension of the mask of chalky boulder clay that covered much of Essex. Outwash gravels and tills occur in the Vale of St Albans as far as Watford and the Finchley area, indicating an ice flow from the north-east spreading through pre-existing lowlands as far south as Woodford, Hornchurch and Billericay. One major consequence of the Anglian ice was that it first 'ponded' back the Thames around Ware and Watford, and then diverted it southwards, from its early route through the Vale of St Albans in Hertfordshire, into its modern valley.[5]

Although the region was never again covered by ice, much of it was nevertheless hugely influenced by its proximity. As permafrost developed and sea levels fell because water was locked into ice, rivers carved out deep valleys that have subsequently within the last 10,000 years been infilled with peat or alluvium as the climate has warmed and sea levels have risen again. No fewer than eight

Fig. 2.5 A downland dry valley in the Chilterns escarpment. Barton-le-Clay, just off to the left of the photograph, is on the Bedfordshire/Hertfordshire border. There is in fact a spring at the head of this steep valley, and woodland and scrub clothe the north-east facing slopes. The Barton Hills National Nature Reserve is on the facing slope, with chalk grassland and characteristic beech woodland.

periglacial episodes have been identified for southern England, during which juniper, birch and arctic willow were the only trees in a grassy tundra grazed by mammoths and reindeer. One important result of these conditions was that the frozen chalk lost its permeability, which in turn led to the creation of one of the most characteristic features of the region, its dry valleys or 'coombes'. These mostly occur on the dip slopes, but also occasionally on scarp faces and as through-valleys. Some resemble great amphitheatres, as at the Vale of Wardour on the Wiltshire–Dorset border, or deep incisions such as the Devil's Dyke near Brighton. Others form patterns of dendritic shape, although many are simply shallow depressions (Fig. 2.5). And during the same period solifluced chalk (coombe rock produced under cold climatic conditions) sludged down into, or emerged from, the dry valleys. It is also to be found at the foot of escarpments or blanketing the raised beaches, as on the Sussex Coastal Plain. At Black Rock, Brighton, the gravels of the 8-m raised beach are overlain by 20m of superficial deposits. Wind-blown deposits of fine-grained loess are also to be found in the region, and provide significant agricultural soils on the Sussex Coastal Plain, in north Kent and over much of the Hampshire and London basins.

THE COAST

The wide Thames Estuary in effect makes south-east England a peninsula, which means that the three main geological basin structures outlined above all possess a coastline. This coast is very well known for its beautiful, indeed iconic scenes – as in the White Cliffs of Dover. Where the geological grain runs parallel to the coast in Dorset, bays such as Lulworth Cove or St Oswald's Bay have become well known to generations of field-studies students. It is here that the 'Jurassic Coast' of Dorset and East Devon, with its complete sequence of Triassic, Jurassic and Cretaceous rocks, became England's first Natural World Heritage Site in 2001. Stretching 150km, from Orcombe Rocks near Exmouth (Devon), to Old Harry Rocks near Studland (Dorset), it contains nine internationally significant sites well known to fossil hunters, such as the Fossil Forest at Lulworth, the ammonite beds at Charmouth and the Ichthyosaur slabs at Lyme Regis.

The coast has been far from static in this region, however. Interglacial sea levels, marked by fossil beach levels and deposits, have been higher than at present. Conversely, during the glacial phase, sea level was reduced to 130m or more below its modern level, and rivers excavated deep channels as they flowed to a coastline perhaps 450km off the present south coast. But today, coastal waters do not exceed depths of 50m anywhere around the South East. And sea levels have risen by over 100m from a shoreline that may once have linked Cornwall and Brittany; over 45m of the rise has taken place in the last 10,000 years. By about 8000 BC rapid submergence began as the ice melted, and waters breached the land bridge to the continent. In the process they scoured a deep channel where extensive tracts of dry land had once lain, and by 7600 BC had formed the Straits of Dover. The Thames Estuary was inundated by 6000 BC, an ancestral Southampton Water by 4500 BC, and a close approximation to the present shoreline was achieved by 1000 BC.

Calculating the position of past coastlines and sea levels is not straightforward, but the south coast appears to be sinking relative to sea level. In the Thames Estuary it is subsiding at the rate of 2mm a year, a fact brought dramatically home by the loss of life and property in the floods of February 1953. Due recognition of this, together with anxieties about the effects of global warming, led to the building of the Thames flood barrier to protect London against high surges and tides. Since its completion in 1982, and especially during the last ten years, it has been used far more than planned (Fig. 2.6) and current predictions of changing sea levels suggest a potentially dramatically changed coastline (Fig. 2.7).

ABOVE: *Fig. 2.6 The Thames flood barrier.*
Between its completion in 1982 and 2005 the barrier
has been closed against surges on more than 80
occasions. Eleven times during winter months is
normal, but in the winter of 2000/01 the Environment
Agency reported that the barrier was closed 23 times,
and in January 2003 alone, there were 18 closures.

BELOW: *Fig. 2.7 Potential change in the coastline of south-east England: the
Indicative Flood Plain.* By 2004 more than 235,000 properties were assessed by the
Environment Agency to be at risk of flooding from either fluvial or tidal sources, and a
further 34,000 residential allocations within major proposals have been approved within
the Indicative Flood Plain by local authorities (and see also Fig. 3.11). Many historic
environments have already been lost by rising sea levels, such as the valley of the 'Solent
River', north of the Isle of Wight.

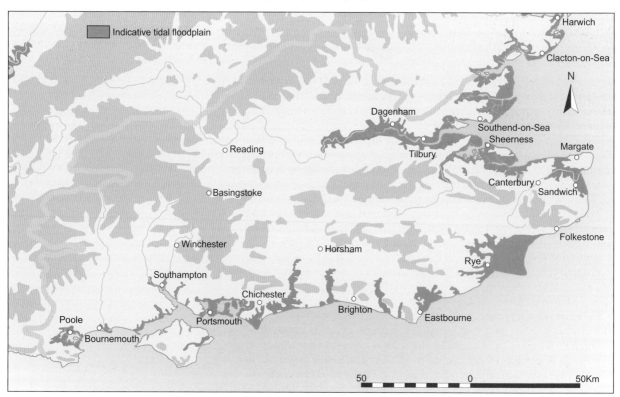

Low-lying coastal parts such as the Thameside marshes and lower Thames valley, the Wantsum Channel, Romney Marsh and the south-eastern coastal zone of the Hampshire Basin – all below 5m OD – could be inundated. It may be that in some coastal areas there is scope for managed coastal realignment, which might offer great opportunities for the re-creation of saltmarsh habitats. At Abbots Hall Farm, 84ha of arable land was converted to saltmarsh and wetland on the north shore of the Blackwater estuary in Europe's largest project of this kind thus far. Further south, in Sussex, restoration of the lower reaches of the Cuckmere valley will create about 46ha of intertidal mudflats over the next few years.

Coastline retreat is ongoing in areas in which weaker rocks face the sea. In some areas, such as north Kent on the London Clays of the Thames Estuary, it is resulting in active cliff retreat of up to 1m per annum. At Selsey the exposed coast retreated by as much as 2 to 4.5m per annum between the mid-19th and mid-20th centuries alone, and may have retreated by as much as 5 to 7km over the past 2,000 years. The sites of the original Saxon cathedral and the former deer park of the bishops of Chichester, together with settlements such as Charlton and Ilsham, have been lost to the sea. Similarly, storms in the climatic deterioration of the late 13th century led to the abandonment of Old Winchelsea in Rye Bay. There are many unstable cliffs. Well known are the chalk cliffs of Dover, the Seven Sisters and Beachy Head in Sussex, as well as the isolated chalk stacks caused through erosion along lines of weakness at Old Harry Rocks in Dorset or the Needles off the Isle of Wight (Fig. 2.8). The cliffs at Beachy Head

Fig. 2.8 Old Harry Rocks, Dorset. *The chalk meets the sea here at Ballard Down, separating Studland Bay (right) from Swanage (in the distance). The South West Coast Path runs along the top of the cliffs. Erosion has formed sea stacks and the crenulated cliffs, picking out weaknesses along joints in the chalk. This forms the eastern end of the Jurassic Coast, a World Heritage Site.*

are retreating by about 1.1m per annum and in January 1999 between 50,000 and 100,000 tonnes of rock were displaced in one large fall; in the same month there were further cliff falls at St Margarets Bay in east Kent. Mass movements have also accounted for erosional coastlines on the chalk at Folkestone Warren, on the clays and sandstones of the Hastings Group at Fairlight and on London Clay at Warden Point, Sheppey. At Folkestone the underlying Gault Clay has failed on as many as 12 occasions since 1765, the most dramatic being in 1915 when a huge slip displaced the Folkestone to Dover railway laterally by up to 50m. Further west, the Undercliff on the south coast of the Isle of Wight is the largest area of rotational landslip in western Europe.[6]

The prehistoric south coast would have been more deeply indented than today's, including several broad, tidal estuaries that have since been filled. There are now few large inlets remaining other than the Thames Estuary, the Solent and Poole Harbour. But the combined Chichester, Langstone and Portsmouth harbours, interconnected by small channels, also form the largest intertidal area on the south coast. Elsewhere most have been reclaimed by human agency. The Isle of Oxney in Romney Marsh and the Isle of Thanet, for example, were islands during the Roman period but are now parts of the mainland. And in a movement repeated along the south coast to the east of Selsey, waves and currents move the eroded debris and finer sediment eastwards along the shoreline to form shingle spits. At Shoreham, Sussex, the mouth of the Adur has thus been deflected eastwards, while at Newhaven the shingle deflected the River Ouse eastwards to escape to the sea near Seaford before breaching and harbour works stabilised the entrance at Newhaven. To the west, there is a fine recurved spit at Hurst Castle and double spits at the entrance to Poole Harbour. Shingle beaches are ubiquitous around the coasts, but at Langney Point and Dungeness large volumes of debris have accumulated to form cuspate forelands. Langney Point seems to have developed since the medieval period and overlies an extensive peat bed dated to between 6810 and 7560 BC at depths of −24 to −28m OD. Dungeness, the largest shingle foreland in Europe, shelters a former inlet with a degraded cliff line still visible today at former ports such as Winchelsea (see Fig. 4.12). A shingle spit grew north-eastwards towards Hythe, resulting in a sheltered swampy forest area, a peat layer from which has been dated to about 1000 BC. Periodic inundations and successive reclamations have since created a complex environment inside the constantly evolving shingle foreland. As a result of the latter, Camber castle, originally built on the shoreline in 1539, now lies some 1.75km inland. The precise ways in which these spits were formed, as well as their dating, are still debated but it has been suggested that they may have originated as offshore bars, the shingle from which was then driven onshore.

Most recently human intervention has also played a key role in shaping the coast. Groynes capture eastward-drifting shingle that accumulates in one area but deprives another area of its supply; sea walls repel the waves but can cause beach scouring and loss. Measures to absorb the sea's energy have recently been tried, such as stone revetments, offshore breakwater islands and the re-charging of beaches. However, the protection of saltmarsh along the Thames Estuary, and its re-creation as at Abbot's Hall, offers a more natural absorption of the sea's energy.

CLIMATE

The South East has a largely equable climate with the highest average daytime temperatures in the British Isles; it also provides Britain's highest sunshine averages. At least on its coasts, this attracts holiday-makers and retired people. Eastbourne and Worthing dispute each other's claim to be the sunniest resort in

Britain; London is one of the driest parts of Britain, and indeed amongst the driest capital cities in Europe.

The chief influences on this favourable climate are the general low relief and proximity to the Continent, coupled with oceanic modifications from the Channel and southern North Sea. Warm and humid south-westerlies vie with anticyclonic conditions to produce most of the south-east's weather, and the region lies furthest from the influence of the North Atlantic depressions that pass between Iceland and Scotland (although, as happened in 2000, they can move south with great impact in terms of flooding). East winds from the Continent in winter, however, can cause considerable cooling.

Marked differences arise between the drier parts of the region, such as northern Kent and the Thames valley (about 525–600mm of rainfall per annum), compared with the wetter western and southern downland areas (about 800mm per annum). Rainfall generally declines from south-west to north-east, with localised altitudinal variations such as on the Hampshire chalklands, the South Downs and High Weald, where it increases to 1,000mm. Limitations to agriculture only really come from coastal exposure and localised inland frost pockets, where descending night-time cold air becomes trapped. Frosts linger in the Low Weald in winter because the cold air takes some time to drain out through the gaps in the chalk. The contrast between the northern-facing escarpment, which often remains frost covered throughout winter days, and the south facing dip slope, is quite noticeable. The most favourable areas in terms of temperatures, especially for plant growth, are coastal Hampshire, sheltered parts of Sussex and the lower Thames valley, and the least favoured are the Chilterns and the higher ground of Berkshire and Hampshire. The growing season in the region exceeds 280 days along the south coast, and 260 days everywhere else except in the higher interior or exposed coastal chalklands.[7]

Over the long span of time covered by this book, we should note the impact of a changing climate. A warm and dry post-glacial climate seems to have ended around 3500–3000 BC. This was followed by a further deterioration to c. 1000 BC, ushering in a climate similar to that experienced today. Even within this present period, however, there have been fluctuations, such as the Medieval Warm Epoch between AD 1000 and 1250, succeeded by poorer weather in the late 13th and 14th centuries, and most recently by the 'Little Ice Age' of the early modern period.

The impact of humans on climate has become marked in the recent past. For example, there has been a dramatic change in London's climate. Noticed as early as the second decade of the 16th century, pollution in London was a human-induced phenomenon, and the early use of imported coal led to a rise in smoke and sulphur dioxide levels. In the later 19th century vast amounts of smoke and soot were emitted into the atmosphere, so that by the 1880s London was 'losing' up to 80 per cent of its winter sunshine. In the disastrous smog of December 1952 about 4,000 deaths were attributed to the atmospheric conditions.[8] But by the late 20th century pollution fell dramatically with the switch away from coal as the prime source of energy, a change already under way at the time of the passing of the Clean Air Acts in the 1950s and 1960s. The ensuing reduction in the frequency of winter smogs and fog and a considerable increase in London's sunshine means that central London now experiences the highest daytime maximum temperatures within Britain. This is because its sheltered inland basin location and a 'continental' effect cause it to warm up and become an 'urban heat island'.

The major soil types of the region, while strongly modified by humanly induced environmental change, were originally determined by climate as well as underlying geology.[9] In overall terms 'brown earth' soils, typical of former wooded environments, have characterised the freer draining soils of the South

East. On heavier ground where drainage is impeded, such as on the Low Weald, 'stagnogleys' have developed. Once the woodland cover has been removed, leaching begins and can result in conditions where free-draining soils are degraded, eventually becoming the acidic and depleted podsols that characterise the western Weald greensand heaths, or central Ashdown Forest. On the high downland, thin calcareous 'rendzina' soils, poor for agricultural purposes and rarely more than 300mm deep, cover those areas where superficial deposits, such as clay-with-flints, are absent. Many areas of the chalk are still covered by wind-deposited loess deposits, which are decalcified and which may yield unusual chalkland heather communities.

ANTHROPOGENIC INFLUENCES ON THE ECOLOGY

In an area as intensively settled and farmed as the South East it is difficult to ignore the impact of human activity on the soils, flora and fauna. The region exhibits an unusual richness of native and anciently introduced species, with areas such as the Hampshire Basin, Dorset heaths and western Thames Basin particularly rich in species. Indeed, the richest 10-km National Grid square (SY 98) in the whole of England has been identified around Wareham, where it includes heathland, chalk grassland, the grazings and ditches of the rivers Frome and Piddle, and a range of coastal plants near Poole Harbour. Altogether 844 species were recorded there, including 56 that are nationally rare or scarce.[10]

The floristic composition of the region has been determined by many millennia of climatic and human influences (Table 2.1). The Pleistocene glacial and interglacial periods, for example, were hugely influential. About 40,000 years ago the first anatomically modern humans in the Thames floodplain found dense forests of alder and yew teeming with fauna such as red deer, elk, wild boar and wild aurochs. But by about 7000 BC temperate vegetation dominated by familiar tree species in a more closed forest canopy over brown-earth soils had become established in the region. The immigration of new species was also facilitated at this time by the land bridge that connected Britain to mainland Europe over what were later to become the Channel and southern North Sea. The result was the 'wildwood', a term popularised by Oliver Rackham.[11] It must always be remembered, however, that local variations remained important: heavier soils supported climax woodland of mixed oak, elm, lime and hazel, with beech and hornbeam in some places; the wetter clay valley bottoms were covered primarily by alder carr woodland, with yew an important element of its drier sites. In the middle Thames area, as in the South East more broadly, lime woodland was dominant almost everywhere until its final local removal by Neolithic and Bronze Age land clearance. This is Rackham's 'Lime province of Lowland England', in which hazel was the second most common species, followed by oak and elm. At this time the region had the most favourable climate, and greatest variety of tree species and woodland types in Britain.

Palaeolithic and Mesolithic hunters and gatherers had a more appreciable impact on vegetation than was once realised, and it is salutary to remember that the hunter-gatherer period actually represents some 60 per cent of our last 10,000 years of history. Modification of vegetation cover seems to have begun with Mesolithic cultures before 4000 BC. This would have entailed localised clearance of mixed oak woodland to assist hunting or gathering, and its replacement by hazel scrub, leading eventually to open heathland, as at Iping Common, West Heath or the Ashdown Forest in Sussex. Pollen analysis from valley sediments confirms the disturbance of vegetation in their catchment areas before 4000 BC. At Pannel Bridge, on Pett Level near Winchelsea, more than 11m of organic sediments, extending back more than 10,000 years, provide the most complete record of Holocene vegetational history in south-east England.

Emerging from the cold of the last glaciation, the narrow floodplain marsh alternated between alder and sedges in response to changes in the estuarine environment downstream, and the slopes were wooded with pine and birch. By 8000 to 5600 BC deciduous trees particularly hazel, oak and elm were present, with Mesolithic flint scatters denoting possible openings in the canopy. Bracken and meadow grass were also in evidence. Up to about 1700 BC lime had been abundant on the slopes, where it was initially accompanied by oak and hazel and by 800 BC joined by elm. A decline in lime between 2300 and 1700 BC has been attributed to human activity in the valley, with similar evidence coming from the neighbouring Brede valley. At later dates, plantain, grasses and cereal pollen give still further evidence of human activity in and around the valley.[12]

Successive clearances and partial regeneration progressively led to the deforestation of large parts of the region, including the downland, where clearance seems to have favoured a greater preponderance of shallower-rooting beech in the modified environments. Certainly black, humus-rich soils are encountered in the dry valleys overlying frost-shattered chalk and coombe rock, in turn overlain by plough-wash rich in loess. Snail species buried within the dark soils indicate wooded environments at that time, whereas open-country species become dominant in the later layers, where they are found with pottery or other artefacts of Neolithic, Bronze or Iron Age date. The Middle Bronze Age seems to have initiated a period of severe soil erosion on these chalk slopes which continued, at least on the South Downs, until intermittent conversion to grass during the late Roman or Saxon centuries.[13]

The timing of the great elm decline, when the species suddenly disappeared from the botanical record across the whole of north-west Europe, has been disputed, but it is commonly accepted to have occurred around 3000 BC. It has been demonstrated, however, that between about 2300 and 1800 BC an elm decline took place in the area of east London and Hampstead Heath, probably through natural disease, to be followed by sedimentation with rising sea levels and peat formation. Thereafter, human modification dominated, and the pollen record contained in the Thames valley peat indicates cereal, grass and herb species associated with Neolithic activities dated to *c.* 2600 BC, the earliest evidence thus far for human modifications to the environment of the Thames valley.[14] As in Sussex, the clearance of woodland, and especially lime, is now accounted for by humans rather than by climatic change, but most of the dated clearances belong to the Middle to Late Bronze Age period at a time of worsening climate and expanding wetland. Lime trees may well have been selected for clearance because deep loams beneath them were found to be suited for arable farming. It is thus to these soils, rather than to the more marginal and thinner chalk and gravel soils, that we should look for traces of the earliest cultivation and therefore settlement in south-east England.

We should also remember, however, that the present marginal areas may themselves once have borne woodland cover. The initial stages of settlement at Avebury, for example, were within localised woodland clearings, accompanied by small cereal plots, but by the time that the ceremonial monuments were built they were within a more open landscape producing cereals and pigs and in which hazel scrub and bracken had replaced much of the tree cover. The early phases of Stonehenge were also built in a grassland landscape, but one which was not totally open, since the nearby Coneybury Henge was constructed in a small woodland clearing.[15] Only by the later Bronze Age did the area become an open landscape much as we know it today.

It can thus be shown that deliberate modifications of the region's environment were ushered in during the more settled existence and agricultural exploitation of the Neolithic period. Beginning in about 4000 BC, this was a period of innovation that heralded continued and indeed accelerated change. By the later Neolithic (*c.* 2500 BC) farming had become a stabilised way of life over all the environments that could be so exploited. Woodland clearance nevertheless continued as a major process in gaining a livelihood throughout the succeeding centuries, as is well attested by Saxon place names in which woodland sites play a large role, or by the last great *defrichement* between the Norman Conquest and about 1300. The enclosed woodland canopy thus gave way to a more open mixture of grasses and heathlands, and arable cultivation made land available for colonisation by native species. But by the 17th century there are clear signs that over-exploitation of the woodland had been recognised, as a result of which commercial conservation measures were put in place, together with a new cultural emphasis on the symbolic importance of woodland, movements which have continued in one form or another through to the present day.

Until relatively recently, the use of artificial fertilisers had helped to reduce the biodiversity of grazing habitats. Intensive grassland management and the use of herbicides have similarly militated against recolonisation by woodland and other species. As a result the region is now experiencing an ongoing decline in the diversity of its plants, with significant reduction in arable, broadleaved woodland and calcareous grassland species. Over Britain as a whole as much as 90 per cent of the original forest cover has been cleared in the last 5,000 years, although there are still significant residual concentrations of ancient woodland (defined as being continually present since before 1600), such as on the clay-with-flint covered dip slope of the Chilterns at Burnham Beeches in Buckinghamshire. It is possible that this trend may have been halted or even slightly reversed during the last ten years as a result of reversion to more extensive farming. More than 70 per cent of lowland heaths also vanished between 1830 and 1980, as intensive farming, afforestation and road and house building ate into the heathland.

The historical ecology of the South East is therefore an ongoing and complex interaction between changes in climate, sea levels, soils and vegetation. During the past 10,000 years, moreover, all the region's habitats have in various and increasing ways been modified by human activity.

NOTES

1 Siddell *et al.* 2000, 122.
2 Siddell *et al.* 2002.
3 Robinson & Williams 1984, 22.
4 Pitts & Roberts 1998.
5 Bridgland 1994, 113–34.
6 Jones 1981, 276; Countryside Agency 1999, 139.
7 Jarvis *et al.* 1984, 21–6.
8 Brimblecombe 1987, 168; Chandler 1965, 246–7.
9 Hall & Russell 1911.
10 Preston *et al.* 2002, 10.
11 Rackham 1987.
12 Waller 1998, 103–15.
13 Robinson & Williams 1983, 119–23.
14 Sidell *et al.* 2000, 111–13.
15 Malone 1989, 31–5; Simmons 2001, 54–5.

3

Culture and Topography: Regional Patterns in an Ancient Landscape

Having examined the underlying structures of the land, we can now turn to more local topographic variation, and also begin to explore the interaction of people and nature that lies at the heart of landscape.

Within England as a whole, two distinctive types of country have long been recognisable. In the 16th century, for example, William Harrison called one the 'champaigne grounde' and the other 'woodland'; in modern times, Joan Thirsk's maps of early-modern farming regions reflect similar differences and Oliver Rackham has labelled the two types as 'planned' and 'ancient'. Most recently, Brian Roberts and Stuart Wrathmell have described the same distinction in considerable detail and plotted some of its changes through time, working through the medium of nucleated and dispersed settlement types and field patterns.[1]

But Harrison's description is still clear and insightful: he described 'champaigne' (Champion) England as having houses 'uniformlie builded in euerie town together, with streets and lanes', but in the 'woodland' country the houses 'stand scattered abroad, eache one dwelling in the midst of his owne occupieng'. Here we see champion England, largely the central spine of England, with its nucleated villages and open, communally cultivated fields later subject to enclosure; there we see the contrast of woodland England (the French *bocage* to their *champagne* countrysides) with smaller, more irregularly shaped fields, less later enclosure, more hedgerow trees and more woodland generally, dispersed hamlets or isolated farms. This volume deals with an area within the 'South-eastern Province' as defined in the Roberts and Wrathmell *Atlas of Rural Settlement in England*, a province that also includes East Anglia and Lincolnshire, and it will explore further the 'sharp local regional variations' that Roberts and Wrathmell have already admitted exists in this province.[2] In the South East the *pays* (to use the convenient French term for sub-regional identities produced by the fusion of landscape and cultures) are, however, still more complex, and their landscape histories more diverse than the national-scale subdivision into 'ancient' and 'planned' or 'champion' and 'woodland'.[3]

An alternative way of describing local landscape character is through the national 'Countryside Character' maps that the Countryside Commission produced with English Nature and English Heritage in the mid-1990s and which are increasingly the basis of planning and management decisions at national and regional level.[4] English Nature defined a similar but slightly more detailed set of 'Natural Areas', and work is continuing on the production of more refined joint versions (Joint Character Areas) at a more regional scale. The two approaches serve to demonstrate the rich landscape mosaic still to be found in the South East, notwithstanding the fact that there are no longer any 'natural areas' in south-east England, since all have been affected by human activities. In all there are 159 'Countryside Character' regions in England (others are being added to cover maritime zones), of which 25 fall within the territorial scope of the present book. The Countryside Character Areas for the South East are outlined in Fig. 3.1. These are areas with a characteristic identity and landscape created from the interaction of ecological patterns, landforms, geology, land use, farm type, settlement patterns, archaeology and industrial history.

While bearing in mind these higher classifications, this chapter will investigate the south-east's sub-regions at a more generic level, through the following broader topographic categorisation:

- chalk (largely champion land)
- wealden and woodland landscapes
- lowland heaths
- marshes
- other coastal areas of the region.

Fig. 3.1 The Countryside Character areas of south-east England. The interaction of so many different pays in such a small region has always been a valuable asset economically as well as aesthetically. The numbers assigned to each area correspond to those published in the Countryside Character approach developed by English Heritage, English Nature and the Countryside Agency in 1999.

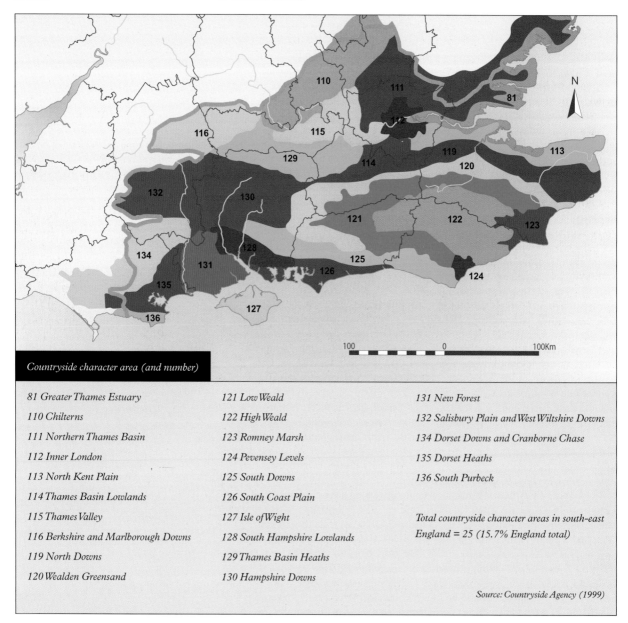

Countryside character area (and number)

81 Greater Thames Estuary	121 Low Weald	131 New Forest
110 Chilterns	122 High Weald	132 Salisbury Plain and West Wiltshire Downs
111 Northern Thames Basin	123 Romney Marsh	134 Dorset Downs and Cranborne Chase
112 Inner London	124 Pevensey Levels	135 Dorset Heaths
113 North Kent Plain	125 South Downs	136 South Purbeck
114 Thames Basin Lowlands	126 South Coast Plain	
115 Thames Valley	127 Isle of Wight	Total countryside character areas in south-east England = 25 (15.7% England total)
116 Berkshire and Marlborough Downs	128 South Hampshire Lowlands	
119 North Downs	129 Thames Basin Heaths	
120 Wealden Greensand	130 Hampshire Downs	

Source: Countryside Agency (1999)

This is not, of course, to deny the huge importance of urban space in the South East, one of the most urbanised regions of Europe. London, the great global city, justifies a chapter (Chapter 7) to itself.

THE CHALKLANDS

Perhaps more than any other characteristic of the south-eastern landscape, the chalk is seen as an emblematic feature, one of the great icons of Englishness. The chalklands of eastern Wessex, indeed, serve as a central hub from which radiate the great downlands that lead north-eastwards to the Chilterns, eastwards to the North Downs, south-eastwards to the South Downs and south to the Dorset heights. At its outward edge the defining chalk escarpment often presents a dramatic profile, sometimes with dry valleys breaching the skyline. Where it is folded by earth movements the chalk landscape can also be more dramatic, as in the steeply dipping ridge at Purbeck in Dorset. More often the dip slopes characterise scenery which is gentle, and which has yielded to settlement and the plough where water and soils permit. And latterly, wherever possible, fields have been amalgamated and commercial forestry has intruded.

The South East contains one of the most complete sequences of chalk anywhere in Europe. There is more than one type of chalk, however, conveniently termed Lower, Middle and Upper in recognition of the order in which it was deposited. Each has different characteristics that affect both topography and subsequent human land use. The Lower Chalk normally outcrops as the familiar gently inclined platform at the base of the main escarpments and is sometimes referred to as 'Chalk marl' (Fig. 3.2); the overlying Middle Chalk, purer in consistency, forms the main scarp face while the Upper Chalk caps the downland, helping to form the soils of the dip slopes, and containing a high quantity of flints, which have been much used for tools and as building material. The chalklands are unified by many common landscape features. The natural environment is dominated by broad swathes of uninterrupted rolling upland, where the chalk strata are horizontal and sometimes punctuated by dry valleys or by intermittently flowing bournes. Chalklands are generally dry because the chalk is porous, but larger rivers flow through valleys where alluvium cloaks the underlying rock.

Where the chalk is overlain by younger, less permeable materials, including 'clay-with-flints' – a broad term for deposits of clays, flints, sands and gravels, but normally involving a stiff clay with large flint nodules – the landscape can take on a quite different complexion, with impeded drainage and large woodland stands dominating the scenery. These acidic deposits can support oak woodland, such as the ancient sessile oaks within Harewood

Fig. 3.2 The Lower Chalk scarp-foot platform – the South Downs at Bostal Hill, Alciston, Sussex, looking westwards. The edge of cultivation has ebbed and flowed over time, across the platform and onto the base of the escarpment, depending on favourable economic conditions.

Forest near Andover. Such deposits, also commonly known as 'plateau drift', can be as much as 15m thick in the Chilterns.

A description of seven distinct areas of chalkland will give some sense of the extent of their local variation.

The Hampshire Downs

The Hampshire Downs consist primarily of elevated, rolling chalk, deep and sheltered valleys, and ridges and escarpments that give extensive views. But, particularly in its eastern parts, this is also a landscape with a sense of seclusion and remoteness. Hamlets, villages and farms are dispersed throughout a network of narrow, winding lanes bounded by ditches and wide verges. Buildings are generally of brick, or brick and timber in the valleys, sometimes decorated with distinctive knapped flint on the uplands. Thatched roofs survive, and chalk, used infrequently as a building stone due to its inherent softness and solubility, appears in the form of 'cob' in walls surrounding some farmsteads.

The springy unimproved downland turf provides one of Britain's richest wildlife habitats, although it has been much reduced over the past 50 years by unprecedented levels of chalk grassland destruction. Only 3.3 per cent of British chalkland now retains 'natural' chalk grassland, largely in places out of the reach of modern agriculture or within military training areas. Much of what survives also tends to be fragmented into small separate sites, many managed as nature reserves or protected as National Nature Reserves (NNRs) or Sites of Special Scientific Interest (SSSIs). Many fine examples remain in the Hampshire Basin, however, including Broughton Down, the National Trust's Stockbridge Down, Danebury hillfort, and Ladle Hill, Watership Down and Beacon Hill near Burghclere.

Chalk grassland, however, is no longer the most distinctive characteristic of the Hampshire Downs. The clay, or clay-with-flints, that lies over the chalk has always influenced farming activity, and since the Second World War intensive arable cultivation has yielded a pattern of medium to large fields defined by woodland edges and low, trimmed hedgerows, post-and-wire fences or coniferous shelter belts. Wooded valleys are particularly characteristic, populated by ancient semi-natural woodlands and subdivided by hedges containing oak hedgerow trees. The Hampshire Downs, like much of the region's landscape, is also characterised by the transport infrastructure required by its relationship to London: during the 20th century the area had to absorb the impact of road building, as exemplified by the M3 cutting its way through Twyford Down at Winchester and urban expansion around Basingstoke and Andover.

The chalk streams are rich in wildlife, and the rivers Itchen and Test are considered internationally and nationally important to nature conservation (Fig. 3.3). But much of the Test and Itchen floodplain was once intensively managed as water meadows. These were of great importance to sheep farming and ensured an early spring flush of grass and a rich source of hay for winter. While the distinctive pattern of interlocking channels and ridges is still widespread, the traditional practice of annually flooding the meadows has died out, leaving a rich wet meadow ecology in some areas and reeds, wet woodland or carr elsewhere (*see* Chapter 5).

The Berkshire Downs and Marlborough Downs

To the north of the Hampshire Downs lie the Berkshire Downs and Marlborough Downs, which run on to meet the Thames along the wooded Goring Gap to the east. To the north and west lie the Upper Thames Clay Vale and the Avon Vale, while the escarpment of the Berkshire and Marlborough Downs is itself a prominent relief feature. The vales of Kennet and Pewsey form the southern boundaries and the chalk forms inward-facing escarpments to north and south. From here the Avon flows south through Salisbury Plain, while the

Fig. 3.3 The River Itchen, a chalk river of international significance for its biodiversity and conservation value. *The river imparts landscape character as well as having a place in the cultural landscape. Parts of the river here are said to have provided Charles Kingsley with the inspiration for* The Water Babies *(1863).*

upper reaches of the Kennet have cut a significant valley that runs west to east through the Marlborough Downs towards Hungerford and into the Vale of Kennet.

These downs form broad expanses of essentially open and waterless chalk on a gentle dip-slope plateau that is dissected by numerous shallow dry valleys, richly farmed, and that possesses extensive areas of woodland. Sarsen stones – remnant blocks of Tertiary sandstone carried by downslope solifluction on to the floors of dry valleys – are a particular feature, best seen at Overton and Fyfield Down to the west of Marlborough, and with some very large 60–70 tonne examples incorporated in the Avebury stone circle and forming the main trilithon ring at Stonehenge.

The area has been settled since Neolithic times and barrows and other prehistoric earthworks are still much in evidence. The Neolithic stone circle at Avebury, the ceremonial mound of Silbury Hill plus the adjacent West Kennet long barrow and other ceremonial monuments are collectively designated as a World Heritage Site. Further significant archaeological features are found on the north scarp of the Berkshire Downs around White Horse Hill and include the Iron Age hillfort of Uffington Castle, the Neolithic chambered long barrow of Wayland's Smithy, built from massive sarsens, and the striking figure of the White Horse itself, now known to date from the late Bronze Age rather than the 1st century BC as previously thought. On the exposed higher chalk, numerous tracks, byways and footpaths cross the sparsely settled landscape. These include the ancient Ridgeway, a broad track that links Avebury with Ivinghoe in the Hertfordshire Chilterns and that is considered one of Britain's oldest 'green' roads (Fig. 3.4). Otherwise, isolated farm buildings, modern fences and the odd clump of trees or shelterbelt form the only significant features.

Because of the increase in intensive arable farming, most of the chalk grassland here, as on the Hampshire Downs, has been replaced in recent years by large, rectilinear fields of cereals, a broad scatter of modern farm buildings and large horse-racing establishments. It is only on the scarp itself and on some of the steeper dry valleys that traditional chalk grassland is found. To the south and east, the open downland gives way to a more wooded landscape that includes the rolling hills of Savernake Forest, south-east of Marlborough. On this isolated area of acidic clay-with-flints ancient semi-natural oak glades are juxtaposed with planted beech and recent commercial plantings of conifers. The settlements here are small and scattered in contrast to the general emptiness of the open downland. The fertile Vale of Pewsey's meadows and orchards offer another contrast: fields on the Lower Greensand slopes are more irregular than on the chalk and are subdivided by hawthorn hedges, which contain oak, and interspersed with numerous blocks of woodland and shelterbelts. The downland valleys contain fairly evenly spaced and generally compact villages and hamlets in which thatch, red brick and weatherboard are characteristic of the cottages and barns. Many buildings display knapped flint and weathered chalk in their walls and sarsen stones in their foundations. The agricultural market towns of Marlborough and Pewsey are the main settlements, while the smaller farm settlements and hamlets are linked by narrow lanes to the wider road network and the M4 motorway.

The South Wessex Downs

The South Wessex Downs comprise Salisbury Plain and the West Wiltshire Downs, the North and South Dorset Downs (including Purbeck) and Cranborne Chase. The landscape pattern is similar to those already described: chalk grassland, chalk rivers, woodland and arable, interrupted by smaller areas of meadow and wetland habitat. The West Wiltshire Downs are gently domed and dissected by shallow dry valleys. Only in the extreme west, where the headwaters of the Wylye form deep coombes, is the relief more dramatic. Arable cultivation dominates again, relieved by copses around farms and barns. And once more, ridgeways, field systems and hillforts emphasise the prehistoric foundations of the landscape.

Within Salisbury Plain the dominant and unifying features are the rather austere rolling chalk landscapes with scattered sarsen stones – known locally as 'greywethers' because of their resemblance to resting sheep – abrupt escarpments, especially to the north and west, and attractive chalk river valleys that flow southwards and eastwards towards Salisbury. Sheep farming has largely disappeared and much is now a vast landscape of arable fields and unimproved grassland punctuated only by small hilltop woodlands of beech and conifer on the clay-with-flints. There are few hedges, and low post-and-wire fences maintain the feeling of openness. Apart from farming, the main modern landscape influence is military activity, as at Tidworth, Larkhill and Bulford. In the 20th century the two major trends were the expansion of the Ministry of Defence training areas and agricultural change. However, the Salisbury Plain LIFE project (2001–5) typified more recent concern for the conservation of the remaining species-rich grassland and its associated flora and fauna. As the largest unbroken expanse of calcareous grassland in north-west Europe (it covers approximately 14,000ha and represents 41 per cent of the United Kingdom's total area of such habitat), this huge expanse is now a rare asset and the project was designed to tackle issues such as grazing, scrub invasion and afforestation.

Cutting across these broad arable landscapes are the valleys of the Wylye, Avon and Bourne, where villages still retain old cottages built of cob beneath thatch roofs, with flint used in combination with brick edging and banding. The Upper Chalk was traditionally used for houses and farm buildings while to the south the greenish, grey-brown Chilmark Stone, from the limestone quarries west of the

Fig. 3.4 The White Horse at Uffington, Berkshire. The prehistoric image, cut into the scarp face at White Horse Hill, is overlooked by the double walls of Uffington Castle hillfort. Optical Stimulated Luminescence (OSL) or 'silt-dating', gives a date between 1400 and 600 BC for the horse, and such a late Bronze Age date may also cover the initial building of the hillfort. Beyond is the straight alignment of the prehistoric Ridgeway, now a National Trail, and beyond that the modern large fields of the Lambourn Downs.

escarpment, was used for churches and other buildings of quality. The Wylye valley is particularly notable for buildings that make decorative use of a distinctive chequered pattern of napped flint and clunch. Scattered farmsteads are found in the more sheltered downland sites and between the villages along the valleys, matched by large isolated barns on the open downland above. Abandoned water meadows are again found in the valleys.

The deeply indented escarpments of the Dorset Downs rise steeply above the Blackmoor Vale and Vale of Wardour to the north and west. In places they jut out into Blackmoor Vale and are cut through by steep valleys such as the Cheselbourne, where there is extensive woodland, rough grassland and patches of scrub. At the top of their slopes, and on outliers such as Win Green, Fontmell Down and Hambledon, there are abundant prehistoric features, especially Bronze Age round barrows and Iron Age hillforts. Below, villages cluster around the springs that emerge at the escarpment base. Between the Stour valley and Shaftesbury, the escarpment runs near to the outlier that forms Hod Hill and Hambleton Hill and then continues to Melbury Hill.

On the dip slope, the familiar treeless chalk landscape is dominated again by arable farming, broken up by some geometrically shaped game coverts. The slopes fall to sheltered, secluded valleys occupied by linear villages, water meadows fringed by willows and poplars, valley-side woodlands and narrow lanes, which, in different combinations, impart local character to individual valleys. Here again, a wide variety of building materials includes timber-framing, flint with brick dressing and banding, and clunch, sometimes used with brick to give chequered patterns. Low, rendered buildings are also common and there are many pre-18th and 19th-century brick buildings. Although thatch is traditional, there are many tiled roofs and some slate. The villages are the main settlements, apart from Blandford Forum in the Stour valley and Dorchester at the southern edge. In contrast, the remnants of the medieval hunting forest of Cranborne Chase are characterised by woodlands, shelterbelts, clumps and copses that contain ancient hazel coppice, and also by enclosed arable, pasture and parkland. Between Melbury and Blandford Forum woodland cover spills over the scarp from Cranborne Chase, crowning spurs and filling the steep coombes. Along much of the dip slope a thin scattering of mostly modern farmsteads lies within a road pattern dominated by straight enclosure and turnpike roads. The Chase, by contrast, is characterised by large houses, substantial parks, villages and a scatter of hamlets.

South Purbeck, the distinctive 'Isle of Purbeck', bounded to the north by the Dorset heaths, is separated from them by the narrow, largely uninhabited, chalk ridge that extends right across Purbeck. On the north is a steep slope of ancient semi-natural beech and oak woodland. The chalk is again mainly open grassland with gorse and other scrub on the steeper slopes. The spectacular coastline forms the southern and eastern boundary of the area. South Purbeck's geology has effectively created four distinct yet intertwined landscapes, in which the use of Purbeck and Portland limestone as a dominant building material lends unity across Purbeck in both town (eg Swanage) and countryside. The narrow, but prominent, chalk ridge overlooks the sheltered Corfe Valley, mainly under hedged pasture, interspersed with copses and small woodlands. These then give way to groups of Scots pine on the slopes rising up to the austere Purbeck limestone plateau, where fields are littered with small, shallow quarries and bounded by drystone walls. The coastline demonstrates similar variety. From the sheltered heathland coastline of Studland Bay, around to the chalk cliffs of Swanage Bay and the abrupt limestone of Durlston Head, a complex and beautiful coastline sweeps round to Worbarrow Bay. Sheer chalk and limestone cliffs contrast with sheltered coves at Chapman's Pool and Lulworth Cove, and extend out to sea as the chalk stacks of Old Harry Rocks. To the west are the unstable clay and shale cliffs at Kimmeridge.[5]

The Chilterns

The Chilterns are defined by the dominant escarpment that rises steeply from the Vale of Aylesbury to 275m. The face is wooded, interspersed with fragmented unimproved grassland and scrub on thin rendzina soils. The Chilterns are cut by a series of through-valleys formed by glacial meltwater, as well as a small number supporting streams, and many hidden coombes and dry valleys that sometimes give rise to intermittently flowing bournes. Much of the dip slope is overlain by clay-with-flints and supports extensive woodlands. These include ancient semi-natural woods, together with medium-grade farmland and even remnant heath. Very importantly, the Chilterns contain the most extensive area of native beech woodland in England, and are indeed one of the most wooded lowland landscapes in England. Between 20 and 30 per cent of the land is covered by trees, ranging from dry beech woods on acid soils through to oak-beech woods on heavy clays and beech woods on thin rendzinas. Beech was selectively managed because of its value in the 18th- and 19th-century furniture industry. The 'hanging' woodlands of the valleys are a characteristic feature of the area. The extent and grandeur of the beech woods clearly distinguish the Chilterns from other more open chalk landscapes of the region.

Settlements traditionally consisted of scattered farmsteads and hamlets, but during the 20th century large-scale development took place from the 1930s onwards along major road and rail corridors, including the route of the Metropolitan line, which had penetrated the Chilterns by the 1890s. More recently the M1 and M40 motorways have also stimulated commuting. Most Chiltern villages have therefore grown rapidly and house styles from the previous 300 years can be found in most of them. Notable again is the consistent use of flints, often combined with brick, both in buildings and boundary walls. Most vernacular buildings also have tiled roofs, rather than thatch. The oldest farm buildings have large timber-framed barns clad with black, horizontal weatherboarding, and brick-and-flint gable walls. Along the Thames, the towns of Marlow, Henley and Cookham expanded greatly in the 19th century, with river frontages characterised by ribbon developments of summer homes. There are also the substantial towns of Luton, Dunstable, Hemel Hempstead, Berkhamstead, Chesham, Amersham and High Wycombe. Nevertheless, overall the area retains a predominantly quiet and prosperous farming character.

The North Downs

The North Downs extend from the narrow Hogs Back ridge near Farnham, widening eastwards to end in the White Cliffs of Dover. The escarpment here faces south and is cut by a series of steep-sided coombes, chalk pits and quarries for agricultural lime. Up to the present day its rich grassland has maintained sheep and cattle grazing. The north-facing dip slope, with shallow dry valleys, is primarily given over to arable farming, orchards and improved pasture. Woods and shaws (thickly hedged and wooded field boundaries) also cover the numerous dry valleys, and the North Downs are also well wooded in west Kent and the eastern parts of Surrey between Guildford and Leatherhead. Oak and ash are typical of the upper part of the dip slope while a mix of beech, ash and maple is commonly found on the dry valley sides. In Surrey, extensive areas of yew and box woodland exist, giving a distinctive dark green appearance to parts of the scarp, as at the riverside cliffs at Box Hill (Fig. 3.5). Many of the downland ridges are wooded and on the clay-with-flints or sandier superficial deposits soils are markedly acidic; here heathland can be found, in striking contrast to the chalk downland.

The chalk is cut by the valleys of the Wey, Mole, Darent and Great Stour and at Rochester the Medway has been for long associated with busy transport routes, industry and mineral extraction. Narrow, enclosed lanes, overhung with yew,

***Fig. 3.5 Box Hill and river cliffs,
Surrey.*** *Now in the care of the National
Trust, the woodland overlooking the Mole gap
has long been a place of recreation. Yew and
beech trees thrive on the thin soils here,
although much beech was destroyed in the
storms of 1987 and 1990.*

wayfaring tree and whitebeam, run diagonally down the escarpment as the remnants
of once-extensive drove roads that connected north Kent and north Surrey with the
wealden 'dens' (pastures). Local building materials consist again largely of flint, with
rich orange-red wealden brick commonly used for corners and door and window
surrounds. The area now contains some large towns such as South Croydon,
Chatham, Dover and Guildford. And as a reminder of Kent's close links with the
Continent, the Channel Tunnel terminal development dominates the views from
the escarpment at the White Cliffs, while the busy M25 and M20 motorways cut
through the North Downs, reminding us also of the proximity of London.

The South Downs

The South Downs extend eastwards from Winchester and the chalk of the adjoining
Hampshire Downs to finally meet the sea at Beachy Head, dipping southwards to
the narrow Coastal Plain and the English Channel beyond. Much of the south-
facing slope has long been cultivated for arable crops, and the landscape is now
often covered in large-scale grass leys and cereals, but nevertheless still offers a
prized open and remote character, greatly valued in the heavily populated South.
The most dramatic feature is the steep, north-facing scarp that contains much of the
region's remaining semi-natural chalk grassland, chalk heath and scrub.

Traditionally the Downs have been an important rearing ground for
Southdown sheep, whose grazing, together with that of rabbits, has historically
maintained the open and homogeneous semi-natural chalk grassland habitats
that are seen as the traditional clothing of the Downs. The soft, springy,
unimproved chalk grassland is again species-rich but has declined as a result of
the decrease in sheep farming, changing patterns of land use and the invasion of
scrub. Legal protection for the remaining areas is increasing, through
mechanisms ranging from SSSI status to Annex 1 of the EC Habitats Directive.
The best examples are now under consideration as Special Areas of
Conservation (SACs). More recently, there has been a reversion of significant
arable areas to grassland and restoration of sheep grazing under the provisions of
the government's Environmentally Sensitive Areas scheme.

Chalk heath, an extremely rare habitat, occurs where acid loessic soils overlie
the chalk, and Lullington Heath, north-west of Eastbourne, is the best surviving

example in Britain. The ash or beech hangers on the east Hampshire escarpment are also notable, but English elm is now largely confined to areas around Brighton. Areas of ancient woodland are concentrated in the western South Downs, and include some areas of relict large-leaved lime woodland. An internationally important area of yew woodland at Kingley Vale NNR, north-west of Chichester, in West Sussex, is considered to be the finest European example of this habitat.

The chalk of the South Downs is broken only by the valleys of the Meon, Arun, Adur, Ouse and Cuckmere. These possess a range of riverside habitats that includes pastures that are often enclosed by hedges, copses, and lines of alder, willow and poplar, some of which are pollarded. Settlement on the chalk itself is sparse and often reached by long chalky tracks, while scattered villages, hamlets and isolated farms with traditional barns occur in the dry valleys of the dip slope, clustered along the scarp foot, or within the river valleys. The villages consist of nucleated brick-and-flint buildings, with brick quoins and window details and roofs of tile or slate. These are often set within mature trees and sometimes surround a village pond. The central part of the Downs is hemmed in by the conurbations of the Coastal Plain, and the northward growth of Brighton, Eastbourne and Worthing in particular has intensified urban pressure on the area.

The Isle of Wight

The final chalk landscape is that of the central ridge of the Isle of Wight. Attaining a height of 214m at Brightstone Down, this is an area of deeply dissected dry valleys covered by generally thin and infertile soils. At Tennyson Down, eroded offshore stacks form The Needles. A second area of chalk forms the high downs between Shanklin and St Catherine's Point and along the southern coast, eventually reaching a height of 240m at St Boniface Down, where capping gravels support relict gorse, bracken and heather. The downland in west Wight is frequently capped by clay-with-flints that supports gorse scrub and in a few places chalk heath, as on Brook Down. On Ventnor Down, precipitously steep slopes rise up behind the town of Ventnor to be capped by acidic flint gravels that support typical dry heathland vegetation. But again, much of the chalk grassland here has been lost over the last century as the introduced holm oak has spread from Ventnor's Victorian gardens.

The chalk downs support a variety of land uses including pasture, intensive arable, ancient hanger woodlands, scrub and commercial forestry. Chalk grassland fares rather better here than in many other parts of the South East; 862ha still survive and cover 15 per cent of the chalk outcrop – nearly five times the national average. Grazing has maintained these grasslands for centuries, thereby preserving the rich flora, although some of these grasslands, such as those on Afton Down, are remarkable in having remained ungrazed for decades without any loss of botanical diversity. These may be the region's truly natural grassland, possibly surviving intact since the last Ice Age.

Such are the defining but fragile chalk landscapes of the South East. Historically, these were difficult areas to farm because of their windswept aspects, thin soils and paucity of water, but they were integrated into farming systems through their capacity to support sheep flocks, which in turn fertilised the lower arable soils. In places the chalk also supports woodland: oak and ash woods on the upper dip slopes; beech, ash and maple on the dry valley slopes; and yew and box woods with their distinctive darker green foliage on the Surrey chalk. The vegetation cover is varied: a journey from open downland in Hampshire towards Twyford Down and Winchester might then pass eastwards through extensive wooded clay-with-flints in West Sussex, and thence again to open downland turf east of the River Arun towards Beachy Head. Today the downlands are most likely to feature in everyday consciousness as bare or rolling open country, and as such are highly prized and protected by a variety of planning and environmental legislation.

WEALDEN AND WOODLAND LANDSCAPES

The contrast between open, chalk landscapes and wooded environments is one that echoes through much of Western Europe. Where these two environments are juxtaposed, each has been exploited by mankind for the different resources that they offer – the contrasts have been summarised as being that of different *pays*, regions of human and physical distinctiveness. Opinions differed on the felicitousness of living in one or the other environment: William Gilpin wrote in his *Remarks on Forest Scenery* (1791):

> *Perhaps of all species of landscape, there is none, which so universally captivates mankind, as forest-scenery: and our prepossession in favour of it appears in nothing more, than in this; that the inhabitants of bleak countries, totally destitute of wood, are generally considered, from the natural feelings of mankind, as the objects of pity.*[6]

Notwithstanding Gilpin's feelings, within south-east England the interactions between the two environments have been equally strong in both prehistoric and historic times (*see* Chapter 5). The wooded landscapes that will receive particular attention here are the High and Low Wealds of Sussex, Kent and Surrey, and the old hunting grounds such as the Forest of Windsor in Berkshire or the Forest of Bere in Hampshire. While the former are, to a degree, natural environments whose settlement history and cultural appreciation has been an outcome of the possibilities offered by the physical surroundings, the latter are purely cultural products. The forests were the hunting grounds of the elite; reserved spaces for their leisure which actually comprised a variety of scenery. By no means all of the ground was wooded – 'foresta' being a legal term rather than a reference to a specific landscape type – and it is possible that little more than 20 per cent of these legal forests was actually covered by trees. Whilst it is convenient to treat the two together in this section, the important distinction should be borne in mind.

The High Weald

The High Weald is the core of the south-eastern peninsula. It has a complex geology of interbedded sands, soft sandstones and clays, with nutrient-poor soils. Many of its poor soils are prone to waterlogging, ensuring that this remains an area of forested ridges, among which rise the headwaters of the Medway, Ouse and Rother. Although not exceeding 240m in height, the High Weald is a hilly country of east–west ridges and valleys, the sandstone cliff exposures of which provide the only inland rock climbing in south-east England.

Despite its strong topography, the area's overall character is equally one of human creation. The High Weald comprises a dense mosaic of small fields surrounded by shaws, and broken up by sunken lanes, roadside verges, ponds and ancient semi-natural woodland, all giving a feeling of privacy (Fig. 3.6). Clearance of the woodland has been cyclical but continuous and many of the scattered farmsteads, field patterns and woodlands are directly attributable to a prolonged period of clearance and habitation in medieval times. Grassland is the dominant agricultural land use, supporting sheep, cattle and pigs. There were until recently hops and orchards in the eastern river valleys. Heathland was formerly more widespread in the High Weald, but a cessation of grazing, as well as woodland incursion and conifer planting, has led to its loss. The only sizeable remainder is the Ashdown Forest, a former hunting ground at the very centre of the Weald.

Woodland is certainly the major land cover, with significant interconnection along hedgerows between the wooded areas. Numerous conifer plantations, as at St Leonard's Forest near Horsham, are also locally dominant. Approximately 15,460ha of ancient semi-natural woodland (ie that which is demonstrably pre-1600 in date

and has not been artificially replanted) remain here, accounting for 14.5 per cent of the land cover compared with the English national average of only 2.6 per cent. In many cases the semi-natural element of woodland has been replaced by sweet chestnut and hornbeam coppice, which was used for the production of charcoal for the iron and glass industries. Hammer ponds, relict features of the post-medieval iron industry, are another distinctive feature of the landscape and add to its diversity.

In great contrast to the chalk downland, the settlements in the High Weald were sited on ridges. They avoided the wooded valleys and many have since grown into hilltop villages, such as Burwash (seen in Fig. 3.6), Mayfield, Wadhurst and Hawkhurst. Former oast houses and stone church towers and spires are also located on the ridges, and elsewhere in the area there are the larger towns of Tunbridge Wells, Crowborough, East Grinstead, Bexhill, Hastings and Horsham. Vernacular buildings exhibit various combinations of materials, including abundant white weatherboard, brick, tile, stone and timber-framing. Horsham stone slab tiles from the western end of the High Weald were used for the roofs of larger buildings.

Fig. 3.6 The High Weald. A view from the southern slopes of the Rother valley, looking towards the ridge-top village of Burwash. The small fields, sloping ground and dense woodland cover of the High Weald are well illustrated.

The Low Weald

Wrapping around the High Weald on three sides is the Low Weald, an elongated horseshoe-shaped clay vale, bounded for much of its outer length by the Greensand. In this flat, low-lying and frequently wet environment altitudes rarely exceed 40m and are often as low as 15m. The area is well wooded, with many fields created by woodland clearance. Their species-rich shaws contain many mature trees and run between small copses of oak and birch, while occasional lines of trees mark out former field boundaries. Small streams with riparian willows and alders drain lazily to the wet grazing lands of major rivers such as the Arun, Adur, Beult and Medway. Small ponds, relict features of brickmaking, marl digging and the iron industry, are frequent on field edges and in woodlands, although many have become silted up.

As in the High Weald, broadleaved oak woodland is dominant in this 'oaktree clay', and significant areas of semi-natural ancient woodland survive, as in Chiddingfold Forest in Surrey and adjacent parts of West Sussex, their age reflected in their large coppice stools, banks and ditches (Fig. 3.7). Coppiced woodland, a rich habitat, varies between chestnut, hornbeam and hazel. There are also examples of wood-pasture environments that arose from the former grazing of livestock among mature trees, as at Ebernoe Common and The Mens, between Petworth and Wisborough Green in West Sussex. Agriculture here remains largely pastoral on the nutrient-poor clays, although there is some arable and fruit growing on deposits of brickearth in Kent, where the fields are larger and there are fewer hedges and trees.

Because of the original wooded nature of the Low Weald, settlements tend to be small and scattered and often comprise linear groups of houses along roadside wastes. Many have greens or commons and are linked by narrow lanes. Sometimes the latter were widened by the addition of verges and attendant ditches to allow early travellers and horse-drawn vehicles to avoid waterlogged areas. Vernacular building generally employed brick made from local clays, often with Horsham stone for roofs and sometimes the use of timber-framing or tile-hanging. Contrasting with the essential rurality of most of the area, the urban and airport development around Gatwick and Crawley provides a very different landscape in which expansion has destroyed all traces of what went before.

Hunting forests

The hunting forests of medieval England were reserved to the crown or its lessees, or might sometimes be privately owned. Because so many royal and ecclesiastical residences were located in London, Winchester and elsewhere in the region, members of elite society looked particularly to the South East for their leisure pursuits. In fact the counties of Hampshire, Dorset and Wiltshire, together with Essex, possessed most of the royal forests, of which the best known are the New Forest, Epping Forest, Alice Holt and Woolmer. Countryside with interspersed open ground ('lawns') and cover – the so-called 'wood-pasture' landscape – was ideal, and here deer were reared and protected through a network of rangers and forest courts that administered strict forest law. Laws of this kind were proclaimed over much of the region at various times during the medieval period and the fines exacted by the forest courts, which operated outside normal judicial systems, were a source of much-needed (but highly unpopular) royal revenue.

Remnants of former medieval hunting grounds survive in the form of ancient oak and beech pollards or the associated boundary banks and ditches. On the heavy London Clay the old hunting forest of Epping displays many relict landscape features from its past, although it should not be assumed that all the woodland lies on the lower, heavier clays of the region. There are many smaller areas of great significance to be found on a variety of soil types. Windsor Forest, for example, spans both London Clay and Bagshot sands and gravels and several hundred hectares of its ancient habitats have been designated as SSSIs. Altogether more than 3,000 of its veteran oak and beech trees are at least 300 years old, many of them having been pollarded. Near by, north of Slough, is Burnham Beeches, an area of forest now owned by the Corporation of London in which many further ancient pollarded beeches and oaks similarly thrive on acid gravels and clay. Many of the pollards here are more than 400 years old, but since the 1930s their numbers have decreased dramatically as they have aged and decayed.[7]

Fig. 3.7 The Headcorn Oak. *The oak, a symbol of the wealden clay soils, was destroyed by fire in 1986 but had stood by the door of Headcorn Church in Kent for at least 500 years. The illustration is from the cover of Furley's* A History of the Weald of Kent *(1871, Vol. I).*

OPPOSITE PAGE: **Fig. 3.8 Epping Forest, pollarded beech trees.** *Polling, or pollarding, was the regular cutting of branches at a height of 2–3m to produce repeated crops of wood. The new wood then grew well out of the reach of deer and livestock. The practice has largely fallen into disuse, leaving large numbers of ancient overgrown and top-heavy pollards, many of which have not been cut for decades. Pollarding was typical in deer parks, as here in Epping Forest.*

Epping Forest, now also managed by the Corporation of London, is seen as a 'green lung' for Londoners. The modern Epping Forest covers 2,430ha and was formerly part of the great medieval Essex Forest that once included Waltham and Hainault. In 1878, when threatened by enclosure, its varied mosaic of grasslands, heaths, ancient trees and wood-pasture inspired the protection of the Epping Forest Act. This early example of conservation legislation protected the rights of commoners to graze cattle, as well as extending recreational privileges to the wider public. In 2001 the concept of a London 'Green Arc' was launched, of which Epping Forest was to be a key component in the move to create a more sustainable capital city. The ancient and semi-natural woodland of the forest has large resources of oak, beech and hornbeam and there are more than 50,000 veteran pollards (Fig. 3.8).

The hunting forests – and still larger areas of legal forest, some of which were never actually used for hunting – covered much of the present landscape at various times. We now see fragments only: in Hampshire, West Walk, at 350ha, is the largest remaining portion of the former Forest of Bere that formerly stretched from the River Test at Kings Somborne in the west in a great arc to Rowlands Castle in the east. West Walk supports a rich biodiversity; at least 63 ancient woodland plants survive there and it is one of Hampshire's most important woodlands outside the New Forest. Most of the original Forest of Bere is today a typical mixed habitat of woodland, open space, heathland, farmland and downland. Alongside the remaining 19th-century oak and 20th-century conifer plantations there are areas of scrub and coppice, streams, ponds and an extensive network of rides and paths. And very typically, the landscape has been opened up to the public through the provision of information points, waymarked trails, horse-riding and cycle routes.

THE LOWLAND HEATHS

The origins and historical character of the region's extensive heaths are discussed below, but we should note here that, like the royal forests, they occupy only a fraction of their former extent.[8] They were reviled by many early commentators, and were later reclaimed for farming or forestry, or encroached upon for urban development. Ironically, those heaths that do survive are now greatly valued and are offered varying degrees of protection; indeed some efforts have been made to re-create new heathland in places where it had been lost. Although their subsoils may vary, there are some shared similarities of vegetation and landscape: heath is typified by poor, degraded and acidic soils which, appropriately grazed and drained, can support ling (*Calluna vulgaris*), cross-leaved heath (*Erica tetralix*), or bell-heather (*Erica cinerea*), purple moor-grass (*Molinia caerulea*), gorse (*Ulex* spp.) and rank grasses, scattered trees, scrub, sphagnum mosses, rushes and open grassland. Acid peat may also be found in some valleys. Well-known areas of heath, other than those described below, include the High Weald sites at Ashdown Forest, which now accounts for between 2 and 5 per cent of the entire lowland heathland in England, and St Leonards Forest, together with the Low Weald site at Chailey Common, south-east of Haywards Heath. There are still remnants of former expanses on the Lower Greensand soils, especially in the western Weald, while others survive on the Bagshot Sands and the sands of the New Forest.

There may be as many as 23,000ha of heathland in the South East – about 40 per cent of the United Kingdom total. Some examples are described here to illustrate the general landscape character of these environments.

The New Forest

The New Forest is an area of shallow ridges and valleys, falling to gently sloping land around the Forest edges. Complex patterns of soils and drainage occur, resulting in poor, free-draining, infertile and acidic soils from which nutrients

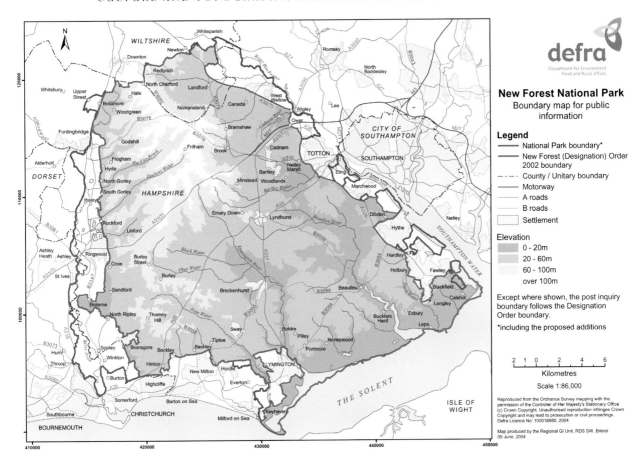

Fig. 3.9 The New Forest National Park, designated in 2004 and operational from March 2005.

Lyndhust and Brockenhurst are much-visited centres, and the much-travelled M27/A31 transect is well known, but the western edge overlooking the Avon valley is the least-visited area of the park.

have leached out. About two-thirds of the Forest is lowland heath, with associations typical of south-eastern heaths elsewhere: rough heather, acidic grassland, bracken and gorse bushes. The impoverished land also offers a mosaic of ancient woodland (one of the largest tracts of semi-natural woodland in the region) and conifer plantations, wood-pasture, grassland commons maintained by close grazing, and small-scale pastoral farming.

Above all, this is a cultural landscape, shaped from the creation of the Norman kings' hunting *Nova Foresta* to the grazing of Commoners around the forest, and the small-scale farming of today. From 1923 the Forestry Commission administered the area, and when formal Forest Law was finally rescinded in 1971, it was replaced by the Verderers' Court, whose members were elected to protect the rights of Commoners. This landscape is thus a manifestation of centuries of changing balances between the land-management needs and interests of royal hunting, commoners' grazing and the production of timber, together with the 20th-century addition of recreation and development. The last century also saw variations in grazing that led to steady encroachment on to the heathland by self-sown pine, while the agricultural improvement of 'lawns' through draining and re-seeding, cutting and burning of heathland and clearance of bracken and pine have all played their part in producing subtle change. Meanwhile on the eastern edge of the New Forest urban development has been extensive. As well as the oil refineries of the Fawley industrial complex, the urban fringes now extend through garden centres, caravan parks and light industry. In recognition of its continuing status as a humanly created and maintained landscape, and of the need to balance the conflicting pressures on this fragile environment, the New Forest was designated in 2004 as a National Park (Fig. 3.9).

The Bagshot Formation heaths

The Tertiary deposits of the Bagshot Formation, overlying the London Clay, produce acidic sandy soils that result in heaths extending from the Thames Basin lowlands in the east, across north Hampshire and through to the dip slope of the Berkshire Downs and Marlborough Downs. Despite fragmentation, there remains much unenclosed heathland in these areas, together with oak, birch, bracken and Scots pine. In the second half of the 20th century these heathlands experienced intensive residential development around such towns as Ascot, Camberley, Farnborough and Woking, which are now accessible to London via the major M3, M4 and M25 motorway routes. Extensive areas of low-density suburbs intermix with paddocks for 'horsiculture', golf courses and parkland. Large areas are also owned by the Ministry of Defence, in which barracks and army housing are very evident. South of the River Kennet, the land rises to a plateau of mixed woodland with extensive conifer plantations, farm and parkland, an area which includes the (in)famous defence establishments constructed on heathland, or former heath, at Aldermaston Atomic Warfare Establishment, Farnborough Airfield and Greenham Common.

The Lower Greensand heaths

There is also extensive heathland and common land on the Lower Greensand in Surrey and western Sussex. Here are Wrotham Heath, Reigate Heath and the commons at Farnham and Frensham, together with the woodland-heathland complex of Woolmer Forest. Between Petersfield and Pulborough another series of heaths is to be found at Iping, Stedham and South Ambersham. The Lower Greensand formation also underlies the spectacular Hindhead, with its 450ha of connected common, heath and woodland to the north of Haslemere. Acquired in 1906 as one of the founding sites for the young National Trust, it still maintains much of the area's heathland.

The Dorset heaths

The fragmentation of heathland is perhaps best illustrated by a final example: the decline of the wild Dorset heaths, internationally known as settings for Thomas Hardy's novels (*see* Chapter 8). From the mid-18th century, when they occupied about 39,960ha and formed a continuous presence around Poole Bay and in eastern Dorset, they shrank to just 5,670ha by the mid-1980s – a decline of 86 per cent.[9] Reclamation for farming, post-Second World War forestry, recreation and especially urban expansion of the Poole conurbation, as at Canford Heath, have all helped to reduce the heathland cover to fragmented patches (Fig. 3.10). Increased growth of scrub and young trees can also be seen as traditional grazing practices have declined. A National Lowland Heathland Programme has been

Fig. 3.10 The fragmentation of the Dorset heathlands 1759–1978.

The processes of urbanisation and agricultural improvement have both whittled away older heathlands, which only began to be the object of keen conservation interest in the late 20th century.

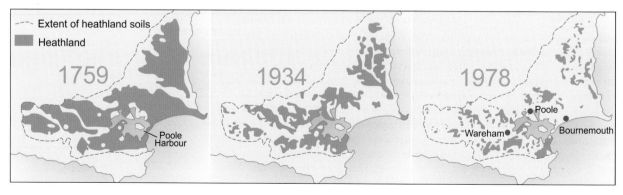

launched by English Nature to address the management issues here, now that 95 per cent of the remaining heathland, including all of the major tracts, is covered by protective designations and ownership.

THE COASTAL MARSHES OF THE SOUTH EAST

The South East has a very long and diverse coast that makes generalisation about landscapes very difficult. One obvious element, however, is the marshlands and former marshlands, which offer character and variety to the shoreline. These include the marshes of the Thames Estuary, and former marshes of east Kent in the Wantsum area; Romney Marsh and the Pevensey Levels; the undeveloped areas of the West Sussex and Hampshire marshes; and finally the Poole Bay area. All have, at various times, been subject to changing sea levels, but the outcomes have been complex and variable. Some remain undeveloped marshland, while others have been converted to profitable farmland or to recreational sites.

Romney Marsh

We begin with Romney Marsh, the prime example of an area that has been converted to a rich farming landscape. From about 6000 BC rises in sea level drowned the lower reaches of several rivers and created tidally influenced estuaries and shallow marine bays (*see* Chapter 2). The area of Romney Marsh (including not only Romney Marsh proper, but also the Walland and Denge Marshes, and the Broomhill, East Guldeford, Brede and Pett Levels) was one such bay into which flowed rivers draining from the Weald – and there remains a recognisable ancient cliff-line around the inner border of the marsh (*see* Fig. 2.9). As sea level stabilised, a series of shingle and sand spits and islands grew slowly across the mouth of the bay, progressively creating lagoons and saltmarsh. From the Roman period at least, wholesale reclamation for agriculture was undertaken, and by the medieval period the area had undergone both periodic inundation and reclamation and was changing from saltmarsh to reed and sedge meadows interspersed with enclosed lagoons.

The Romney Marshes thus owe their modern landscape character both to natural and cultural processes. They retain a distinctive flat, remote and open topography, characterised by pasture or arable fields, often divided by an irregular network of drainage ditches and banks, with few trees or hedges. The exceptions to the flatness are the raised ground and clumps of trees at settlements such as Old Romney and Newchurch. Walland Marsh is particularly distinctive, containing many surviving medieval fields, dykes and unimproved pasture. Sheep grazing was the traditional land use up until the Second World War and still persists over most of this area. In post-war years, however, there has also been much conversion to arable in places where the high quality reclaimed alluvial marshland has been the subject of modern drainage. The scattered settlements along open roads, punctuated by sharp bends, reflect the piecemeal reclamation process as the marsh was 'inned'. Among the traditional houses there is widespread use of weatherboarding and hung tiles, while churches, set among the marshes and some now in ruins, are of stone.

Dungeness Point was formed between about 1000 BC and the medieval centuries and is now the largest shingle foreland in Europe. It characterises Romney as much as its reclaimed land. The landscape here offers a range of paradoxical contrasts. On the one hand there are the two imposing nuclear power stations of Dungeness A and B and on the other the expanding holiday resorts that add to what the Countryside Agency has referred to as the 'general clutter along the coast'. At the same time, there is also a strong and pervading sense of isolation. The residents of Dungeness live in scattered brick houses, beach shacks or chalets.

Demand for properties in this seemingly unpromising location has resulted in a waiting list, fuelled by the popularity of the bohemian nature of the community, and reinforced by Derek Jarman's garden at Prospect Cottage (*see* Fig. 8.13).[10]

The Pevensey Levels

Between Bexhill and Eastbourne lie the Pevensey Levels, about 4,500ha of low-lying reclaimed wetland broken by pockets of raised land occupied by farm buildings and settlements, some of which have now been abandoned. By the 1st century AD the drowned river valleys from the High Weald had formed a wide bay here, as in Romney Marsh. These drowned valleys were partly sheltered by storm beach shingle spits that gradually developed across the bay, allowing alluvium to be deposited behind. As a result of a continuing process of medieval 'inning', the Levels were slowly changed from saltmarsh to reedy meadows. This remains a predominantly pastoral landscape, and an important wetland SSSI habitat. In contrast to the Romney Marshes the area is still dominated by intensively grazed wet cattle pasture, dissected by an irregular network of drainage ditches and banks, and with a few hedges and trees. Although there has been a long history of drainage, especially during the late 20th century to reduce winter flooding, relatively little of the Levels have been subject to arable conversion.

The Thameside marshes

The marshes fringing the Thames Estuary bring touches of wilderness and isolation to this otherwise highly urbanised area, and the coast is indented by several estuaries between the mouth of the Crouch in Essex and the Swale in Kent. The extent of the marshes here ranges from a narrow fringe beside the estuaries to broad coastal tracts and extensive islands such as Foulness. The intertidal zone is one of broad saltmarshes, shallow and meandering creeks, brackish water and mudflats, now interspersed with sea defences against once-frequent flooding. The issue of sea defence is critical in this part of the world and the great tidal surge of 1953 is still remembered in places such as Foulness, where virtually the whole island was flooded. Underwood for thatching sea walls has long been extracted from Essex forests. Lines of posts and branches were also installed on the mudflats to trap silts at high tide, thus allowing saltmarsh vegetation to colonise naturally – a method still employed on Mersea Island. Since the medieval period marshland has been inned and coastal defences constructed, yielding sheep-grazed marsh within the sea walls and in the saltmarsh beyond. At West Thurrock, by contrast, walls were erected using chalk from Purfleet, but maintenance of the hugely expensive length of sea-wall defences is now giving way to a policy of managed retreat and foreshore recharge as an alternative to total exclusion of the sea – however controversial this may be among those who see their land being lost.

Low islands such as Sheppey, Dengie and Mersea bring diversity. Sheppey is typical: the higher ground between Sheerness, Minster and Leysdown is densely occupied with farms and settlements, stunted trees and hedges. In contrast, the open marshes are largely inaccessible and few roads cross this bleak landscape. The farmland on these marshes is now primarily arable, but with some grassland and substantial grazing marshes. However, reclamation of the marsh since the Second World War has reduced this habitat, and on the Essex side of the estuary the development of Southend-on-Sea as a popular seaside resort has induced a ribbon of settlement between Shoeburyness and Canvey Island. The area is certainly vulnerable to London's outward reach. In 1969 Foulness's isolation was threatened by proposals for a third London airport on the Maplin Sands. Although that particular development never took place, there has more recently been a similar proposal for a four-runway development on the Kentish mudflats at Cliffe, Halstow and St Mary's Marshes. This was fiercely resisted by naturalist groups concerned for the European-wide importance of the site for bird life, and the proposal was dropped in 2004 in favour of further expansion at Stansted.

South coast marshlands

Along the south coast between Sussex and Dorset there is also a mix of present and former marshland, mudflats, wetland scrub and low-lying fields, occasionally interrupted by small creeks. Chichester Harbour is a large natural anchorage and its diverse landscape of inlets, agricultural land and woodlands has been designated as an Area of Outstanding Natural Beauty (AONB); Langstone Harbour between Hayling Island and Portsea Island is a smaller version. Harbourside settlements, small boatyards and marinas complete the scene. By contrast, Pagham Harbour remains relatively remote, dominated by extensive tidal mudflats and marsh vegetation.

   This central south coast possesses a long stretch of ribbon development, but the fertile soils are also intensively farmed alongside the grazing marshes, and there is a thriving tourist and leisure trade. Buildings reflect the ease of importing raw materials along this coast. Timber frames, flint, cob and thatch are all common, and the medieval churches around the harbours are of flint and stone. Modern marinas and boatyards now mix with suburbs, industrial landscapes and caravans, and the pressure for further development is intense.

   The largest indentation of all is Poole Harbour, the world's second largest natural harbour behind Sydney Harbour and covering some 3,600ha. Here, along a coastline of 100km, reed beds, marshes and mudflats compete with the modern conurbation of Poole and Bournemouth. Commercial shipping, pleasure craft, and extremely expensive housing at Sandbanks contrast with the fragile environment of mudflats, sand dunes and saltmarshes on the southern edge, where they grade into the heaths of the Isle of Purbeck. There is a total of 440ha of saltmarsh within the harbour, but this represents a decrease of some 190ha within the last 15 years of the 20th century. On the quieter southern shore, ball clay deposits are exploited, as are oil resources. Since the 1970s Wytch Farm has ranked as the largest onshore oil field in Western Europe, whence oil is piped to the terminal at Hamble on Southampton Water. The harbour itself is dotted with small islands, such as Brownsea, and sites around the shores are designated as NNRs or as SSSIs.

THE DEVELOPED COAST

Marsh is only a small component of the South East's lengthy coastal landscape. From Essex to Purbeck this has now to be characterised as being predominantly developed or urbanised, despite the survival of well-known 'natural' coastal features such as the White Cliffs at Dover, the Jurassic Coast or the Thames marshes. There are three elements that we need to consider here: first, many lengths of coast are intensively urbanised; secondly, there are others that display some of the most productive agricultural landscapes in the South East; and finally, all these coastlines are formed on softer and younger rocks which are now attracting attention because of erosion and rising sea levels.

Urban coasts

Beginning in south Essex, we can immediately see that the coast is dominated by Southend-on-Sea, the largest town in Essex. It experienced rapid growth over the last quarter of the 20th century and by 2001 had a population of 160,000. Because it is just 60km east of London, the town has grown as a popular seaside resort for the capital. As well as possessing the longest pleasure pier in the world – more than 2km and sadly ravaged by fire in 2005 – it has all the accompanying accoutrements of the typical British seaside resort. In 2001 the Government confirmed the extension of the Thames Gateway project from Thurrock to Southend-on-Sea, highlighting the area as a regional and national priority for regeneration. On this, the most urbanised estuary in England, it is hoped that regeneration will ride on the back of environmental improvement and a radically enhanced image for the area.

The concept of the Thames Gateway (promoted as 'the hub of Europe') has important landscape implications since the area is believed to have the potential to relieve growth pressures on the other three sides of London. Thus far, most growth has taken place closer to London, although the largest shopping mall in Europe has been created at Bluewater (*see* Chapter 5); Chatham Maritime business park, leisure and housing complex (complete with 'traditional' Kentish fishing village) has been developed on the former dockyard site, and the new Dartford International Eurostar station is under construction at Ebbsfleet in Kent.

The urbanised part of the Sussex coast has a very different history of development and a very different landscape to that of the Thames Estuary. A discontinuous line of coastal towns stretches from Hastings and Bexhill westwards through Eastbourne and Newhaven, to Brighton and Hove. Thereafter the urban areas become more or less continuous through Shoreham, Worthing, Littlehampton and Bognor, with all manner of large glasshouses, farm shops, nurseries and equestrian facilities, golf courses, paddocks and industrial and institutional buildings. Their landscapes have been shaped by their differing urban histories, primarily, though not entirely, related to their functions as resorts. Eastbourne, and to a lesser extent Hove, have an overall seafront grandeur that owes its origins to their unitary landownership and planned development (*see* Chapter 6). Hastings has a longer urban history but is presently one of the most deprived towns in the South East, derelict in part, and sadly in need of regeneration – something to which attention is now being paid. Newhaven, Shoreham and Littlehampton are working ports with a commercial atmosphere that is quite different again. Brighton, Worthing and Bognor have built on their resort reputations, although also attempting to diversify commercially. Their traditional seaside landscapes are still present, but often survive as a thin façade to a diversified leisure, retailing and business hinterland.

Further west again, the Portsmouth and Southampton urban complex also exhibits contrasting landscapes. The naval dockyards of Portsmouth give way to hi-tech landscapes of offices and laboratories for research and development. The naval functions remain important but diversification is again a key to the modern landscapes. With a population in 2001 of well in excess of 750,000, the area between Hayling Island in the east and Southampton, Eastleigh, Hythe and Fawley in the west is a major urban complex. Mid-19th-century housing, recent housing estates and industrial and commercial developments dominate much of the area and there is continuous pressure for more urban expansion. Urban renaissance projects at Portsmouth and Gosport have transformed the former dockyards. Portsmouth dockyard is now a heritage site that welcomes visitors to the Mary Rose, HMS *Victory* and HMS *Warrior*, as well as to the 165m-high Spinnaker Tower beside Gunwharf Quays – the centrepiece of the £86 million Renaissance of Portsmouth Harbour project. Southampton has large roll-on-roll-off container facilities and its natural deep-water harbour and double tide allow unrestricted access for the world's largest vessels. It is the United Kingdom's leading vehicle-handling and cruise port. Around 23 million tonnes of oil and petroleum-related products are also handled each year at the nearby oil refineries at Fawley and Hamble, giving the area's waterside landscapes an intensively industrialised character. Modern Southampton has developed in the late 20th century to become the *de-facto* regional capital. As a result, office space has grown enormously, primarily in the city centre and at the waterfront, but pressure is now also mounting on greenfield sites near the M27 motorway.

The westernmost urban coastal complex reaches from Barton-on-Sea through Christchurch to Bournemouth and Poole, around the shores of Christchurch and Poole Bays. Although Bournemouth continues to advertise its long sandy beach, its economy has been diversified by the addition of a strong service sector, making the town one of the most prosperous areas of the United Kingdom, in which businesses have access to a local market of some 435,000 residents. Its beautiful sea front and gardens notwithstanding, the town is continuing to expand to the north; and when the Castlepoint shopping centre was opened in 2003 it was at the time the largest such development in the country. There is now no break between Bournemouth and Poole, which with a population of 138,000 adds a bustling port landscape to the rich variety of Poole Bay.

Coastal farmland

Alongside these important urban landscapes there are also areas of extremely fertile farmland. Two may be briefly mentioned here: those of north Kent and the Sussex Coastal Plain. Both historically have been highly productive, and their landscapes still reflect the investment made possible by the judicious use of their soils. The landscape of the north Kent plain is essentially open, with a low relief. Apart from the heavy London Clays and higher ground of the wooded Blean, which supports the largest area of continuous woodland in Kent, this is rich agricultural land based on fine and deep brickearths. Shelterbelts of alder or ash characterise the gentle Great Stour valley, with its orchards and horticultural crops. The chalk of the Isle of Thanet is a more open and treeless arable landscape that offers extensive views over cereals and roots, and is frequently heavy with the smell of cabbage. Rather different are the floodplains of the Stour and Wantsum, the latter occupied by the silted Chislet marshes, reed beds and wet grassland. The western part of the plain has large fields, now dominated by lines of pylons, but with intensive arable cropping taking place between such towns as Dartford, Gillingham and Chatham. It is an area that is increasingly encroached upon by major communication routes, with further development spawned by the M2 motorway and Channel Tunnel High Speed Rail Link.

The Sussex Coastal Plain is similarly a highly productive agricultural zone that was for long one of the most fertile and intensively cultivated areas of Britain. Wider in the west, where it forms the Manhood Peninsula and Selsey Bill, it tapers eastwards towards Brighton. The flat plain, although exposed to south-westerly winds, has a relatively warm climate, high quality soils and a long growing season. Alongside its large and intensively farmed arable fields, it also supports a prosperous horticultural and glasshouse industry.

A threatened coast

The third characteristic of coastal south-east England is the degree to which its coastline and human communities are under threat from erosion (*see* Chapter 2). Climate change is exacerbating this: wetter, stormier winters and drier summers are now affecting the South East, and in the near future rising sea levels will have to be seriously faced. The Thames Gateway, for example, now has a high standard of coastal defences, built as a response to the 1953 floods. London itself now has one of the best tidal defence systems in the world, although it threatens to become over-loaded (*see* Fig. 2.6). The Environment Agency uses the mean sea level at Sheerness as one of its indicators of change (Fig. 3.11). Since 1850 the level has risen here at a rate of 2.2mm per year, compared with an average of just 0.7mm at Aberdeen.[11]

More than 235,000 properties in the South East are now at risk from flooding, the biggest risk coming from the sea in the form of high tides, storm surges and wave action. In places the shingle beaches form a defensive barrier that helps to protect the land from wave attack – indeed in low-lying areas they are the principal

Fig. 3.11 Changes of mean sea level at Sheerness in Kent, 1850–1997. The relatively high increase in sea level around the south-east coast places the region at greater risk of flooding and erosion than other parts of England, particularly important given the huge concentration of development here as well as that planned for the future in the Thames Gateway expansion (and see also Fig. 2.7).

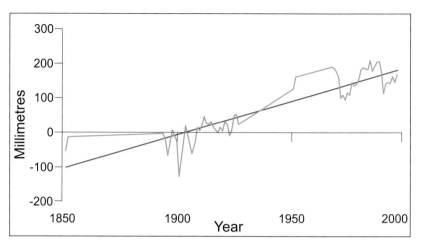

natural defence against erosion and flooding. But the shingle that used to supply the beaches is composed almost entirely of flint from the chalk cliffs, and the rate of supply may not now be sufficient to replenish losses resulting from the building of sea walls and groynes, which significantly restrict the natural supply of flint. Equally serious is the suggestion that much of the flint that now forms shingle was eroded from the chalk strata during earlier glacial periods, when rivers running off the frozen Downs deposited flint gravel on the floor of what is now the Channel at a time when the sea was no nearer than western Cornwall. Rising sea levels subsequently drove much of the flint gravel back towards the land, thereby creating the shingle beaches. But when the sea reached its present level, 5,000 or more years ago, this supply of offshore shingle largely ceased. If this is true, the shingle that protects the present-day shoreline is essentially a non-renewable fossil deposit that is diminishing under the attack of the waves, and there is thus a substantial risk that current sea defences will be overwhelmed. One alternative – managed coastal re-alignment noted in the previous chapter – is now being used in an attempt to give orderly way before the relentless advance of the sea.

A REGIONAL MOSAIC

Here then is a complex region, whose human history and landscape will be further explored in later chapters. It is a region of contrast, whose landscape reflects long centuries of human activity, use and development, as well as external influences. At the same time it contains some of the essentials of a wider 'Englishness' – the area is home to landscapes that have become symbols of a greater national identity, whether urban or rural. But this landscape must also inevitably reflect the region's role as a motor of change and a focus for international investment. It is the region of London. The overwhelming presence of this global city is felt everywhere, yet it is still possible to escape the pressures of modern living in its varied rural retreats.

NOTES

1   Thirsk 1967, 4 and 1984, xx–xxi;
    Rackham 1986, 2–5; Roberts &
    Wrathmell 2000.
2   Roberts & Wrathmell 2000, 40.
3   Roberts & Wrathmell 2000, 2002;
    Rackham 1986.
4   Countryside Agency 1999, 5–12.

5   Countryside Commission 1993.
6   Gilpin 1791, 269.
7   Corporation of London 1993.
8   DOE 1994, 35.
9   DOE 1994, 36, 65.
10 Countryside Agency 1999, 117.
11 Environment Agency 2003, 87.

4

The Peopling of the South East and the Evolution of Settlement Patterns

Thus far we have examined the long-term evolution of the region's environments and the resulting regional mosaic that we see today. To this we now add a cultural and historical dimension as we examine the successive human interventions that have shaped the landscape we see today and created the intimate patterns of settlement in the South East. The effects wrought by humans vary in scale from the very local to the region-wide, and from the everyday to those deserving the status of World Heritage Site.

THE EARLIEST INHABITANTS

We still know little about the people who lived in what is now the South East before the retreat of the last ice about 10,000 years ago, although recent archaeological advances are beginning to throw light on much earlier periods. Although our earliest human predecessors left little evidence of themselves within the landscape, this book cannot completely ignore the long-distant past (*see* Table 2.1). This is because the South East offers us two privileged glimpses into this very remote age – the internationally important Palaeolithic sites at Boxgrove in Sussex and Swanscombe in Kent.

At present we believe that nomadic bands occasionally crossed the land bridge between what is now south-east England and the Continent during interglacial and warmer periods, although they left only rare traces of their presence in the landscape. We are not sure, however, how often or for how long they stayed this far north. From sites outside the South East evidence is now accumulating to date such 'visits' to between 700,000 and 500,000 BC. The sites we know about are primarily concentrated on river gravel deposits and raised beaches, particularly where those deposits are being commercially exploited, as at Fordwich and Sturry in Kent but also from some surface sites, as on the North Downs in east and west Kent.[1] No structures are known, and the hominid presence is attested instead through finds of stone tools and the waste associated with their manufacture and use. But it is Boxgrove and Swanscombe that have told us most about this period.

The Boxgrove sites stand on the Goodwood–Slindon 40-m raised beach overlooking the Sussex Coastal Plain. Here, extensive marine deposits have yielded handaxes, cores and waste flakes of a tradition called 'Acheulian'. Similar materials have been found at Fordwich in Kent and in the Farnham river terraces in Surrey, where they represent a tradition that altogether lasted for more than a million years. Long-known concentrations of find spots around Slindon began to be revisited in the 1970s and at Eartham Pit, Boxgrove, hominid remains were found between 1993 and 1996 – the earliest then known from Britain and indeed much of the rest of Europe.[2] Two hominid teeth and a shin bone probably belong to two different individuals of the Middle Pleistocene *Homo* cf. *heidelbergensis*, relatives of *Homo erectus*. The evidence from the site was interpreted as revealing 'confrontational scavenging', or perhaps even hunting, and butchery practice, on mudflats and grassland where hominid populations competed for food with giant deer, rhinoceros, bison, bear, horse, lion, wolf and hyena. The site, occupied for tens of thousands of years, dates between Oxygen Isotope Stage 12 (*c.* 450,000 BC) and OIS 13 (*c.* 500,000 BC) thereby predating the Anglian glaciation (Table 2.1).

Temporary occupation during warmer periods within the ensuing Anglian glaciation itself may be evidenced at Swanscombe, the South East's second major Palaeolithic site. Use of this site was, however, clearly intermittent, although it carried on through the Hoxnian phase (Table 2.1). Swanscombe remains the most extensively studied Palaeolithic site in England, from which up to 100,000 handaxes have been recovered. Particularly important for our purposes are the studies that show the gradually changing landscape of the site over many thousands of years. The lower and earlier levels suggest occupation on grass-covered mudflats cut by small streams and edged by hazel scrub that merged into mixed oak forest, probably on an estuary opening on to the Thames. Elephant, rhinoceros, horse and deer may have been hunted, and the estuarine habitat would have provided birds and fish among reed swamps, fen and light woodland. An excavation in advance of the Channel Tunnel rail link yielded a tusk from the extinct *Palaeoloxodon antiquus*, an elephant twice the height of its modern African cousin. The gravel terraces were a ready source of flint for tools, and large quantities of cores and flakes have been found. Environmental evidence from Barnfield Pit suggests a shift to relatively open grassland conditions that supported large numbers of horse and wild oxen. Pollen analysis indicates that hazel, alder, pine and oak trees bordered the river and human remains were found in 1935 in gravels that were perhaps laid down in the Later Hoxnian – skull fragments, thought possibly to be from a female with some early Neanderthal features.[3]

The two small windows afforded to us by Boxgrove and Swanscombe (and other, so far lesser sites) in many ways remind us more about our ignorance of the ancient past than they add to our knowledge. We cannot yet write a detailed narrative but we can at least be sure that the peopling of the South East has a history of more than half a million years. The fact that there is a 'gap' – a period of about 100,000 years after about 200,000 BC, when there seems to be no definite evidence of human presence in Britain – simply tells us to look harder, or with different methods. Intermittent ice advances would certainly have rendered much of Britain inhospitable, although there is evidence from Trafalgar Square of hippopotamus, rhinoceros and elephant, even though we do not yet know of any people associated with them.

In the later Upper Palaeolithic, as the final ice age was drawing to a close, we at last start to find more enduring remains of our predecessors. House (or tent) constructions first appear in continental Europe, and in Britain have been found at Hengistbury Head, overlooking Christchurch Bay. One of the best late Upper Palaeolithic sites in Britain was found at the Three Way's Wharf site in Uxbridge, Middlesex. It has been dated to between 9000 and 7000 BC and comprised a flint-working floor that yielded three distinct flint assemblages and a large collection of animal bones. It was at about this time that the last (so far) Ice Age drew to a close and 'our' interglacial, which we call the Holocene, began. With it we start to see the emergence of a record of the human landscape that has continued uninterrupted through to the present day.

POST-GLACIAL HUNTERS AND GATHERERS

As we move into the most recent 10,000 years we can trace a concerted and widespread modification of the landscape. By about 7700 BC juniper, birch and pine began to recolonise southern England, together with hazel by around 7100 BC. By 6000 BC the more temperate oak, elm, alder and lime had replaced the colonising birch and pine, together with holly, ash and ivy on all geological formations. Elk, roe deer, pig and beaver accompanied the woodland. This is the Mesolithic period, when nomadic hunter-gatherers deliberately burned the vegetation to increase the amount of available browsing and to make hunting easier by concentrating herbivores into more open spaces. Thereafter the South East became covered by lime-dominated woodland, matched by ash and oak on the more upland sites and alder in valley or lower-lying coastal locations. This is Rackham's 'wildwood' into which people began to push their artificial clearings, complementing and speeding up natural processes such as fire through lightning strikes, wind-throw and the depredations of beavers and large herbivores. The results of this activity are tell-tale charcoal horizons in the stratigraphic record and an increased incidence of grasses and plantains. The 'wildwood' can no longer be considered as a dense, dark canopy, but as a wood-pasture ecosystem in which glades and lawns were produced and enhanced by these natural and human processes. Deliberate management of the region's environment had begun.[4]

Although the original sites are no longer easy to find, the early loss of woodland cover through human intervention almost certainly led to the creation of most, if not all, of the region's heathland. On the wealden heaths, Mesolithic sites had rested originally on more fertile brown earths that only later lost their structure through the removal of biomass and were eventually covered by blown sand. At West Heath, on the Lower Greensand in Sussex, pine and hazel was replaced by heathland and post-clearance scrub and lime. Ivy covered dead trees that had resulted from the forest clearance. At Iping, near Midhurst, dense hazel woodland was similarly replaced by heathland.[5]

Evidence has been growing for the impact of humans on forest cover in southern England, in limited areas from the 7th to the 6th millennia BC, and later across most geological formations. In the Ouse valley below Lewes there are more than 6m of alluvial deposits, of which 2m accumulated after the removal of the vegetation cover in the Upper Ouse during the Mesolithic period. Investigations in other valley floor deposits in the region reveal a similar story, probably one of localised clearances. Furthermore, there is evidence within the Weald for Mesolithic hunting camps, and temporary rock shelter sites with associated sandstone hearths and microlith and flint assemblages, as at Hermitage Rocks at High Hurstwood in Sussex. Access to both beach and downland flint indicates wide exploitation of the landscape during the annual rounds of food procurement. The Farnham area has yielded large numbers of flint scatters that may indicate the bases from which hunter-gatherer communities operated. Not far away at Thatcham, in Berkshire, a site occupied in about 9000 BC amidst birch, hazel and pine and overlooking a tributary of the River Kennet revealed a possible tent-like structure and the remains of red and roe deer and pig. It is also possible that by the later Mesolithic (c. 6500–3500 BC) groups of these hunter-fisher-gatherers would have been settled along coastal and estuarine areas, with their more abundant food resources, from where seasonal inland migrations may have taken place. We should also remember that the later Mesolithic landscape and coast was now developing independently of continental Europe as the Straits of Dover had already been formed by around 6000 BC. Excavations in Bermondsey indicate early Mesolithic long-term exploitation of deer, aurochs, pig, wildfowl and fish around a silting lake basin. As sea levels rose in oscillating sequences, so later Mesolithic sites are to be found higher in the Thames valley, including its tributaries such as the Colne and Lea, where evidence of woodland firing, possibly to create browsing for game, has been found.[6]

THE ORIGINS OF THE AGRICULTURAL LANDSCAPES OF SOUTH-EAST ENGLAND

Fig. 4.1 Diagram of land snails from buried soil beneath the bank of the Neolithic henge at Avebury in Wiltshire. This shows the decrease in shade-loving species and their replacement by taxa indicative of open conditions.

No revolution has impacted upon the landscape more than that which occurred during the 4th millennium BC. The origins of farming, long debated, need not be explored here other than to suggest we must now infer the adoption of farming techniques by Mesolithic and Neolithic groups already within the region, rather than looking for migrations of agricultural peoples from elsewhere. The gradual adoption of more sedentary economies has had many repercussions, forming as it did the material foundations for later society. Environmentally, it resulted in a greatly increased rate of soil erosion as the stripping of woodland cover exposed the loessic soils and deposited them as floodplain alluvium during the period 5000–3000 BC. Evidence from beneath Neolithic enclosures on the chalk, or from hillwash deposits, indicates that a more wooded environment was gradually being replaced during the mid-4th millennium BC. The decline in the elm population between about 3300 and 3000 BC, linked to elm disease, may have initiated woodland clearances that in turn could be exploited by humans. Clearance was certainly undertaken before the mid-4th millennium BC on the Wessex chalklands and in east Kent, as evidenced by grassland pollen and snail species beneath the late Neolithic Silbury Hill and Avebury henge, as well as below long barrows and other henges (Fig. 4.1).

The Neolithic also witnessed the construction of communal undertakings large enough and sufficiently robust to have survived as recognisable field monuments. Nationally, 70 or so causewayed enclosures have been identified. The Trundle (Fig. 4.2) on the Sussex downland is now carbon-dated to the 4th millennium BC, and dates going through into the mid-3rd millennium have also been confirmed elsewhere on the downland. It has been suggested that in Wessex causewayed enclosures such as Maiden Castle, Hambledon Hill or Robin Hood's Ball were linked to barrow groups as part of a territorial complex. Although their precise use is uncertain, their construction clearly required coordinated effort and they may have had both ritual and communal functions. It is also

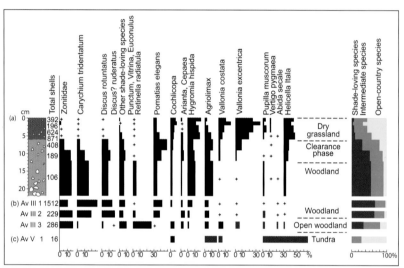

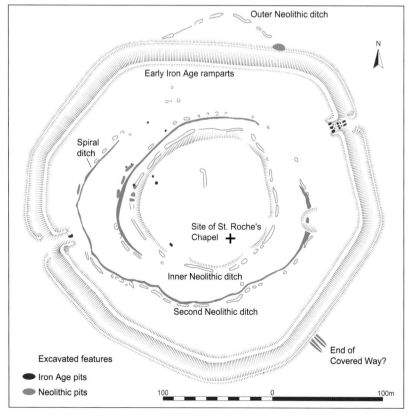

probable that such enclosures will have undergone many changes during their thousand-year lifespans. At Springfield in the Chelmer valley, near the junction with the Essex boulder clay, a complex of Neolithic features includes a causewayed enclosure and the crop mark of a cursus (the first of its kind to be found in this part of the region) with a timber circle of contemporary date. Other sites, now visible only as crop marks from the air, are to be found at Staines and at Orsett, north of Tilbury.[7]

Another well-known feature of the Neolithic is the long barrow. These barrows are approximately contemporaneous with the enclosures and are usually, but not always, associated with small quantities of human remains. At Hambledon Hill, on the edge of Cranborne Chase, a Neolithic complex has been revealed within what was at the time a predominantly wooded landscape. It was composed of two closely associated long barrows and a causewayed enclosure, together with cross-dykes, a secondary causewayed enclosure and yet a third probable Neolithic camp near by. One interpretation put forward is that Cranborne Chase served as a large sacred area that was marked by barrows and periodically visited for ritual and burial ceremonies.

In the years since the Second World War many prehistoric monuments have been destroyed, either by ploughing or quarrying. However, the Salisbury Plain Training Area ensured good survival, shielded as it has been from intensive farming. Here one causewayed camp, Robin Hood's Ball, was found to be associated with a cluster of pits yielding cattle and red-deer bones dated to the mid-4th millennium BC. There are also 30 long barrows in the training area, some regularly spaced along valley floors as well as interfluves.[8] The West Kennet barrow, near Avebury, was constructed over a passage and chambers built out of megalithic blocks. Chambered tombs built of sarsen stones also occur in the Medway valley, the best known of which is Kit's Coty House, originally constructed between 4300 and 3000 BC. Here a 70m-long mound covered a chamber, of which the remaining standing stones are preserved. Other barrows in the area have yielded pottery and human remains suggesting continued use well into the 3rd millennium BC.

Flint mines are also well known in central Wessex and on the West Sussex downland, as at Church Hill, Findon, at Cissbury and Harrow Hill. Radiocarbon dating confirms that flint was being exploited here in the earlier 4th and 3rd millennia BC. At Harrow Hill it is believed that initial opencast mining was later replaced by shafts and galleries, of which 160 have been found at the site. There was considerable trade in high-quality flint, and axes from the South Downs have appeared as far afield as Windmill Hill on the Marlborough Downs and Maiden Castle in southern Dorset.

Perhaps most intriguing of all, in the context of landscape history, is the question of Neolithic settlement sites. The evidence is still inconclusive. Densely concentrated scatters of worked flints, especially those containing a wide range of tool types, may represent more permanently occupied sites – but could also be little more than the result of manufacturing in areas in which flint was particularly easily obtained. The middle Thames valley yields several possible sites, including Runnymede Bridge, where well-preserved pottery vessels contained residues of fish, salt and proteins that suggest meat, pork fat and beeswax.[9] It may be that most Neolithic settlements were temporary affairs, but evidence for more permanent open agricultural settlement has been put forward in the shape of storage pits at Dunstable, Amesbury, in the Stour valley at Wimborne, beneath Heathrow airport, and from shallow gullies at Bishopstone in Sussex. Such sites may have been in turn the foci for larger territorial groupings that encompassed different ecological zones. These would have comprised areas suitable for woodland hunting, saltmarsh exploitation, and perhaps most important of all, valleys where supplies of wild food were most abundant and cattle could most easily be maintained. In south Dorset three major territories have been hypothesised on the basis of primary Neolithic

OPPOSITE PAGE, BOTTOM:

Fig. 4.2 The Trundle, on the western Sussex Downs: a Neolithic causewayed enclosure and later Iron Age hillfort, originally excavated and mapped by E C Curwen in the late 1920s (scale converted to metric for conformity with present volume). *Neolithic pottery from the Avebury area suggests a link with Wessex. St Roche was a 14th-century French saint, but the chapel was already a ruin in 1570.*

settlement areas, each marked by clusters of barrows and other monuments. It is suggested that the territories initially represented seasonal circuits for livestock herding. Henges and stone structures were added later, at which point these linked places also began to take on a symbolic significance.

WESSEX AND THE LATER DEVELOPMENT OF THE PREHISTORIC LANDSCAPE

Thus far, the impact of humans on the landscape has largely been limited to the building of symbolic or funerary structures. In the Bronze Age and Iron Age, from about 2000 BC, the landscape begins to fill up, people settle in permanent places, they farm the land and their cultivation begins to create what we can genuinely and comfortably call cultural landscapes. We now believe that most areas within south-east England underwent some form of exploitation and modification in the late prehistoric period. Indeed, almost every area of lowland Britain displays evidence of this in the form of plough-levelled crop marks and soil marks or upstanding earthworks. The Thames gravels, Wessex and the South Downs are particularly rich in such features, and it is salutary to remember the number that have been lost on lower ground to later ploughing and other developments. The shibboleth of prehistoric settlement being confined to lighter upland soils has been destroyed by aerial photography's demonstration of intense valley settlement across broad sweeps of south-east England.

Nevertheless, it is the upland chalk of Wessex that has long held centre stage in British archaeology, in large measure as a result of the pioneering late 19th-century excavations of Lt Gen Pitt Rivers. Because of its relatively open and undeveloped landscape it has retained many prehistoric features to the present day and thus continues to hold an intense fascination for research projects in such areas as south Dorset, Cranborne Chase, Stonehenge, eastern Salisbury Plain, Avebury and the Marlborough Downs, and the Berkshire Downs. Much of the later prehistoric landscape of south-east England has therefore come to be interpreted in the light of findings from Wessex.

The causewayed enclosure at Windmill Hill, on the northern flank of the Avebury World Heritage Site, is thus one of the most important Neolithic sites ever excavated in Britain. The associated finds dominated the study of the Neolithic for more than a generation, and even now work on Windmill Hill remains highly influential. An early excavation took place here in 1922, prompted by the existence of at least one ditch around the hilltop that had been recognised some two hundred years earlier by the antiquary William Stukeley. By the early 20th century there were still huge gaps in our understanding of the Neolithic and although evidence of occupation had been recognised, larger and more formal places of settlement had not been found in southern Britain until causewayed enclosures, or 'causewayed camps' as they were initially known, were discovered in the first decade of the 20th century. Then Alexander Keiller's excavations at Windmill Hill in 1925–9 uncovered huge amounts of pottery, worked flint, chalk and stone, human and animal bone, and charred plant remains. Most of these have now been dated to between about 3600 and 3300 BC. Some of the material had even come from as far away as Cornwall, North Wales and the Lake District. Stuart Piggott then used this material to define an early Neolithic 'Windmill Hill Culture', which included causewayed enclosures and long barrows, leaf-shaped arrowheads and flint axes among its characteristic products. Here then, was an important gathering place. The predominance of cattle bones and a seeming absence of domestic structures led Piggott to interpret the site as a corral and market for cattle, but more recently the focus has been on ritual activity and the exchange of goods and animals. Windmill Hill is one of the Wessex landscape sites that has been constantly reinterpreted in line with changing archaeological theory. Many of the Wessex complexes are now being reinterpreted as ritual landscapes, or at least landscapes whose practical origins as places of shelter, arable or pasture later came to be integrated with a more complicated 'mental landscape'.

The best known of all such cultural landscapes is, of course, Stonehenge. Together with Avebury, it is the most important prehistoric site in Britain. The Avebury complex of sites and monuments on the edge of the Marlborough Downs comprises the great henge and its stone circles, Windmill Hill, Silbury Hill, the West Kennet long barrow, the Sanctuary and the West Kennet and Beckhampton avenues. The components – henges, stone circles, stone alignments and causewayed and palisaded enclosures, together with Bronze Age round barrows, an Anglo-Saxon village, substantial manor houses and designed parklands – contribute to a cultural landscape of such importance that in 1986 it was inscribed, along with Stonehenge, as World Heritage Site C373 under the UNESCO World Heritage Convention. Altogether, the World Heritage Site covers more than 2,000ha.[10] The mysterious Silbury Hill is thought to be the largest artificial mound in Europe, covering more than 2ha and reaching a height of 40m (Fig. 4.3).

Stonehenge is the most complex and spectacular of the class of late Neolithic henge monuments and stone circles. Three phases have been identified: in Phase 1 the main ditch is now dated securely to 3020–2910 BC. During Phase 2 the main ditch continues to silt up and into it are set the Aubrey holes and wooden post settings. Phase 3 has a burial dated to around 2400–2100 BC; it also sees the first erection of the sarsen stones in 2800–2400 BC, the addition of the trilithons in 2400–2100 BC, the creation of the bluestone circle in 2280–2030 BC and the addition of the bluestone horseshoe in 2270–1930 BC. The concentric circular

Fig. 4.3 Silbury Hill, Wiltshire.
This enigmatic Neolithic mound probably had a path originally spiralling up its side. A Roman road is aligned on the mound (top) and there is evidence of Roman and medieval pottery and artefacts in the near vicinity. The modern A4 now passes close by. The top of the mound has a cordoned-off area protecting a shaft, excavated in 1776, which collapsed in 2000. The shaft will be back-filled with a capping of chalk.

BELOW: **Fig. 4.4 Stonehenge in Wiltshire, arguably the best-known prehistoric site in Europe.** *The air photo shows the standing stones, inner and outer rings. 'The Avenue' leaves the outer ring top left. Some of the thousands of visitors file past (bottom).*

RIGHT: **Fig. 4.5 Stonehenge.** *An interpretation of the Late Neolithic/Early Bronze Age sacred landscape around Stonehenge in Phase 3.*

N

DOMAIN OF THE LIVING

Ceremonial circles of the living

Durrington Walls

Newly Dead

Woodhenge

Living Wares

LIMINAL ZONE OF EARLY BRONZE AGE BURIALS

Route of ancestral initiates

Circle of the Ancestors

The Avenue

Stonehenge

DOMAIN OF THE ANCESTORS

Transformation from life to death

R. Avon

2 0 2km

holes outside the main circle are dated to 1640–1520 BC, and finally the Avenue that links Stonehenge to the River Avon has now been dated to 2590–1880 BC. We know little about the post-monumental prehistoric use of Stonehenge, although some Late Bronze Age pottery and an Iron Age burial have been found. At Stonehenge, the unsurpassed stone circle is believed to constitute a sacred space, surrounded by a ceremonial landscape that in addition to the Avenue included the neighbouring Durrington and Coneybury henges, the Stonehenge cursus, Neolithic long barrows, more than 300 Bronze Age burial mounds and many other prehistoric remains (Figs 4.4 and 4.5). Recent nearby discoveries such as the grave of the 'Amesbury Archer' (an early metal-worker born in the Alps and buried in about 2300 BC with one of the richest collections of Early Bronze Age grave goods ever found), or the 'Boscombe Bowmen' (who came from the same Prescelli area of southern Wales from which the Stonehenge bluestones originated), add depth and human interest to this astonishing area.

Elsewhere in the region we can discern 'fixed' settlements with greater clarity once we reach the Middle Bronze Age. Thus, on the Sussex downland the sites at Itford Hill and Blackpatch (Fig. 4.6) are real settlements, with contemporary fields. At Itford there was also a ceremonial hut that may have contained a family 'shrine'.[11] Across the downland small round-houses are clustered, some with enclosing embankments, near low barrows that contain individual cremations. Some of these sites almost certainly continued through into the later Bronze Age.

By the end of the Bronze Age many river valleys presented an unstable environment for settlement. As a result of rising sea levels, intertidal mudflats with peat deposits began to cover earlier Bronze Age farming landscapes, including those represented by buried ard marks at Southwark and Westminster. There is some evidence for Early Bronze Age activity on the landward shingle ridges of Romney Marsh but little for the Iron Age. There was also settlement on the Willingdon (Shinewater) Levels before the climatic deterioration that occurred towards the end of the Bronze Age. At Shinewater, a timber platform excavated in 1995 supported a range of Late Bronze Age material, including a complete bronze reed hook and skeletal remains. It was connected to the mainland by a timber causeway across the marshy ground. Both the track and the platform were constructed in about 830–800 BC, before being rendered unusable by flooding in the Iron Age.

Overall, there is evidence of farmsteads on most types of soil,

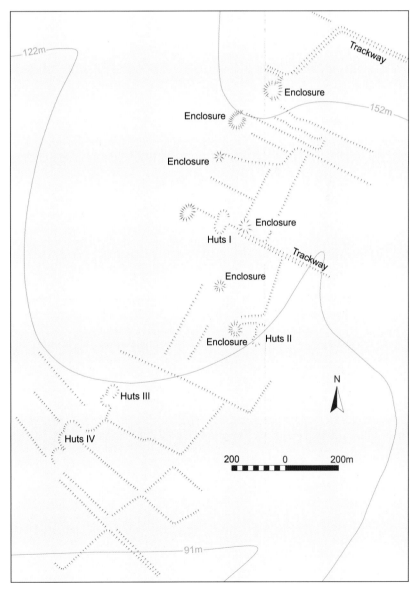

Fig. 4.6 Blackpatch Late Bronze Age farmstead, Sussex. *The site was originally mapped soon after the Second World War but has largely been ploughed out since. Small rectangular, lynchetted fields surround hut platforms and enclosures. A hollow way and lynchetted trackway enter the settlement and there are 11 barrows associated with the site, with evidence that the latter was inhabited by an extended family group.*

including the heathlands. Much of the evidence for settlement in the Late Bronze Age and Early Iron Age actually comes not from Wessex but from the South Downs, together with an accumulating amount of material from recent excavations on the Sussex Coastal Plain. It is possible that some significant enclosures, such as Highdown Hill, stood at the junctions of resource and cultural areas. The Coastal Plain, for example, has concentrations of settlements and metalwork (some of it exotic) that suggest it had become an area of high prestige by the early 1st millennium BC. The Thames valley was seemingly dominated by pastoralism that made use of extensive ditch systems, and in the Runnymede Bridge area a wide range of animal bones has been found associated with settlement post-holes and a bronze founder's hoard. These more heavily populated areas had a greater affinity with continental Europe at this time, as witnessed by imports of pottery and the evidence of continental sea connections provided by the Dover Boat (c. 1500 BC), which was discovered in 1992.

The final 700 years before the Roman conquest saw many changes in the landscape. Population expansion exerted pressure on poorer soils and led to an increase in large dykes, linear earthwork structures and fortified enclosures. Trade networks were widening, and included industrial goods from iron or salt production sites. Caesar commented of the Kentish area that its 'population is exceedingly large, the ground thickly studded with farmsteads'. The earlier Bronze Age settlement patterns of round-houses within enclosures associated with field systems now disappears, to be replaced on every type of soil by Iron Age settlements that are larger in size, more complex and often packed tightly together.

The huge influence of Wessex archaeology is perhaps even more marked in terms of Late Bronze Age and Iron Age studies. At this time Salisbury Plain was covered by a proliferation of different settlement types, and its round-houses, enclosed farmsteads and hillforts have been taken as the norm against which the prehistoric landscape of the rest of lowland England can be measured. Although the great isolated round-houses of Little Woodbury, which became the type-site for the Iron Age, are now believed to have Bronze Age antecedents, and despite Trow-Smith's warnings against Wessex hegemony, the influence has been long-lasting. It is no accident that the great round-house reconstruction at the Butser Ancient Farm in Hampshire was based on the buildings excavated by Sonia Hawkes at Longbridge Deverill, Wiltshire (see Chapter 5, Fig.5.2). On the basis of ceramic styles and continental imports, however, we should regard Wessex and its 'outliers' in Sussex and part of Surrey as being different at this time from Kent, which looked northwards towards the Thames valley and eastern England. And in Sussex, moreover, there is little evidence at present of substantial Iron Age farmyard compounds of the Little Woodbury type. Nor are there many of the Wessex 'banjo-enclosures', with their distinctive funnel-like ditched entrances. Long linear boundaries were often focused on central points at this time and may have demarcated grazing grounds. Both enclosed and unenclosed small settlements also dominate Salisbury Plain, and it has been suggested that the former might be shepherds' enclosures since there is increasing evidence for very large numbers of sheep being kept here in the Iron Age.[12] Towards the end of the prehistoric period there was clearly widespread agricultural and settlement activity in Wessex: small enclosures extend across the whole area, varying from less than a hectare in area up to what might be called valley forts at places such as Dorchester-on-Thames.

The Iron Age landscape of Sussex was characterised by many small, undefended mixed farming sites, with unusual evidence of rectangular houses at Charleston Brow and Park Brow. A greater density of settlement characterises western, rather than eastern Sussex, with individual farmsteads on the Coastal Plain exploiting rectangular fields separated by ditches. These must have been communally maintained and were linked by double-lynchet trackways. Many farming sites of this period are now coming to light in areas such as the Coastal

Plain, characterised by their round-houses and ditched enclosures and confirming that a mature mixed farming economy was now in place. On the adjoining downland, four Early Iron Age and ten Late Iron Age huts have been found concentrated in a small area at Chalton in Hampshire.[13] Similar densities of settlement existed in the Thames valley, where extensive ditch systems also date from the Late Bronze Age. On the Kent Downs a site at Farningham Hill, dated to either side of the BC/AD divide, offers a similar picture of an enclosed settlement set in grassland and with strong evidence for the pastoral herding of cattle, sheep, goats, pigs and horses for milk, meat and wool.

Visually the region's Iron Age hillforts remain its most impressive landscape features. Sometimes they began as Neolithic causewayed camps, as at Maiden Castle, or as single-ditched Late Bronze Age contour structures encircling the crests of hills. Others were constructed from scratch, with additional defensive banks and ditches or new ramparts and gateways being added over time. The earliest of the hillforts on the northern edges of the Sussex Downs, as at Hollingbury, contain clusters of round-houses, and it seems most likely that these Early Iron Age 'forts', including Chanctonbury Ring, Seaford Head and Ditchling Beacon, were primarily pastoral enclosures rather than defensive sites. Structures built from the mid-4th century BC onwards were different, however, and transparently intended for defence. They stretch from Wessex through to Kent, the multivallate enclosure at Bigbury, overlooking Canterbury, being the most easterly. Cissbury and the Trundle (see Fig. 4.2) commanded individual blocks of the South Downs, each one in turn surrounded by undefended settlements. They may have acted as focal points and trading centres for these communities, although their functions as well as size and types of defence were highly variable. Seemingly indicative of control in an intensively exploited landscape, they are to be found throughout the region's chalklands, but also in the Weald, where Garden Hill (in the Ashdown Forest) has revealed traces of ironworking.

The huge multivallate hillforts of Wessex, sometimes located in pairs as with Hod Hill and Hambledon Hill in Dorset, are absent in Sussex, although the 50ha Oldbury hillfort in Kent is exceptionally large. Some hillforts must have been major political and social centres: at Hambledon Hill the 13ha enclosure contained at least 207 hut platforms; and at Danebury in Hampshire a large resident population is implied by a planned internal network of roads, housing, ritual areas and storage pits, some of which contained deliberate ritual deposits. And just below the Trundle at Westhampnett is one of the largest cremation cemeteries so far found in Britain. It contained 161 burials and associated features, including a central timber-built sacred space. Rather smaller in scale were a group of Late Iron Age defended enclosures on prominent sites, such as Mount Caburn, Devil's Dyke and Castle Hill, Newhaven. Caburn's function has not been fully determined, but is now also thought to include ritual use.[14]

The landscape at this time also contained substantial numbers of single, double or multiple banks and ditches, including cross-ridge dykes, that may have had territorial or pastoral functions. Sometimes running for considerable distances, these are to be found on Salisbury Plain, the Berkshire Downs and the Chilterns. The Wessex linear-ditch system comprises spinal linear earthworks that can reach several kilometres in length, are prominently placed and are the main backbone from which subsidiary linear features spring. In all instances they post-date the region's Bronze Age co-axial field systems (see Chapter 5). A surviving complex of dykes with impressive 3m-high banks north of Chichester, dated to the 1st century BC and early 1st century AD, parallel those at Lexden, Colchester, and may in part herald the approaches to an oppidum, the term for centres of native power that the Romans encountered. As yet no such centre has been identified on the Sussex coast, and it is even possible that the considerable erosion of the Selsey peninsula has long since destroyed any site that may once have been there. Such centres, proto-urban in nature but often extensive in area, commanded routeways and were not necessarily defended. As well as Selsey there were probably *oppida* at Silchester, Canterbury/Bigbury, Hengistbury, Verulamium, Wheathampstead and Winchester. So far, the most detailed information comes from Silchester, where recent excavations have revealed a grid-like pattern of streets set out between AD 40 and AD 60 on a north-west to south-east axis. They extend over a substantial area and were respected by the first Roman buildings and streets at the site, but are at 45 degrees to the later mid-3rd-century Roman street plan.[15]

From the late 2nd century BC through to the Roman conquest in AD 43, the South East had a closer trading relationship with the Mediterranean world than other regions in England, facilitated by the introduction of coinage. For a hundred years prior to the invasion, the South East was effectively on the frontier of the Roman Empire, and cross-Channel links with Gaul brought both imported material goods and Romanised cultural influences. The recipient coastal areas would have included east Kent, especially Dover, Chichester Harbour, the Solent area and Poole Harbour. At Christchurch Harbour a settlement grew up from about 100 BC and there is plentiful evidence of Mediterranean luxury goods, shipped via the Breton coast and then taken northwards into Wessex along the Stour valley.

In summary, by the time Rome took a serious interest in Britain, the South East was already a core region, and indeed had relationships with the Empire to its south. Trading centres, the circulation of luxury goods and coinage, and links with Gaul foreshadowed an ongoing historical dominance for this region, which by the eve of the Roman conquest was crowded, sophisticated and possessed of a mature rural landscape and incipient urban centres.

THE IMPACT OF ROME ON THE LANDSCAPE OF SOUTH-EAST ENGLAND

Given the nature of late-prehistoric developments, it comes as no surprise that the direct impact of Rome on the regional landscape of Britain was nowhere more strongly felt than in its south-eastern corner: not only was it a 'civilian zone' compared with the 'military zone' to the north and west, but it was also a zone already well down the road of urbanisation and indeed 'Romanisation'. The region was accessible to the Continent and the four centuries of Imperial rule saw an intensification of population growth, an increased density of settlement, expansion of farming and the introduction of planned towns and communications. The Roman legions almost certainly landed at Richborough, where a fortified beachhead camp has been located, but also possibly on the Sussex/Hampshire coast within the territory of the usurped client king Verica. They then headed for *Camulodunum* (Colchester) where the *oppidum* of the late *de facto* ruler of southern Britain, Cunobelinus, and his sons, was taken.[16] The Emperor Claudius himself received the surrender of various British tribes from there. The rest of the region was taken swiftly within four years, and relatively few permanent military forts were established apart from those required to subdue the Durotriges in southern Dorset, such as that built within the perimeter of the Iron Age hillfort at Hod Hill.

A hierarchy of settlement types is frequently adduced for Roman Britain, ranging from native non-villa settlements to villas, smaller towns, and a variety of fully developed urban centres further subdivided by function. With the conquest the Graeco-Roman culture of urban living and landscape was imported to south-east England. Planned *civitas* capitals were at the peak of the hierarchy and were the central places for each canton. They contained both central forum-basilica complexes and gridiron street layouts, public baths, temples, amphitheatres and theatres. By the end of the 2nd century most *civitas* centres could display a complete array of these buildings, together with stone-built private houses that became even more opulent by the 4th century, as at *Verulamium* (St Albans) (Fig. 4.7). Prior to this, timber structures lined the streets; combining house, workshop and shop, they were close-packed and would have offered a vibrant commercial atmosphere. *Verulamium* may technically have been given the higher-status title of *municipium*.

As a client kingdom of Rome, the land of the Regnenses, occupying parts of the modern counties of Sussex, Surrey and Hampshire, was the first to feel a new influence on its landscape. The cultural and military conquest would doubtless have bypassed many inhabitants but the *civitas* capital *Noviomagus Reg(i)norum* (Chichester), the 'new market' of the tribal group, would have been a centre for cultural adaptation as the British here became Romano-British. Much Roman archaeology has tended to focus on site-specific evidence, and only in the recent past have attempts been made to evaluate wider landscape issues. Although we know quite a lot about *Noviomagus*, therefore, we know far less about its hinterland despite some knowledge of roads such as Stane Street, which led from its east gate and was lined by cemeteries, and the nearby, possibly associated, villas.

Not fitting easily into any defined settlement category was London (*see*

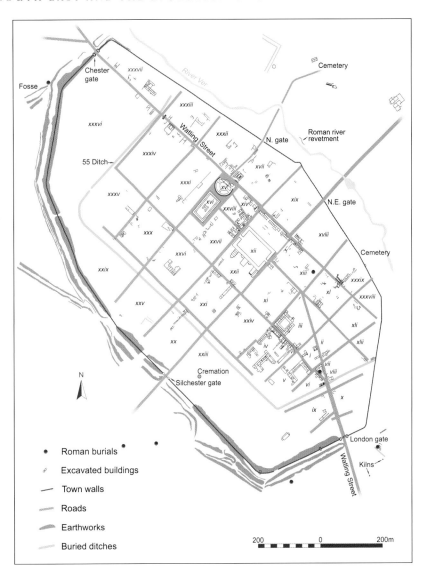

Fig. 4.7 Roman St Albans – Verulamium. *This shows the town on Watling Street, with its numbered insulae, forum and basilica site (XII), theatre and temple (XVI), refined houses (III and IV) and a triumphal arch (XXXIII–XXXIV). Timber-framed shops are known from insula XIV although many were destroyed in the Boudiccan revolt of AD 60. There are also extramural cemeteries. The map represents a compound picture since there were many changes in the development of the Roman town.*

Chapter 7 and Fig.7.1). From about AD 50 the city developed rapidly. *Londinium* was neither the provincial administrative centre for *Britannia* (this was Colchester) nor a *civitas* capital, since it was on the boundary of *civitates*. Its early importance stemmed instead in large measure from trade, both seaborne and via the crossing point of the Thames at London Bridge. Undoubtedly the juxtaposition of economic and later administrative functions also enhanced growth, for by the 3rd century *Britannia* was divided north–south into *Britannia Inferior* and *Britannia Superior*. London was the capital of the latter and the convergence of the provinces' road network here was clearly important in administrative as well as landscape terms.

Then there were the *vici* – unplanned smaller towns with winding streets, suburbs, industrial sites, cultivated fields and town cemeteries. They were serviced by major roads and fulfilled a variety of local administrative, redistributive, artisanal and commercial roles. The development of these smaller urban centres is less well understood. Some were of military origin; some showed continuity from the Iron Age; some developed market functions; many were effectively staging posts with inns and facilities for the speeding of the *cursus publicus* (imperial post) along the impressive Roman road network.

At Springhead (Kent) an irregular ribbon development encompassed a temple complex that sprawled along the line of Watling Street.

One pronounced feature of the Romano-British South East was the sheer number of rural settlements. In some parts of Bedfordshire, for example, Romano-British settlements occur at 500m intervals, although it is difficult to assess whether they were all inhabited contemporaneously over the whole 400-year period. Much of the late pre-Roman Iron Age landscape and farming activity continued as before, but in many instances these earlier patterns were modified, extended or overlain by Romano-British developments, though with continuity of actual settlement site demonstrated in areas such as Cranborne Chase and around Basingstoke. At Gussage All Saints and Tollard Royal in Dorset, Iron Age settlement continued through into the 2nd century AD. By the 3rd century, possibly 90 per cent of the population of Britain, estimated at 3.7 million, lived in the countryside in a bewildering variety of isolated huts, nucleated hamlets and village formations. At Chalton, noted above for its cluster of Iron Age huts, the village layout remained in use from the Late Iron Age through to the 4th century and was characterised by timbered rectangular buildings integrated with tracks and fields. Similarly, at Chisenbury Warren, east of the Avon in Wiltshire, surviving earthworks represent a single street or hollow way lined by some 80 rectangular house platforms and with an open 'green'. The whole complex is surrounded by Romano-British fields and gives the impression of a planned unity covering 6ha (Figs 4.8 and 4.9). In all, 11 Romano-British settlements of either compact or linear form are known from intensive fieldwork undertaken in the Salisbury Plain military training area. Many represent the huts of the poor, and the round-house almost certainly continued in use throughout lowland Britain in the 1st and 2nd centuries AD, although with increasing adoption of the more typically Continental style of rectangular house. Walled, banked or ditched compounds also existed around family farms, as at Studland or Woodcuts in Dorset. We are seeing here an important development, as a peasant underclass, separated from villa life, developed its own settlement system within a landscape that had already been continuously occupied for several centuries.[17]

Although probably represented at under 10 per cent of rural sites, the dwelling that popularly most signifies the Roman countryside is the villa, a form of house that demonstrated surplus wealth and conspicuous consumption through the adoption of a Mediterranean culture. Indeed Dark and Dark refer to the South East as a 'villa landscape', and although this is clearly insufficient as a characteristic description, since such sites were greatly outnumbered by more humble groupings, it does remind us again of

Fig. 4.8 Chisenbury Warren, Wiltshire, plan. This excellent example of early linear village topography has Late Iron Age origins and subsequent developments through to the later Romano-British period.

Fig. 4.9 Chisenbury Warren, Wiltshire.
The air photograph, taken from the north, shows the house platforms and 'celtic fields' on the valley sides.

the relative political, economic and cultural importance of this region.[18] Most villas would have been lived in by native Britons, but would have afforded many different degrees of luxury and complexity; their proliferation in lowland Britain, often within easy distance of towns, was a sign of the stability of the *pax Romana*. The use of stone for the construction of rectangular buildings with wings or corridors, the mosaic and tessellated floors and the hypocausts and bath-houses all signified a fundamental shift from the British round-houses which many villas directly succeeded. There were also several different forms, ranging from the very elaborate through to smaller versions. The most common types in the South East were the aisled villa and the winged corridor villa, although the most superior villa of all, the palace at Fishbourne, had a courtyard surrounded on all sides by building (Fig. 4.10). Fishbourne began as a military base that was established

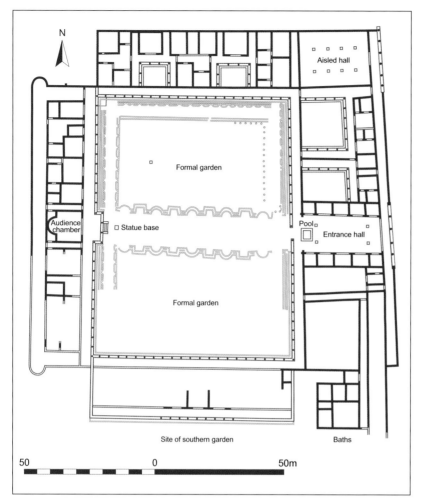

N

Aisled hall

Formal garden

Audience chamber

Statue base

Pool

Entrance hall

Formal garden

Site of southern garden

Baths

50   0   50m

***Fig. 4.10 Fishbourne Roman Palace,
near Chichester, Sussex.*** *Map of the site
and a scale model, viewing the imposing
palace from the east. Discovered by chance in
1960, the palace has been linked to the client
king Togidubnus. It would have survived here
until about AD 275. Between 1995 and 1999
the remains of a military headquarters of
AD 50–60 have also been uncovered to the east
of the palace.*

soon after AD 43, but grew into its splendid palatial state by the end of the 1st century AD. Villas were plentiful here on the Sussex Coastal Plain and in north Kent, especially in the Medway and Darenth valleys, as typified by Lullingstone. They were also located on better Lower Greensand soils around the edges of the Weald – as at Bignor, near Pulborough in Sussex, one of the largest villas in Britain – and in valley locations, such as those recently discovered at Beddingham and Barcombe in the valley of the Sussex Ouse. Non-villa settlements in Sussex, by contrast, were more widespread on the downland, and also feature strongly on Cranborne Chase and Salisbury Plain – an area curiously lacking in villas. North of the Thames, although there is a concentration of villas around *Verulamium*, there are fewer known sites than to the south of the river, although non-villa sites are again frequent.

The end of Roman rule in the South East was a prolonged affair. In landscape terms, significant changes were occurring in many towns during the 3rd and 4th centuries. There appears to have been a cessation in the construction of public buildings, and in London some buildings appear to have become disused. At Silchester (*Calleva Atrebatum*) the forum/basilica complex lost its public functions and became a location for ironworking. The larger towns were less vibrant now, and the countryside resumed greater relative importance. On the other hand, significant town defences were being constructed by the end of the 3rd century – at Canterbury and Silchester for example – although such defences may have demonstrated a competitive civic pride rather than any Imperial command.[19] Trade declined, especially with European centres, as Britain became more self-sufficient. This affected the wealth of London in particular, where commercial functions fell into relative decline compared with their importance in the 2nd century. In the countryside increased numbers of villas at first seem to compensate for this loss of urban dynamism. By the 4th century, however, the number of occupied villas declined sharply, although some were still being developed to provide elite displays of luxurious personal prestige. By the mid-4th century rural industries had also stagnated; wealden ironworking sites were declining from the mid-3rd century and large-scale pottery manufacture finished in about AD 400.

External threats to Roman Britain were certainly increasing through the 3rd century. The vulnerable south-eastern coast received protection through considerable investment in the string of fortifications known as 'The Forts of the Saxon Shore'. These may well have succeeded in warding off serious attack by pirates or 'barbarians' as Europe started to become a more unstable place. Reculver, at the mouth of the Wantsum channel, was the site of the first of these forts, followed by Richborough, Dover and Stutfall near Lympne in Kent, Portchester in Hampshire and Bradwell-on-Sea in Essex. In Sussex the fort at Pevensey (*Anderitum*) was constructed in about AD 293.

Nevertheless, from about 406 onwards we enter a period of confusion as Britain was withdrawn from the protection of Rome, faced barbarian invasions, but still remained effectively Roman in character. By the 440s Britain 'passed under the control of the Saxons', with territory being ceded or lost in the South East in particular. The *Anglo-Saxon Chronicle* records the invitation to Hengist and Horsa in the 440s to come to Britain and the ceding to them of the Isle of Thanet before their eventual revolt. Old Romano-British towns retained their defences and physical presence, albeit somewhat decayed, but their functional continuity is more difficult to demonstrate. The shore fort at Pevensey had sub-Roman occupation until the late 5th century. Villas, too, decayed and any real continuity probably existed primarily at the level of the self-sufficient peasantry.

THE *ADVENTUS SAXONUM* AND THE REGIONAL LANDSCAPE

The full significance of the period between the end of Roman rule and the Norman Conquest for the settlement landscape of south-east England only really came to be appreciated by scholars towards the end of the 20th century. Enough has been written above to show how this was already an old-settled landscape with a high population, and recent DNA back-projection from modern populations hints at a continuity of Romano-British (Celtic) survival in southern Britain, with far less genetic dominance from Saxon incomers than might have been expected.

Nevertheless, the 650-year Anglo-Saxon period was one of ongoing settlement dynamism. Again, the South East must be seen as a powerful force within Britain following the development of the kingdoms of Kent, together with the emergence of East, South and West Saxons as four of the seven kingdoms of the Heptarchy (alongside the East Angles, Northumbria and Mercia). Within it, landscapes were organised so thoroughly and at such an early date that the templates they left have moulded much of the landscape history that followed. The later Anglo-Saxon period also saw the rise of the great line of Wessex kings, whose expansionist policies and battle victories ultimately brought all the land south of the Thames under the control of Wessex by the middle of the 9th century. This authority was challenged by the Danish armies throughout much of the 9th century, but by the time of King Alfred's death in 899 Wessex was again secure and powerful. By the middle of the 10th century much of Britain was controlled by Wessex, but successive Danish armies again menaced, and finally overran the South East in the early years of the 11th century, causing widespread devastation, including the sacking of Canterbury in 1011, before Cnut was finally proclaimed king of England in 1016. Of course, these political power struggles passed over much of the landscape, leaving it relatively unchanged; but the fortunes of towns and the ability of people to farm in peace would certainly have been affected. Large linear earthworks were also thrown up as defensive measures, such as those in Surrey and western Kent against external threats, or the East Wansdyke in north Wessex, also facing north and built against Mercian incursion.

One of the key landscape questions of this period concerns the fortunes of the Roman towns. In contrast to the older Roman buildings, the succeeding vernacular structures were once again constructed of organic materials – wood, straw, clay and mud, a fact that bedevils archaeological work on the early Saxon period, although a great deal of activity has recently been directed at sub-surface evidence. Thus at Chichester a layer of dark earth developed between the 5th and 8th centuries from the decaying remains of buildings. The simple wooden sub-Roman structures at

Poundbury in Dorset were found only because they directly overlay the real objective of the investigation, the Romano-British cemetery. Only some early church buildings have any stone still surviving. It is nevertheless known that *Verulamium* was still occupied in the late 5th century, and may be the one real example in Britain of a continuity of urban settlement from Roman to Saxon. Despite the fact that the early Saxons had little urban society or economy, many of the region's towns developed as central places during this period, though they probably did not acquire the range of functions of fully fledged towns until the 8th century.

At Canterbury timber buildings among the Roman ruins demonstrate reoccupation inside the Roman walls in the later 6th and 7th centuries. Looking back at this period from an 8th-century perspective, Bede described political stability and a Christian resurgence among standing buildings here; outside to the east and north-east St Augustine's Abbey and the ancient St Martin's church had already been built, and further out still there was the prosperous outport of Fordwich. The *-wic* element, implying a trading area (Latin *vicus*), was an important aspect of the prosperity of most towns. Canterbury, however, was additionally the defensive *burh* of the men of Kent and possessed a cathedral, churches, a mint, a palace, monasteries, a market (*port*) and a wall. Other *wics* under the control of the kings of Kent included the London Aldwych on the Strand, and Sandwich on the Wantsum.

Other towns seem to have developed from the 8th century onwards as trading centres, sometimes on old Romano-British sites, sometimes *de novo*. Many were clearly planned, including *Hamwic*, a port for the kingdom of 8th-century Wessex that now lies beneath the suburbs of modern Southampton. The town covered an area of 45ha on the west bank of the Itchen, where ships from the Continent could be safely beached. It possessed good trade links with Winchester and had a planned layout of streets and dwellings. In about 800 it housed a community of artisans and merchants drawing on the agricultural resources of its Wessex hinterland, but by the 10th century the need for deeper port facilities and a lack of defences against the Danes resulted in its decline. The remaining population moved to a safer site to the south-west, where defences were erected around what was ultimately to become the new town of Southampton.

In the 850s the Vikings began to over-winter on the islands of Thanet and Sheppey, as a result of which the undefended *wics* were no longer viable. Instead, urban activity switched to the new defensive *burhs* that were created under King Alfred, sometimes at larger pre-existing strategic centres as at Southwark, Winchester and Chichester and sometimes on entirely new sites, as at Wallingford on the Thames in Oxfordshire (Fig. 4.11) and Wareham in Dorset, where regular street plans were adopted to allow quick access to the turf rampart defences, which can still be seen. Later, some single-function *burh* sites such as Eashing, on a promontory overlooking the River Wey in Surrey, were replaced by planned, multi-functional towns such as Guildford, complete with mints, street plans, defensive ditches and links to their hinterlands. Although not listed as an Alfredian site in the early 10th-century Burghal Hidage the defences at Rochester (Old English *Hrofesceaster*), capital of west Kent, reinforced older Roman walls to protect the second-oldest cathedral in England, established in 604. Following the defeat of the Danish army in 878, Alfred invested greatly in making the Winchester *burh* an appropriate capital. By the 11th century, Winchester – 'the fourth city of the realm' in a survey of about 1057 – had a cathedral, royal palace, mint, garrison, courts, tradesmen, shopkeepers and craftsmen in profusion, as well as pilgrims, beggars and prostitutes. Distinct specialist areas had arisen that were more prosaic than the palace and ecclesiastical space around the cathedral: animals were butchered in Fleshmongers street, from which hides were moved to Tanners street, whence some might then go to be worked on in 'Shieldworkers street'. There were also extra-mural holdings and suburbs and market gardens.[20]

In the countryside the Romano-British villas seem only seldom to have survived as ongoing concerns. However, the areas around London and *Verulamium* do have evidence of later 5th- or 6th-century timber building on villa sites and it seems likely that the associated farmland continued in operation while the villa buildings themselves decayed. Evidence for Saxon huts is certainly available from all over the South East, especially in Kent, Essex, Bedfordshire and Dorset. They are to be found along the chalk scarp near Dunstable, in small groups at Aylesbury, or within Iron Age and Romano-British sites as at Keston in Kent. At Heybridge in Essex they have been dated as contemporary with late Romano-British occupation.[21]

As concentrations of rural buildings developed after the early 5th century, their morphologies can be discerned more clearly. The Thames valley is particularly

Fig. 4.11 The landscape of the Saxon burh: Wallingford. Possibly the best-preserved Saxon burh in England, it guarded a ford across the Thames, displays the typical semi-regular street topography of a planned layout, and retains open spaces within the walls at the Bullcroft (top left) and Kinecroft (bottom left), both of which contain buried traces of medieval topography. A medieval castle was erected in the north-east section of the town (top right) in what is now Castle Meadows.

rich in small mid-Saxon settlements at such locations as Egham, Staines, Thorpe and Stanwell. Many lacked any plan but two distinct types, a proto-'green village' and proto-'street village', can be seen, although their remains may not have been co-existent. In many cases the settlement itself might 'drift' within an overall tenurial structure, and we must recognise the fluidity of rural sites over these long time periods – often, as in the Thames valley, leaving considerable traces of Saxon occupation behind. Closely spaced hamlets might fuse in time to become 'polyfocal' settlements, but in other circumstances small or marginal sites, including some on the downland, can be regarded as short-lived elements in a wider pattern of settlement mobility – sites abandoned as later nucleated settlements developed on more productive valley-floor soils. On the South Downs the early medieval settlements were almost entirely valley-based, leaving the higher downland for stock pastures.[22] Bishopstone in Sussex is a 5th- to 6th-century settlement but with its 7th to 8th century buildings on different foci – another example of a *wandersiedlung* or 'wandering settlement'.

One point is clear and important: the nucleated village as a feature of the south-eastern countryside was not introduced by the Saxons. Indeed, it is likely that the landscape was initially dominated by hamlets and farmsteads and resembled far more closely the prehistoric and Romano-British pattern than the standard conception of a medieval village. Furthermore, along the rivers Avon and Wylye and in the Vale of Pewsey in Wiltshire connections can now be positively identified between later Iron Age sites and villa-based estate centres and the medieval and modern villages that succeeded them. Links between Romano-British estate boundaries and early medieval estate and parish boundaries have been demonstrated within the Avon valley, and the general density and variety of Anglo-Saxon settlement in Wessex is only being fully revealed through the application of geophysical prospection and air photographic reconnaissance. Early Saxon 'heathen burial' cemeteries were also located on the borders of pre-existing estate boundaries, thus showing that the incomers respected the landscape divisions that they found.

Between 40 and 50 early Kentish territories have been identified as having a riverine or springhead community at their heart. They were also near to routeways and encompassed a variety of soils and resources that included outlying woodland – the kind of landscape organisation that is likely to have been seen by St Augustine when he landed in Thanet in 597. Most had their centres located on the Lower Greensand, a fact reflected in the large number of mentions of settlements in this zone in the many pre-Norman Kentish charters. Elsewhere in the region, running down the chalk scarp to the clay Vale of the White Horse in Oxfordshire, there is a series of elongated estate boundaries that were established by the late Saxon period and that encompassed different soils and resources. On the chalk the boundaries clearly cut through older Romano-British fields. The same territorial arrangement is repeated throughout the South East, both for the larger sub-county units such as lathes, rapes and hundreds, or the more local units such as the later parish boundaries; frequently it reinforced the pre-existing estate patterns, but with a focal settlement on better soils that were most frequently located below the chalk escarpment. The same theme recurs in the Wylye and Avon valleys and then eastwards through the length of the South Downs, the west Sussex Rother valley and the Surrey downland. Three classes of land were generally incorporated: valley meadows for cattle; better-drained soils below the escarpment for arable; and downland sheep pastures, sometimes with woodland making a fourth component.

There is little archaeological evidence, even as late as the 7th century, for settlement clusters that might be considered Saxon villages. Nevertheless, by the end of the 11th century most of our present-day villages were in existence, although not necessarily in their modern shapes. But they do not overlie early and mid-Saxon settlements and must therefore have been created between the

8th and late 11th centuries. Together with the formation of the surrounding open fields, the rearrangements constitute the landscape historian Christopher Taylor's second great landscape revolution – the first being that of the Late Bronze Age (*see* Chapter 5). Now 'villages appeared within the space of 300 years or so'. They were also frequently planned, often by ecclesiastical as well as lay lords, in a phenomenon generally referred to as the 'Middle Saxon Shift'.[23] One example at Cowdery's Down, near Basingstoke in Hampshire, included building alignments, rectangular enclosures and timber hall buildings.

An unusually extensive excavation of early Saxon settlement took place at Mucking on the 30m terrace that overlooks the Thames Estuary in Essex. The finds include two pagan cemeteries, at least 53 buildings and more than 200 sunken huts, laid out in a seemingly haphazard fashion within abandoned prehistoric and Romano-British fields. The remains were generally of humble type and date overall from the early 5th to the early 8th centuries. The area also possesses many early Saxon topographical place-name elements, such as -*dūn*, indicating the importance of dry ground above the Thameside marshes. Within the excavation area there had also been a gradual 'drift' in the settlement's focus over the period of occupation, but always within a specified territorial unit. The population at any one time has been estimated at between 85 and 100 – exceptionally large for this period, although once again there is no sign here of a typical nucleated settlement.[24] The early Saxon settlement in this coastal area of south-east Essex seems typical of the wider region, since similar early sites, as dated by pagan burials, are to be found in east Kent and along the Sussex and Hampshire coasts. In 2003 a spectacular 7th-century prince's burial site was excavated at Prittlewell on the outskirts of Southend-on-Sea, further enforcing the importance of this part of Essex for early Saxon settlement.

Firmer signs of systems of settlement also emerge at this period. Linkages between settlements were based around the multiple estate (with its centre or *caput*) that was linked to specialised landscape areas and in which stock was moved by transhumance between the component parts. Within Wessex the *caput* was often a royal *tūn*, an enclosure used by the kings in their progressions around their kingdom. There are many examples: Wiltshire offers Wilton, Warminster and Amesbury, the latter with rights in the extensive Forest of Chute to the north-east; Berkshire has Old Windsor; Surrey has Battersea, Chertsey and Farnham. In Sussex the extensive Malling estate is traceable through 9th-century charters. In time this interlinked system broke down into smaller, more self-sufficient units, which might anyway have pre-existed the multiple estate as the most basic tenurial item and which were inherited by the Saxons from their Romano-British predecessors. These small units included the more familiar estates and the manors, which developed in many areas alongside the late Saxon nucleation of settlement. The Domesday manor of Croydon, for example, may originally have been part of a larger unit that ran the length of the Kent/Surrey border but became fragmented in the 870s. Blewbury in Berkshire, granted to Bishop Aelfric of Ramsbury in 944, broke up into units which became parishes with names such as North and South Moreton, Aston Upthorpe or Aston Tirrold, all with the habitative place-name element -*tūn* that came into more frequent use from the 8th century as a result of the process of fission.[25] This fragmentation of larger units again exemplifies the dynamism of rural settlement organisation during the Saxon period.

It is important to note, however, that there were other areas within the region where Saxon reorganisation and settlement activity was more restricted. The 'Middle Saxon Shift' did not apply uniformly, since in much of the Kentish downland, the clay-capped Chilterns or the Weald there was no remodelling – this was early colonised wood-pasture countryside, and not part of 'village England'. Here, instead, was a landscape of scattered woodland and green commons, isolated farmsteads and hamlets, linked by twisting lanes – 'ancient countryside' where the rural framework developed piecemeal and unplanned.[26] In the *Anglo-Saxon*

Chronicle for the year 893 the Weald was 'the great forest which we call Andred', attested to by the proliferation of place-name elements with *-leah* (glade or clearing), *-feld* (open land), *-hyrst* (wooded hill) and *-denn* (swine pasture). Although there still remains discussion about the precise extent of settlement here before 1066, it seems clear that it was far more limited than in much of the South East. In other less-populated, heavily wooded areas such as the Savernake Forest in Wiltshire or Windsor Forest in Berkshire any reorganisation was similarly less obvious. Clearings were recognised, possibly as *pearroc* or private enclosures within the woodland. The Surrey Weald has so far produced not a single Saxon cemetery, however, and has few early place-names; earlier pre-Norman sources almost invariably refer to swine pastures, *-denns*, although in Surrey these tend to be represented by *-falod* (enclosure) names. Large estates were more normal here and were able to utilise the scarcer resources across a wider area; and this again may be seen in the larger sizes of many later medieval parishes in areas such as the central Weald. Similarly, the area around Windlesham, Chobham and Frimley on the poor Bagshot sands had virtually no settlement until the 12th century, and Windlesham itself originated as a forest pasture of Woking. In general the settlement pattern of such areas was one of isolated farmsteads, and stayed just that way.

Within the Christian church, sacred centres were based on pre-existing urban nuclei. The key cathedral was at Canterbury, destroyed by fire in 1067 and rebuilt in the new Norman style, but there were others at Rochester, Selsey (lost and replaced by a new building in Chichester in 1075), Old Sarum, London and Winchester. Territorial subdivisions developed in which regional 'mother churches' – the minsters developed by the bishops and their Christian kings – were serving their surrounding *parochiae* by the mid-8th century. On Southampton Water, kings Caedwalla and Ine founded minsters on royal estates at Eling, Southampton, Bishop's Waltham, Titchfield and Romsey in the late 7th or early 8th centuries. In Surrey, Chertsey, Bermondsey, Farnham and Woking appear as minsters by the mid-Saxon period. Chertsey, in particular, was lavishly endowed with land by Frithuwold, sub-King of Wulfhere of Mercia, after its early foundation in about 666; as an abbey it retained a prime position among Thames valley religious foundations.[27] In some cases the minsters were close to the royal *tūns* themselves, as at 7th-century Winchester or at Milton Regis in Kent, but equally they might have their own enclosure a little distance away, which itself might have been an older Roman town or even Iron Age site. In turn, these then might grow to become sizeable medieval towns. Even where the sites were new, as at the *burh* of Wareham in Dorset, a pre-existing minster was included within the walls. It is very likely that the *parochiae* were incorporated into the organisational units that have come down to us as hundreds. But it also appears that as a part of the huge administrative changes of the late Saxon period the *parochiae* were subdivided into the units that later emerge as medieval parishes. Although their influence may have remained stronger in some areas for longer, we can generally see that from the older *parochiae* there emerged the proto-parish spatial units that were to remain features of landscape and society over the following millennium.

THE MEDIEVAL URBAN AND RURAL LANDSCAPE

Landscape evidence accumulates rapidly as we start to examine the centuries from 1066 to 1500, the English medieval period. The conventional political chronologies which have defined the period, however, are now difficult to sustain in a study of landscape history, and there is much to be said for a complete reappraisal. This would give a break in landscape terms at around AD 700, before which the landscape may still have been a recognisably Roman or sub-Roman one, and after which the huge landscape reorganisations offer a more 'medieval' view. One powerful reason for not making this earlier break, however, is the existence of the Domesday Book (1086), the document that serves to summarise late Saxon settlement and to point forward to the making of a specifically southern English landscape – one that can now be viewed through the lenses of Norman and medieval documentary sources. In characterising the Norman arrival as ushering in an early medieval colonisation of the region, much as Hoskins had done in the brilliant chapter 3 of his *Making of the English Landscape*, we must nevertheless remember that we are dealing with just another phase in a much longer period of landscape reorganisation.[28]

One important feature of the period was undoubtedly the scale and extent of urban growth, the increased number of towns and the inward drift of people from the surrounding countryside. Population estimates are unreliable, but general consensus offers a population for England in 1086 of between 2 and 2.25 million, rising threefold to a peak of 5–6 million by 1300. Between 1315 and 1375, however, famine and plague wiped out much of the growth, and by 1377 population levels had fallen back to around 3 million and declined still further to a total of 2.8 million or less in the 1540s. The precise regional impact of these demographic changes is difficult to chart, but importantly for the South East there was also an accompanying internal migration from marginal areas to richer soils and from countryside to town. As a result, the South East experienced in-migration from other regions, and therefore avoided to some extent the late medieval demographic crisis that impacted so severely elsewhere.

With the growth of the economy in the 12th to 13th centuries a strong commercial and industrial presence was established in many of the region's towns. This was generated in great part by increased levels of production in the surrounding countrysides. The main towns of the region listed in Domesday (London was not mentioned as such) were Canterbury, followed by Sandwich and Lewes, and then by Chichester, Hastings, Hythe, Guildford and Kingston. The manufacture and trading of cloth was very important to London and Winchester. Some urban development stemmed from the *burhs*, as at Lewes, or from trade with France, as at Rye and Steyning. At Lewes a broad spread of gravel below the bridging point on the Sussex Ouse was utilised in the 12th and 13th centuries for the beaching of ships, around which an eastern suburb had already developed at Cliffe. The early boroughs, with their markets, were often located in places accessible to the coast, as at New Shoreham, Arundel or Chichester, but the population increases of the 11th to 13th centuries also opened up parts of the Weald, allowing the development of markets at Cranbrook, Tenterden, Crawley, East Grinstead, Uckfield and Horsham.

The South East benefited particularly from its cross-channel and coastal trading links, which included the export of cloth, wool and corn and the importing of wine from Gascony. In the 11th century the Abbey at Fécamp in Normandy was granted lands in Sussex, including Winchelsea, which thereby benefited from the increased trading links. Several centres were of greater importance to the king for their strategic positions and their capacity to provision ships in war and this was symbolised by their nomination as Cinque Ports. By the early 13th century Romney, Hythe, Hastings, Dover and Sandwich – the original ports – had co-opted affiliated members such as Rye and Winchelsea, together with corporate members such as Pevensey, Faversham and Fordwich, and other lesser 'limbs', into a confederation that stretched around the coast from the lower Medway to Seaford. Topographically, such development meant the improvement of harbours, the planning of market places, and the building of merchant and commercial properties, merchants' and craft guildhalls, large churches and religious houses, bridges and walls. The gradual establishment of burgesses' rights and privileges, freedom from tolls, jurisdictional independence and exemptions from seigneurial servitude meant that more profit could be retained and recycled into the urban landscape.

The benefits of an urban location were obvious to magnates, and if they were sufficiently powerful they might found a town *de novo* (Table 4.2). Small-scale

TABLE 4.2 NEW TOWNS OF THE MEDIEVAL PERIOD IN SOUTH-EAST ENGLAND.

Bedfordshire	**Hertfordshire**
Dunstable *c.* 1119	Chipping Barnet *c.* 1199
Berkshire	St Albans *c.* 950
Abingdon (?)	Watford 1119–46
Hungerford by 1131	**Kent**
Maidenhead by *c.* 1270	Hythe by 1086
Newbury (?)	Queenborough 1368
New Windsor 1107–31	New Romney before 960
Wokingham 1146	**Middlesex**
Dorset	Uxbridge by 1145
Corfe (?) 1080–1215	**Oxfordshire**
Newton (Poole Harbour)	Henley on Thames by 1179
1286	**Surrey**
Poole *c.* 1170–80	Haslemere 1221
Essex	Reigate *c.* 1170
Chelmsford 1199–1201	**Sussex**
Hampshire	Arundel *c.* 1071
New Alresford 1200	Battle 1070–1
Beaulieu 1204–27	Hastings *c.* 1069
New Lymington 1184–1216	Midhurst by 1184
Newport (IOW) 1177–84	Pevensey (near) 1207
Newtown (in Burghclere)	Rye by 1086
1218	New Shoreham 1096–1103
Newtown (IOW) 1255–6	Wardour 1262–7
Overton 1217–18	New Winchelsea 1288
Petersfield 1182–3	**Wiltshire**
Portsmouth 1194	Downton 1208–9
Stockbridge *c.* 1200	New Salisbury 1219
Yarmouth (IOW) *c.* 1170	Old Sarum 1075

Source: Beresford 1967, 394–526, listing only those new towns within the region as defined in this present book. Other new towns, such as Farnham or Bramber, are additional to Beresford's text.

OPPOSITE PAGE:

BOTTOM: *Fig. 4.12 Medieval new town. New Winchelsea, planned c. 1280, as it was in the early 15th century. The vaulted undercrofts were primarily for the storage of imported wines.*

TOP: *Fig. 4.13 New Winchelsea from the air. The modern settlement occupies only the north-eastern corner of the original walled enclosure.*

towns were set up by local lords over much of the region: Farnham by Bishop Henry de Blois and Reigate by the earls Warenne in the mid-12th century; or even villages such as the seigneurially planned Leatherhead and Bletchingley. In central-southern England Winchester, Christchurch and Southampton were noted as boroughs in 1086, but by the end of the 13th century nine Hampshire villages had been promoted to borough status and a further ten towns, such as New Alresford, had been planted. Norman barons were initially prominent in this process, replacing the *burh* at Burpham with the new town of Arundel across the River Arun, for example. Elsewhere in Sussex, Bramber was planted around the Norman castle to curtail the trade of Steyning upstream, only to be replaced in its turn by New Shoreham at the mouth of the river, with its rectilinear street pattern, large Norman church and customs house. In some cases a new town might replace an earlier location rendered hazardous by natural processes or by the need for greater accessibility. New Romney provides one example – as does New Winchelsea, re-founded in the 1280s as Edward I's royal port and at the time one of the foremost in England. The town was planned on a grid-iron basis by commissioners and for a while was the leading importer of Bordeaux wines and a fishing centre (Figs 4.12 and 4.13). But French raids and the gradual silting of its approaches were difficult to resist and by 1378 Chichester had usurped its position as chief Sussex port.[29] By the 16th century Winchelsea was reduced to the size of a village.

Quite different in origin was New Sarum (Salisbury), laid out in 1220–5 by Bishop Richard le Poore adjacent to his new cathedral and on common fields and common marshes beside the Wiltshire Avon. Individual house plots were marked out within each of the chequers, themselves bounded by roads that, though regular, also respect the pre-existing watercourses and field ways. Open water channels flowed through its streets to provide drainage and water supplies. The St Edmunds district, near the city ditch, shows the use of orthogonal geometric surveying by the 1260s, perhaps the first time it had been employed in England. A large market place, a guildhall, and the city's location on the main London–Exeter road all helped prosperity, as a result of which Salisbury grew to become one of the wealthiest provincial towns in England. One landscape feature resulting from its marshy location has been the sunken houses that, because of their weight, have fallen below the level of the streets.

London was now dominant among English towns and by about 1300 had a population of 100,000, which made it the second largest city north of the Alps. England's main roads focused on London and the elite now resided seasonally in the surrounding countryside. To some extent all the region's ports acted as outports for London, although Southampton, Sandwich and Winchelsea were long-distance trading ports in their own right. Southampton in particular grew as a distribution centre for Wessex and much of southern England in the 15th century. But London's dominance meant that market-oriented and more specialised rural production was now aimed at Londoners, and few other large towns in the region could compete. Several of the Cinque Ports were decaying

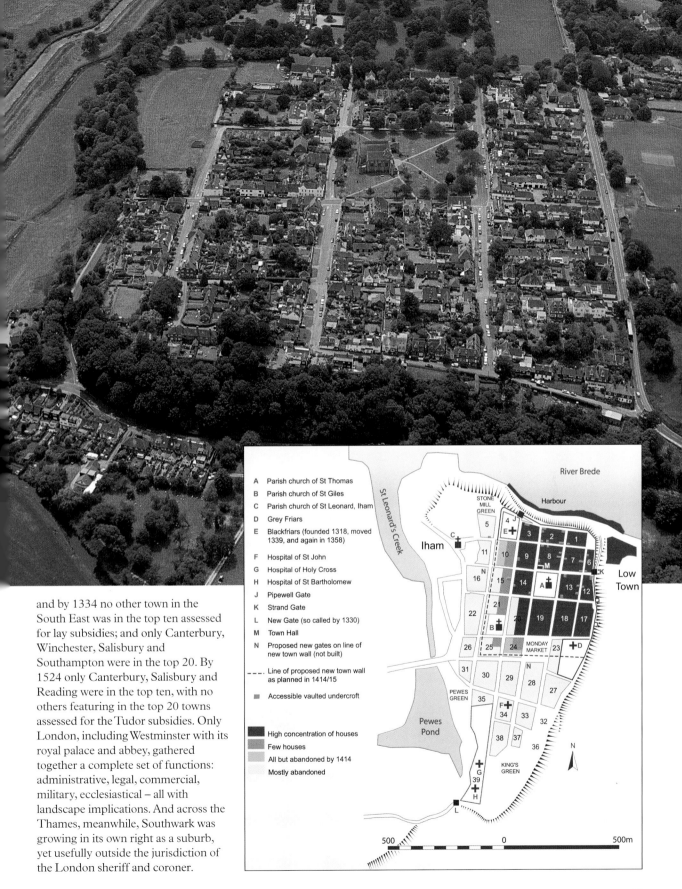

A Parish church of St Thomas
B Parish church of St Giles
C Parish church of St Leonard, Iham
D Grey Friars
E Blackfriars (founded 1318, moved 1339, and again in 1358)
F Hospital of St John
G Hospital of Holy Cross
H Hospital of St Bartholomew
J Pipewell Gate
K Strand Gate
L New Gate (so called by 1330)
M Town Hall
N Proposed new gates on line of new town wall (not built)
- - - Line of proposed new town wall as planned in 1414/15
▨ Accessible vaulted undercroft
■ High concentration of houses
▨ Few houses
▨ All but abandoned by 1414
□ Mostly abandoned

River Brede

St Leonard's Creek

STONE MILL GREEN
Harbour

Iham

Low Town

MONDAY MARKET

PEWES GREEN

Pewes Pond

KING'S GREEN

500   0   500m

N

and by 1334 no other town in the South East was in the top ten assessed for lay subsidies; and only Canterbury, Winchester, Salisbury and Southampton were in the top 20. By 1524 only Canterbury, Salisbury and Reading were in the top ten, with no others featuring in the top 20 towns assessed for the Tudor subsidies. Only London, including Westminster with its royal palace and abbey, gathered together a complete set of functions: administrative, legal, commercial, military, ecclesiastical – all with landscape implications. And across the Thames, meanwhile, Southwark was growing in its own right as a suburb, yet usefully outside the jurisdiction of the London sheriff and coroner.

Towns were frequently associated with defensive castles, conspicuous symbols of authority, beneath whose curtain walls communities might grow as supply and garrison bases, or administrative centres. By 1100 the pivotal defensive centres were being fortified, such as the six Sussex castle towns at Chichester, Arundel, Bramber, Lewes, Pevensey and Hastings, which were located at the southern end of their administrative divisions (or 'rapes') to guard their coastlines while offering a line of communication between Normandy and London. The construction of the castle at Lewes, however, undoubtedly destroyed many of the previous roads and buildings in the north-western quarter of that town. From William I's White Tower keep on the south-east section of London's wall, to the great castle at Dover on the Eastern Heights, these could be spectacular landscape features. The early castle keep at Canterbury included local flint, Caen stone and Roman materials in the construction of its walls. River crossings were also well guarded, such as that of the Medway by Rochester castle and its elevated keep. Castles were also used to guard rivers or roads in rural areas, such as at Bodiam where the castle, built in 1386, commands the marshes and eastern Rother valley. Other rural defences included fortifications to religious buildings, such as the great Gate House at Battle Abbey (*see* photo p.10); crenellated manor houses; new or redesigned moated settlements, such as Eltham Palace and Ightham Mote; or for hunting lodges. The medieval landscape of fear has bequeathed to us a formidable array of such sites, including the town walls themselves, which became especially important in the 15th century as French attacks proliferated. The walls at Arundel, Lewes, Winchelsea and Rye all date to this period, as do fortifications to Battle Abbey and the priories at Lewes and Michelham. The castle is a unique landscape feature of the period: they had become anachronistic by 1500 and the last to be constructed was the brick-built residential castle at Herstmonceux, begun in around 1440.

If defence is a key element in our understanding of the medieval landscape, equally important is the cultural, political and economic power of the Church. At the time of the Norman Conquest the old minster churches were in decline and the new Norman clergy of the late 11th century were eager for reform. By 1086 the minster at the large estate of Stanmer in Sussex had already been replaced by St Michael's at South Malling, near Lewes, and autonomous parish churches had similarly sprung up within the limits of the former estate at Westmeston, Ditchling and Wivelsfield. While there are few signs of small churches being built prior to the 10th century, the period thereafter was one when localised small manorial and secular churches, built by Saxon thegns, seem to have blossomed, at the expense of the older centres. In landscape terms there is evidence of a large-scale rebuilding of the older churches, or the building of new ones, between about 1030 and 1130. It has been estimated that by 1066 some 60–70 per cent of medieval parish churches already existed.[30] But in a prodigious burst of activity, every major church in the region was rebuilt in the decades after 1066, except the abbeys at Westminster, which was already Norman in style, and Waltham, where a stone church had been built in the 1050s.

Ecclesiastical power now featured strongly in the landscape: the Bishop of Winchester's Farnham estate covered some 25,000 acres in total and the grip of such magnates on the lives and landscapes of their subjects was as strong as that of any lay seigneur. The Domesday Book and its near-coeval texts, such as the *Textus Roffensis* (a cartulary of Rochester Cathedral from about 1125), the *Excerpta* (a Domesday satellite text from St Augustine's) or the *Domesday Monachorum* (a Domesday-related text detailing estates of the Archbishop of Canterbury and other landholders), offer an unparalleled insight into the numbers of churches and ecclesiastical establishments in the South East. The Domesday details can sometimes be amplified by reference to the other sources: thus the *Monachorum* lists an additional 104 churches in the diocese of Canterbury while the *Textus Roffensis* adds another 48 in the bishopric of

Rochester – thereby increasing the number of Domesday Book churches in Kent alone by more than 100 per cent. But even with this degree of uncertainty about the true landscape significance of the church, it is safe to state that the main impacts were within the towns. The Benedictine Christ Church Priory associated with Canterbury Cathedral was built in about 1070 in a style similar to Lanfranc's abbey church at Caen (Fig. 4.14), while just outside the wall St Augustine's Abbey was completed by Abbot Hugh (d. 1124). Urban parishes and churches multiplied: Canterbury had 22 by the mid-12th century and London no fewer than 126 parish and 13 'greater' churches, including the rebuilt St Paul's. The move of the Sussex diocesan centre from Selsey to Chichester resulted in the construction of another great Norman cathedral – indeed an architectural revolution was now under way that would eventually lead to the Gothic style. The number of Benedictine foundations now grew: at Battle, William's victory was celebrated by the building of the Benedictine abbey, despite the concerns of the imported monks from Marmoutier about the inhospitality and isolation of the site. There was also a smaller number of Cluniac houses, such as the priory of St Pancras that created a new suburb to the south of Saxon Lewes; it also possessed a spectacular high steeple and a 28m vault over the high altar – half as high again as the nave of modern Chichester cathedral. The Cluniac order endowed further houses at Reading and Faversham, while at Bermondsey its richly endowed abbey entered fully into the mainstream of London, and therefore national, affairs. However, from the 12th century new religious orders began to advocate a return to a simpler and more austere life, resulting in foundations of the Cistercians, firstly at Waverley Abbey (Farnham) in 1128, and at Boxley in Kent and Robertsbridge in Sussex; Premonstratensians at Bayham and Durford; and Augustinian (Austin) canons at Merton, Tandridge and Reigate in Surrey and Michelham in Sussex. Alien priories belonging to Norman mother houses were also founded, such as Boxgrove Priory from Lessay (*c.* 1105). Within the towns, friaries were founded in such places as Arundel (Blackfriars), Chichester (Blackfriars, Greyfriars, Austin friars), Lewes, Rye and Winchelsea, where they often occupied marginal sites near rivers or the sea.

As noted above, the extent of wealden settlement has long remained controversial, not helped by Domesday Book's method of recording manors rather than settlements, for which purpose both demesne land and the outlying elements of multiple estates are simply allocated to a manorial centre. Thus, the

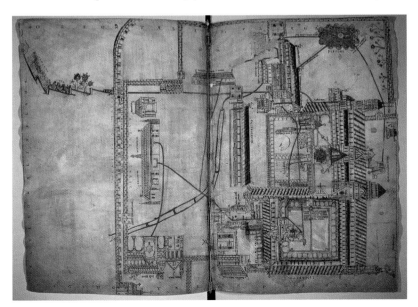

Fig. 4.14 Canterbury Cathedral 1153–61. East is at the top. The map is primarily to show the water supply from the River Stour, coming from the west, outside the curtain wall of the precincts. The cathedral choir and Norman central tower, shown here, were destroyed by fire in 1174, soon after this map was drawn. The Romanesque nave was also replaced in late-medieval rebuilding. The map also pre-dates the murder of St Thomas à Becket here in 1170.

lands of Earl Warenne at Ditchling and Patcham included scattered farms and hamlets in the area of Worth, around its Saxon church on the Sussex/Surrey border. The most likely picture is one of small, dispersed settlements more closely spaced in some parts of the Weald than in others; a woodland environment was still very apparent and the hunting forests would have been the most sparsely settled of all. Church foundations of the 11th and early 12th centuries indicate settlement, as at Alfold or Horley. But while 10th-century sources mainly describe -*denns*, later medieval sources refer to tenements and homesteads. The 11th and 12th centuries undoubtedly witnessed a great deal of settlement activity here; this continued in eastern Sussex into the 12th and 13th centuries, which saw the largest amount of assarting (woodland clearance), while in wealden Kent, by contrast, the -*denn* system was still active in the 13th century. Varying chronologies of clearance and settlement must therefore be recognised, closely related to tenurial linkages and lordship policies as well as to demographic and economic fluctuations. In Kent and eastern Sussex the large remaining expanses of woodland and marsh meant that the pressures of population on resources could be accommodated without the wholesale conversion of farmland to a common-field system as in the Midlands or the Danelaw counties. Although the Weald was undoubtedly less populated than its surrounding areas in 1086, and to an unknown extent, Domesday Book does offer some insight into the distribution of population at a broad scale. Thus, it is possible to discern in its folios that Wessex, the Bagshot sands and the Lower Greensands of western Surrey were also thinly populated, but that the richer lowland soils in north Berkshire and on the coastal fringes of Sussex and eastern Kent were more populous.

By 1100 most of the region's villages were in existence. Thereafter they expanded in planned or unplanned ways – hamlets coalesced, ribbon development grew, and greens were impinged upon. Their churches, so characteristic a feature of our landscapes, were also rebuilt. In general the region's nucleated villages took shape at this time – those with house-plots grouped in double rows occurring most commonly in the Thames valley, on Salisbury Plain or on chalk dip slopes. Along the Till and Avon valleys on Salisbury Plain the village plans were composed of elongated tofts that ran parallel to the rivers, with a back lane behind. Such 'repetitious symmetry' implies a common origin, and alongside the reorganisation of field systems in the 11th and 12th centuries (*see* Chapter 5) the hand of seigneurial planning can once again be posited. The villages belonging to

Fig. 4.15 Regular medieval village topographies: row settlements of Chertsey Abbey manor, in Surrey. Most villages in the Surrey part of the London Basin were of this simple compact linear form, with house plots facing each other along a road. Such villages were in existence by the 14th century but their origins remain uncertain.

Chertsey Abbey in Surrey, such as Egham, Great Bookham, Chobham, Chertsey and Effingham, also display great regularity in their layout (Fig. 4.15).[31] In the severalty (individualised) farming environment of the Weald, by contrast, villages were scarcer and also more diffuse or polyfocal; at times their churches may have acted as the nuclei for settlement accretion. Early medieval population growth here did not result in nucleated villages, since resources were more easily available and the land use was dominated by pastoral activities which did not require the degree of communal cooperation necessary in the open-field arable areas.

This expansion of rural settlement was, at least in part, the signature in the landscape of a process of 'subinfeudation' in which the constituent elements of the older multiple estates broke apart into smaller manors, earlier in some places than in others. The large Bramley manor in Surrey dissolved into independent holdings between 1086 and about 1250, but nearby Chertsey and Farnham continued longer. Assarting of chalk woodland commons also continued from the late Saxon period into the mid-12th century, as documented for the North Downs and Chilterns, or even the early 13th century as at Fyfield Down in Wiltshire. Along the downland dip slopes and scarp-foot settlements, small strip-shaped manors grew from the larger units. This kind of splitting might also be reflected in place-names such as West and East Clandon, or West and East Horsley in Surrey. On Salisbury Plain and more generally throughout Wessex such pairings can be on either side of a river, such as East and West Chisenbury on the Avon.[32]

Even allowing that medieval documents may list places for the first time that had actually existed long before, some soils were definitely colonised at this time. Everywhere on the London Clay, *bruera* (a mix of oakwood and brushwood) was being cut back, and common wastes being brought into cultivation. Thus Penge, part of Battersea estate, was described as pasture in a 957 charter, but by the mid-13th century it comprised compact arable holdings and tenements with crofts. Assarting was clearly responsible for settlements such as Oxshott in Stoke D'Abernon parish, first mentioned in the mid-12th century and described in about 1200–20 as a mixture of woodland, enclosures and recent 'purprestures' (areas under former Forest Law). Colonisation in the 12th and 13th centuries also brought marshland into cultivation. In Romney Marsh reclamation occurred behind the accumulating Dungeness foreland. Here, 12th-century inning at Walland, Denge and Guldeford marshes created long and narrow parishes west of the Rhee Wall, itself actually a massive drainage channel built in the mid-13th century in an attempt to save the declining port of Romney. Much of this hard-won reclamation was subsequently lost, however, in the great floods that hit the area in the early 15th century and led to the abandonment of much of Romney Marsh, Pevensey Marshes, the north Kent and Essex marshes and the lower estuaries.

One inhibiting factor in settlement expansion between 1100 and 1300 was the declaration of Forest Law over large areas of the South East. While this did not totally inhibit settlement, since fines and rents might be levied as tacit recognition of an encroachment, it did raise problems of the legal protection of deer, as well as the protection of lords' pannage (swine grazing) rights in these wooded areas. Settlement was therefore delayed until late in the 13th century in such areas as Frimley, Chobham and Chertsey, all within Windsor Forest. The New Forest, Epping Forest and Ashdown Forest, along with many smaller areas, chases and parks, demonstrated similar histories.

Although the declaration of Forest Law acted as a brake on settlement expansion in many areas of the South East – perhaps best illustrated by the earlier displacement of Saxon communities in the New Forest – the pace of settlement expansion also stalled for other reasons after 1300. Indeed, one theme that has gained popularity among landscape historians has been that of tracing deserted or shrunken settlements. While acknowledging that desertion must be seen as an inevitable component of the longer-term settlement shifts noted above, there were nevertheless some distinct medieval processes that affected the longevity of settlements. Climate and sea-level changes dealt blows to coastal communities such as those at Old Winchelsea, or at Milton, which lay somewhere near the present pier at Southend but disappeared at this time. Economic shifts also reinforced a retreat from more marginal downland sites; and the Black Death may have dealt the final blow to many impoverished settlements, as at Hangleton near Brighton in Sussex. While the latter is now beneath suburban development it is still possible to see abandoned house platforms on the Sussex downland at such places as Charlton or Monkton. In south-east England, as elsewhere, the impact of the Black Death on the landscape must be placed alongside the effects of more general economic decline as the period of expansion that had lasted from the 8th century came to a halt. Population growth was intermittent from about 1300, arable land was reduced and more marginal settlements were consequently threatened. By the 15th century pastoral farming had become a more viable alternative to arable as a result of an increasing demand for wool at home and abroad; and although the South East escaped the worst impacts of this process of conversion, which was more severely felt in the Midlands and North, the shift from arable to pasture may have been accompanied by the eviction of tenants from some smaller settlements.

EARLY-MODERN LANDSCAPE CHANGES 1500–1750

Whether viewed as a period of transition from medieval to modern, from feudalism to capitalism, or as an important historical period in its own right, covering as it does the Tudor, Stuart and early Hanoverian dynasties, the early-modern centuries are an important constituent in any consideration of the settlement patterns of south-east England. Furthermore we now have plentiful maps and illustrations, a good array of documentation and individual topographical accounts to help in the reconstruction of the landscape. This is as well, because the application of archaeological methods to the post-medieval and modern periods is a relatively recent development.

All else in the settlement history of the South East during these centuries is overshadowed by the continuing rise of London and by the concomitant increase in the South East's influence in national terms. The region was also now of vital strategic importance in military and commercial struggles against continental opposition, a fact that also influenced its landscape. London, 'a monstrous head grown too big for the body of the country of England', outstripped all other towns. Its consumption of food, coals and raw materials reached into many corners of the country, both inside and outside the South East. In 1649–50, for example, London received 989 shipments of corn from the rest of England, of which 527 came from Kent, shipped through Faversham, Milton Regis or from Thanet. Drovers brought stock from the furthest parts of the kingdom. By 1700 London handled an extraordinary 80 per cent of all England's imports and 69 per cent of her exports. And manufacturing in London alone may have had as many as 200,000 livelihoods dependent upon it.

Urban landscapes, then, were dominated by London. With a population of 70,000 in 1550 rising to 400,000 by 1650 and 575,000 by 1700, by which time 10 per cent of the entire country's population were Londoners, this was truly a world city. During the 17th century population growth took place predominantly outside the city walls, and by 1680 more than 60 per cent of London's population lived in such suburbs. Elsewhere fortunes varied from town to town, although all were minnows by comparison: by the 17th century Canterbury had reached about 6,000; Rochester, Maidstone and Dover about 3,000; and there were several other towns with 1,000–2,500 people. Some towns fared poorly: Winchester and Salisbury suffered from declining textile industries, losing out to a growing rural Wessex industry. Canterbury was similarly affected, multiplying the negative impact here of the Dissolution of the Monasteries. Trade ebbed and flowed and by the 16th century the markets at Bletchingley, Ewell, Haslemere and Leatherhead were declining with consequent loss of population. Reigate contained only 90 tenements by 1622. Celia Fiennes's 'sad old town' of Sandwich had a silted harbour by 1690, and Defoe noted the decay of ports at Dover, Rye and Winchelsea. The rapidly growing population in the South East was both the outcome and the engine of growth, but urban environments were beset by plagues that declined only gradually and then returned in 1665–6, followed by influenza in the 1670s and 1680s. This heralded declining birth rates and continuing high levels of mortality that yielded an actual, though locally variable, decline in population that lasted through to the mid-18th century.

Conversely, Chatham and the lower Medway towns fared well because Tudor and Stuart overseas expansion and maritime aggression required growth in naval facilities. By 1700 Chatham's population had risen to 5,000, putting it on a par with Canterbury. Faversham similarly prospered as a major corn-exporting port to London, and also had a gunpowder works, granaries, warehouses, inns, offices, a paved town centre by 1549, a grammar school and a fine Elizabethan guildhall. Inland, Godalming had been a 16th-century clothing town but was granted borough status in 1575, which led to the holding of a market and fair and a market house and 16th-century timber-framed buildings in the High Street and Church Street. Reading also prospered during Elizabethan and Jacobean times, with cloth-making, markets and fairs bringing wealth, a rising population but a multiplication of smaller cottages and subdivided properties that were 'obscure receptacles of poor people ... creeping and intruding into that borough'.[33]

But the towns were also the showcases and centres of culture, fashion and exchange. Architectural design now guided the form of public, commercial and private buildings, and Renaissance and classical proportions were admired over the local vernacular, and seen as cultural capital that would help to achieve prestige and status. Parliamentary Improvement Acts also provided normative design in street layout, building materials, water supplies and gardens. In 1737 the rivulets that ran down the centres of Salisbury's medieval streets were brick-lined and bridges were provided for foot passengers and the greater ease of wheeled transport. Public space was now planned for promenades, and such space, together with theatres, assembly rooms, racecourses and coffee houses, ushered in new conceptions of urban landscape. The development of new towns had not ended in the 14th century either: Tunbridge Wells, whose springs were 'discovered' by Lord North in 1606, grew as a fashionable spa town throughout the 17th century (see Chapter 6). The overall outcome of these developments was to emphasise the dynamism, market potential and consumer demand generated by a region with a higher proportion of urban population than any other. The population of the counties of Kent, Surrey and Sussex in 1676 was 41 per cent urban, including Southwark and the Kent and Surrey Thames-side developments.[34]

The landscape importance of the medieval church came under severe attack with the Reformation. The religious upheavals of the Reformation and its extremist aftermath of the 16th and 17th centuries had their own local landscape impacts – on the furnishings of parish churches, for example – but it was the Dissolution that had the greatest impact on the landscape. Kent was the first English county to be entered into the *Valor Ecclesiasticus*, the 1536 valuation of church property, and the first to receive a visitation as a preliminary to the Dissolution. Some smaller religious houses had already been dismantled in the 1520s – such as Bayham in 1525, notwithstanding a local riot – but the main suppressions began in 1536 at Waverley, followed by Chertsey in 1537, and in 1538 by St Augustine's, Battle, Reading and Faversham abbeys, and Dover and Lewes priories. The last abbey to be dissolved in England was Waltham in 1540. Thereafter the destruction of the shrines began, including that of St Thomas at Canterbury, followed by the suppression of the hospitals, chantries, charities and colleges.

The great age of church power was now ended, and with it the pilgrimages that had brought wealth to ecclesiastical centres such as Canterbury or St Albans. At Southwark the Dissolution had a severe impact, since employment was provided by the town houses of the abbots of Battle, Lewes and Beaulieu, together with Bermondsey Priory, and lands belonging to the Archbishop of Canterbury and the Bishop of Winchester. By the mid-1540s a large amount of Canterbury's diocesan property had been handed over to Thomas Cromwell and the Crown, and thence to lay magnates and large landowners, city speculators, local squires, merchants and lawyers. An extraordinary 40 per cent of the total area of Essex, for example, was thus transferred. This was the largest transfer of land since the Norman Conquest and much more than the average 25 per cent that occurred over England as a whole. The Priory of Sheen, dissolved in 1539, went to Edward, Earl of Hertford (afterwards Duke of Somerset); Lewes Priory was handed to Cromwell; Waverley was passed to the Earl of Southampton and the 22 manors of Battle Abbey to the influential Sir Anthony Browne. Indeed, by the 18th century there were few large estates that did not owe something to these upheavals. Thus, Sir Thomas Sackville, created Lord Buckhurst in 1567 and first Earl of Dorset in 1604, owned Buckhurst, on the edge of Ashdown Forest where he was also appointed Master Forester for life in 1561. He also acquired Knole, which he proceeded to rebuild in 1603, together with property in Lewes and London. In 1576 he purchased the barony of Lewes and in 1599 succeeded Burleigh as Lord Treasurer. His father had been Chancellor of the Court of Augmentations in 1548, overseeing the Dissolution, and had in the process gained property as well as advowsons and impropriations.

The acquisition of the former church properties heralded a great increase in secular country-house building in the region from the early 16th century. Powerful Londoners and provincial landowners vied to create new standards of splendour and domestic comfort, often re-using the dressed or rough stone taken from the former monastic sites. Stone from Abingdon Abbey went to Oatlands; from Lewes Priory to the nearby Southover Grange and Hangleton Manor, north-west of Brighton; while Reading Abbey was used as a quarry for both public and private building stone. Some church properties became manor houses, such as Michelham in Sussex. Henry VIII had ten royal palaces of his own, including his favourite Hampton Court and its formal landscaped garden that he had taken over from Cardinal Wolsey in 1525. The old palace at Richmond was sold and dismantled in 1650, and his highly decorated new Nonsuch, near Cheam in Surrey involved the displacement of the village of Cuddington, although only traces remain of the building today following its demolition in the late 17th century. In general, we now see external Tudor gatehouses, courtyards, stables, outbuildings and gardens, and internal galleries, staircases and parlours. The E-shaped entrance front, so characteristic of the Elizabethan age, is well represented at houses such as Danny and Wiston in Sussex. Brick became fashionable, as at Sutton Place (Surrey) in the 1520s where Sir Richard Weston employed a style observed in the Loire, or at Old Buckhurst. The formal garden now came into its own, again reflecting French and Renaissance Italian styles, as at the residences of the Boleyns at Hever, the Sydneys at Penshurst or Sackvilles at Knole. Under James I the palace gardens at Somerset House, Greenwich and Richmond were redesigned on geometric lines with fountains and grottoes, and such fashions percolated down through society to the gardens of the greater nobles and gentry further from London.

Equally characteristic of the period, however, were the changes made to the houses of the lesser gentry and yeomen. Between the 13th and 16th centuries most middling domestic housing had been built with box frames and an open hall. The fine timber-framed hall house that is now Amersham Museum is just one 15th-century example, though much modified. From the early 16th century, though with many variations and intermediate forms, the larger houses displayed staircases, floors and chambers were inserted in former open halls; windows were glazed and hearths and chimney stacks added. Dormer windows allowed more use of the roof space. Wood remained the dominant building material, but the use of brick, weatherboarding and tiling increased. The traditional 'wealden' (but by no means confined to the Weald, as shown by the Bell Inn at Waltham St Lawrence in Berkshire) hall house with its jettied first-floor levels continued throughout the 17th century. Indeed, there remained many medieval designs, especially in the countryside, although the half-timbered wealden house might now be built upon a stone or brick base or use these materials to replace the earlier wattle-and-daub infill (Fig. 4.16). In the prosperous farmland of north Kent there was a multiplication of more specialised rooms, many of which can be discerned in probate inventories at this time, such as butteries, boulting houses (for the processing of flour), cheese lofts and wool chambers, and the Dutch gable appeared, although it hardly penetrated into the Weald. The concept of a 'Great Rebuilding' between the 1520s and 1640s, as originally proposed by W G Hoskins, has now been much modified and is seen as one upsurge in a more cyclic phenomenon of change, and one with great regional variation. The South East, wealthy and willing to blend new ideas with vernacular tradition, certainly embraced the rebuilding. Of course, much of the landscape of housing was far less sophisticated: labourers and commoners lived in single-cell, single-storey cottages, and many lived in hovels or even turf-covered huts if they were migrant charcoal burners.

Rural settlement patterns between 1500 and 1750 largely continued medieval trends in the consolidation of village morphologies through infilling and the building of more substantial houses. In some areas, such as the Forest Ridges around Ashdown Forest, or on the barren Bagshot sands, cottage and garden plots were enclosed on roadside waste as dispersed or linear squatter settlements grew up. On the small North Downs common of Stelling Minnis, the 18th-century Kent topographer Edward Hasted saw 'numbers of houses and cottages built promiscuously on or about the Minnis, the inhabitants of which are as wild, and in as rough a state as the country they dwell in'.[35] Defoe, in his early 18th-century travels, encountered Bagshot Heath:

Fig. 4.16 Wealden house. Old Bell Farm, Harrietsham, Kent. A late 15th-century house that had an open hall of two bays with a through passage, flanked by two two-storey bays, jettied on front and sides. The close-studded walls have original timberwork. In about 1600 the hall was floored and a chimney-stack inserted backing on to the old through passage.

> … here is a vast tract of land, some of it within seventeen or eighteen miles of the capital city; which is not only poor, but even quite sterile, given up to barrenness, horrid and frightful to look on, not only good for little, but good for nothing; much of it is a sandy desert, and one may frequently be put in mind here of Arabia Deserta, where the winds raise the sands, so as to overwhelm whole caravans of travellers, cattle and people together; for in passing this heath in a windy day, I was so far in danger of smothering with the clouds of sand, which were raised by the storm, that I could neither keep it out of my mouth, nose or eyes: and when the wind was over, the sand appeared spread over the adjacent fields of the forest some miles distant, so as that it ruins the very soil. This sand indeed is checked by the heath, or heather, which grows in it, and which is the common product of barren land, even in the very Highlands of Scotland; but the ground is otherwise so poor and barren, that the product of it feeds no creatures, but some very small sheep, who feed chiefly

BELOW: *Fig. 4.17 Distribution of the sheep-keepers'*
lookers' huts on Romney Marsh. There were possibly
as many as 300 on the Marsh in the early 19th century but
only 15 survived through to the late 1990s. The hut depicted
in Fig. 4.18 at St Mary-in-the-Marsh is noted.

BOTTOM: *Fig. 4.18 An example of the sheep-keepers'*
accommodation, as shown by a reconstructed
looker's hut and its associated sheep pen, St
Mary-in-the-Marsh, Kent (see Fig. 4.17). This hut
was originally at Midley but has been reconstructed on its
present site. The poor-quality wealden bricks and clay tiles
are typical of the construction of these primitive buildings.

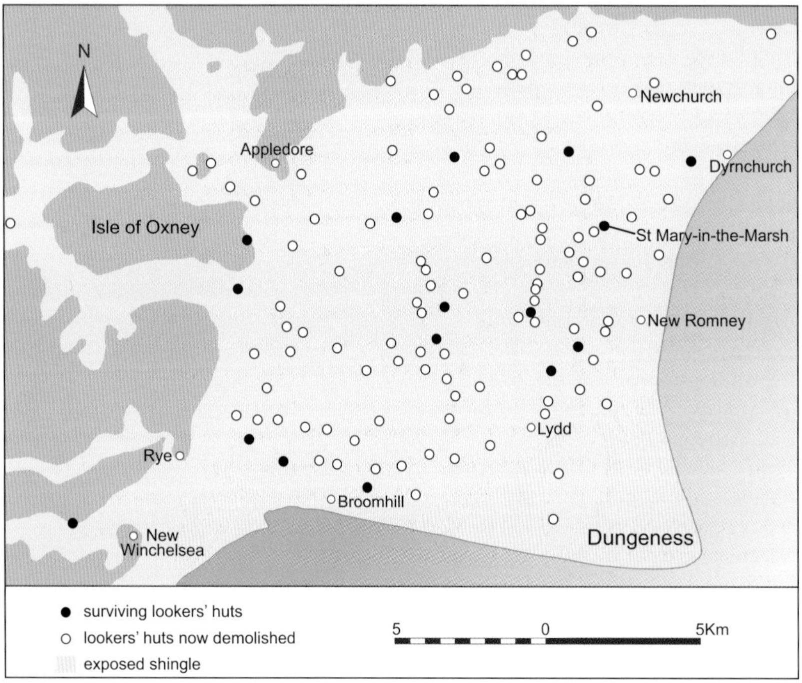

on the said heather, and but very few of these, nor are there any
villages, worth remembering, and but few houses or people for
many miles far and wide; this desert lies extended so much, that
some say, there is not less than a hundred thousand acres of this
barren land that lyes all together, reaching out every way in the
three counties of Surrey, Hampshire and Berkshire.[36]

Even where productive land was being brought into use, settlement might not follow. In Romney Marsh inning, protection and draining continued to bring new land into use near Winchelsea and Rye, and at Pevensey the former harbour was by 1595 a common marsh. The Wantsum Channel separating the Isle of Thanet from mainland Kent was silted to the extent that a bridge could be constructed in 1485, and today the Wantsum is little more than a ditch. Such areas provided excellent farmland for the graziers but were unhealthy and 'very aguish', and in consequence developed little new settlement, except for the 'lookers' huts' for the sheep-keepers (Figs 4.17 and 4.18). By 1600 Romney Marsh had the lowest population density of anywhere in the region. The great Dymchurch wall protected the marshland in the east, but silting emphasised the decline and changeover to pasture and there were as many as seven abandoned churches here, such as Broomhill, Midley and Hope all Saints, by 1670.[37]

Fig. 4.17

Fig. 4.18

THE MODERN PERIOD: EXPANSION AND CONTAINMENT

After 1750 the South East experienced a veritable explosion of settlement that is challenging to summarise. In particular the period saw an unprecedented increase in urbanisation and urban growth, and the townscape must therefore take some precedence in this account. From the first census of 1801 to the present, the region's population growth consistently outpaced the national average. Perhaps one *leitmotif* of this growth is the in-between settlement, the suburb, whether in the form of the Victorian villa, Edwardian terrace, inter-war suburb, post-war New Town or owner-occupied estate of the 1980s and 1990s and early 21st century – the last including the gated communities that have recently emerged as landscape symbols of a divided society.

Many forces have shaped this development: internal trade and population movement were facilitated by revolutions in communications (*see* Chapter 6); colonial expansion brought wealth to the region, just as 20th-century globalisation and multinational corporate strategies continued to do. London's grip on the affairs of England tightened still further as great bureaucratic and administrative institutions were located close to the heart of government and the City of London. The modern period has also witnessed cultural and social changes that led to new values being placed on the sea-coast, in the process bringing fashionable society and service economies to a growing number of resorts. In the same way, the region's countryside has come to be preferred by many as a living space over the town, a trend that in more recent decades has brought jobs to the countryside as well. The West End of London might be the World's most expensive location for office space in 2006, but for 50 years there has been a steady outward flow of jobs and people from London, only very recently reversed in part by residential development in the City and in east London. Population growth rates for the London area as a whole tended to mask the fact that inner London was actually losing population. London's peak population was attained in 1939; inner London's had been reached in 1901, and that of outer London was achieved in 1951. This was the period of the great suburbanisation of the South East (*see* Chapter 7).

With the explosion of suburbia and multiplication of communications, it might at one point have seemed that concrete would eventually cover the whole of the South East. A degree of control was exerted, however, at the very moment that the railways were allowing unprecedented access and development. Middle-class opinion began to articulate an underlying fear of rural destruction (of both landscape and culture) – a fear heightened by the onset of the Great Depression from the 1870s. In 1865 the Commons Preservation Society was formed to protect remaining open spaces around London such as Wimbledon, Wandsworth and Banstead commons and Hampstead Heath, where it proved helpful in mustering support for the retention of the open spaces. The National Trust was founded in 1895 and the spirit of rural protectionism was reinforced by the foundation in 1928 of the Council for the Preservation of Rural England (now the Campaign to Protect Rural England). Piecemeal growth was also controlled by the planning of garden suburbs or cities, utilising the ideas of Ebenezer Howard (*see* Chapter 8). The experiment began in 1903 at Letchworth in the Hertfordshire countryside, where the first Garden City still retains the outlines of its central square, from which roads radiate, as well as many of the original buildings in Parker and Unwin's Arts and Crafts style. At Hampstead Garden Suburb another model community was laid out from 1907 with leafy winding lanes and spacious housing densities, this time as a suburban ideal.

In response to the 1909 Housing, Town Planning etc. Act local authorities were provoked to move in similar directions in terms of the planning of suburban growth. The London County Council was particularly active: in 1927 the Greater London Regional Planning Committee was formed, which included representatives from local authorities within a 25-mile radius of central London, and in 1933 an open 'green girdle' was proposed to separate old and new developments and provide recreation space for Londoners. In 1938 a Green Belt Act was passed to safeguard open local-authority land, an act which has had huge landscape implications for the South East ever since. Only in recent years, in the face of enormous pressures to release more land for housing in the region, has the concept come under serious attack. While the Green Belt may include some derelict or unaesthetic land, its protective value against London's continuous built expansion has been demonstrable (Fig. 4.19).

Located just beyond the Green Belt came London's eight designated post-war new towns. These were planned as self-contained settlements that would not look economically to London and that would have neighbourhoods to provide socially

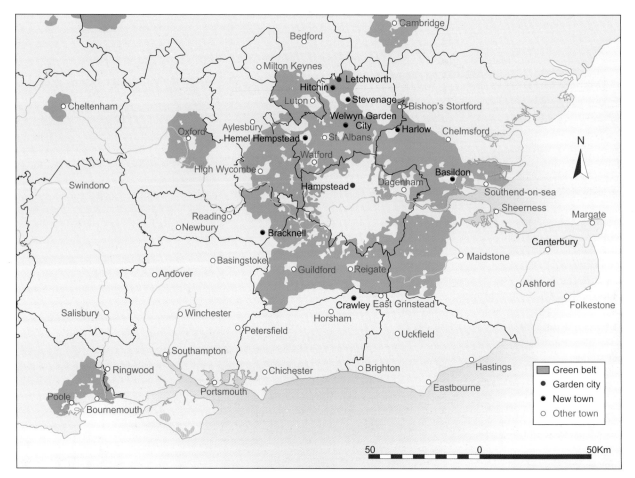

Fig. 4.19 London's Green Belt, and the location of 20th-century new towns and garden suburbs. *The belt is an irregular ring of open country of 486,000ha with no internal unity, within which there is a presumption against development. Since 1955 several provincial towns have also had green belts declared, although only that around Bournemouth and Poole, abutting onto the New Forest National Park, is within the region included in this book.*

for their populations. Open space and civic amenity was emphasised. Stevenage, in the Chilterns, was the first to be developed, followed by Basildon, Bracknell, Crawley, Harlow, Hitchen, Hemel Hempstead and Welwyn Garden City. But although the modern designed architectural spaces were put in place, the idea of self-containment broke down quickly and all too soon the new towns became commuter settlements for London as rail and road links with the capital improved.

The region's precocious development after 1750 has also had a significant impact on rural settlement. The progressive advances in travel have served to bring most of the region's countryside within commuting range of London or one of the regional centres such as Southampton. Some villages may have been swamped by suburban expansion, but few have been lost altogether, except to military requirements as at Imber in Wiltshire (Fig. 4.20) or Tyneham in Dorset. Some others have been moved at the behest of landowners for aesthetic reasons, such as the much-photographed Milton Abbas in Dorset, which was rebuilt for Lord Dorchester between 1773 and 1786 on a site chosen by Capability Brown. It was composed of 40 sturdy thatched cottages lining a wide road, each with an expanse of lawn at the front and, between them, great chestnut trees (which have since been felled). There was also an inn, almshouses, and a church by James Wyatt. Elsewhere displacement was not an issue, but the aesthetic taste of the wealthy was nevertheless significant. At Holly Village, near Highgate, Baroness Burdett Coutts had a small village built in the Picturesque style; it included an ornate 1865 archway and just seven cottages, with open gardens around a grassy area, all with Gothic touches and decorated chimneys. Earlier in the 1820s Nash had also employed the Picturesque style in the park villages at Regents Park, then on the

suburban fringe of London. There are many other urban and rural examples of philanthropic housing schemes in the South East, such as the cottages for alcoholic ladies set up by Lady Henry Somerset in 1896 at Duxhurst, between Reigate and Horley. The founding in the 1870s of the Bedford Park estate, half-an-hour from the City, was different again: Arts and Crafts designs were employed in this elite community of 'flannelled faddists', for whom spacious detached houses were built in tree-lined streets that converged on the railway station, inn, stores and church.[38]

In the 20th century there were, to begin with, fewer new rural settlements. There are examples of planned company developments, such as Crittall's Silver End village in Essex, the Bowater village at Kemsley in Kent, or the 1930's Czech Bata shoe company's village at East Tilbury, the cottages of which were built in the International Modern style. In 1914 the wealthy London draper Sir Ernest Debenham bought land and farms at Briantspuddle in Dorset to create a model

Fig. 4.20 Imber, Wiltshire. A 20th-century deserted settlement on Salisbury Plain. The church and derelict manor house (top) still stand and medieval earthworks surround the churchyard. The village has been used for military training since the Second World War, hence the breeze-block buildings shown. The Ordnance Survey map refers to this as a 'Danger area'.

estate. Farm buildings and cottages were built in the Arts and Crafts style using brick, cob and thatch, there was a large war memorial by Eric Gill, and also a central milk factory and dairy. The venture was an attempt to demonstrate British self-sufficiency, and its activities included forestry, bee-keeping, chicken farming, the raising of pedigree stock and a veterinary service. Following Debenham's death in 1952 the estate was broken up and sold, but the neatly thatched cottages remain. In the 1960s New Ash Green in Kent was built to house people from a wide social spectrum, with some housing allocated to the Greater London Council. However, the original plan has been overtaken by the growth of modern standardised housing. Across the region the image of the 'village' has more recently been used as a marketing tool, and some new 'villages' that have sprung up are basically suburban dormitory residences, such as Bolnore, newly created on the outskirts of Haywards Heath as an 'instant rural idyll'. The Prince of Wales's Poundbury village outside Dorchester has attracted attention for its revivalist architectural style, and other early 21st-century developments include Elvetham Heath at Fleet in Hampshire and the Fishing Village at Chatham. The latter is part of the dockyard regeneration scheme and includes homes that are fully wired for teleworking.

Fig. 4.21 The 'Cocktail Belt': large detached houses and their gardens in south-east England, as mapped in the 1980s. There is a strong correlation between the distribution of these larger expensive houses and the western and south-western extent of London's Green Belt.

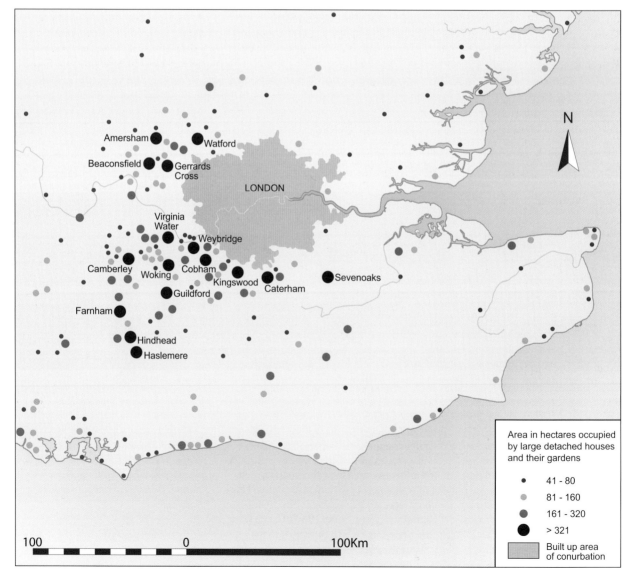

Post-war development has boosted counter-urbanisation within the region. The decline in London's population between 1951 and 2001, like that of many large cities, resulted partly from a search for environmental quality, rural living and opportunities for homeworking by the professional and service classes. Rural areas have grown significantly in population wherever planning restrictions have allowed, with the result that village landscapes now include private estates composed of detached, four-bedroom, double-garage residences for householders whose lifestyles frequently do not contribute to village life. In those villages where development is prohibited, either because they are historically 'close' and controlled by a powerful landowner or as a result of modern conservation planning, house prices have risen steeply. Although the exteriors of cottages may look unchanged, the interiors are fully equipped with modern furnishings – often with a 'rural idyllicism' theme – but with online facilities for shopping or work. This is the region's 'Cocktail Belt' (Fig. 4.21).

The development of the planning system advanced the protective concept of the Green Belt much further in the last 50 years of the 20th century. The New Forest National Park, the Areas of Outstanding Natural Beauty (one of which, the South Downs, was in the process of being designated as a National Park as this book was being written), Heritage Coasts, World Heritage Sites, Conservation Areas, Sites of Special Scientific Interest, and lesser designations now offer a hierarchy of protection to the remaining countryside of the South East (Fig. 4.22).

Fig. 4.22 The protected countryside of south-east England. Areas of Outstanding Natural Beauty (AONBs) cover about 30 per cent of the South East; the areas of Heritage Coast are also shown, the first in England to be so defined being Beachy Head. The large amount of countryside designated as having the necessary qualities to qualify for protection does, however, limit the land available for further development and pushes land and house prices upwards. The New Forest was operational as a National Park from 2005.

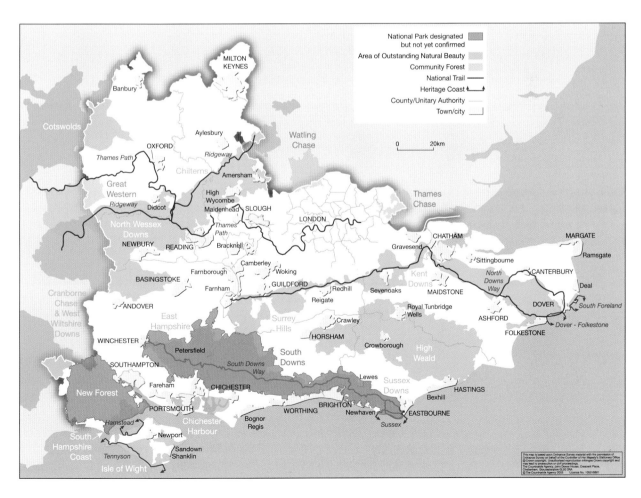

From the mid-Victorian period the quality of the region's landscape became a public issue with the huge environmental impact of modern technology harnessed to an expansionist society. In a wider democratic society, issues that had previously concerned elite landowners in their own domains now became a matter for public discourse as middle-class opinion moved towards the preservation, and latterly conservation, of both urban and rural landscapes. Over a period of about 150 years this reaction to a variety of threats has become intertwined with politics, with social and cultural changes and attitudes to living in town and country. One of the great future challenges for planners will be to reconcile the historic landscape in all its deep complexity with the demands for further development in this booming regional environment.

NOTES

1. Woodcock 1999, 11, 143 fn 3; Scott 2004, 7.
2. Roberts & Parfitt 1999.
3. Drewett *et al*. 1988, 4–5.
4. Vera 2000.
5. Drewett *et al*. 1988, 14.
6. Sidell *et al*. 2002, 16–23.
7. Drewett 2003, 40; Oswald *et al*. 2001; Cunliffe 1993, 56.
8. Tilly 1994; McOmish *et al*. 2002, 21–33.
9. Needham *et al*. 2000.
10. Parker-Pearson & Ramilisoniona 1998.
11. Drewett *et al*. 1988, 117.
12. McOmish *et al*. 2002, 73.
13. Cunliffe 1974; 1978.
14. Drewett & Hamilton 2001.
15. http://www.rdg.ac.uk/AcaDepts/la/silchester/publish/2003/roundup.php/.
16. Manley 2002.
17. Taylor 1983, 83–5; Millett 1990, 181–6; Cunliffe 1993, 248; Hingley 1989, 191; McOmish *et al*. 2002, 87–98.
18. Dark & Dark 1997, 11.
19. Millett 1990, 137–42.
20. Hill 1988, 208–12.
21. Rippon 2000, 53.
22. Gardiner 2003, 153.
23. Taylor 1983, 41; Hamerow 1993; 2002, 121–4.
24. Hamerow 1991.
25. Hooke 1989, 16–19.
26. Rackham 1976, 17; Roberts & Wrathmell 2002, 54–6.
27. Blair 1991, 94.
28. Hoskins 1955.
29. Beresford 1967, 14–28; Martin 2003, 179–90.
30. Blair 1991, 133.
31. Blair 1991, 58–65.
32. Blair 1991, 31–49; Everitt 1986, 141–80; Taylor 1983, 195.
33. Slade 1969, 7.
34. Brandon & Short 1990, 196.
35. Everitt 1977, 4.
36. Defoe 1971 edn, 156.
37. Brandon & Short 1990, 194; Eddison 2000, 88–101.
38. Darley 1978, 47–121

5

Changing Ways of Life and the Landscape

The changing settlement patterns of the South East were considered in Chapter 4, and yet a full appreciation of the region's evolving landscape also requires due regard for the many ways in which men and women throughout history have changed their surroundings in their pursuit of the necessities of life: seeking shelter and warmth, finding or cultivating food, making tools and machines. In this chapter we focus upon the development of agricultural landscapes and upon rural industry. At the beginning we measure landscape impact over thousands of years, not only because we infer a slow rate of change, but also because of a lack of evidence. In later centuries, thanks to the wider range of sources, we can more accurately register change to within decades.

THE LANDSCAPES OF PREHISTORIC FARMING

We must assume at present that Mesolithic peoples in south-east England first became familiar with farming techniques during the 4th millennium BC. People nevertheless continued to collect shellfish and wild plants, and to fish and hunt – and such activities remained as important as farming during the Neolithic period. The bones of auroch, wild pig, and red and roe deer together with the remains of hazelnuts, crab apples and sloes on many sites around Avebury demonstrate the enduring importance of wild food as well as domesticated produce. Now, however, this was accompanied by the intensified clearance of woodland, the sustained grazing of domesticated cattle, pigs and sheep and, at a later stage, based on evidence from such places as Windmill Hill, the cultivation of emmer and spelt wheat and six-rowed barley. Meat and animal products made up a substantial part of the diet, and evidence for sheep and cereals has also been found under the South Street and Horslip long barrows in the Avebury area. In Sussex such complexes of activity were in place by the mid to late 3rd millennium BC, with plenty of downland evidence being provided at sites such as Whitehawk, The Trundle, Offham and Bishopstone. We can therefore imagine that much of the region had similarly adopted agriculture by 2500 BC.

Few parts of the South East remained untouched by this most fundamental of agricultural revolutions, although some areas, such as Epping Forest, have had an almost continuous cover of woodland since about 2000 BC. Into this regional woodland cover we must imagine the introduction of laborious tree-felling and burning to give temporary clearances for a shifting form of cultivation. Some degree of permanency is also possible, however, and the Neolithic pits discovered at various locations reinforce a picture of increasingly sedentary communities involved with food production and crafts. Evidence for the breaking up of the soil, serrated harvesting tools, animal husbandry, pottery, leather-making and

TOP: *Fig. 5.1 Ancient (Iron Age) fields in Wessex.* These fields on Thornham Down (centre) and Charlton Down (top left) are separated by lynchets which can reach up to 6m in height. The dry chalk valleys are west-bank dry tributaries of the River Avon.

BOTTTOM: *Fig. 5.2 Butser Ancient Farm, Hampshire.* Founded in 1972, the farm moved from 'Little Butser' to Bascomb Copse (shown here) in 1991. There are four roundhouses within the enclosure. The largest ('The Great Roundhouse') is based on Dr Sonia Hawkes' records from Longbridge Deverill, Cowdown, Wiltshire. The roofless structure is based on an excavation from Dyfed, and the two smaller structures on construction designs from Glastonbury Lake Village.

wood-working, all point to more stable communities. Storage pits have been found in a cluster near Sittingbourne in Kent and singly at other sites in east Kent. Evidence for cross-ploughing with a simple ard comes from beneath South Street long barrow and the henge monument at Avebury, but there is little evidence so far for field sizes, nor might there have been much need for permanent boundaries, given the relatively small population. There is evidence, however, that there was some reversion to scrub or light woodland as soils became exhausted in later Neolithic times; as a result many cleared areas would have reverted to pasture to accommodate growing numbers of livestock.

Evidence for early agricultural landscapes multiplies greatly from about 2000 BC, and by the Early Bronze Age, permanent farming settlements and distinct fields can be seen. Large-scale archaeological investigations on the site of the new Terminal 5 at Heathrow during 2002–3 uncovered field boundaries and a permanent settlement of Early Bronze Age date on the brickearth of the Thames valley terrace. At Ebbsfleet in Kent an open farming settlement had access to water and good agricultural land. At Belle Tout in Sussex the remnants of an enclosed settlement containing hut structures and pits have been dated by pottery analysis to around 2000–1800 BC; there is also evidence that emmer wheat and six-rowed barley were being grown in nearby lyncheted fields.

On Salisbury Plain the most widespread remains are the so-called 'Celtic fields' that were first recognised by O G S Crawford and E C Curwen in the early 20th century. They are often arranged in chequerboard or 'co-axial' formations aligned NE–SW and are generally between 0.2 and 0.6ha in area; their regularity implies large-scale planning independent of topography and they are currently believed to date from the Middle Bronze Age, about 1500–1000 BC (Fig. 5.1). Recently it has been argued that large-scale co-axial systems can also be detected in south-east Essex; on the Chilterns dip slope, where they are associated with Early Iron Age pottery; and in the Lea Valley, south of Hertford. Excellent examples survive on the Wessex chalk at such locations as Chaldon Herring in Dorset, Fyfield and Overton Downs in Wiltshire, or in a fragmentary form on Woolbury Down in Hampshire and in the Isle of Wight. Similar features have also been found during the Heathrow excavations – large linear blocks of land divided by banks and ditches that extend all over the 25 square kilometres of Hounslow Heath. Interestingly this landscape division respected the line of the Neolithic Stanwell cursus and some settlements were established on top of earlier 'ring-ditches', suggesting both continuity of site and a continuing respect for the cursus.

It has been suggested that this intense Middle Bronze Age activity constituted a large-scale planning and reorganisation of the landscape: indeed, the first great revolution in the English landscape.[1] If so, the implications for our understanding of contemporary social power and relationships are fascinating, since it would have been a huge undertaking to co-ordinate such large-scale landscape change. The boundaries are of earth, stone (eg sarsens on Fyfield Down), flint from continuous field-clearance, ditches or even unploughed baulks. Constant ploughing, effecting downslope soil movement, also created positive lynchets (from the Saxon *hlinc*, meaning 'ridge'), which might in time bury the original boundaries; in turn, negative lynchets formed where soil had been removed by repeated ploughing further upslope. The resulting stair-like sequences of terraces endure on many Wessex hillslopes, such as Charlton Down on Salisbury Plain where they reach a height of 6m.

Such field systems were long-lived, possibly from the early 2nd millennium BC to the 5th century AD or even later. It is impossible to be sure of the full extent of fields that were worked contemporaneously, and we are presumably dealing only with the arable component of any overall farming system. There are nevertheless large areas of fields near Leatherhead and Coulsdon in Surrey; those on Fyfield Down in Wiltshire cover 113ha and are clearly demarcated, and the system on Nutwood Down in Berkshire covers 425ha.[2] Field systems are sometimes bordered by

lynchets as on Salisbury Plain, but also by trackways, ditches, barrows, woodland or natural topographical features. The associated pastoral landscape is less discernible, and may be represented by the remnants of long linear ditches or 'ranch boundaries' that survive on the southern parts of Salisbury Plain or in the Ram's Hill area of the Berkshire Downs. Equally these may have been territorial demarcations, constructed as a response to increasing population pressure. The overall picture is nevertheless clear: the prehistoric period saw the hard-won clearance of much of the region for arable farming alongside the creation of grassland in and around woodlands for pigs, goats, sheep and cattle – with the result that many of the region's more-favoured soils have remained excellent farmland ever since. One valuable insight into the Iron Age farmscape is provided by the experimental work undertaken by the late Peter Reynolds at the Butser Ancient Farm in Hampshire. This replica of a farm as it would have existed around 300 BC, complete with its buildings, structures, animals and crops (such as spelt, emmer, woad and einkorn), is essentially a large open-air laboratory for learning more about life in later prehistory (Fig. 5.2).

By the time of the Roman invasion, these areas of mixed farming were producing surpluses of cereals and cattle for export. The Romano-British villas were invariably centres of farming (and in some cases industrial) estates, and examples in the Darent valley in Kent have provided evidence for substantial barns for the storage of produce. We must nevertheless assume that the native farming landscape elsewhere mostly continued to use the field patterns described above: 'Celtic' fields separated by linear ranch-boundaries and worked by wooden ards with iron share-tips, a technique that continued for most of the first 500 years of the first millennium AD. On Fyfield Down in Wiltshire, 'Celtic' fields were certainly in use in the Roman period, and were being drystone-walled. We have already noted that at Chalton in Hampshire the late Iron Age system continued through to the 4th century AD, and similar continuity has been demonstrated at Bullock Down and Bishopstone in Sussex. In some areas Romano-British pottery is found within such fields, as at Harlington in Bedfordshire. There is also evidence for the replanning of field systems on the chalklands – as at Chisenbury Warren in Wiltshire, where the reorganisation took place in the 1st and 2nd centuries AD – and the extension of fields into new areas of the Wessex downs. There have been tentative suggestions that fields in some parts of the South East may have been subject to Roman 'centuriation', as in the case of a system at Ripe in Sussex that appears to have been laid out on a surveyed grid. As yet, however, there is no conclusive evidence that the method of measured land division that was commonly used in the southern Roman Empire was ever adopted in Britain. The Ripe example may therefore instead represent re-use of a Bronze Age layout, further emphasised by north–south drove roads of later Saxon date.[3]

The cultivation of spelt wheat and barley continued during the Roman period, but with increasing use of bread wheat, rye and oats. Some forms of crop rotation, marling and manuring would almost certainly have increased the productivity of the fields at this time. Later in the Roman period ploughs became heavier and were fitted with a coulter that facilitated the breaking-up of soil; asymmetric shares from possible mouldboard ploughs have been identified from villas at Folkestone in Kent and Brading on the Isle of Wight, although it is unlikely that heavier ploughs of this kind persisted for long after the Roman collapse.

SAXON AND MEDIEVAL FARMING LANDSCAPES

With the arrival of Saxon farmers we might expect significant changes in the agrarian landscape. Each part of the South East witnessed an *adventus saxonum* manifested in specific ways. For example, because there was no longer a requirement to produce food for the Roman taxation system, some of the more marginal land in the South East went out of cultivation, perhaps locally reverting to scrub or woodland – as appears to have been the case at Amberley in Sussex and Snelsmore on the Berkshire Downs – but there is no evidence that this happened on a large scale. On the chalklands it is probable that land reverted to pasture rather than continuing to produce the grain, and we may assume that the collapse of the villa economy resulted in its constituent farms and fields reverting, at least initially, to a more localised form of subsistence farming. Pollen evidence, scarce as it is in the South East, certainly suggests continuity, albeit at a lower level of productivity.[4]

Though locally variable in its character, this sub-Roman farming landscape may have continued for another two centuries. From the 7th century onwards, however, there were enormous landscape changes that ultimately swept away most remaining functioning 'Celtic' fields. The re-planning of Saxon settlement was discussed in Chapter 4, and here we examine the related issue of the re-planning of the fields that surrounded those settlements. Between the 'long 8th century' (*c.* AD 680–830) – in western Europe perhaps the first fully post-Roman century – and the 12th century another great landscape revolution took place. Over much of England this was to create the 'traditional' open or common field systems that many regard as typical of the medieval agricultural landscape.

Across much of southern England in the later Saxon period the increasing dominance of individual manors at the expense of the disintegration of the old multiple estates (*see* Chapter 4), meant that the production of specialised resources from the component areas of the estates ceased. As a result, the outlying *denns*, or large areas of pasture, might not now be available. One likely outcome was the local reorganisation of the system to ensure that it continued to allow communal food production. This implies co-operation within the vill or a degree of local manorial (including ecclesiastical) control, intensification in the use of existing fields and livestock, and the concentration of populations into more nucleated arrangements around new churches as outlying hamlets were abandoned. Within the community the land would initially have been in compact blocks, but these were progressively subdivided to more than one heir, a practice known as partible inheritance. The extent to which the fields were planned to an integrated blueprint is not known, but they might have been allocated equally or according to the proportion of tenure within the nucleated settlement. The fields would then be reorganised communally in strips, to facilitate ploughing with an oxen team. Large open fields were subdivided, and communal decisions on such matters as internal boundaries, grazing on the stubbles, fallowing and manuring were dealt with through a manorial court. The latter was a late addition to the community and came into effect from about the early 13th century.

We must assume that cultivation using two oxen and a wooden ard continued throughout most of the Saxon period, but the lack of real evidence for Saxon ploughs before the 10th century is tantalising. Aelfric's *Colloquy* written in about AD 1000 at the monastic school at Cerne Abbas in Dorset, refers to a conversation piece between a master and a role-playing pupil acting the part of a ploughman. By this time the plough's share and coulter are both mentioned:

> PLOUGHMAN: *Oh I work very hard, dear lord. I go out at daybreak driving the oxen to the field, and yoke them to the plough: for fear of my lord, there is no winter so severe that I dare hide at home; but the oxen having been yoked and the share and coulter fastened to the plough, I must plough a full acre or more every day.*
> MASTER: *Have you any companions?*
> PLOUGHMAN: *I have a lad driving the oxen with a goad, who is now also hoarse because of the cold and shouting.*
> MASTER: *What else do you do in the day?*
> PLOUGHMAN: *I do more than that, certainly. I have to fill the oxen's bins with hay, and water them, and carry their muck outside.*

MASTER: Oh, oh! It's hard work.
PLOUGHMAN: It's hard work, sir, because I am not free.[5]

It is not until the 10th and 11th centuries that we begin to see the more familiar medieval plough. This heavier one-way plough probably favoured larger open fields, although they were not necessarily originally farmed communally. By this time bread wheat, some rye (especially on sandier soils), barley (for fodder or brewing by the later Saxon period) and oats, supplemented by beans and peas, would have been common field crops, varying with soil type and demand. Apart from arable crops, diets were supplemented seasonally where possible by fish (eels were especially prominent), game (fallow deer and pheasant were Roman introductions), honey, berries, herbs and fruit. Luxuries such as wild boar, stag and wine would have been confined to the tables of the elite, including the monasteries.

The full panoply of the nucleated village, surrounded by intermixed strips in open and common fields and controlled through a manorial court, therefore did not reach its full extent until the 12th or 13th centuries, and then mainly in midland England. Over much of the South East this peak of development was never reached, and dispersed settlement and land held separately by farmers in many localities must often have remained the dominant pattern. Where they did exist, the common fields might cover only the better soils within a community, as in the pre-Norman Wylye valley, where the higher chalk was abandoned and still bears evidence of relict Romano-British fields. Medieval ridge-and-furrow, the distinctive corduroy pattern that results from strip cultivation, has been plotted elsewhere on the Wessex downland, however, where it is dated to the 13th and 14th centuries, and on the Upper Chalk landscape of Overton Down in Wiltshire it overlies Romano-British criss-cross ard marks.[6] On hillsides around the edge of the Wessex chalk, the cultivation strips can also reveal themselves as strip lynchets that follow the contours and are sometimes inserted into older 'Celtic' fields, as along the edge of the Avon and Wylye valleys. It is unlikely that many strip lynchets in the South East were deliberately built in response to land shortage. The terraces are instead more likely to have resulted from the continuing processes of lynchet formation described above (Fig. 5.3).

Although such farming systems were a prominent medieval feature throughout much of lowland England, by later medieval times much of Kent, Surrey and Essex had developed very different agrarian customs from those of the Midlands. The north Kent coastal plain was the richest area of south-east England according to the 1334 Lay Subsidy Rolls, but here there were no agreed rotations for the large fields, no systematic distribution of holdings between two or three open fields as the basis for cropping, and no annual allocation of a field for fallow. Agreements on the latter were less necessary in the region's plentiful wood-pasture areas. If there ever had been greater similarity with the Midlands, it had become far less obvious by this time. Instead, small freeholders were able to consolidate and develop holdings in severalty, moving early towards a landscape of agrarian capitalism. The ability to change depended on the availability of land, the opportunity to lease demesne land, and a reduction in surplus labour – the last consequent upon the Black Death. The effects of the plague on the region's population were felt differently from manor to manor: on the Bishop of Winchester's manors in Wessex and elsewhere, and in the hundred of Farnham and at Brightwell in Berkshire, about 30 per cent of the population had died; but at Downton in Wiltshire it was double this figure.[7]

Thus within the South East there was no single medieval farming system. One possible generalisation is that as the common land or woodland that was available to a community decreased, the more integrated and controlled that community might become. In part, the region superficially resembled the Midlands, with its open fields subdivided into strips, and H L Gray in 1915 was therefore able to incorporate the lighter soils of Wiltshire, Dorset and Hampshire, the Isle of Wight, the South Downs

Fig. 5.3 Strip lynchets at Worth Matravers, Dorset. The lynchets, a scheduled ancient monument, form 'staircases' on both sides of the steep valley leading from the village (top right) to the sea.

and Chilterns into his two or three-field 'Midland' farming system. But the open fields here were smaller than in the Midlands and only a few cultivators might share a field. To add complexity, in Wessex there was frequently more than one system in operation within a single parish, but in the Chilterns each farm typically was composed of arable land held both in common and severalty. The turning out of livestock onto common grazings – sometimes stinted at times of scarcity – and onto the stubble and arable fallow was vital, and manorial courts would often also ensure ongoing rights of access by a common sheep flock on to enclosed lands.

Gray excluded from the 'Midland system' all of Kent, northern Sussex and southern Surrey, the lower Thames valley and Essex. The latter area was classic wood-pasture countryside.[8] The area of London Clay and Bagshot and glacial sands stretching over southern Essex, south Hertfordshire and north Middlesex was a region of hedged crofts, heaths, private woods and parks, and open forest; any small areas of common field were enclosed by 1600. Most closes were assarted directly from wastes in the early medieval period, offering a quite different landscape from that of the open field areas on the downland (Figs 5.4 and 5.5). The closes might reach between 5 and 10ha, larger than in other wood-pasture areas such as the Weald or Chilterns.

Other areas, such as Romney Marsh, were quite different again: having had about 4,000 ha 'inned' during the late 12th and 13th centuries only for reclamation to become necessary again following medieval flooding. The later period produced larger fields for grazing, especially after the high mortality of

Figs 5.4 and 5.5 'Created' and 'evolved' landscapes of south-east England. *Fig. 5.4 (right) shows a regular enclosed field pattern 'created' on former open fields and downland at Figheldean in the Avon valley, Wiltshire, in the 19th century. Fig. 5.5 (below right), by contrast, shows 'evolved' medieval fields near Best Beech Hill, Wadhurst, in the East Sussex High Weald, with irregular morphologies, large shaws and woodland remnants.*

the 14th–16th centuries, when wealthier graziers began to take up leases from Canterbury Cathedral Priory and to engross land for wool production for wealden clothiers.[9] Different again were the marshland and saltings of southern Essex that presented a mixed landscape of common and severalty fields between London and Thurrock; here large sheep flocks and extensive cornfields were maintained on the flat lands that had been drained. Corn was sold to London from Dengie (dispatched by sea because the roads were so poor), but more generally the growing 16th-century demand for tallow, meat and wool encouraged pastoral specialisation on these Essex marshes and clays.

To continue this theme of landscape differentiation, we should also notice that by the mid-14th century the county of Sussex was divided almost in half by an east–west line that separated severalty farming in the Weald from open-field farming to the south. On the fertile Coastal Plain there were manors that at this time possessed two, three or four large fields cropped on a fixed cyclic basis. At the foot of the chalk escarpment the fields were smaller but might contain more than one crop: at Alciston there were in 1433 three common fields (West, Middle and East leyne) and 32 furlongs containing more than 400 parcels belonging to 21 tenants. The demesne land of the manor, however, was in severalty, and also included 'outfields' on heavier land to the north that were cropped intermittently. The basis for cropping was the furlong, the bundle of strips, not the field. The division into a northern and southern Sussex was not altogether a neat one but rather one of emphasis. Not all land to the south was in open fields, but the severalty closes increased in number to the north. In Surrey the position was reversed, since only in northern, extra-wealden Surrey were open fields to be found. But here too, they were small and interspersed with closes, as in the assarted lands of the Bagshot sands that surrounded common fields such as those at Chertsey Abbey. Small hedged closes grew up here on the former sheepwalks of Windsor Forest, and within the forest boundaries Chobham, Frimley, Horsell, Pirbright, Pyrford and Worplesdon were all filling up. By the 13th century much demesne land here also was already held in blocks rather than in intermixed strips. Here too the essential unit of husbandry was the subdivided furlong, within which cultivation was organised quite flexibly, rather than the 'field', although the enclosed demesne holders were free to choose their own rotations. Again, the fully integrated regulation of cropping, fallowing and grazing seems never to have become established.[10]

Again we should note that such developments did not affect all areas to the same degree. Some earlier landscapes persisted through into medieval or later use, and so were not swept up in a general re-planning of the countryside. In south-east Essex, for example, within a short distance of Rochford three distinct landscapes have been observed (Fig. 5.6): a rectilinear field pattern dated to the Romano-British period and still surviving into the present; an area of 'radial landscapes' around Shoebury that shows 5th to 11th-century Saxon planning; and an area of post-Roman woodland clearance that has resulted in an irregular assarted landscape. The incidence of three types of countryside within so little space warns us not to make easy generalisations about continuity or change in the landscape.[11] Nevertheless, for much of Kent, Everitt's assertion of a continuity, a 'landscape of evolution', holds true:

> Seen in the light of that age-long process, in places extending over a thousand years, and involving a more exhausting process of clearance than is sometimes envisaged, the belief in a countryside more or less fully exploited by the seventh century is not everywhere easy to accept; and certainly the Kentish evidence does not support it.[12]

In some parts of Kent, as on the eastern downland, surveys, rentals and 17th-century maps testify to the presence of open fields, but although farms and fields were here partitioned under the gavelkind custom of inheritance, the partitions

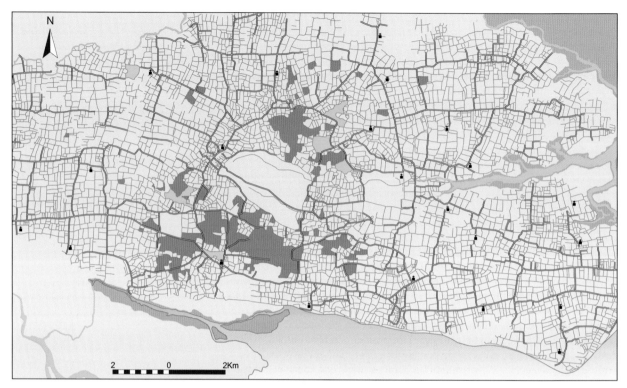

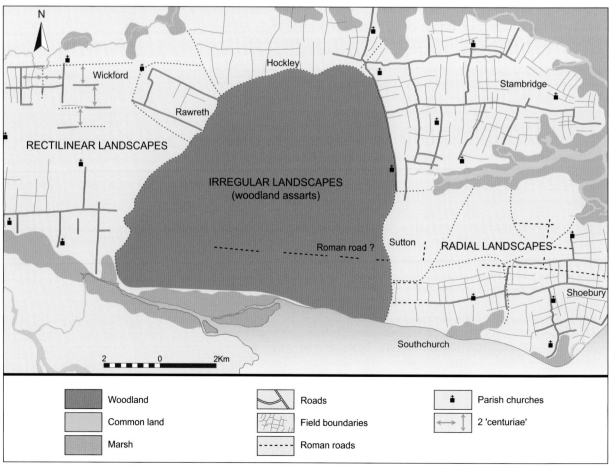

were cancelled out by the freedom to exchange and amalgamate land *inter vivos* (among the living). Except in a technical sense manorial power did not survive here after the 16th century and it was more typical for the land to be held by the freeholder in severalty. Fields might be open, but they were not held in common, nor is there any evidence of parliamentary enclosure of these open fields in the period after 1700 – once again, the extreme regional diversity of the South East must always be remembered (*see* Chapter 3).

Some intrinsically poorer terrains were (and long remained) appurtenent to more powerful distant estates or to manors beyond their boundaries, their roles being the supply of wood and the provision of oak, beech, hornbeam and chestnut *denns*. Transhumance routes in the Weald radiate outwards, cutting across the grain of the geology as sunken drove roads. The wood-pasture areas of the Weald comprised England's largest concentration of woodland and about 70 per cent of the area was probably covered by trees at the time of Domesday. These areas were not subject to re-planning, and although the holdings and earlier *denns* might be subdivided as population pressures built up, wide shaws still separated the small fields. Such ancient landscapes retained an aura of slowly-evolving woodland colonisation, rather than showing the results of the wholesale reorganisations seen within largely planned farmlands (*see* below).

Pastoral areas within the region supported large flocks of sheep from the mid-Saxon period onwards and their products became internationally renowned in the medieval period. Sheep were kept primarily for their wool and meat, but also as dunging animals. Permanent sheep enclosures were erected in Wessex downland areas, sometimes with shelters for animals and shepherds, and their positioning at the edges of common fields demonstrates the importance of the sheep for their folding qualities. Indeed, a sheep–corn husbandry was nearly universal throughout the chalk downlands. The village flocks of some Wessex townships could number more than 1,000 head, and in Hampshire even some individual farmers possessed similar numbers. In general, common fields survived longest in areas where the sheep flock provided the essential manure for light soils. In Aelfric's *Colloquy* the shepherd says:

> *In the early morning I drive my sheep to their pasture, and in the heat and in cold, stand over them with dogs, lest wolves devour them; and I lead them back to their folds and milk them twice a day, and move their folds; and in addition I make cheese and butter; and I am loyal to my lord.*[13]

The sheep's pride of place among livestock would have been shared with the oxen that were so vital for ploughing and haulage; and access to meadow, pasture and wood-pasture resources was essential for both cattle and pigs. Access to such resources was jealously guarded: within the community stinting might be introduced to limit the number of beasts that an individual might graze, while between communities arguments could arise over intercommoning rights on grazing lands. As arable expanded to feed the growing population in the South East, such pastoral resources were put under ever greater pressure. At West Overton in the Kennet valley, 10th-century charters refer to an area of rough pasture as *dune* or *scyfling dune*, but by 1311 this area had become Southfield, and part of the arable.[14]

One of the great medieval features that covered much of the South East was the hunting forest. Although there had been forests in Saxon times – certainly in Windsor and Savernake – royal hunting grounds were expanded following the introduction of Norman forest courts and Forest Law, in some cases taking over parts of pre-Conquest manors. For the New Forest, Domesday Book is revealing: about 30 or 40 small or moderate-sized villages were placed under Forest Law in the central part of the forest to make way for the deer. At the peak of forest coverage it was possible to ride from London or Windsor to the Hampshire coast almost

OPPOSITE PAGE:
Fig. 5.6 Landscapes of continuity and discontinuity in south-east Essex. *Rectilinear, irregular and radial landscapes are juxtaposed near to modern Rochford and Southend.*

115

Fig. 5.7 The park pale. *The north-western Ashdown Forest, Sussex, still shows traces of the distinctive bank-and-ditch boundary. This would originally have been topped with stakes or otherwise raised to retain deer. The ditch on the inward side of the boundary would make it even more difficult for deer to escape.*

continuously in royal forests. Within the region, these included forests at Windsor in Berkshire; Epping and Writtle in Essex; Bagshot, Alice Holt and Woolmer in Surrey; Pamber, Bere juxta Winton and Bere juxta Porchester, the large New Forest, Buckholt and Chute in Hampshire; and Savernake and Clarendon in Wiltshire. The forest (from *foris*, outside normal laws and subject to special laws of their own) might be wooded, or heathy 'waste', but was essentially a hunting ground or deer ranch. One calculation offers the view that about 20 per cent of forest area was wooded. Among the 'chases', with very similar landscapes and ecosystems to those of the forests but not belonging to the king, were Cranborne in Dorset and Enfield in Middlesex. Ashdown, the largest such area in Sussex, seems not to have been subject to Forest Law, but was ecologically indistinguishable from the forests. Other areas enclosed for hunting, but as 'inferior franchises', were the enclosed parks that were held by landed magnates or ecclesiastics. The Bishop of Winchester at one time had 23 such parks, and in Kent, Surrey and Sussex alone there were no fewer than 380 parks by the early 14th century.[15]

As well as an overall pattern of heathland, intermittent woodland, assarts and scattered settlement, these hunting landscapes have left minor features such as enclosing earth banks, or pales. These sometimes included deer-leap fences (over which stakes were originally placed) and hatches (gates) across the routeways

through the pale that marked the circumference of the forest; such pales were frequently marked on the county maps of the period (Fig. 5.7). Other landscape features included 'lawns' to provide grazing for deer; deer houses; keepers' cottages; and hunting stations – King John's in the New Forest was at Romsey while that of Henry VIII and Queen Elizabeth was at Chingford in Epping – or standings for the comfort of nobility, hence the name of King's Standing in Ashdown Forest.

But during the early medieval period such areas came under attack from land-hungry local populations, and permission might be given for assarting and cultivation in the forests, in return for a fine (rent); and such activities came to offer a distinctive landscape in which islands of cultivation or grassland were surrounded by heathland (Fig. 5.8). In Hampshire and the Isle of Wight, early medieval population and new assarts multiplied faster than anywhere else in the region, due to the attack on the woodlands.[16] In the New Forest wheat was grown with the help of manure from sheep folded on the poorer sandy soils.

Although many former hunting forests still retain ancient woodland today, including ancient coppice and pollards such as those in Windsor Forest or Epping, disafforestation and assarting had reduced the area under Forest Law by the 16th century, and much timber was destroyed. As early as 1288–9 monks on the Westminster Abbey estate at Pyrford on the edges of Windsor Forest were

Fig. 5.8 A medieval island of cultivation in the southern New Forest between Beaulieu and Lymington, at Norley Farm, mentioned in 1298 as Northlyghesdych.

felling a demesne wood and shipping cartloads of great oaks (*robura*) and young rafter-standards (*cheveron*) to Westminster; and in the early 1290s the roots were grubbed out and the area sown with oats. The landscape of elite pleasure was without doubt giving way to a working landscape managed for profit.[17] Waterdown Forest in Sussex was reclaimed by the Earls of Abergavenny from their Eridge estate in the 16th century, but much of western Essex – for example in Epping and Hainault – remained a landscape of woodland with hamlets, dispersed farms and small enclosed fields. In the pannage and pasture of these areas farmers could profit from pig-keeping and horse-breeding.

ENCLOSURE AND IMPROVEMENT 1500–1850

Although many parts of the South East, such as the Weald and Essex, were already enclosed by the medieval period, elsewhere there were early indications of the changes to come. In extra-wealden Surrey and Sussex in the 13th century and on the 14th-century Chilterns, some demesnes and peasant holdings were already being gathered into compact blocks to avoid problems connected with communal husbandry operations. The London market for their produce beckoned and a thriving land market entailed relatively easy consolidation through the interchange of land by exchange. Hedging and ditching around the newly consolidated land might then be provided in an attempt to defend against later fragmentation. In Surrey this typically produced a field of up to 4ha surrounded by a ditch or hedge, the consequence of which was 'a patchwork of fragmented severalties'.[18] The process frequently fossilised the ridge-and-furrow resulting from the ploughing of the strips, and where the fields have not been extensively ploughed since, the patterns are still visible and sometimes display a characteristic reversed-S aratral curve.

As a result of the reduction in population during the 14th century, the subsequent conversion of arable land to pasture and the growing demand for wool, a surge of enclosure and engrossment began to impinge on the landscape, and this continued into the 16th century. Along the Winterbourne valley, south of Dorchester, several deserted settlements were the result of an expansion in sheep numbers. A local commentator, Thomas Gerard, reported that at Winterbourne Faringdon stood 'a lone church, for there is hardlie any house left in the parish such of late hath been the Covetousness of some private Men that to increase their demesnes have depopulated whole parishes'. Winterbourne Ashton was 'nowe soe decayed that there is not one house remaining'. Wiltshire, by contrast, was largely a 'champion' countryside in 1600, but by 1700 it was at least two-thirds enclosed with the typical small-hedged enclosures of the period.[19]

Early 16th and 17th-century government Enclosure Commissions, concerned about the possible depopulating effects of enclosure, concentrated their attentions on the Midlands. By 1517–19, however, over 6,300 acres (2,550ha) of Berkshire had also been enclosed, involving the displacement of more than 600 people from 86 villages. The trend was now towards larger units on the chalk, but with consequent depopulation as economies of scale left fewer jobs for labourers. The process was not all-encompassing, however, and in Surrey common fields persisted long beyond the medieval period. In the Chilterns the slow process of exchanging strips had similarly started during the 13th and early 14th centuries; although the enclosing of this land was barely begun before 1500, by 1600 about 35 per cent was enclosed. Single strips or blocks of amalgamated strips were hedged-in, often while the remaining strips were left open. At Great Gaddesden in Hertfordshire, 16th-century exchanges of land are recorded and by 1600 most of the farmland was in severalty. Closes were made in the South Field at Little Gaddesden in the 16th century but the open field itself was not entirely eliminated until 1836. A lease of 1584 for Pishill in the Oxfordshire Chilterns refers to former common fields as 'closes'.[20]

The rural landscape also saw other agrarian changes. One important landscape development at this time was the 17th-century 'floating' of water meadows. Controlled spring flooding of lower-lying meadows, especially in areas of calcareous streams such as Wessex, has left a relict network of small irrigation ditches, often arranged in herringbone fashion (Fig. 5.9). Leats taken off the stream led water through the channels along the tops of artificial ridges; as it overflowed, the water ran into the ditches, which eventually returned it to the stream again. Sheep were grazed here during the day through to April and folded on the arable at night. Later the meadows were mown for hay. Silt deposits benefited fertility, and the water, raising the ground temperature, stimulated an early spring flush of grass for lambs. Encouraged by manorial lords, the technique was introduced on to Broadmoor at Puddletown in Dorset by 1630, into the valleys of the Wylye and Ebble by 1635, and along the Kennet and Avon by 1645, spreading thereafter to other Wessex chalk valleys. Sir Richard Weston described their use in Surrey in about 1638, and they had become common there by the 1670s. These were valuable meadows, and all the main Wessex valleys contained such features by the mid-18th century, when the technique was described as 'the sheet-anchor of Dorset husbandry'.[21]

In many eastern parts of the region such 'floating' was impractical. Soils were too heavy or too sandy, rainfall insufficient, gradients less steep and calcareous water less common. Instead, there were other changes, primarily connected with crop rotations. One hugely significant development was that of ley farming or alternate husbandry, whereby greater flexibility between arable and temporary grassland was achieved. This flexibility, already practised on many more advanced medieval estates, was now helped by the revolutionary introduction of higher-yielding clover, trefoil, sainfoin, lucerne and rye-grass. These had arrived from the Low Countries, in part due to the proselytising of Sir Richard Weston, from Sutton Court in Surrey, in his *Discours of husbandrie used in Brabant and Flanders, shewing wonderful improvement of land there* (1645). These new crops spread quickly to chalky soils, where their advantages in increased livestock productivity (and hence manure) were appreciated by farmers with capital to invest. Root crops also entered the rotations: turnips were grown in the fields after about 1650, and Daniel Defoe in 1724 referred to turnip cultivation being 'spread over most of the south and east

Fig. 5.9 Floated water meadows. The Britford Meadows in Wiltshire show the remains of hatches, channels, weirs and drains, to be found along almost every Wessex chalk stream. The majority of these landscapes were developed from the late 16th century onwards.

parts of England'.[22] The open fields around London continued to produce such crops until suburban expansion extinguished them in the 19th century, whereas in Wessex they were hardly grown at all since the water meadows continued to produce the necessary animal fodder. The wider adoption of clover and turnips in the 17th and 18th centuries helped the region to break out of a closed system in which output could be increased only by extending the area under cultivation, much as had been done for millennia. Now, fallows were replaced where possible (although not so much on the clays) by these new crops; these fixed atmospheric nitrogen in the soil and also boosted winter fodder supplies that in turn allowed increased livestock numbers and manure. Such intensification of farming was also accompanied by some limited spatial expansion. Saltmarsh drainage made halting progress around the coasts, but Canvey Island was drained and improved by Dutch settlers after 1660, and progress began again from the mid-18th century around the Essex coast. More arable crops could now be grown there, and although marshland was still in demand for the 'finishing' trade – the fattening of imported Welsh or Scottish bullocks for the London butchers – the once-famous ewe-milk cheese thereafter disappeared.

Greater specialisation was also important and was fuelled particularly by demand from London: as early as the 13th century the Thames and Lea were busy transport arteries for grain to London, with Ware, Henley-on-Thames and Faversham the leading transhipment points. By the early 16th century much of the clay-covered Chiltern dip slope in Hertfordshire was a grain and horse-producing landscape whereas many Middlesex villages were turning to the production of cattle and sheep, in both cases to exploit their proximity to London. By the end of the century fruit and vegetables were also being grown, sometimes in gardens and also in the common fields, around Fulham ('The Fulham parsnip'), Chelsea and Kensington, in the Lea valley at Edmonton and Stoke Newington, at Hackney ('the Hackney turnip') and in orchards in northern Kent and Surrey. By the early 17th century hops were also becoming better known, especially around Maidstone, Farnham and on parts of Salisbury Plain. During the 18th and 19th centuries the hop garden's characteristic landscape of poles and oast houses diffused from its mid-Kent heartland across the Weald into eastern Sussex, with the result that by the 1870s the Sussex High Weald accounted for 25 per cent of the entire British output.

Specialisation should not, however, be overemphasised. On the thinner upland soils of the South East, sheep–corn husbandry persisted over centuries, with only its emphasis changing from place to place or in tune with prevailing market trends. Defoe heard that 600,000 sheep fed on the chalkland around Dorchester, and no landscape depiction would therefore be complete without the evocation of such scenes.[23] Over the centuries selective breeding yielded sheep such as the Dorset, Wiltshire and Hampshire or the Berkshire Nott – breeds which were large and long-legged, hardy and able to range the hills all day, requiring little water and tending to drop manure at night when folded on the arable. Similar breeds ranged the South Downs, although here between 1780 and 1830 John Ellman bred the aboriginal sheep into a shorter-legged, heavy-wool animal that was more suited to the butcher and cloth-factory than the fold.

The first parliamentary enclosure act in England was for Radipole near Weymouth in 1604, although this only affected a small area of common; the first true enclosure may be that at Ropley in Hampshire in 1709. Private agreements between common-field farmers, as described above, were more normal before 1700 (accounting for about one-third of Dorset's common field enclosures, for example) and continued as an important part of the enclosure process in Wessex, Sussex and Hertfordshire throughout the 18th and 19th centuries. But by the 1720s, private acts of parliament were increasingly used to bypass any dissenting voices and to hasten the decay of the common field system. Enclosure commissioners thereafter proceeded to reorganise the landscape of the affected areas in ways that have prompted Christopher Taylor to term this process the third great landscape 'revolution' after the Bronze Age and late Saxon/early medieval 'revolutions' that he had previously identified.

This latest reorganisation affected the chalk uplands in particular. By 1700 there were exactly 100 open field systems surviving in southern Sussex, accounting for about 30 per cent of the county's parishes. Just under half of Dorset's parishes contained open fields, and of these 64 per cent were still in existence in 1800. Winterbourne Kingston, for example, remained as a 'classic' open-field system into the 19th century, and Fontmell Magna, on the edge of Cranborne Chase, although enclosed by 1774, still possessed remnants of open field in the 1840s. Wiltshire in many respects most closely resembled the Midland enclosure processes in that the 288 systems that were operating in the county in 1700 had been cut to 146 by 1800. The Hampshire/Wiltshire border was a heartland of parliamentary enclosure in the South East, whence it spread across the Wessex chalk and into the Sussex downland during the Napoleonic wars. About 30 per cent of the total area of Hampshire and Wiltshire was enclosed by parliamentary act after 1700. Nearer London, by 1750 there were still open fields remaining to be tackled from Egham and Chertsey in the west to the Hoo peninsula in the east. Wimbledon had been largely enclosed by 1640 but Battersea still presented a bewildering landscape of arable, pasture, market gardens, drained marshes and severalty nurseries. In 1706 the three fields of Wandsworth totalled about 400ha, but by the mid-18th century about 150ha had been taken into a new park.[24]

This time the enclosures were not a cause of depopulation, although scholars have long argued about their indirect effects on rural population and society; for example, smaller farmers and those receiving allotments of land in lieu of common rights often had to sell up to their larger neighbours. There are arguments, too, about the productivity of the new fields compared with what had been achieved by the capitalised farmers in the open fields of the 17th century. But the visual impact on the landscape is undeniable. Quickset hedges were laid out around surveyed and rectangular closes, which now replaced remnant open fields. Roads and tracks were re-planned and now intersected at right angles, often set out between ample grass verges. The proportions of open-field arable, and also common and waste, that were enclosed by Act of Parliament are set out in Table 5.1. Unfortunately most analysts have not separated the constituent parts of counties by their soil or geological subdivisions. Counties such as Bedfordshire, Oxfordshire and Buckinghamshire that impinge to lesser degrees on the South East as defined in this volume, are included, even though most of their enclosures affected their clay belt northern component beyond the chalk escarpment. In Buckinghamshire, for example, the average of 33.2 per cent in Table 5.1 conceals the fact that the chalk escarpment separates areas on the northern clay, where over 50 per cent of land was enclosed at this time, from the southern chalk, where it was 30 per cent or less. Similarly Wiltshire and Dorset overlap with the western clay vales, and Essex runs northward on to boulder clay beyond this volume's remit.

TABLE 5.1 PROPORTIONS OF COMMON-FIELD ARABLE AND OF COMMON AND WASTE ENCLOSED BY ACT OF PARLIAMENT (FROM TURNER 1980, 180–1).

County	Percentage open field arable	Percentage common and waste	Soil type/ location
Oxfordshire	51.4	3.2	Much on Midland clays
Bedfordshire	47.6	1.8	Much on Midland clays
Buckinghamshire	33.2	1.7	Much on Midland clays
Berkshire	32.1	2.0	Wholly within South East
Wiltshire	26.9	2.5	Much on West Country clays
Middlesex	20.6	7.4	Wholly within South East
Hertfordshire	12.3	3.2	Wholly within South East
Hampshire	8.8	8.0	Wholly within South East
Dorset	8.3	6.7	Some on West Country clays
Surrey	7.4	7.0	Wholly within South East
Sussex	2.3	2.1	Wholly within South East
Essex	2.2	2.0	Much on boulder clay
Kent	0.0	0.8	Wholly within South East

Many of the remaining open fields and commons were enclosed by the end of the Napoleonic wars, when high food prices or the conversion of land to building, as at Portsmouth or Brighton, justified the costs of enclosure. Some of the poor, thinner soils were now brought into cultivation again, and yields too were rising. This was certainly helped by increased marling and, where there was an acidic overlay, liming. On the heavier clays too, 19th-century corn yields were also rising. The main reason was the application of larger-scale under-drainage, using earthenware tiles or pipes. This enabled the landscape to dry out and to be ploughed when required, which in turn allowed good crops to be grown. The overlying clays of Hertfordshire and the Chilterns, much of the intractable London Clay and the wealden clays thereby became a part of arable England by the mid-19th century. The Ashburnham estate in the High Weald was providing tenants with drainage tiles from its own yards by 1830, but progress was possibly faster to the north of the Thames than the south.[25] Chalk, lime and marl were also applied, as testified by the many surviving chalk quarries eating into the face of the downland escarpments, ruined lime kilns and the small pits in wealden field corners from which marl had been extracted. From the Gravesend area large quantities of chalk were shipped off to the London Clay areas and Essex. This was certainly necessary, one Dengie farmer describing his sub-soil as 'stiff, tough, numb, dumb and impervious'. It required three horses to plough it, and could not be touched in wet weather.[26] The eradication of shaws had also begun, because the overgrown and wooded nature of these high and wide hedgerows was preventing ploughs from reaching all parts of fields. Clearly, even the region's 'ancient countryside' was changing at this time.

Whereas most effort was directed towards arable land, thus creating an easier environment for new rotations and root crops or converting it in the process to more profitable pasture, the environments associated with former hunting forests, chases and common 'wastes' had incurred the wrath of agricultural improvers from the 17th century onwards, St Leonards in Sussex being described as 'incorrigible at any expense'. Now that the older forest administration was virtually defunct such areas also began to receive attention, and the sandy heaths of Middlesex, Hampshire, Surrey and Dorset were all enclosed to some extent at this time. Sussex, Essex and Kent, by contrast, were hardly affected at all. As Sir John Sinclair, President of the Board of Agriculture, proclaimed in 1803: 'Let us not be satisfied with the liberation of Egypt, or the subjugation of Malta. Let us subdue Finchley Common; let us conquer Hounslow Heath, let us compel Epping Forest to submit to the yoke of improvement.'[27]

Attempts at economic return had often previously been limited to artificial rabbit warrens – elongated 'pillow-mounds' surrounded by perimeter banks and ditches that remain visible to this day. Further decay during the Civil War years did not help, but many landscapes were altered considerably as a response to calls for later improvement, for example the planting of conifers such as the Scots pine in the New Forest in the 1770s. From the end of the 18th century the remaining woodlands were disafforested, enclosed and 'improved'. In 1812 two-thirds of Alice Holt and Woolmer Forests became a nursery for timber, and between 1810 and 1855 most of the other southern forests were similarly disafforested, enclosed and divided between the crown, landowners and commoners in lieu of their common rights. Not everyone approved: William Cobbett wrote in 1830 of the firs planted in Woolmer Forest that he could see no reason to plant more and 'what he can plant the fir for, God only knows, seeing that the country is already over-stocked with that rubbish'.[28] In some cases entire farms might be carved from the poor heathland, as at the aptly named Coldharbour Farm at Berkhamsted Frith in the Chilterns; this was formed from part of the 450ha sheepwalk in the course of a 19th-century campaign of parliamentary enclosure that was primarily concerned with the fencing and allotting of common woods, heath and downland.

As a result of the enthusiasm for improvement, there are surviving reminders of the medieval forest in just two locations: the New Forest and Epping Forest. In the former, proposals for it to be developed as a source of timber came to nothing, and in 1871 plans to disafforest it were withdrawn because of strong opposition. Instead, a new sentiment was gaining ground, and in the New Forest Act 1877 commoners' rights were given prominence under the supervision of a reconvened Court of Verderers, together with due provision for safeguarding the scenic qualities of the Forest. In 1923 the Forestry Commission assumed control, becoming responsible for the management and sale of timber, recreational amenities and conservation. Epping Forest is the oak, beech and hornbeam remnant of the formerly great Essex Forest that also included Waltham and Hainault. The latter was disafforested in 1851 and most of the land was enclosed for farming in squared fields once steam ploughs had grubbed up the roots of the ancient trees. But in Epping Forest the commoners' rights were championed by the City of London, whose corporation held an estate at Little Ilford with attached common rights, and which wished to see Epping preserved as an open space for Londoners. During the 1870s various measures were taken to ensure free access, culminating in its disafforestation through the 1878 Epping Forest Act, which also ensured that the Forest would henceforth be conserved for popular enjoyment. At a ceremony in 1882 Queen Victoria officially threw it open to the public.

Although not strictly farming landscapes, many Tudor and Stuart parks in the South East were also being transformed at this time. Some were very large such as Blagdon in Dorset, which covered nearly 3,500ha, but convenient sites for hunting by courtiers frequently meant the creation of parks near London – Hyde Park and St James's Park were created by Henry VIII for this purpose. By 1600 there were at least 69 such parks in the Chilterns and they covered about 10 per cent of the entire area of the Weald. Hunting and, more prosaically, income from timber or later grazing or arable, rendered these parks socially as well as (marginally) economically successful, and they have left a significant impression on the landscape. Given the concentration of wealth around London, it should occasion no surprise that many of the best-known landscape parks were created here to the designs of Kent, Bridgeman, Brown and Repton, in the process sweeping away earlier parks and formal gardens such as Henry VIII's Hampton Court or Lord Pembroke's Wilton.[29]

At Petworth in Sussex, for example, there had been a park attached to the manor house since at least the 13th century and succeeding centuries saw the provision of large stands of timber, rabbit warrens, a fishpond, a garden and large quantities of deer, as well as additions to the area of the park. Between 1752 and 1765 'Capability' Brown laid out the southern end of the park; the result is now internationally recognised as one of the best examples of his designs for the English landscape park. Petworth is also home to the largest and oldest herd of fallow deer in England. Brown's greatest achievement was perhaps the serpentine lake (Fig. 5.10), which he engineered by damming a series of small ponds and which is still fed by a mile of 18th-century underground spring-fed brick culverts. The dam was created by filling the valley with about 47,000 tonnes of soil and a further 17,000 tonnes of retaining clay laid over the sandy sub-soil. It was one of the largest earthworks of its time in southern England.

Brown was associated with at least 50 of the parks in this region including such well-known examples as Ashburnham, Sheffield Park and Cowdray in Sussex, Highclere in Hampshire, Claremont in Surrey, Wilton Park in Wiltshire and Cliveden in Buckinghamshire – all of them Grade I English Heritage Parks. Others include Broadlands in Hampshire, Clandon Park and Addington Park (where Brown worked in the year before his death) in Surrey, as well Kew Gardens, which was inscribed as a World Heritage Site in 2003. At least another 12 parks are associated with William Kent, and more than 40 with Humphrey Repton. The latter

Fig. 5.10 Petworth Park, West Sussex.
A Capability Brown landscape with the lake,
tree clumps and knoll captured by J M W
Turner in The Lake, Petworth: Sunset,
Fighting Bucks, *c. 1829.*

worked on urban developments such as Russell Square and Kensington Gardens in London as well as on country estates such as Heathfield Park and Bayham Abbey in Sussex, or the nearby Sheffield Park and Brightling Park on which he collaborated with Brown (*see* Figs 8.17 and 8.18). His *Red Books*, demonstrating before-and-after views of landscapes, give an excellent appreciation of the degree to which he was attempting to transform landscapes, as at Wycombe Park in Buckinghamshire.[30]

These were symbolic landscapes, the contours of which were carefully shaped to allow the eye to perceive power and wealth. They were gentle in terms of their artfully planted trees, deer, and diverted streams, yet still they exuded control. William Cobbett, riding through Kent in 1823, noticed the contrary imagery: 'Paradice Place – Spring guns and steel traps set here'.[31]

THE FARMING LANDSCAPE FROM 1850 TO THE PRESENT

The ancient countrysides and planned landscapes of the region have undergone yet another transformation since 1850. Indeed, perhaps rather too much of the rural landscape has been transformed over the past 150 years. Agricultural booms and depressions have fluctuated across this well-documented period, and each swing of the economic pendulum has left its profound imprint on the landscape. It is impossible to examine all these varied effects in detail, but the landscape impacts are summarised in Table 5.2.

Above all, the region responded at this time to the huge influence of the urban markets within its boundaries, and especially to London. By 1850 railways ran into the capital from major towns such as Colchester, Hertford, Reading, Southampton, Brighton, Dover and Maidstone, which therefore acted as collection and dispatch centres for the agricultural produce of their hinterlands. Fresh milk could now be sent from Dorset to London overnight, memorably described by Thomas Hardy in *Tess of the Durbervilles*, when Tess and Angel Clare watching the churns being loaded:

> *Then there was the hissing of a train, which drew up almost silently upon*
> *the wet rails, and the milk was rapidly swung can by can into the truck…*
> *'Londoners will drink it at their breakfasts tomorrow, won't they?' she*
> *asked. 'Strange people that we have never seen.'* [32]

The London market, better transport and favourable soils all fostered specialisation within the region by the mid-19th century. Thus the rural landscape included such features as market gardens in north-west and north-east Kent around Sandwich; large areas of soft fruit and orchards in Kent, especially around Maidstone; and the characteristic hop gardens and oast houses of mid-Kent. Elsewhere sheep–corn husbandry still dominated the lighter uplands; sheep and cattle-fattening the Thames valley, Thames-side, Romney and Pevensey marshes; and dairying the fringes of London, especially in Middlesex, Hertfordshire and Berkshire. In the Weald the small farmers looked increasingly to the fattening ('cramming') and marketing by higglers of poultry from small, often roadside, operations centred on Heathfield in Sussex.

The period from about 1840 to the mid-1870s has been characterised as a 'Golden Age' for farming. Yields were high, thanks to the diffusion of newer scientific approaches (fostered by the Royal Agricultural Society (1838) and many local societies), inputs of new fertilisers, extended drainage of heavier soils and the increased mechanisation of ploughing and harvesting. Investment in farm buildings, cottages and maintenance paid off, and the landscape saw more arable crops than for many years as both downland and clays were put under wheat and barley wherever possible. However, all this 'high farming' changed during the 1870s and 1880s as prices fell, overseas competition increased and a run of poor seasons threatened crops. The 'Great Depression', lasting intermittently through to the First World War, impacted particularly hard on the region's more marginal soils. On the clays of south Essex, for example, many arable fields 'tumbled down' to 'coarse weedy pastures' as farmers looked to livestock production, and especially dairying, for an income. Many were unsuccessful, and bankrupt farms were often taken on by Scottish and West Country dairy and potato farmers, who were prepared to accept lower living standards in return for low rents and the crucial access to the London market. A brief wartime plough-up campaign in 1917–18 saw the return of some arable farming, but following the 'great betrayal' in which cereal farmers who had been guaranteed prices were reneged upon by the post-war government, the south-eastern countryside was again plunged into a depression that lasted through to 1939. Grassland, often poorly maintained, again dominated the landscape as farmers struggled to make a living, especially on the more difficult soils. When the first Land Use Survey was undertaken in the mid-1930s, arable farming was virtually non-existent in the Weald. The buildings erected in the era of high

TABLE 5.2 AGRARIAN LANDSCAPE FLUCTUATIONS IN SOUTH-EAST ENGLAND 1850 TO THE PRESENT.

Phase	Years	Landscape impact on light soils	Landscape impact on heavy soils
'Golden Age'	1840–73	Increased cereals; buildings	Increased cereals and dairying; buildings
Great Depression	1873–1914	Rough pasture and poor grassland increases	Increased dairying; scrub and poor pastures
Great War	1914–18	Plough-up for arable	Some plough-up
Inter-war depression	1919–39	Rough pasture and poor grassland increases; land sold for urban development	Rough pasture and poor grassland increases; land sold for urban development
Second World War	1939–45	Plough-up for arable	Plough-up for arable
Post-war productivism	1945–84	Wheat and barley; enlargement of fields, machinery and buildings	Increased cereals and milk output
Post-productivism	1984–present	Set-aside; Environmentally Sensitive Areas (ESAs); diversification; stewardship	Set-aside; ESAs; diversification; stewardship

farming still stood – there was no money to replace them – hedges grew unkempt and undistinguished secondary woodland expanded.

All this changed quickly as the South East was forced into high productivity during the food crisis of the Second World War. The landscape once again was dominated by cereal production wherever this was possible, helped by plough-up grants, imported American tractors and Women's Land Army volunteers. Government assistance and surveillance were provided through the County War Agricultural Executive Committees, which advised, monitored, chastised and in some cases evicted, the region's farmers. The landscape rapidly regained its productivity, and the grateful wartime government promised that never again would farming be neglected. One result of this was the ushering in, particularly through the 1947 Agriculture Act, of a period of 'productivism' during which government and European funding, large-scale borrowing and the intensification of commercialised production resulted in the enlargement of fields to accommodate the increased size of machinery or for improved stock control. Frequently a discontinuous line of older trees across the middle of a large field is all that now remains of a former boundary. The hedges of parliamentary enclosure and of ancient severalty fields alike were destroyed, bringing a greater uniformity to the farming landscape, but at the cost of increased soil erosion and a loss of biodiversity.

From the introduction of imported fertilisers in the 19th century to the present-day use of biochemicals, the intensification of farming has had a controversial impact on the landscape. Wetlands have been drained, but the use of modern fertilisers and pesticides has too often led to the eutrophication of water courses since excessive nutrients washed from the fields have generated algal blooms that deplete oxygen levels and also cause downstream pollution. Modern farmscapes, particularly on the lighter soils, superficially came to resemble those of the pre-enclosure period Midlands – large open fields were used to grow monocultural barley as the remaining ancient chalk downland was ploughed up. The prefabricated buildings associated with this new intensified agriculture were, however, more massive and standardised than those of earlier centuries. And within the past 50 years, another theme in this pressurised region has been the loss and fragmentation of farmland by the steady encroachment of urban land uses and communications (Fig. 5.11). Few areas have been immune, and suburban growth and ribbon development during the interwar depression expanded over much former agricultural land. However, the loss in the 1920s of grade 2 farmland on the South Downs to the new

Fig. 5.11 Landscape change. The route of the new M1 motorway before and after. Opened in 1959, this section ran through farmland south-west of St Albans, and the first stage of the London–Birmingham motorway was actually a St Albans bypass.

planned town of Peacehaven was particularly instructive to many who thereafter sought greater protection for rural scenery.

A post-productivist countryside was ushered in by the introduction in the mid-1980s of milk quotas and in the late 20th century by other European measures to reduce surplus production and increase the number of agri-environment schemes. This attempt to re-create sustainability has also affected landscapes. Within the South East, extensification and 'greening' policies are yielding some increases in biodiversity in grassy field margins, renovated meadows, an increase in broadleaved woodland and a lesser rate of hedgerow loss (indeed, more than 9,000km of hedgerow have been restored nationally). Restoration of downland grasses and heathland is also proceeding apace. At the beginning of the 21st century suspicion of intensive farming among the general public has reached new heights, and both government and the farming industry have reacted positively to efforts to reintroduce diversity to the countryside. In the summer of 2005 this was symbolised most clearly by the phasing-in of the 'Single Farm Payment', which began the process of de-coupling European subsidies from agricultural production.

RURAL INDUSTRIES AND THE LANDSCAPE

Although the South East does not have the highly visible industrial history of some other regions, no historical period has lacked industrial activity, and to some degree each has left a mark on the landscape. The processing of agricultural and woodland produce has left many landscape legacies, in the shape of mills, breweries and tanneries. In this section we shall concentrate primarily on rural industries, leaving urban activities until Chapter 6.

Even prehistoric industries have left their faint imprint: the considerable downland flint-mining activities of the Neolithic period have already been noted (Chapter 4). There is evidence for early bronze-working at Petter's Field and Runnymede Bridge in the Thames valley, but although several bronze hoards have been located in the region, there is as yet little other evidence for Bronze Age metalworking. The existence of Iron Age smithies is evidenced by metal swords, shields (such as that found at Chertsey in river gravels), buckets and other finds; many of them are again from the Thames valley and appear to indicate the copying of exotic objects by local craftsmen. The smithies themselves are rarely found, however, and may have been itinerant. At Garden Hill, the hillfort in the central Weald, the discovery of a smelting furnace indicates a specialised presence and the exploitation of the local iron ore. And as well as pottery and metalworking, including the production of coins in the later Iron Age, domestic crafts such as weaving and bone-, wood- and leather-working were ubiquitous.

Industrial remains from the Romano-British period are more visible. Water-mills were introduced from the Mediterranean world and are known from Silchester and Fullerton in Hampshire. Thereafter they disappear from view until the 9th century, when one is recorded for Old Windsor in Berkshire, and they become a common feature by the time of the Domesday Book. Pottery, ironworking, stone quarrying and salt-making were all locally important; of these ironworking was the most significant and perhaps represented the largest such operation in the Roman Empire. Julius Caesar mentions the production of iron from the South East in his *Gallic Wars V* and Strabo listed iron as an export. The Weald was already being exploited for its iron deposits and since every pound of finished metal needed about ten times that amount of charcoal, the environmental impact would have been significant. More than 60 iron-working bloomery sites have been dated to this period: one large site alone, Beauport Park, left behind 50,000 tonnes of slag. It is possible that the much of the Weald produced iron under the aegis of an Imperial Estate, and tiles stamped with the letters CLBR indicate links with the *Classis Britannica*, the Roman fleet that was based along the vulnerable channel coasts. One estimate suggests that between 600 and 4,000 people may have been involved directly or indirectly in the huge wealden operation.[33]

Building stone was widely available, though not of high quality. Flint and chalk are ubiquitous, but imported stone was used for important public buildings. Limestone from the environs of Bath was incorporated into the walls of Silchester, for example, but local material was also employed, such as greensand in fort walls at Pevensey or Richborough, or the hard white shelly Quarr Limestone from Bembridge on *Vectis* (Isle of Wight) in the walls of *Clausentum* (Southampton). A 2nd-century barge found near Blackfriars Bridge, was carrying a cargo of Kentish ragstone. *Tegulae* (tiles) were an important Roman introduction and were commonly used for roofing, hypocausts and sundry other purposes. Most tileries were short-lived and mobile, being located on accessible clays and near suitable transport, although the elaborate furnace system with flues made from finely decorated hollow bricks recently uncovered in Reigate may indicate a more settled 2nd- or 3rd-century industry. Pottery was also mass-produced at some sites following the introduction of the potter's wheel in the late Iron Age, although hand-made pots in many different styles continued in local use. The potteries produced mounds of waste as well as associated roads and buildings, all of which served to create industrialised landscapes in the New Forest, around Poole Harbour, in the Thames Estuary/north Kent area and at Alice Holt in Surrey. The smaller Roman town of Neatham marketed the substantial products of the Alice Holt/Farnham pottery industry across a wide area of the South East, thanks to a good location on the River Wey; at its peak it may even have had a population of several hundred people. Salt was also produced around the estuarine coast, with particular evidence of hearths and fragments of clay vessels found on the Thames and Medway marshes.[34]

Much of this industrial infrastructure seems to have come to an end by the early 5th century, and evidence for industrial landscapes remains fragmentary for several centuries thereafter. A smelting and smithing industry dating to the late 8th and early 9th centuries has been excavated at Ramsbury in Wiltshire, while at Little Totham in Essex, just to the north of the Blackwater estuary, there is earlier evidence for 7th-century furnace working within *grubenhaus* sunken-floored buildings.[35] There is little evidence for ironworking within the Saxon Weald, but a primitive 9th-century iron furnace and hearth from Ashdown Forest is the earliest example yet known and only one ('*una ferraria*') is mentioned in the Sussex Domesday, within East Grinstead hundred. Others are mentioned at Chertsey in Surrey and at Fyfield Bavant in Wiltshire, which might imply the existence of smithies. Coastal salt-making remained ubiquitous and is mentioned for Kent, Sussex and Hampshire in particular. At Lancing in the Adur valley, saltern mounds – the debris from salt-impregnated silt or sand – occur in groups along the valley, and Domeday Book refers to 58 such works here alone. Quarrying is also recorded in Domesday; Lower Greensand was worked at Limpsfield in Surrey and near Petworth, and was used, in the form of Kentish Rag, in Lydd church. Flint was also used in church building on or near the downland, while the Isle of Wight's Quarr stone was exported not only for the construction of parish churches such as Warnford in the Meon valley, but also the Tower of London and Winchester and Canterbury cathedrals. When better-quality materials were needed, however, they were imported from northern France.

By the medieval period rural extractive and manufacturing industries, such as pottery-making (in relatively crude and small-scale enterprises), leather-working, metalworking and shipbuilding, featured in many communities. London and Winchester were important cloth centres, although other locations are recorded after 1225 within the Weald and Kennet valley, as are water-powered fulling mills. London's cloth was being put out for fulling to rural areas by the mid-13th century. Stone was much in demand for the great rebuilding of the Norman period; Purbeck marble from Dorset became particularly fashionable in the 12th century and was used at cathedrals such as St Paul's and Chichester as well as in Westminster Abbey.

Iron manufacture in bloomeries now spread to many wealden landscapes. From the 1490s the more efficient blast furnace was in use, the first known site being at Newbridge on the edge of Ashdown Forest. Here a small headwater stream of the Medway was ponded back to provide continuous power for the furnace bellows and a forge that used local iron ore and charcoal. Production of the latter required steady supplies of cordwood and as a result coppicing became a widespread activity. Today this has left its own residual landscape throughout much of the Weald in the form of overgrown coppice woods. This area in due course became the industrial heartland for the manufacture of Tudor cannon, armaments and implements. All nine of the blast furnaces known to be operating in England in 1542 were in the Weald, and expansion of the industry occurred so dramatically that by 1574 there were at least 51 blast furnaces and 58 forges operating here. With a relatively high demand for ordnance during the mid-17th century, the industry was still employing more than 1,500 people by 1664, though this fell nearer to 1,000 by 1717. At Heathfield, where the industry operated most continuously, perhaps half the population was employed in some capacity during favourable periods. But by the 1660s uncertainties of water power in dry years, temporary shortages in charcoal supply, deteriorating roads and falling government contracts were beginning to spell the end. By 1653 at least 35 furnaces and 45 forges were still operating, but by 1788 just two furnaces were left, although the last furnace and forge persisted anachronistically at Ashburnham into the 19th century. With the arrival of 18th-century technical changes, decline was inevitable as the industry shifted nearer to sources of coal. Importantly for landscape history, no relationship has been traced between the iron industry and deforestation, since both furnace and forge were fed from carefully managed coppice woods that were expanded rather than ruthlessly exploited. If possible, encoppicing was undertaken within short distances of the ironworks, and at Ashburnham little change occurred after 1672 in the location of 40 to 50 areas of woodland – a stability aided by freedom from tithe payments and a low poor-rate assessment on woodland. The overgrown remains of the industry may still be found, in the form of elongated hammer ponds, bays, slag and waste, and substantial stone and half-timbered ironmasters' houses (Fig. 5.12).

By the 13th century large quantities of glass were produced around Chiddingfold in Surrey, and from the mid-15th century the centre of glass-making was at Wisborough Green, Kirdford, Chiddingfold and Hambledon. Sheds, furnaces and kilns used local timber supplies, and the industry was further developed from the 1560s with the arrival of French glass-making families skilled in making the newer window glass. The wealden industry effectively closed down from about 1620 as coal-fired competitors elsewhere took over, but pieces of the old locally made window glass can still be seen in Chiddingfold and Kirdford churches.

The region's extensive woodland cover spawned a myriad related by-employments. These were small-scale industries with minimal impact on the landscape, primarily operated from

Fig. 5.12 Ironmaster's house, Batemans, at Burwash, Sussex.

This 17th-century residence was later the home of Rudyard Kipling from 1902 until his death in 1936. This is now a popular National Trust property.

small workshops and yards. The wealden woodlands were closely linked with the fortunes of iron, and sales slumped as the demands for timber and charcoal lessened and as sea coal became more widely used. Furthermore, during the Civil War many woodlands, including the remnants of Ashdown and St Leonard's forests, had suffered from depredation and ineffectual management. Elm and oak were conveyed slowly along the miry roads to the Medway, and thence to the naval dockyards at Woolwich and Chatham, northwards to Rotherhithe, or southwards to Shoreham and the Sussex shipbuilding centres. Timber merchants and landowners recognised timber as a valuable crop, and employment was guaranteed in faggoting, hedging, cutting, grubbing, cleaving and carting. From the wealden craft workshops came ash barrel-hoops and hurdles and chestnut fencing; birch and heather besoms came from the Hindhead 'broom-squires', trugs from the Herstmonceux area and willow cricket bats from Robertsbridge, while ash walking-sticks were a Chiddingfold speciality. Further afield, the south-western part of the Chilterns exported large quantities of beechwood timber, firewood and tanning bark via Henley-on-Thames to London. Chair-making offered work for women and itinerant male 'bodgers' as well; it was centred around Chesham and later High Wycombe, and the Windsor chair and turned chair parts became a nationally famous speciality (Fig. 5.13). Forestry was the mainstay of the economy of the Burnham plateau, the poor soils of which still retain the well-known Burnham Beeches. In the New Forest the smallholding, cottage stock-keeping and commoning society also shared space with an increased sylvicultural interest; from here oaks were being transported to Bursledon and Portsmouth for naval shipbuilding. Defoe noted 2 miles of huge timbers lying upstream along Southampton Water, ready for shipment to Portsmouth as required.[36]

Fig. 5.13 Wood-turners in the Chilterns.
Wood-turners photographed in Hampden Woods, Buckinghamshire, in about 1890.

A significant change to the industrial landscape occurred from the late medieval period as cloth-making began to replace the production and export of raw wool. Within the South East very many villages were involved and the occupations of shearman and weaver were commonplace in such Surrey villages as Caterham, Nutfield and West Horsley in the early 17th century. The 'Great teynter field' of Kingston-upon-Thames in 1699 would have had racks filled with drying cloth, while the residents of Mitcham in the Wandle valley were engaged in whiting and bleaching, and later in the production of calico for sale in London. But the key textile areas were the kersey-producing area of Dorset and the broadcloth and kersey area of Berkshire, Hampshire and the Sussex/Kent border around Cranbrook, and especially Wiltshire, where by 1674 the manufacture of woollen cloth employed about 30,000 people. In these areas clothiers prospered, leaving behind them cloth halls and fine houses, often with large first-floor windows or wide overhanging upper rooms that gave space for weaving. It was London, however, that dominated the export of broadcloth (as it had the trade in raw wool), followed a long way behind by Southampton and Poole. The centre of wealden clothing had been around Cranbrook and Tenterden, the outworkers for which stretched into northern Sussex. By 1640, however, only Tenterden was classed among England's main cloth towns. Inter-regional competition from centres specialising in the 'new draperies', as well as from the urban clothiers of Sandwich, Canterbury and Maidstone, together with familiar disputes over timber supplies, export restrictions and poor communications all hastened the wealden decline. Defoe noted that in Kent the trade 'is now quite decay'd, and scarce ten clothiers left in all the county', for during the first half of the 18th century even urban cloth-manufacturing and its linked trades fell away, thereby depriving surrounding villages of outwork. Emigration rates rose as the rate of employment among the rural population fell. In Surrey, only Godalming survived through to 1750 making kersies, stockings and other cloths; and there is little evidence for a continuation of the Chichester kersey and broadcloth manufacture after 1700.

Like many of the region's employments, the late 16th-century development of paper-making owed much to demand from London. By 1558 a mill was in operation at Dartford and there was further production at ports such as Dover and Southampton where old rags and ships' cordage and sails could be recycled for paper. By 1720 the High Wycombe and West Wycombe areas boasted the highest concentration of paper mills in England, an ascendancy that lasted through until the early 19th century when it faced competition from coastal Kent, as well as northern England.

The combination in south-east England of wood-pasture landscapes, poor soils for farming and available resources of water power, charcoal and minerals, helped to create an environment in which proto-industrialisation could flourish at this time. This was an early form of industrialisation, however, that predated any 'industrial revolution'. Small farmers, working severalty holdings, required something more than their poor farm incomes could supply. By turning to cloth-making and glass-making, or by finding a niche within the iron industry, they created dual employments in such areas as the Weald and the New Forest, and in parts of the Chilterns they specialised in straw-plait, pillow lace and woodworking. This diversification allowed early industry to flourish before large-scale production or exhaustion of resources moved the industries away to Midland, northern or Scottish towns in the 18th and 19th centuries. The region's lace industry was on a large scale: its centre was to the north of the Chilterns, but there were lacemaking schools at Marlow and High Wycombe in the 18th century, the latter employing several hundred lacemakers by 1717. The presence of such by-employments in turn attracted more people to these areas, which had plentiful common grazings, woods and marginal land on which they might build housing. A cheap source of labour was thereby ensured, together with raw materials, power supplies and proximity to London's market and resources of capital.

The Weald presents a very good example of a failed transition towards full industrialisation, however. Industrial linkages with purchasers were weak with the result that contracts for wealden iron petered out long before the shift to coal-fired iron production occurred; the glass, iron and cloth industries were also too independently organised to allow them to benefit from any economies of scale. Dependence on external capital funding was also risky and much was anyway switching to more promising regions elsewhere.[37] Although agricultural development in the 17th and 18th centuries reabsorbed some of the labour force, with no industrial renewal, the Weald – like East Anglia, the West Country and north Wales – became de-industrialised from the mid-17th century, with the result that its modern landscape effectively hides its industrial past. Fragments of church-window glass, clothiers' and ironmasters' houses, streamside earthworks, slag waste, iron fire backs and iron grave slabs (there are more than 30 at Wadhurst) are the few landscape clues that remain, although the large amount of old coppicing also offers testimony to a once-indispensable raw material.

In the Thames valley, perhaps more than anywhere else in the region, husbandmen could diversify their activities, take extra work, and become part-time industrial workers or one of the many intermediaries between food production and consumption. The corn mills of the Wandle were joined by copper and dyeing works, and along Thames-side, and particularly at Southwark, a multitude of semi-rural processing and manufacturing industries proliferated alongside older trades such as the basket-making of the Thames eyots. Shipbuilding, barge manufacture and maintenance, fishing, brewing, tanning and slaughtering jostled with metal trades and formed an urban industrial scene that permeated the remnants of the open fields and paddocks. In north-west Kent paper, metal, lime, brewing and glass industries were expanding within reach of London. Between the London Basin and the fringes of the Low Weald there were primary extractive industries, such as the quarrying of building stone and fuller's earth from the Lower Greensand of Kent and Surrey, or the manufacture of gunpowder and paper at Dartford and Faversham, as well as in small rural mills. Around the coast there was corn milling near Chichester, while the north Kent copperas (or green vitriol, a form of ferrous sulphate) workers supplied stones for dyeing, ink manufacture and the leather industries. Fishing was also combined with farming, and along the Sussex coast shellfish and mullet were greatly renowned. On the north Kent coast oysters were a speciality (as they remain today, witnessed by the 25 July Whitstable Oyster Festival) and even their starfish predators were used locally for manure.

The absence of heavy industry and the full impact of the Industrial Revolution is an important silence in the landscape history of south-east England. In many ways, the South was forced to give way to the industrial might of northern England. Capital and craftsmen moved north. The survey of rural industries carried out by FitzRandolph and Hay in the 1920s offers a glimpse into an element of the rural landscape about to undergo a fundamental change; already they could chart a decline during the previous 50 years.[38] Woollen mills had decayed or were converted to corn grinding and the site of England's first blast furnace, in Sussex, has now been completely recolonised by woodland. Important industries based on local resources, such as chair-making in the Chilterns, initially grew as a reaction to the immense market provided by London. Between 1880 and 1920 chair-making developed into furniture-making around High Wycombe, providing cheaper as well as more exclusive furniture for West End stores. Machine-based manufacture initially supplemented the home-based rushing and caning work, but later developed into large factories such as that for the production of G-Plan furniture. But again the industry has now shrunk; between 1939 and 1990 its 10,000 workers fell to about 4,000, and the G-Plan factory itself closed in 1992 with the loss of 700 jobs.

From the 19th century onwards, however, the industrial landscape of the South East presents a more complex picture. Links between local landscape and industrial development have been broken by the rise of multinational companies (MNCs) and globalisation. The South East is now one of the world's key locations for many business interests, and as a 'core' region, it commands a high rental premium. Companies with central London offices have frequently found it cheaper to relocate beyond the M25 ring road, in turn creating higher site values and high housing demand in the rural outer South East. The modern rural industrial landscape has many faces, and a great deal has been written about the rise of hi-tech, R&D and corporate 'command and control' facilities in the South

Fig. 5.14 The Bluewater shopping complex, Greenhithe, Kent. Opened in 1999 in a former chalk quarry, this is the largest retail-leisure complex in Europe. It is surrounded by parkland, with one million trees and shrubs, lakes and car parks.

East, particularly in the 'sunbelt' crescent from Hertfordshire through Berkshire and into Hampshire. If we focus here purely on rural development, it is possible to see three kinds of visual impact.

First, there are now many small/medium enterprises (SMEs), typically employing fewer than ten people, that have started up in redundant agricultural buildings. In areas where farming has ceased to be profitable these now house a variety of light industrial, service and domestic consumer industries, storage, handicraft and electronics companies. Flexible production of customised goods flourished during the 1980s in the South East, and in 1992 a survey in Kent found 370 sites where former farm buildings were being used for other businesses. There are, of course, tensions inherent in this conversion process, particularly where the landscape is protected by conservation status, and issues of signage or heavy lorry deliveries can compromise landscape quality, peace and sustainability.

Secondly, large numbers of purpose-built industrial and retail estates have sprung up since the 1980s and have contributed to the surge in rural development in the 'city beyond the city'. Partly as a result of the impact of the Channel Tunnel rail link, Ashford in Kent, for example, has mushroomed and its shopping centres, new roads and industrial estates now face the nearby village of Sevington.

The concept of such estates is not new: they had enjoyed an earlier surge in the 1930s when they were associated with 'new' industries that even then were highly concentrated in the South East, at places such as Welwyn Garden City, Ealing or Elstree. They provided a number of important advantages to manufacturers, including external economies of scale, reduced production costs and accelerated growth. Most were actually situated on the outskirts of smaller and medium-sized towns, extending the built-up landscape further into the countryside, and this trend has continued through to the present. Formerly discrete wealden towns such as Burgess Hill, Uckfield, Hailsham and Haywards Heath are now surrounded by a maze of roads and estates – both industrial and residential. New higher education establishments add to suburban development, especially from the 1960s as at the universities of Sussex at Brighton, Kent at Canterbury or Surrey at Guildford, with fashionable pressure for science parks (for example Chilworth at Southampton University) and 'Innovation Centres' (Sussex). There are also the vast new retail parks such as Lakeside at Thurrock in Essex, opened in 1990 and with parking for 13,000 cars, or Bluewater in Kent, with its 320 stores and three malls, which began trading in 1999 (Fig. 5.14). Their landscape impact has been enormous.

Thirdly, there are larger company buildings, often belonging to high-tech MNCs and located near communication routes, which also make a considerable impact on the landscape. These are characterised by the former IBM test laboratory buildings at Havant, near the junctions of the A3(M) and M27 – an imposition of modern architectural design in what was previously a rural setting. Havant now has twice the regional average of manufacturing jobs, with an emphasis upon skilled and scientific research establishments – the types of R&D company that are searching for environmental quality of life for their employees. The Berkshire section of the M4 motorway – the 'M4 corridor' – has seen a particular proliferation of such buildings in recent years, from Heathrow at one end to Swindon at the other.

In the long term, the rural industrial base of the South East has been diversified from agricultural processing and food-related industries to the heavy armaments industry of the Tudor and Stuart periods, to the peri-urban industrial growth of the 18th and 19th centuries, and latterly to the greenfield 'sunrise' industry sites of MNC prestige. The region's locational advantage with respect to the Continent has been maintained, and is now even more important in landscape terms because of the late 20th-century Channel Tunnel and its associated rail links, which has transformed the landscape of north and east Kent.

NOTES

1 Taylor 1983, 47; Taylor in Hoskins 1988, 16.
2 Fowler 1981, 144–61.
3 Fowler 2002, 138–9; Dark & Dark 1997, 97; Applebaum 1972, 97–102.
4 Dark & Dark, 1997, 143–4.
5 Fowler 2002, 192–3.
6 Fowler 2002, 210–11.
7 Baker 1973, 187–95.
8 Gray 1915.
9 Gardiner 1998, 129–45.
10 Blair 1991, 71.
11 Rippon 2000.
12 Everitt 1986, 3.
13 Fowler 2002, 239.
14 Fowler 2002, 227.
15 Brandon & Short 1990, 70.
16 Hallam 1988, 981.
17 Short 2000, 139.
18 Blair 1991, 88–9.
19 Aston & Bettey 1998, 124.
20 Thirsk 1967, 241; Roden 1969, 115–26; Hepple & Doggett 2000, 272.
21 Aston & Bettey 1998, 129.
22 Defoe 1724 (1971 edn), 82–3.
23 Defoe 1724 (1971 edn), 193.
24 Chapman & Seeliger 2001, 49–50, 141ff; Short 1984, 289.
25 Williamson 2002, 89.
26 Hunt & Pam 1995, 167.
27 Overton 1996, 92.
28 Cobbett 1967 edn, 86.
29 Strong 1998.
30 Daniels 1999.
31 Cobbett 1967 edn, 207.
32 Hardy 1891 (1974 edn).
33 Cleere & Crossley 1985, 57–86.
34 Jones & Mattingly 1990, 205–14; Millett 1990, 169–71; Drewett et al. 1988, 244.
35 Drewett et al. 1988, 330–1; Hamerow 2002, 189.
36 Wordie 1984, 344.
37 Zell 1994; Short 1989.
38 FitzRandolph & Hay 1926.

6

Urban Living: Urban Landscapes

The landscape history of south-east England must take account of the complex mosaic of town and countryside, since the interaction between the two is striking and persistent. In previous chapters the emergence of an urban landscape has been charted, but in this chapter we examine more particularly the townscape as it emerged from the 18th century, thereby emphasising the period in which urbanisation has had its most profound impact. London will be the subject of its own chapter, since a world city of that magnitude is not easily encompassed within the present chapter. Here we concentrate on the layout, building fabrics and land uses of the provincial towns of the region and the interactions between lives, livelihoods and urban landscape. In so doing, we examine the coastal ports and resorts, later commuter settlements, and the skeins of communication that link them together across the landscape.

THE COUNTRY TOWN

Although this chapter deals more specifically with the centuries from about 1700 onwards, it must be remembered that most townscapes were to some extent moulded by the legacy of previous generations. Continuity from medieval or Tudor predecessors can still usually be seen in the surviving buildings, town walls or cathedral closes, and the morphology of streets and house plots, whether originally planned or having grown organically. The town's churches were real as well as symbolic landmarks, giving physical presence to community, and the patterns of ownership, either private or corporate, also impacted on decisions about urban space.

By 1700, we start to have sufficient information to chart the emergence of an urban hierarchy, solidly expressed in the number and grandeur of private and public buildings. London obviously dominated, with a population of 675,000 by 1750 (11 per cent of the total English population, and *see* Table 7.1) and served also as the provincial capital, removing the possibility of there being any other second-ranking provincial capital such as an Exeter, Bristol or York. Otherwise, only Canterbury, Salisbury, Chatham and Portsmouth possessed more than 5,000 people, and the two latter were essentially specialist naval dockyard towns. Instead, in second-ranked place came the county towns. Those located inside the region were Maidstone (in Kent, with its more modish reputation toppling Canterbury in the late 17th century), Dorchester (in Dorset, but showing little vitality at this time), Lewes and Chichester (for East and West Sussex), Hertford (Hertfordshire), Chelmsford (Essex), Winchester (which became a renowned social and retailing centre and replaced Southampton for Hampshire), Guildford (Surrey, but latterly Kingston-upon-Thames), Salisbury (Wiltshire, but latterly Trowbridge which is outside the scope of this volume). Reading has acted in the capacity of a county town for Berkshire, together with Abingdon. Lower down the urban hierarchy were the region's many small market towns and ports.

These offered a selection of townscapes and those at the foot of the hierarchy have little to distinguish them from large villages.

Even before 1700, and certainly after, this hierarchy was subject to change. Older towns might stagnate and newer centres expand. Salisbury, Winchester, Wilton and Canterbury all declined in the 17th century. Changes in communications, fluctuations in trade, attitudes of governing elites and cultural shifts in consumer taste might all impact on the physical fabric of an expanding or decaying town. Both Salisbury and Canterbury were among the largest provincial towns in about 1700 but both disappeared from the list thereafter.[1] Salisbury, because of the loss of its textile industries, dropped from its place in the top five English provincial towns in 1524/5 to a lowly position in the top one hundred towns by 1841. Near by, its predecessor, Old Sarum, was stripped of its borough status in 1832. By 1700 the largest south-eastern town outside London was Portsmouth, and it remained among the largest English towns for another century. By 1820 its population, combined with Portsea, exceeded 45,000. Below Portsmouth came Canterbury, Maidstone, Chatham and Woolwich (Kent), Brighton (Sussex), Southampton (Hampshire) and Reading (Berkshire) all with over 10,000. The latter reached nearly 13,000 people by 1820 and was thriving because of the milling, malting, brewing and other more minor industries that flourished at the junction of the Thames and Kennet, on the road from London to Bath and Bristol.

In about 1700 the region's townscapes were being affected by the use of new building materials: for the wealthier, brick, tile and ashlar replaced the wooden frames and thatch and mud infills of an earlier generation. Often these newer materials were used to front those buildings facing on to high streets. The 18th-century façades in Lewes High Street, for example, frequently hide vernacular medieval structures behind. The symmetrical Classical style of architecture became much favoured and was intended to symbolise dignity and a solid permanence, especially for public building. It offered uncluttered and cohesive frontages, interrupted by sash windows and pilastered and pedimented doorways. Printed manuals and pattern books facilitated this transformation of the built environment, and kept styles evolving as taste changed from baroque to rococo, neoclassical and Gothic by the end of the 18th century. The brick-built London terrace, with its narrow street frontages, became the model for many provincial builders. The streets and squares also offered communal space for circulation, commercial and market functions, recreational and ritual activities. Too often the streets had previously been used for storage, animals and the dumping of domestic waste. But from 1715 city authorities could appoint 'scavengers', a power that was extended to all market towns in 1736. As the 18th century progressed the streets were more carefully cleaned, paved, widened and lit by oil lamps, albeit often in piecemeal fashion, at the behest of the new Improvement Commissioners; the first outside London were those appointed at Salisbury in 1737.[2] Later, medieval walls and gates were dismantled as encumbrances to new layouts, as at Dorchester, where the remains of the Roman walls on two sides of the town were demolished to make way for tree-lined promenades. At Southampton in 1770 the Improvement Commissioners took down the East Gate to widen and 'render [the streets] more commodious'. An elderly inhabitant of Chichester, writing in 1784, could say 'I have seen almost the whole city and town new built or new faced, a spirit of emulation in this way having run through the whole.'[3]

By 1700 provincial towns were becoming centres of consumption as well as production. They could display many signs of wealth, and overt displays of civic pride multiplied, many of which have left a lasting mark. The Hertford Shire Hall was built to John Adams's classical designs in 1768–9, a common pattern for 18th-century civic buildings. That at Chelmsford (1789–91) also had an imposing decorated façade. Country banks, too, were expanding, although purpose-built commercial buildings were less common at this time. The first provincial voluntary hospital was opened at Winchester in 1736; and other public buildings included town halls, new churches and chapels, theatres (as at Newbury in 1802 or Brighton in1806), libraries or the exclusive assembly rooms. Grammar or free schools often formed part of the landscape: the example founded at Berkhamsted in 1541 still survives with its central schoolroom bounded to one side by the headmaster's house and the other by that of the usher. Rising numbers of urban gentry meant balls, concerts, society meetings, horse races and 'polite social intercourse'. In addition, country gentry families took town houses for parts of the year, their bustling social venues adding to the town's lustre and economy. Their houses can remain impressive today, such as the three-storey, red-brick Serle's House in Winchester (of about 1715) or Pelham House in Lewes. The latter was occupied by the family of that name between 1654 and 1790, during which time the Elizabethan house was re-fronted in the late Classical style. Many towns could provide considerable amounts of accommodation: Winchester and St Albans both offered stabling for more than 1,000 horses by the 1680s.[4] Urban consciousness can also be seen in the growing number of town histories written after 1700. These follow on from William Somner's *Antiquities of Canterbury* (1640) and include works such as John Hutchins' *History of the Town and County of Poole* (1788).

Most smaller towns remained linked to their agricultural surroundings, with fields, butchers' grazing paddocks, barns and processing industries such as tanning or milling located on the edges of built-up areas. Agricultural servicing, implement and machinery manufacture and processing trades dominated most of the smaller towns in the region. Agricultural societies, part business, part pleasure, developed in many country towns from 1750. Thomas Hardy's 'Casterbridge' (Dorchester), though set in the 19th century, caught the atmosphere:

> *Casterbridge … was deposited in a block upon a cornfield. There was no suburb in the modern sense, or transitional intermixture between town and down. It stood, with regard to the wide, fertile land adjoining, clean-cut and distinct like a chessboard on a green table-cloth. The farmer's boy could sit under his barley mow and pitch a stone into the office window of the town clerk; reapers at work among the sheaves nodded to acquaintances on the pavement corner; the red-robed judge, when he condemned a sheep-stealer, pronounced sentence to the tune of Baa that floated in at the window from the remainder of the flock browsing hard by; and at executions the waiting crowd stood in a meadow immediately before the drop, out of which the cows had been temporarily driven, to give spectators room …*[5]

Urban tradesmen, professionals and commercial suppliers kept a close eye on farming fortunes since their own profits would be affected by a poor harvest or bumper crop. Bankers, lawyers, insurance agents, hoteliers and newspaper proprietors were all to be found here as the 18th and 19th centuries progressed, together with localised crafts and manufacturing activities. Urban industrialists also saw advantages in locating in many of these provincial towns: the older cloth industry has bequeathed fine clothiers' houses at Warminster, where the large corn market was joined by textiles and silk-weaving in the 18th century. Lace provided employment at Marlborough, Blandford Forum and Salisbury. Malting, brewing and a host of small industries drew population to Reading, and the well-known Huntley & Palmer biscuit factory was established in 1846; it used the canal system for distribution and later the Great Western Railway, and many of its workers lived in the terraced houses in New Town. Bentalls' agricultural engineering firm at Heybridge near Maldon in Essex similarly became locally significant; it employed large numbers of workers in the 19th century but is now remembered more for its four-storeyed warehouse of 1863 and the Bentall shopping centre on the site of the former engineering works.

Fig. 6.1 John Walker's map of Chelmsford 1591. *Encroachment of buildings on to the market place can be seen, with permanent houses and stalls in a 'Middle Row'. The Sessions House was also used as a corn market. Thatched and tiled barns are shown, and beyond the immediate 'backsyde' fields were the 'meades' to east and west.*

For many smaller towns it was their market that defined their purpose; serving as collecting points from the surrounding area for the onward shipment of local produce to London, especially in Kent and Surrey where new markets had developed by the end of the 17th century. Markets were held in wider streets or at road junctions, often denoted by market crosses – whether modest as at Winchester or grand like Chichester's – and open stalls and nearby inns were scenes of bustling activity. Encroachment into these spaces by more permanent buildings can be traced in many towns, such as Royston (Hertfordshire) and Croydon (Surrey) where the slum infill was redeveloped in the 1890s, or Chelmsford (Essex) (Fig. 6.1). More specific market areas or market halls, as had been constructed at Wallingford and Windsor by 1700, might also be built away from the town centre. During the 19th century many such towns also saw the building of corn exchanges with spacious halls to cater for the dealers' stands: that at Newbury cost as much as £6,000, but this was an important grain transhipment point and the corn sold at the market by sample was delivered in bulk to the granaries erected near the market wharf on the Kennet. The more typical cost of southern corn exchanges was between £2,000 and £3,000.[6] That at Guildford, built in 1818 by public subscription, doubled as the Assize Court. Although its population was just 1,716 in 1741, Farnham was reputedly the busiest market for wheat in England (outside London) in the early 18th century. Several mills were at work there, although by 1800 wheat from Sussex and Hampshire was being sold instead through Chichester and Southampton, and Farnham's trade declined, to be replaced later by a thriving hop market. The town's decline has, however, left a considerable legacy of 18th-century listed buildings, such as Willmer House (1719), now the town's museum, and those in Castle Street (Fig. 6.2).

Not all dealing was carried out in the market towns, since large livestock fairs continued at well-known rural locations: Barnet fair could attract 50,000 cattle with their large contingent of Welsh drovers and Weyhill, near Andover, was famous for sheep and hops. These fairs suffered badly from the advent of the railways, which could transport animals further and faster and with less weight loss than when they travelled on the hoof. The number of fairs in Kent fell from 130 in 1792 to 13 in 1888; in Sussex from 119 to 41. Reading's Michaelmas cheese fair disappeared in the 19th century. Some towns, such as Dorchester or Lewes, moved their cattle markets closer to the railway station, away from the crowded main streets and the sensibilities of citizens, although others retained their older styles of tethered cattle and sheep pens in the streets (Fig. 6.3). At Chelmsford horses were put through their paces in the street outside the Saracen's Head inn. Although weekly retail markets were more resilient, hiring fairs were also in decline, and as a result many fairs began to change to horse or funfairs at this time, such as the Midsummer Fair at Farnham, the Marlborough Mop Fair held in the High Street, or the rowdy Fairlop Fair held below the monstrous

Fig. 6.2 View of Castle Street in Farnham, Surrey, in about 1880 by John Henry Knight. *Pevsner in his guide to Surrey refers to the town as 'one of the best Georgian towns in England'. Markets were held in this wide street, and the castle itself, in the distance, was one of the seats of the Bishop of Winchester.*

Fairlop Oak in Hainault Forest. Modern retail shops were now developing faster than in any other region and becoming more specialised; they were characterised by their advertising displays and barrel-shaped glass windows, later replaced by plate glass. Winchester already had as many as 90 shops by 1704.

Specialist markets also began to appear, especially in a ring 30–50km from London, to co-ordinate supplies to the capital. Examples include Chelmsford on the Great Essex Road, which was the milling and marketing centre for mid-Essex; it later expanded to include more specialist retailing and by 1794 had at least 31 shops. Farnham, Henley-on-Thames and Newbury were important for their wheat transactions, Dorking for poultry, Reading for barley (by 1760 it was regarded as the primary malting centre in Britain) and Ware for its malting – barges took the malt to London down the River Lea, a trade that expanded after the river was improved for navigation through an Act of 1739. There were at least 20 maltsters in Ware by the 1830s, and this figure was matched at Kingston-upon-Thames and Guildford. At Hitchin, Luton and Dunstable there were large covered straw-plait markets before overseas competition closed them down.

Although the South East's towns were by 1700 generally more prosperous than those in any other region, social and landscape inequalities certainly persisted. As late as the 1660s half or more of the householders of inland towns in Kent, Surrey and Hampshire were too poor to pay rates, and although it is

Fig. 6.3 Cattle market in East Street, Chichester, Sussex in about 1870. The elaborate market cross and the cathedral spire are shown. But the beast markets were causing problems for the city centre, as observed by Charles Swainson in 1866: 'Two streets that lead to the cross are absolutely impassable. The cattle and sheep and pigs stand in their own filth for so many hours that they leave marks behind on the pavement ... and thus it is a fact that better dressed people avoid Chichester ... the working days of our shops are reduced ... no wonder that Chichester is dull.'

difficult to draw firm lines around rich and poor urban areas, notable concentrations were starting to form. The wealthier residences tended to locate in the central areas of provincial towns and poorer families in the more peripheral parishes. Many of the poor were still packed in inferior alleys and narrow lanes or 'twittens', subject to damp, fire and disease. The older medieval burgage plots were infilled and small courtyards were lined with dwellings. Squalid cottages mixed with the premises of butchers and leather cutters. At the end of the 18th century nearly 50 per cent of the population of Hungerford in Berkshire were very poor and 20 per cent were receiving poor relief.

Health was also poor and visitors cautious: Hitchin had a street known as Dead Street until it was later renamed Queen Street. Privies and water supplies were few or non-existent and cholera and diphtheria frequent. The combination of poverty, overcrowding, pollution and malnutrition also brought smallpox, typhus and influenza. Dysentery could follow droughts, attacking poorer families and their children. The bubonic plague years of 1665 and 1666 are well recorded for London, where 70,000 died, but high death rates were also reported in Chelmsford and in the Thames-side and Medway towns, and as many as one-quarter to one-third of Dover's population died in this epidemic.

Fire also remained a major hazard in these older quarters, where trades with a high fire risk were often housed in unsuitable buildings, although the South East, Thames-side apart, was less subject to such disasters than some other regions, due to its earlier adoption of brick, tile and stone. Nevertheless, in recognition of this ubiquitous problem, thatch was banned at Reading by 1638 and Winchester in 1656, and at Andover in 1668 the tanners were ordered to shift their kilns to the riverside and to tile them. But in 1689 New Alresford was ablaze, and in 1727 a fire at Gravesend destroyed more than 100 houses and rendered at least 500 people homeless. The London Building Acts of Queen Anne's reign were widely adopted in provincial towns with the result that many towns now acquired their more uniform Georgian landscape elements. Rebuilding was effected in brick and tile, and after a fire at Blandford Forum in 1731 that began at a tallow chandler's, John and William Bastard remodelled the town on more spacious lines, with a new church (1739) and civic buildings (Fig. 6.4).[7] Hence the inscription carved into the paving stones outside the Town Hall:

Recipe for regeneration:
take one careless
tallow chandler and
two ingenious Bastards

In the 19th century an enthusiasm for urban redesign – what Conzen referred to as 'Victorian indiscretion' – affected most country towns.[8] Ornamental town halls were proudly commissioned and built to a scale much larger than hitherto: Reading's was designed by Alfred Waterhouse, for example. They still accommodated other functions, such as the corn market and assembly rooms at Farnham town hall (1866), or the police station and cells at Wokingham. And many more public buildings were erected: red-brick schools, imposing police and fire stations, classically inspired museums, Gothic churches and town halls with

Fig. 6.4 Blandford Forum, Dorset. *The Market Place with Town Hall and church of St Peter and St Paul.*

imposing clock towers (at Croydon this was a neo-Jacobean hall built in 1892–6), libraries, union workhouses (which after 1929 often became depressing hospitals), asylums and prisons. The gaol at Reading (1842–4) looms over the ruined Abbey. Statues of notable local figures were erected, such as that to the poet William Barnes at Dorchester in 1889. New commercial buildings, typically of three storeys or even more, now favoured somewhat uniform Classical façades in Portland stone or Italianate designs in red brick. Still more seriously antagonistic to local design, multiple stores began to spread and often used their upper floors as storage space instead of for living accommodation. The provision of a gas supply was also seen as prestigious: Reading's was established in 1818, although most followed in the ensuing two decades. At first this was mainly for the provision of public street lighting, a revolutionary development that allowed greater freedom of movement after dark and was the envy of rural visitors.

Many country towns expanded physically during the late 18th century, but especially in the 19th century. Their functions were boosted by population increases, higher income per head and middle-class living standards that were higher than in many other regions. Middle-class town houses and villas, continuous streets, squares and terraces were provided for all levels of wealth. Well-built artisan brick terraces also typically constituted these landscapes of expansion and social separation was now commonplace in these smaller settlements. Towns such as Dorchester, Wareham and Wallingford had previously hardly expanded beyond their medieval limits, but now Dorchester began to grow across neighbouring Fordington when the latter's open fields were enclosed in the 1870s. In some cases the new housing formed a link between the older town and the new landscape feature, the railway station where the latter was outside the old town, as at St Albans, Watford and Hitchin. Railway stations were, of course, to prove a vital catalyst and the South East had a higher level of rail connectivity between its towns than other regions. Settlements such as East Grinstead, Uckfield, Crowborough, Haywards Heath, Burgess Hill and Crawley expanded quickly where the railway was coupled with abundant common land that could be enclosed for building. But where the railway, for whatever reason, failed to arrive or promote growth, 'sleepy hollows' continued to serve purely local needs and eventually stagnated, as in the case of Wessex chalkland towns such as Cerne Abbas and Cranborne, or Arundel, Steyning, Midhurst and Petworth in Sussex. By 1871 the decrease in population at Warminster in Wiltshire was attributed to the railway which had 'diverted the traffic connected with the corn market, caused many of the inns to be closed, and induced a large number … to seek employment elsewhere', and by 1845 Staines had lost 'the appearance of bustle and prosperity' with the loss in its stage-coach traffic.[9]

INLAND SPAS AND COASTAL RESORTS

The fastest-growing late-Georgian towns had a service function that distinguished them from villages and that was also reflected in their landscapes. The 17th century had seen the initiation of spas in England: Bath was established in the late 17th century, and became the 18th-century pleasure capital *par excellence*. But others followed. The sick came for treatment; many came for entertainment, especially after the Restoration; and royal patronage gave the necessary seals of approval, as at Tunbridge Wells in the 1660s. The spas near London flourished first, as at Sadler's Well or Clerken Well on the edges of the Fleet valley; at fashionable Hampstead with its Well Walk, pump room and assembly rooms; or Dulwich, Sydenham, Streatham or Epsom Wells, the latter especially between 1690 and 1710. There was an assembly room at Kentish Town until 1853, a spa and tea gardens at St Pancras and St Chad's Well at Kings Cross; the tea garden there remained open until 1840 and the pump room until 1860, overlooked by smoking tile kilns and a smallpox hospital. The Fleet was now a filthy ditch, laden with sewage and refuse from an overcrowded area. Kilburn's chalybeate spring in the Tyburn valley also attracted few visitors by this time. One problem with these sites, other than their deteriorating scenery, was that they were just too close to the capital, allowing less desirable elements to visit.

Status and class remained important. In fact Epsom soon became a residential town, on which Defoe commented: ''tis very frequent for the trading part of the company to place their families here, and take their horses every morning to London'.[10] But Epsom remained relatively small in population by 1700. Pleasant walks and rides were required, together with lodgings and a willingness for both London-based and local investors to speculate on the future success of the location. Epsom, with its coffee house, racing on Banstead Down, gaming rooms, promenades around the two greens, and shops, also had nearby Box Hill. It was here that John Macky noted that it was easy for 'gentlemen and ladies insensibly to lose their company in these pretty labyrinths of box-wood and divert themselves unperceived', so that 'it may justly be called the Palace of Venus'.[11]

Planning was negligible in these surroundings, and the provision of other urban facilities was sometimes slow. Although Tunbridge Wells did have a market to provide luxuries for the visitors, and by the 1630s was attracting visitors in sufficient numbers for the walks (The Pantiles) to be laid out, its other facilities were more limited. After the Restoration, however, visits from Charles II's courtiers confirmed its importance and development began in earnest. London speculators joined local tradesmen in investing in shops, taverns and lodging houses around the common at Mount Ephraim, as well as building a church in the 1680s. From 1700 there were also coffee houses and leisure areas, a cold bath and assembly room. By 1732 Beau Nash was Master of Ceremonies; by 1770 there were two libraries and a theatre, and with the Pantiles paved, the town reached the peak of its fortunes by the mid-18th century. But it still had 'the appearance of a town in the midst of woods' with the houses, according to Fanny Burney, *en route* for Brighton in 1779, 'strewed promiscuously'. Indeed, although its population grew quickly in the 18th century among the scattered wealden settlements of Southborough, Rusthall, Mount Ephraim and Mount Sion, many urban elements still had to await the later 19th century, when the town changed its primary function to that of a famously conservative residential centre, attracting retired military, colonial officials and overseas merchants.

Another class of town should briefly be noted here, though neither spa nor coastal resort. The inland resort, favoured by London's elite, was also a feature of the 18th century, perhaps best exemplified by Richmond-upon-Thames. Increasingly a fashionable settlement during the Tudor period after the development of Henry VIII's palace, it became for Georgian Londoners a place of retreat, since, as Walpole noted in 1749, there was now 'a fashion to go out of London at the end of the week'.[12] The Georgian inheritance is considerable: a green, a park, riverside scenery observable from Richmond Hill, and buildings to accommodate royalty (in particular George III and his family) together with courtiers, artists and their patrons. By 1833 steamboat excursions from London assumed considerable social importance.

Nevertheless, the emphasis moved inexorably to the coastal spas. Brighton had a chalybeate spring that was exploited from the 1750s and the Prince of Wales visited Southampton's spring and sea-bathing facilities in 1750, to be followed later by his sons. In such locations access by sea was easier and the liminality of the beach provided a relaxed social atmosphere that was lacking in the inland resorts. Although Brighton, Southampton, Hastings and Margate (with Scarborough and Weymouth) were initially modelled on the inland spas, by the 1750s they were accommodating a new elite fashion, that of sea-bathing. Margate, however, with its easier access by sea from London, was rapidly developing a more plebian image, the company being 'compos'd of every trade, and each degree'. Lower

Fig. 6.5 Brighton, the fully restored Royal Pavilion. The building began as a farmhouse on the Steyne where fishermen's nets were dried. The initial classical building of 1786–7 by Henry Holland was replaced during the height of Regency interest in Chinoiserie and the Orient, and given full reign for the Prince of Wales. A Chinese interior contrasts with the domes and minarets of John Nash's 'Hindu' exterior of 1815–20. Nash's garden scheme for the palace has now also been fully restored.

fares on hoys – small passenger sailing vessels that were thought to be somewhat inferior – and then from 1814 on steamboats, boosted visitors to the extent that by 1831 about 120,000 passengers were travelling annually between London and Margate. By the 1750s the bathing machine had made its appearance, followed by the pier, now used for recreation rather than for commerce.

These and the other coastal resorts had grown from fishing towns, many of which, like Brighton, had been in decline because of an eroded foreshore. With sources of capital available from local gentry and from London, they could look forward more confidently. A guidebook of 1813 for Margate observed: 'It was merely a fishing town, and one dirty narrow lane … was the principal part of the town.' Medical backing was important, particularly in advocating the restorative powers of the springs and seawater, with Dr Richard Russell at Brighton paramount in this respect. Brighton's Georgian town houses were built facing on to the common land of the Steine, and from 1780 expansion on to the open-field strips (known as leynes) around the town proceeded quickly in the shape of bow-windowed terraced houses. Royal patronage was crucial, and Brighton's modern council logo still bears the image of the unique and fantastic Royal Pavilion in its oriental splendour; it was designed for the Prince of Wales, later George IV, who thereafter became identified with the town (Fig. 6.5).[13]

Brighton by 1801 had a population of 7,000, much of it poorly housed; by 1831 it had become the 20th largest town in England with 41,000 people, and had indeed been the fastest-growing town in England in the intercensal period 1811–21. The Chain Pier here was opened in 1823, and further entreprenurial activity created virtual new towns: Kemp Town was an impressive mixture of squares and crescents laid out along the coast to the east in the 1820s, as was Brunswick Town to the west. Both were designed in the grander Regency style. Visiting became fashionable, and hotels, lodging houses, baths, shops, libraries, theatres and assembly rooms sprang up to accommodate the beau monde of the 1830s, who were now coming in winter and spring as well as summer. Here, then, was one of the first coastal areas in the world to be transformed by tourism from an agrarian base to a modern service-sector economy.

By 1841, with Brighton further boosted by the arrival of the railway, a visitor commented that it was a place of two distinct classes, 'those who make the town an hotel, and those who live by providing for their entertainment'.[14] In 1851 Brighton's population surpassed that of Bath – a symbolic recognition of the changing impetus of fashion. During the late 19th century Brighton also developed a major railway engineering works, which at one stage employed 2,000; it also had iron foundries and breweries, all to the north of the old town and behind the glittering coastal façade. The railway brought a different kind of visitor and from the 1850s it became a day-trippers' or weekenders' destination, with new income for boarding houses, funfairs and the piers. But Queen Victoria ceased to visit and the Royal Pavilion was sold for a pittance to the corporation. Thereafter at bank holidays the seafront overflowed with Londoners and became the epitome of working-class seaside relaxation. The front now had elite housing, shops and hotels stretching for 2km, but behind were the back streets and dingy slums. Exacerbated by the use of sea sand, inferior bricks and damp basements, housing conditions were as poor here as anywhere in England and became the inspiration for the *demi-monde* of Graham Greene's *Brighton Rock* (1938). Slums were already being demolished by the 1860s, but in 1911 Brighton still had one of the highest population densities of any county borough in England.

The erstwhile counterparts – sometimes aping Brighton, sometimes deliberately not – were to be found all around the region's coast by the end of the 19th century. These included Bournemouth (Dorset); Ryde, Ventnor, Shanklin and Sandown (Isle of Wight); Lymington, Southsea, Southampton and Christchurch (Hampshire); Bognor (alias Hothampton), Worthing, Seaford, Hastings and later Eastbourne and Bexhill (Sussex); Gravesend, Margate, Ramsgate, Broadstairs, Folkestone, Hythe and Sandgate (Kent). Each had its own story of social pretension, growth and Victorian expectation. The Isle of Wight resorts grew once the railway reached Portsmouth and Southampton and with the further impetus given by the patronage of Victoria and Albert at their great mansion at Osborne House. Although some projects, such as Sheerness-on-Sea on the Isle of Sheppey, failed altogether, the timing was echoed elsewhere, and the period 1850–1914 proved highly significant for resort growth in the region. More plebian was Herne Bay: it was laid out in a gridiron pattern from the 1830s, 2km from its parent village of Herne, and eventually possessed a square, promenade, clock tower and pier. A station on the London, Chatham and Dover railway line opened in 1861 but Herne Bay's appeal as a resort was overtaken by its dormitory function by the early 20th century. Still small and quite elite by 1840, the South End of Prittlewell in Essex had also been a resort for the wealthy since the end of the 18th century; its attractions included The Terrace and the Grand Hotel with its assembly rooms, covered sea-water baths and The Shrubbery. Caroline, Princess of Wales, had spent three months here in 1803 and the resort's reputation was confirmed. Until 1856 and the arrival of the London, Tilbury and Southend Railway, nearby Southend grew slowly, but thereafter the growth of the modern resort began.

Folkestone and Eastbourne's seafront landscapes still reflect their solid respectability. By 1891 the latter had became the second-largest town in Sussex after Brighton and housed 34,000 people. If Brighton, Southend and Margate (after 1847 when the railway arrived) now catered for working-class Londoners, others such as Bournemouth, Folkestone and Eastbourne explicitly looked to a more genteel clientele and increasingly gained growing numbers of retired residents. Capital investment came from local landowners, such as the Dukes of Devonshire at Eastbourne. And where such coherent development did occur, the seafront landscapes were composed of the iconic features of elegant open lawns, bandstands, piers and terraced promenades, all backed by imposingly large hotels.

Most of these resorts had grown from pre-existing settlements into resorts on an accessible piece of coastline. Southsea, for example, expanded on to reclaimed marshland and waste land facing Southsea common to become a thriving resort and residential suburb of Portsmouth. By contrast, Bournemouth was a totally new town and provided the most striking example of growth. The area was virtually uninhabited until one holiday home was built in 1810, to be followed shortly afterwards by a few more cottages and the planting of pine trees. Hotels and pleasure gardens followed from the 1830s, but in 1851, with a population of 695, it was still primarily a collection of detached houses among flowering shrubs. With the opening of rail links to London and the Midlands from the 1870s, however, it rapidly acquired a pier, hotel, Winter Gardens (1874) and the

OPPOSITE PAGE:

TOP: *Fig. 6.6 The sea front, Bournemouth, in 1921.* The photograph is from the East Cliff, looking across the original path of the River Bourne to the West Cliff area, the site of the 1810 Tregonwell family investment in land, which led to the rapid growth of the resort. The pierhead is also shown, the pier itself stretching to over 300m by 1909.

BOTTOM: *Fig. 6.7 Port Solent Marina, from the east.* Opened in 1988, the development was built on a large land refill site in the harbour at Portsmouth. Residential, leisure and retail facilities characterise these large south-coast complexes.

trappings of a fashionable but genteel resort. By 1911 its population exceeded 78,000 and reached 117,000 by 1931, by which time it was one of the larger towns in England (Fig. 6.6). The town still retains an air of prosperity. Mimicking the fashion of Paris and the Burlington Arcade in London, Bournemouth developed five arcade-shopping projects of its own between 1864 and 1892. Having expanded eastwards to Boscombe and Pokesdown in the direction of Christchurch, and westwards through Westbourne towards Poole, Bournemouth is now essentially a conurbation that runs continuously between the mouth of the Avon and Poole Harbour, and is home to nearly 350,000 people.

The lure of the south-east coast entailed massive 20th-century investment. Inter-war developments such as the modernist Saltdean Lido were joined after the Second World War by the new concept of holiday camps, as for example Butlins at Bognor (1960), and more recently by marinas such as those at Brighton and Portsmouth, which combine retailing, residential, boating and other leisure facilities in schemes that rank among Europe's largest leisure developments (Fig. 6.7). Brighton and Hove's seafront was in 2005 the subject of a proposal for a complex of sports centre and residences with futuristic towers, designed to replicate the billowing dresses of Edwardian ladies by the renowned American architect Frank Gehry. In addition, a host of other yachting and marine-associated leisure sites has taken full advantage of the heavily indented coastline, including the well-known Cowes development on the Isle of Wight. These buildings and their associated structures and sea defences reinforce the impression of a South Coast that is now almost continuously built-up from Poole in the west to Southend at the mouth of the Thames in the east.

DOCKYARD TOWNS AND PORTS

A distinctive element of the South East's urban development has been the alternating necessity to protect the vulnerable coastline from continental attack and to facilitate the movement of people and goods between England and the Continent. Towns have grown up around both these functions. Indeed London, as we shall see in the next chapter, had by 1700 attained a central role in an imperial and international system of defence and trade. It dominated other ports in the region, reducing many to a redistributive role or restricting them to the import of foreign goods. With monopolies over the East India and transatlantic trades it was truly a global port.

Coastal trade was highly significant throughout the region, especially for the movement of heavy products that would have been prohibitively expensive and difficult to deliver overland. Poole and Swanage, for example, sent large quantities of Purbeck stone slabs to London; by the end of the 18th century more than 50,000 tonnes left Swanage quayside each year. Vast quantities of hay and oats were also required to feed the enormous population of London's horses and these, too, tended to come by coastal shipment, as did the large amount of coal required to fuel the capital. All around the coast, quays, solid tall warehouses, coal drops, hoists, cranes and wharves were built to receive the necessities of urban life from the coasters; often the cargoes were transhipped on to lighters and canal barges for delivery to destinations that sea-going vessels could not reach. Most smaller ports such as Maldon (Essex) or Milton Regis (Kent) concentrated on this coastal trade, which primarily shipped grain to London on the Thames sailing barges and received luxury goods in return. Others such as Southampton, Deal, Poole, Rochester and Dover had more independent economies. Deal profited from the trade of her boatmen, plying (or 'hovelling') their luggers between their resting places on the shingle beach and larger merchant and Royal Naval vessels waiting offshore in the Downs, the stretch of water between the coast and the treacherous Goodwin Sands 6km offshore. During the Napoleonic Wars Deal's castle and

naval yard were also central to the region's defences. Further around the Kent coast, a large harbour was built at Ramsgate between 1820 and 1850, at a cost of nearly £2 million, to shelter trading vessels waiting offshore to enter the Thames. By contrast, some formerly significant towns could no longer accept the larger sea-going vessels that were coming into use: Chichester, Rye, Sandwich (Celia Fiennes's 'sad old town') and Winchelsea, for example. Indeed, with the exception of Dover with its passenger and packet traffic, the Cinque Ports 'long on splendour, short on trade' now served local markets only.

The older dockyards near London were Deptford, with its huge victualling yards, Woolwich and Greenwich. Sheerness (closed in 1960) was developed during the Dutch wars of the 17th century because of its deeper water facilities, and Chatham became the leading government dockyard; its fort and shipbuilding facilities employed about 1,000 people, making it probably the largest industrial employer in England, and possibly even in the world at this time. By 1700 both Chatham and Portsmouth were new arrivals to the list of significantly sized seaports. Chatham's population doubled during the 18th century, and in the early 19th century Fort Pitt (1805) and its new barracks brought still more inhabitants. These were naval towns rather than overseas trading ports; with their heavy government investment in shipbuilding and repair facilities they had grown significantly in importance. Chatham's dockyard closed finally in 1984.

The north Kent coast had also seen industrial expansion in the late 19th century and the cement works between Dartford and Gravesend had a huge impact on the landscape. The early Thames-side pits at Northfleet eventually became uneconomic and were abandoned as the industry moved south to Swanscombe, where long rows of terraced houses, in gridiron pattern, were built for the cement workers. The lower Darent valley supported paper manufacture from the 1860s, using logs and pulp from the Baltic and Canada; by the 1930s large mills dominated the scene, such as the Imperial Paper Mill at Gravesend, Bowater's paper mill at Northfleet and the Daily Telegraph paper mill at Dartford. Erith had armaments works (the Vickers factory operated there from 1898), chemical manufacturing and large coal wharves; with the addition of brick and gunpowder manufacture an industrial landscape came into being all along this part of the coast. The lower Medway similarly witnessed the coalition of Rochester, Strood, Chatham and Gillingham to form a single large conurbation in which both Chatham and Gillingham had populations in excess of 50,000 by 1911. By the 1920s the Isle of Grain had also become industrialised through the construction of oil-storage plants and refineries.

On the south coast, building land at Portsea was scattered among open-field strips to the north and east of Portsmouth old town and it was the disposition of the strips that determined the pattern of building development. Defoe had noted that the docks and yards were 'now like a town by themselves … there being particular rows of dwellings, built at the public charge, within the new works, for all the principal officers of the place'. Development was rapid during the Continental wars after 1750, and in the great expansion associated with the Napoleonic Wars nearly 4,000 dwellings were erected on individual or amalgamated strips in narrow streets, or

Fig. 6.8 Stone Street, Southsea, Portsmouth. Houses built in about 1811 during the Napoleonic building boom. No covenants existed at this time to control the façades and thus little unity of appearance was found.

in blocks where some prior enclosure had been effected. Names such as Albion Street mark the topical themes of the time. There were no large landowners or covenants to govern the appearance and structure of the new buildings; architectural merit was reserved only for more fashionable developments at Southsea after 1820. Instead, street frontages were narrow, sanitation appalling, and jerry-built houses of two storeys were often in multiple occupation (Fig. 6.8). Lodging houses, inns, music halls and brothels jostled with housing in the overcrowded alleys, where health was a constant problem. In 1846 Portsea was likened to one large cesspool. The whole of Portsea Island was enveloped in housing during the 19th century; between 1801 and 1821 the number of houses doubled, swallowing up former villages such as Buckland and Fratton. By 1871 the population of Portsea, as it was still known, had grown to 113,000, and to 231,000 by 1911. In the face of the fear of French attack, a massive scheme of fort-building and defence was put in place from the 1860s, as it was also further along the Sussex coast at Newhaven. Portsmouth's 19th-century military landscapes were largely destroyed, however, by the Blitz, when 65,000 homes out of a total 70,000 were destroyed or damaged by bombing; what remained was then swept away by urban redevelopment schemes of the late 20th century. A reminder of the real origins of Portsmouth can perhaps be best appreciated today in the Historic Dockyard, which houses such treasures as Nelson's HMS *Victory* and the Tudor warship *Mary Rose*, together with dry docks, blockmills and machinery, stores and engine houses.[15]

Along the Sussex coast, there was no comparable port development. The older ports and more modest ones such as Rye, Littlehampton and Chichester had decayed, and by this period much of the commerce had contracted to Shoreham and Newhaven. By the 1840s Shoreham was the leading Sussex port; by the middle of the century its lagoon, behind a shingle spit, had been canalised and enclosed. By the early 20th century the landscape was dominated by a power station, coal wharves, and brewing at nearby Portslade. Newhaven, at the mouth of the Ouse, grew when the Dieppe steamer service, operated by the London, Brighton & South Coast Railway, moved there from Kingston-by-Sea in 1847. The harbour was deepened in the 1860s and a large breakwater was built in the 1890s.

The one south coast port that demonstrated spectacular growth during the 19th century was Southampton. Although the town had grown northwards beyond the Bargate by the end of the 18th century, and then eastwards across drained marshland, the greatest period of growth lay ahead. By 1820 spa water from Southampton was sold only in bottles and sea-bathing in Southampton had largely ceased. Instead, a new dock was opened in the 1840s close to the new railway terminus, and a second followed in 1851. The tonnage and numbers of vessels here ranked Southampton fifth among all English ports, behind London, Liverpool, Newcastle and Hull. With its London connections, the port was used by the Royal Mail and the large ocean-going vessels of the P&O and Castle lines, followed later by the White Star and Cunard lines, which had transferred from Liverpool. The town's population reached nearly 120,000 by 1911, the year preceding the maiden voyage of the *Titanic* from the docks. The King George V dock was opened in 1933 to accommodate the largest of the world's liners, such as the *Queen Mary*, and the opulent Ocean Terminal for passenger reception was inaugurated in 1953. Southampton was heavily bombed during the Second World War; it has since been extensively redeveloped and is now a busy and successful deep-water port. Its natural deep-water harbour and unique double tide still allow unrestricted access for the world's largest vessels, including the huge *Queen Mary II*, which was launched in 2003. Southampton is now the UK's leading vehicle-handling port, has long been its principal cruise port, and is a major handler of containers. In addition, about 23 million tonnes of oil and petroleum-related products are handled at the refineries of Esso at Fawley, and BP at Hamble, each year. Early in the 21st century plans are being developed to expand this industrial-port landscape still further.

SUBURBAN GROWTH

The growth of the suburbs as an important component of the landscape of the South East was discussed in Chapter 4 and will be returned to again in connection with London in Chapter 7. Here we need only note that although suburbia is such a ubiquitous feature of the region's townscapes, it has since 1700 been thought of mainly as a locality for consumption rather than production. Immediately around the older urban centres, however, there might be zones of small workshops and artisan quarters, as for example in the North Laines area of Brighton, north of the older town. These areas met the requirements of the service industries and elite tastes of a growing town.

But in general the urban margin was no longer the landscape of noxious industries and those that were best relegated to space outside the city wall. It had now become a place for home-making and conspicuous consumption by those who, like Charles and Caroline Pooter in Brickfield Terrace, Holloway, could afford to separate home from workplace, and for those households where the wife's pivotal role was deemed to be synonymous with the home itself. The Pooters had a

> nice six-roomed residence, not counting basement, with a front breakfast-parlour. We have a little front garden; and there is a flight of ten steps up to the front door, which, by-the-by, we keep locked with the chain up ... We have a nice little back garden which runs down to the railway. We were rather afraid of the noise of the trains at first, but the landlord said we should not notice them after a bit, and took £2 off the rent. He was certainly right; and beyond the cracking of the garden wall at the bottom, we have suffered no inconvenience.[16]

In a world initially dominated by pedestrians, the 'walking suburb' had inevitably been of limited extent. Sedan chairs, horse-drawn carriages and cabs were expensive, but the extent of London's pollution and central finance and commercial activities was pushing more and more affluent families away from the health horrors of Thames-side (Fig. 6.9). The first introduction of detached and semi-detached single-family houses was at St John's Wood, London, in the 1790s (*see* Chapter 7). Initially limited in extent, the fashion for suburban living spread and as early as 1841 Kent's population was 55 per cent urban, a high figure outside the industrial Midlands and North, and in large measure due to suburbanisation. By contrast Wiltshire was 30.9 per cent urban and Dorset 36 per cent.

Physically, as well as culturally, the social classes of Victorian England were becoming segregated. In a world of 'separate spheres' the suburb has been held up as the complete antithesis of the slum, and yet the two urban landscapes have institutional if not spatial linkages. Both were the product of unregulated commerce. For example, the advent of the railways after 1840 found most railway companies vying for access to urban centres. This was not always

Fig. 6.9 'Father Thames introducing his offspring to the fair City of London'. This cartoon appeared in Punch *on 3 July 1858. Raw sewage and industrial pollution caused 'the Great Stink' in that year, bringing about the suspension of Parliament.*

FATHER THAMES INTRODUCING HIS OFFSPRING TO THE FAIR CITY OF LONDON.
(*A Design for a Fresco in the New Houses of Parliament.*)

DIPHTHERIA.   SCROFULA.   CHOLERA.

possible, but where it could be achieved lines, tunnels, embankments and viaducts sliced through existing areas of poor housing, thus creating new problems of overcrowding, homelessness and pollution, as well as still more degradation of the landscape. The railway arches themselves became newly available shelters for many destitute people. Neighbourhoods were dissected and dead-end streets created. In south London alone some 24,000 people were 'dishoused', mostly between the 1840s and 1860s. By contrast, those living in the suburbs travelled through and above the streets and houses of the poor, looking down upon the urban mix of slums, small industrial units and narrow thoroughfares of an older era. Income earned centrally might now be recycled as investment in the suburban housing boom, which in turn generated profits for builders and their suppliers, professionals connected with housing and the land, and financial interests.

Not all suburbs were spacious and green: an equally common image is of repetitive, rectilinear terrace housing around London, the monotony enforced by the economics of building, and the introduction of building by-laws from the 1840s which sought to set basic structural standards. Elsewhere suburbs engulfed older villages in which residual craft or service employments might endure as the suburban tide swept around them. Brighton expanded to encompass Hove, West Blatchington and Preston by the mid-19th century, and Patcham and Rottingdean in the early 20th century. Large numbers of villages were caught up in the spread of the great suburban continent of London (*see* Chapter 7) and the same, as noted above, occurred on a smaller scale at Portsmouth. The Victorian suburbs also had their churches – often large brick creations that reflected Anglican high church or Anglo-Catholic zeal, complemented by a dramatic return to Gothic architecture. The same principles might be applied to old grammar schools, which were escaping to more spacious surroundings in the suburbs. In 1868 Reading School reopened on the southern edge of the town in a new Gothic building designed by Alfred Waterhouse. But in most suburbs there were few, if any, shops, pubs or places of entertainment. Community centres were sometimes built but were often shunned or divisive, and some residents returned to live in the old town centre. Some never returned, however, and were buried in the large suburban cemeteries that were being developed to replace the over-full urban churchyards. And bringing a new landscape feature to the scene were the crematoriums, the first of which opened at St John's, Woking in 1885.

In the 20th century new housing projects were even more tightly constrained, and homogenised housing began to encircle many of the region's towns. To meet Ministry of Health specifications, the layouts of peripheral estates were now made up of curves, crescents and cul-de-sacs, rather than the linear street patterns of 19th-century terraces. Paint colours, door and fence designs, landscaping and 'street furniture' all reinforced the uniformity. Not all were privately developed. In the late 19th and early 20th centuries local-authority rehousing of inner urban families had begun on a large scale. From its creation in 1888 the London County Council (LCC) implemented many such schemes, using both cottage-style developments as at Totterdown Fields (1903) and blocks of flats as at Millbank (1897); these ideas were later adopted in many of the other region's large towns. By 1921 the eastern part of Brighton had areas of substandard housing on Carlton Hill that had already been recommended for clearance in the late 19th century. Now the Moulsecoomb estate grew as a suburb to the north, taking many of the rehoused families into good working-class housing. Unfortunately the process of renovation and rehousing was sometimes problematic. Families were disconnected from kinship and credit networks, and central areas witnessed the obliteration of streets and their associated senses of place. The Becontree Estate (Essex) is known as the largest council-housing estate in the world. It was built by the LCC 16km from the centre of London between 1921 and 1934 to provide Lloyd George's 'homes fit for heroes' for the better-off East End working families. More than 25,000 houses were built on compulsorily purchased farmland at Barking, Dagenham

ABOVE: *Fig. 6.10 The Becontree Estate, Dagenham, Essex, in the 1920s. Many of the LCC tenants were overwhelmed by the space and silence of their new landscape.*

BELOW: *Fig. 6.11 Urban landscape change. The demolition of the 1960s' concrete Tricorn Centre, Portsmouth, in 2004. The start of demolition was marked by fireworks, celebrations and wide media coverage. A developer-funded art project invited local people to comment on the building – most were in favour of its retention! A 'Tricornfest!' was held to mourn its passing.*

and Ilford, and 112,000 people moved to the area, many finding work at Ford's car plant at Dagenham, a mainstay of the local economy until it finally closed in 2002 (Fig. 6.10). At least 2,000 families came from Stepney alone. The new houses had gas and electricity, inside toilets, fitted baths and front and rear gardens, but there was still a high turnover of tenants. Other LCC out-county estates were developed, including Oxhey and Borehamwood in the Chilterns. Again in Essex, but created in the aftermath of the Second World War, Harold Hill was the largest LCC overspill estate, and one of the largest of its kind in Europe. Together with the southern part of the Borough of Havering, which lies in the Thames Gateway regeneration area (*see* Chapter 7), Harold Hill has started to attract significant levels of external funding to ameliorate the large amount of deprivation that had built up since its foundation.

Much of the older historic urban landscape of south-east England has been extensively changed and replaced. The turnover of buildings increased with

Victorian intervention and a desire to build larger, more imposing public monuments to prosperity. The replacement of old housing stock has been described above. But in many towns the greatest impact was made during the Second World War when large areas were devastated by bombing, and afterwards during energetic periods of urban re-planning. In Southampton 30 per cent of the housing stock was destroyed; post-war Canterbury was a patchwork landscape of weed-infested bomb sites and temporary single-storey 'pre-fabs'. City centre redevelopment became an ongoing post-war process, and since the 1950s ring-road engineering and the successive architectural styles of pedestrian shopping precincts have now replaced earlier urban layouts and vernacular building traditions. One mid-1960s' example of the 'New Brutalism' was the concrete Tricorn development in Portsmouth; it was referred to as one of the ugliest in Britain and was in its own turn demolished in 2004 (Fig. 6.11). Often it is council offices themselves that dominate the urban skyline in unfortunate styles, such as those belonging to Buckinghamshire County Council in Aylesbury or East Sussex County Council in Lewes.

Urgent rehousing and slum clearance was also tackled through the building of blocks of high-rise, high-density flats on the edges of towns. London boroughs accounted for 38 per cent of all high-rise developments before 1972 but many other authorities throughout the region followed suit where housing stress was most acute. Many peripheral estates were subsequently stigmatised as council housing of poor quality, as 'no-go' areas, and became highly visible and unpopular reminders of social deprivation and class difference. As a result, councils have more recently embraced the concept of renewal and refurbishment of housing stock, a policy made the more necessary by disasters such as the collapse of the Ronan Point flats in Newham in 1968. Many high-rise buildings have been demolished, and since 1974 designated Housing Action Areas and improvement grants have instead been used to concentrate funds and attention on the improvement of urban environmental quality. During the 1980s the 'right to buy' legislation of the Thatcher government also impacted on suburban council estates: those who bought their homes have often subsequently changed the appearance of them, with the result that new colours, neo-Georgian doors, PVC windows, patios and stone cladding now break up the formerly uniform landscape. Ironically this diversity has happened at the same time that many privately built estates at the town edge have been developed by the large house-building companies to more uniform designs. And finally, at the edge of most towns – often beyond the original ring road, now superseded by a by-pass – the low-level ranch-style hypermarket has appeared, complete with its large retail floor space, filling station and spacious car parking.

LINKING THE TOWNS: THE GROWTH OF COMMUNICATIONS

The advance of communications, promoting and also benefiting from urban growth, is an important facet in any examination of the relationship between urban life and urban landscape. This is not, of course, to deny its significance for the landscape of rural areas; although improved communications normally improved economic and social life in the countryside, the landscape itself could often be transformed for the worse. Access and mobility play a key role in both town and country. The significance of this for the spread of the suburb has been noted above, but the larger regional picture also needs to be addressed, especially the way in which improved communication affected towns and urban activities from 1700 onwards.

The first attempts to do more than rely on individual parishes to repair local roads came with the development of turnpiking. Large areas of the Weald had execrable roads in 1700, the 'bottomless clay' of which resisted winter travel; the easiest overland movements were instead along the drier chalk downlands, as long as bridges were in repair to cross the intercepting rivers. Linking by-roads (bostals) that ran down the chalk scarps were hollowed out into deeply rutted tracks that could be negotiated by saddle-horses but were impassable to wheeled traffic. In winter, many carrier services were suspended on the atrocious roads. Walpole wrote in 1749: 'If you love good roads, good inns, plenty of postillions and horses, be so kind as never to go into Sussex … Sussex is a great damper of curiosity.' And three years later, descending Silver Hill after a visit to Bayham

Abbey he remarked: 'The roads grew bad beyond all badness, the night dark beyond all darkness, our guide frightened beyond all frightfulness…'.[17] Over the Berkshire Downs and Salisbury Plain travellers often needed guides, or helpful shepherds, to make their way across open country with so few landmarks. Muddy, rutted tracks still characterised the roads approaching London, while wagons took several hours to negotiate Highgate Hill. In south Essex the heavy chalk-laden wagons coming from Purfleet caused great damage and congestion.

The turnpike roads, privately funded and operated on the basis of tolls, made a considerable difference. In Kent the first Turnpike Act was passed in 1709 for the improvement of the route to the Tunbridge Wells spa. But the turnpike era began in earnest in about 1750; within two decades most market towns, leisure resorts and ports were connected to London, to be followed from the 1770s by interconnecting cross-routes. As a result, coach services were speeded up and coaching inns now thrived, entering the era of their greatest importance, and bequeathing to us their familiar solid Georgian fronts, large inn signs, double doorways and inner courtyards. Many older routes were now abandoned as easier gradients were sought. The new road built across fields between Epsom and Guildford by-passed the springline villages at the base of the chalk, leaving them connected by the superseded loops of the old road. Thereafter standards were raised still further by engineering improvements, most notably those brought about under the influence of J L McAdam in the early 19th century.

Between 1790 and 1835 English road passenger transport, much of it on the expanding stage-coach network, increased 16-fold, and national carrier operations similarly grew through companies such as Pickfords. By 1820 the fastest coaches could now run between London and Brighton in less than five hours, allowing, as Cobbett noted with disgust, 'dark, dirty-faced, half-whiskered tax-eaters' to commute from Brighton to London. He also noted that 'Those who travel on turnpike roads know nothing of England – from Hascombe to Thursley almost the whole way across fields or commons, or along narrow lanes. Here we see the people without any disguise or affectation. Against a *great road* things are made for *show*.'[18] Nevertheless, by 1837 there were 50 trusts in Kent alone, responsible for over 1,000km of turnpike, and more than one-third of all the roads in Middlesex had been turnpiked – far in excess of most of the northern and western counties of England. Places such as Hounslow and Newbury bustled with activity as the many coaches passed through. But in Sussex the last authorisation of a turnpike scheme was in 1841, significantly the year in which the London to Brighton railway opened. With such competition, the turnpike trusts struggled to continue profitably and all the Sussex trusts were wound up between 1864 and 1885.

Other landscape features very necessary for the functioning of the road system were its bridges and tunnels, the latter exemplified by the twin entrances of the Rotherhithe Tunnel beneath the Thames that was begun in 1824 and finally opened for pedestrians in 1843. Bridges were repaired and built out of county rates and the expenditure could be heavy and unpredictable. In 1725 'great rains and flouds' destroyed stone arches and damaged the bridge at Redbridge that carried the main road west from Southampton.[19] Brentford Bridge was periodically repaired and reconstructed before 1760, and the cost of the new Fulham and Westminster bridges at this time was also large. With the expansion of turnpiking, more bridge expenditure had to be undertaken, especially for long-distance coach and wagon services between London and provincial towns. Robert Mylne's Blackfriars Bridge (1768–70) was impressive and the same man later undertook commissions at Tonbridge and Romsey.

In contrast to this activity on the roads, the South East never enjoyed the heyday of canals experienced in other regions. Although several rivers were improved to allow more efficient carriage of agricultural produce in the late 18th and early 19th centuries, including the financing of the Chichester Canal by the Earl of Egremont in 1817, the only important waterways constructed at this time were those that provided links to the Thames or that served a military use. The Grand Junction Canal was London's main canal link with the Midlands and the North. From the Thames at Brentford, the canal ascends some 130m into the Chilterns until, after a climb of 56 locks in 50km, it reaches the 4km-long Tring Summit. Here the descent northwards commences towards Braunston on the Oxford Canal. Fully opened by 1805, the Grand Junction had an arm to Paddington, where there was a large basin served by wharves, a hay and straw market, sheds for warehousing and pens for livestock. Paddington soon became a busy inland transhipment point from which goods, especially coal, were carted to other parts of London. The Regent's Canal was built to link the Grand Junction's Paddington Arm at Little Venice, which opened in 1801, with the Thames at Limehouse. This was finally opened in 1820, but although it was initially very successful it soon ran into financial problems, like all such ventures, because of competition from the railway. The last horse-drawn cargo was pulled along the canal in 1956, and it is instead now well known as a leisure-boating venue.

London was also linked to the Severn by canal in 1789, and to Bristol by the Kennet and Avon canal, which opened in 1810. Built across the Berkshire Downs, the latter also served Hungerford, Newbury and Reading, and brought Somerset coal into the London Basin to compete with the seaborne trade. The Chelmer and Blackwater Navigation was opened in 1797 to improve access from Chelmsford to the Heybridge Basin on the Blackwater estuary. This avoided Danbury Hill, which was difficult for wagons, and provided a route for timber and coal imports to the Chelmsford area. The Wey and Arun Canal (known as 'London's lost route to the sea') opened in 1816 and was designed to link the South Coast with the Thames via the Wey. Somewhat different was the Royal Military Canal between Hythe and Winchelsea. This hugged the old cliffline around the inner edge of Romney Marsh and was built in 1806 to facilitate troop and supply movements in the event of Napoleonic threats. It remains perhaps the best preserved of the region's waterways outside London, although all such canals now have their devoted followers.

The greatest revolution in communications, until the new electronic age of the 20th century, was that of the railways. There was a modest beginning: the horse-drawn Surrey iron railway operated along the Wandle valley between Wandsworth and Croydon between 1803 and 1846, and the first steam-powered passenger and goods line opened in 1830 between Canterbury and Whitstable, for a while using George Stevenson's *Invicta* locomotive. But thereafter every major line focused on the capital and a piecemeal network of lines radiated from the London termini to all but the most remote parts of the region; by 1845 the entire region was accessible from London within four hours, and by 1910 within two hours, rather than the 12 hours of 1836 or the 18 hours of 1821. The railway reached the outer edges of the region relatively quickly: Southampton in 1840, Brighton in 1841, Chelmsford by 1842 and Dorchester (circuitously via Southampton) by 1847. The impact of this growth upon the canals and turnpikes of the region was swift, as their revenues dwindled. The Kennet and Avon canal was purchased by the Great Western Railway company in 1852 and its traffic was allowed to decline slowly. The maximum extent of the railway network was reached by the 1930s, but contracted in the 1960s as a result of the cost-cutting measures recommended by the Beeching Report.

The railways made an impact on the landscape of the South East in several different ways. The first was the direct effect of the huge construction works involved in the creation of their tunnels, embankments, viaducts, railway inns, docks and stations (Fig. 6.12). The London and Birmingham Railway (LBR) opened in 1838 and its Tring cutting in Buckinghamshire was 4km in length and an average of 13m deep. The earth was shifted by labourers using picks, shovels and wheelbarrows, and horses pulled the men and barrows up the sides of the embankment. The LBR terminus was at Euston station, where the great Euston Arch of 1838 symbolised the new age, proudly standing higher, it was claimed,

TOP: *Fig. 6.12 Balcombe viaduct, Sussex.*
This viaduct contains 11 million bricks and was
opened on 12 July 1841 to carry the London,
Brighton and South Coast Railway. It is
probably the most impressive of the great
railway viaducts of Victorian England, with 37
brick arches stretching across the upper reaches
of the Ouse valley for a distance of some 450m.

ABOVE: *Fig. 6.13 The entrance portico,*
Euston Grove Station, from 'Drawings
of the London and Birmingham
Railway' by John Britton, published in
1838 by John Cooke Bourne. It was
nearly 22m high and had stone lodges on both
sides, each with a grand Doric central door
and linked together by ornamental gates. Its
demolition in 1961–2 was controversial.

than any other building in London at the time (Fig. 6.13). The earliest of the
London termini was actually London Bridge (1836); Waterloo opened in 1848;
the London terminus of the Great Northern Railway at Kings Cross opened in
1852 on a 19ha site erasing many poor streets and the old smallpox and fever
hospitals; and others followed soon after. The present Paddington station, where
a virtual new town sprang up, became operational in 1854 (replacing a short-
lived earlier version opened in 1845), Victoria in 1860 and St Pancras in 1863 –
the train shed of the latter being at that time the largest covered space in the
world. The last to be opened was Marylebone in 1899. The visual impact of these
ostentatious engineering and architectural works was immense, and the grandeur
of their associated hotels, such as Sir George Gilbert Scott's Grade I Gothic
Midland Grand Hotel above St Pancras or the Great Western Hotel at
Paddington, was impressive.[20]

The second impact of the railways was on pre-existing settlement. Although in
many country towns the station was built at the edge of the existing built-up area,
in London the lines sliced through or over (occasionally tunnelling under) the
city's poorer suburban houses, polluting them with blackness from viaducts such
as that which ran between Deptford and London Bridge. The Midland Railway's

route displaced Agar Town, a collection of knackers' yards, refuse and rag collectors, brick kilns and gasworks.[21]

Thirdly, and more positively, there was the impetus given to new settlements that now grew around railway stations, as at the wealden towns of Haywards Heath, Hassocks, Burgess Hill and Crowborough. Centres of gravity could shift: thus old Heathfield was superseded by a newer settlement near the station; old market towns such as Horsham or East Grinstead were now recipients of middle-class villa-dom; and coastal towns such as Brighton expanded to suburbanise surrounding villages. And fourthly there was the impact of the railways on the rural scene as farmers continued to specialise their production to the needs of urban markets: in the depressed years of the late 19th century the dairy cow became a much more prominent feature of the region's claylands since milk could be sent quickly to the capital by train (*see* Chapter 5). A fifth impact of the railway was the reinforcement of London's centrality to England, not just in economic and social terms but symbolically too: the need to align local timetables entailed the universal adoption of Greenwich Mean Time in 1848. In 1851 the huge influx of people by rail to visit the Great Exhibition confirmed London as the centre of the Empire.

Of course, innovations in transport did not end with the surface railway mania. In 1861 the first London tramway was laid temporarily along the Uxbridge Road, and the first permanent horse-drawn services operated in south London from the 1870s, to be followed by open-topped electrified trams from the 1880s and 1890s. And in 1863 the first London underground service had also opened between Paddington and Farringdon Street, at first based on steam traction but later employing the concept of the electric tramway. This and similar ventures allowed genuine mass transport through the availability of low fares and avoided some of the traffic jams being caused by the varieties of transport above ground in central London. The huge success of London's underground mass transport system is confirmed by its spread to Hendon by 1923, to Morden in the south by 1926, and by the fact that more than 140 years later the network, now some 400km long, is still being expanded. The impact of the underground railway was not simply in terms of the distinctive new modernist stations that appeared as foci in the townscape, complete with their illuminated signs (with a common logo from 1908), escalators or lifts, shops and services, but in the impetus it gave to the spread of London's suburbs, especially in the late 19th and early 20th centuries. The percentage of London's population living in the central area fell from 48 per cent in 1851 to 24 per cent by 1891, a trend that continued for most of the 20th century as well.

Equally important was the rapid diffusion of cycling after the invention of the safety bicycle in 1885; the bicycle allowed work, leisure and courting journeys to be faster or longer, and thereby enabled suburban growth to edge that little bit further out. Even more revolutionary, of course, was the application of the internal combustion engine to light vehicles. Initially motor cars were seen as a luxury for the wealthy, but by 1904 about 30,000 cars and motor cycles were registered in Britain, of which 15 per cent were in London – although a census of traffic in London in 1913 found that 88 per cent of London's goods vehicles were still drawn by horses. London's motor hackney cabs had nevertheless become a feature of the landscape by 1903, and motor buses replaced horse-drawn vehicles by 1911.

The consequent growth of the motor car during the 20th century is too well known to need repeating here. For the South East the consequences have been huge and whole landscapes have indeed been changed as a result. By the inter-war period, reliance had once again switched back to road transport at the expense of rail. The impact on the landscape of Salisbury has been described in vivid terms:

> *Between 1932 and 1936 the motor car effected a profound change in what might be called the townscape of Salisbury. Much that is now taken for granted in any street scene originated in those five years, and has been only*

Fig. 6.14 London's Heathrow Airport.
The inset shows the small hamlet of Heath Row surrounded by orchards and market gardens before the development of the airport. In the photograph, Heath Row has been obliterated in this most dramatic of landscape changes. Heathrow Airport today is an international air-travel hub of the highest importance.

little modified since. The first car park was constructed – on the site of the present coach station – and the first car park charges levied. For the first time a decision was taken to demolish buildings – in Salt Lane – to make way for a car park. The first parking restrictions – in Castle Street – were imposed. The first one-way streets – Fish Row and Butcher Row – were designated. Traffic lights were placed at strategic junctions. Pedestrian crossings made their first appearance. Thirty mile per hour speed limit signs were erected at all the entrances to the city. And the first police patrol car was bought to ensure that they were observed.[22]

Arterial roads, by-passes, routes such as London's North Circular and Western Avenue, and typical inter-war parades of by-pass shops accumulated. And in the last 50 years or so the landscape impact has continued in the form of parking meters, large car parks, many of which were originally on bombed sites, yellow lines and assorted signage. People now drive more, walk and interact less, and the street has become a more dangerous environment for children's play. Only new towns such as Bracknell, designed around the concept of the car as integral to modern life, offer a landscape at ease with the motor vehicle. Here wide dual carriageways, plentiful parking, numerous roundabouts, landscaping and tree planting have helped considerably.

Like the railways a century before, the motorway system of the mid-20th century has had an immense impact on the landscape, taking swathes of farmland in an attempt to speed up journey times (*see* Fig. 5.11) and creating new mini-towns at its service centres. As with virtually every form of communication since the Roman period, London is the focus of these motorways: up until the 1950s, the biggest civil engineering project ever to have been undertaken in Britain was the construction of the M1 motorway, which opened in November 1959. Since then, further motorways have linked the capital with the rest of Britain, and in 1994 they connected it to the Continent via the M2 motorway and Channel Tunnel.

Rapid advances have also been made in air-passenger travel. Originally this was based at small local airfields, such as Shoreham in Sussex (the 1936 art deco terminal of which is now a listed building) and Croydon, which served London from 1920, but the late 20th century witnessed great investment and landscape change in the controversial expansion of the larger airports in the South East. Heathrow, opened in 1946 between Hounslow, Staines and Slough, remains the one of the world's busiest international airports and its huge complex of runways, terminals and associated buildings creates an environment of its own. The airport, which now employs 60,000 workers and is almost a self-contained city, began as the Great Western Aerodrome, privately owned by the Fairey company. In 1944 the government requisitioned it as a major transport base for the Royal Air Force, although in reality it was always intended for commercial use. Before the work of conversion was completed the war ended, and with it came the prospect of a huge expansion in civil aviation, especially in the London area. When the Ministry of Civil Aviation took it over in 1946 one runway was ready for use and an army surplus tent served as a terminal. By the following year three runways had been completed and a new, permanent building arose in the central area at the start of the 1950s. An ever-increasing demand for passenger facilities saw the opening of a second terminal building in 1955, followed by the new Oceanic terminal (now Terminal 3) for long-haul carriers in 1961 and of Terminal 1 in 1968. Increased congestion in the central area led to the birth of Terminal 4 in 1986 on the south side of the airport and a fifth terminal is due to open in 2008. In 1977 the London Underground was extended to Heathrow, and express railway links are also open.

The hamlet of Heath Row (located approximately where Terminal 3 is sited now) was once surrounded by fields and market gardens; in the years since the Second World War it has been transformed (Fig. 6.14). The landscape of this

quiet corner of Middlesex was obliterated by the airport's expansion. Hangars, runways, roads, hotels, warehouses and terminal buildings now cover the hamlet's site. The British Aviation Authority has already received permission to build a fifth passenger terminal and yet more expansion, possibly involving the destruction of adjacent residential areas, is likely.

The region also has other major international airports at Gatwick (the world's sixth busiest airport), Stansted and Luton, other important international airports at Bournemouth, Eastleigh, London City (in the old docklands) and Southend, and smaller facilities at Manston, Biggin Hill, Lydd, Farnborough and Shoreham. Although in December 2003 a new airport at Cliffe, on Thameside marshes, was ruled out, further expansion at Stansted (to the probable detriment of nearby Hatfield Forest) now seems likely. Acting as magnets for business and seen by some as drivers of the regional and national economy, these sites, with their distinctive landscapes, are nevertheless seen by others as environmentally destructive and polluting.

Some innovations may have begun to reduce the need for travel. The increase in literacy that allowed communication through the mail expanded further with the launch of the 'penny post' in 1840 – no fewer than 168.8 million letters were handled in that first year. Improved communication also came with the introduction of telegraph and telephone; London had the first exchange in 1879 and by the outbreak of the First World War still accounted for 33 per cent of all calls. Here was the first real opportunity for the substitution of instantaneous electronic communication for physical movement. A call could save a journey, and the technology has continued to advance to the point at which instantaneous global information and communication is now available to a large majority of the region's population through home computers and mobile telephones. The impacts on the landscape – other than the earlier plethora of telegraph posts and wires and the more recent but equally contentious rash of mobile-phone telecommunications masts on prominent hillsides – have yet to unravel, but the flexibility and freedom to work from home or on the move will undoubtedly affect the appearance of both urban and rural landscapes in the decades to come.

NOTES

1 Ellis 2000, 679.
2 Borsay 2000, 99–124.
3 Jones & Falkus 1990, 141; Steer 1962, 18.
4 Rosen 1981, 172–3.
5 Hardy 1886 (1965 edn), 94.
6 Chalklin 1998, 20.
7 Porter 1990, 19–33; Corfield 1982, 176.
8 Conzen 1981, 63.
9 VCH Wiltshire IV 1959, 318–26; VCH Middlesex III, 1962, 25.
10 Defoe 1971 edn, 171.
11 Clark & Slack 1976, 35.
12 Brandon 1977, 92–3.

13 Whyman 1973, 138, 156; Berry 2005; Rutherford 2003; Jones 2005.
14 Dickens & Gilbert 1981, 206.
15 Chalklin 1974, 122–8; Defoe 1971 edn, 151; Bettey 1986, 246.
16 Grossmith 1892, 1.
17 Walpole 1906, 178.
18 Cobbett 1985 edn, 240.
19 Chalklin 1998, 112.
20 Brindle 2004.
21 Armstrong 2000, 215.
22 Chandler 1983, 151.

7

London Lives, Landscapes and Reactions

London – its origins, its growth, its appetite and its leadership – sits at the heart of the South East. Town and country have always been interlinked and during the 20th century the city and its countryside became virtually inseparable; during the 21st century we can even start to imagine that the continued urbanisation of the South East will force us to redefine the distinction altogether. Although this book is focused on landscape, a subject that is frequently seen in rural terms, we cannot omit London from the discussion and its landscape must therefore be treated in full. The city also has a townscape or cityscape of its own that deserves independent analysis.

It is nevertheless with enormous trepidation that the rich complexity of the landscape of London is now approached head-on. In previous chapters the growth, influence and simply the presence of this global city within the South East have been impossible to ignore, since London's very dominance, in both scale and kind, pervades so much of the region. The task is daunting because the visual impact of London's multi-centred landscape is so kaleidoscopic that it is impossible to render an account that is all-encompassing. In writing its biography Peter Ackroyd has returned to the image of London as a human body which 'cannot be conceived in its entirety but can be experienced only as a wilderness of alleys and passages, courts and thoroughfares, in which even the most experienced citizen may lose the way … London is so large and wild that it contains no less than everything …'.[1] It is a diffuse and unruly city – a law and a life unto itself. It did not become a legal entity until the London County Council was established in 1888, although even then its built-up reality exceeded its legal boundaries.

London's growth and power, however, has always out-paced its narrowly drawn bounds. In Roman times it was the province's main city but appears to have lacked a formal legal status: it seems almost to have simply created itself, to have wrested the functions of capital from *Camulodunum* (Colchester) and to have overtaken the municipal vigour of *Verulamium* (St Albans), just as in the late Saxon and Anglo-Norman period it ousted Winchester as the primary site of the royal courts and *de facto* royal capital. Medieval kings courted it, and feared its unconstrained political will; in the Civil War it tipped the scales more than once and soon afterwards, after its Great Fire, it refused to be 'planned' and made 'fashionable', turning its back on the grand designs of those who wanted to change its character. In the 19th century it outgrew its region and its country and became the hub of a world empire. London as a 'world city' is a cliché, but if such a thing actually exists, then it is London: its population is one of the most ethnically and demographically diverse in the world and few of the world's languages are not being spoken in its streets and houses.

TABLE 7.1 THE GROWTH OF LONDON'S POPULATION (IN THOUSANDS).

Date	The City	Rest of London	Total London	England and Wales	London as percentage of England and Wales
c. 200	20		20	1,000	2
c. 1100	15		15	1,500	1
c. 1400	45		45	2,250	2
c. 1500	75		75	3,000	2.5
c. 1600	186	34	220	4,500	5
c. 1700	208	367	575	6,000	9.6
1801	128	831	959* (1,117)+	8,890	10.8 (12.6)
1851	128	2,235	2,363* (2,685)+	17,983	13.1 (14.9)
1901	27	4,398	4,425* (6,586)+	32,612	13.6 (20.2)
1951	5	8,188	8,193+	43,758	18.7
2001	7.2	7,165	7,172^	52,042^	13.8

* Total London defined as The City plus rest of LCC area

+ The City plus rest of GLC area

^ Revised 2001 census data, to help correct under-enumeration, now puts London's population at 7,307 and that for England and Wales at 52,277, the proportion being 14 per cent.

Source: Mitchell and Deane 1962; http://www.statistics.gov.uk/census2001/.

London has always been 'too big' for its country, let alone its region. A useful context is to consider population growth (Table 7.1), and to remark in passing that the proportion of the entire country's population living in its capital city was surpassed in Europe only by Amsterdam during its Golden Age in the 17th century. Part of London's impact comes from the fact that it has for most of its life been several cities rolled into one – mercantile centre, the focus of national government, the primary royal palace and so on.

Before turning chronologically to the development of the London landscape, it would be helpful to recognise six main components and functions:

- the City of London itself, within the walls, the Roman core and port, and much later and still today, its financial centre
- the crown and governmental power base at Westminster
- the later wave of development on the gravel terrace between the two, much of it planned
- expansion to the east of the City, particularly in relation to the post-medieval and modern port
- the development of the south bank of the Thames at Southwark, with its own vibrant independent Roman origins, and
- the once separate settlements that have been gradually subsumed by London's physical growth through the building of villas, estates and ribbon development.

The chronological development and townscape differences within these six components are the subject of this chapter. What cannot be offered is a detailed account of architectural finesse or of the minutiae of building styles and components, which must be left to the many magnificent volumes of English Heritage's ongoing *The Survey of London* (begun in 1900), the closest thing we have to an 'official' topographical history of the capital. Some reference will be made to such essentials of the landscape that in their juxtapositioning, symbolism and holistic patterning give character to London, but in the main we must rest content here with an overview of change in this most complex of all England's built landscapes.

EARLY LONDON LANDSCAPES

The enormous amount of redevelopment in London since the end of the Second World War has enabled the discovery of a great deal of new knowledge of its Roman, Saxon and medieval past. Although there was much prehistoric settlement in the Thames valley, and the river itself provided a trading route and potential farmland on its lower terraces, London emerges as an important settlement site and landscape entity only with the Roman occupation (Fig. 7.1). Major Roman arterial roads still create the fundamental skeleton of parts of the city, and the Roman city walls still mark the boundaries of 'The City'. The military Watling Street, aligned on Marble Arch and an early crossing at Westminster, was moved downstream and timber revetting was used to secure the bank of the river, then considerably wider than today. The earliest wooden London Bridge was constructed from the river terrace on the north bank of the Thames to the sandbanks that offered access to the south side of the river, and it also had a harbour at its northern end. On rising ground at Ludgate Hill and Cornhill, *Londinium* developed, with the lower ground of the Fleet, Shoreditch and Walbrook (to the north) offering good defensive views. During the Boudiccan revolt (AD 60) London was attacked and burnt, an assault now dramatically marked by a red layer in the archaeological horizon. A similar layer has also been revealed in recent excavations at the new Jubilee Line site at Southwark, proving that a suburb – indeed an independent town – existed here at that time. *Londinium* was rebuilt – heavy timber quays dated to AD 70 mark the new harbour site, and the provincial administration now moved here, with a palace, forum (by AD 80–100), amphitheatre and the Cripplegate fort.

Fig. 7.1 Roman London in the early 2nd century, looking north-west. The broad width of the Thames has been bridged from Southwark, with the road continuing towards the forum-basilica. The Walbrook stream enters the Thames to the west of the bridge, and beyond is the amphitheatre, which could potentially seat some 8,000 spectators, and the fort in the north-west corner of the city boundary. A major fire destroyed much of this structure in about AD 125.

The houses were mostly wooden and of a single storey, with floors of beaten earth and with pigs and chickens kept among piles of refuse. Although squalid to modern sensibilities, the shops, baths, arena (on the site of the 15th-century Guildhall) and the port proclaimed London's importance. In the late 2nd century its defensive circuit enclosed over 130ha, the largest of any town in the province.

By the 3rd century, however, the public baths at Huggin Hill and Cheapside had fallen into disuse and were demolished, as was the governor's palace in the 4th century. There is evidence for a build-up of soils over Roman floors and streets, signifying dumping, decay and possible re-use for stock pens. The Wallbrook, flowing through the city, was now left to form a marsh outside the wall at the Moorfield, near Broadgate. To date, there have been few early Saxon finds within the walls of *Londinium*, and it appears that the city was effectively abandoned, although its site, bridging point, line of walls and place-memory were too important to be completely erased. And because this 'failure' was probably a failure of its Roman context rather than any inherent failure of the city itself, it was not long before it came back to life. In the post-Roman centuries the need to locate lordship, religion and trade (state, church and the city) returned here. In 604 King Æthelbehrt of Kent, London's overlord, ordered the construction of St Paul's Cathedral near the old Roman fort at Cripplegate, with a possible royal residence to the north, and by the 630s there was a mint. And importantly, by the late 7th century a thriving port had been established to the west of the Roman city at *Ludenwic*, along the Strand foreshore between the rivers Fleet and Tyburn; the beaches where ships were pulled up from the river is now buried deep beneath the reclaimed streets and gardens of this part of London. The earliest confirmed date for this development is 679, but it is unlikely that palace and 'cathedral' could possibly have preceded trade. *Ludenwic* expanded inland to reach its peak in about 800, by which time there is evidence of streets, tenements and alleys. It became the largest of all the English mid-Saxon trading settlements that bore the name *wic* (eg Ipswich, Norwich, or Hamwic at Southampton) and its local and more distant trade dealt with imports of wine, pottery, glass and quern stones, and exports of slaves, cloth and agricultural produce. This commercial importance was underlined by elite and ecclesiastical residences, as bishops and nobility moved in. The area as far north as Cheapside was acquired by Westminster Abbey by the mid-10th century, but the trading centre was not to be long-lasting. Instead, it moved downstream again, back into the former city, leaving behind the 'old wic' (Aldwych), which to this day is still the important physical and psychological connection between the City and Westminster. The move downriver brought the land on the east of the Fleet into Alfred's stronghold system as *Lundenburh* following the seizure of London from Viking control in 886. A commercial centre, streets and beaching area now developed back within the safety of the old walls. Its streets led into the city from the river frontage and linked with the east–west Cheapside, which was intended as the principal market place.

LONDON'S MEDIEVAL LANDSCAPES

London was more than just a flourishing international port when William I came to it. For at least half a century it had been the largest city by far in England; it already governed itself, through institutions such as the 'folkmoot' that met in St Paul's churchyard. William's whole military campaign after Hastings was designed to isolate and win over the city; he chose to be crowned in Westminster, as, hurriedly, Harold had been less than a year earlier. This was in contrast to the traditional royal choice of Winchester – although interestingly Edward the Confessor, while crowned at Winchester, had been elected king by the men of London, and was buried in his new church at Westminster. All this is surely an indicator of London's important place in the wider European world of that time.

William came to a city that already had a life of its own; having expanded rapidly in the 11th century it had an estimated population of 15,000 by 1100, although this was probably still far less than in the mid-Roman period. A Benedictine abbey was formed by St Dunstan in about 960 in place of the Saxon church of St Peter-on-Thorney (785), which had been built originally to serve *Ludenwic*; thereafter royal interest in the site ensured its continuous development. Further upriver, the great Romanesque cruciform abbey at Westminster and the nearby palace were finished months before the Norman conquest, with Edward the Confessor drawn – 'summoned' indeed – to the site by London itself:

> *... it lay hard by the famous and rich town of London and also was a delightful spot, surrounded by fertile lands and green fields and near the main channel of the river, which bore abundant merchandise of wares of every kind for sale from the whole world to the town on its banks.*[2]

Edward was buried here in January 1066; Harold was crowned here on the same day, as was William I on Christmas Day of the same year. Although the 126th folio of Domesday Book, where an account of London should be found, is missing, its royal status was now confirmed. At the end of the 11th century Westminster became the location of the astonishing 73m-long and 20m-wide Great Hall of William Rufus, larger than any comparable building in England at that time. In the 12th century came the Exchequer and later still the royal courts of justice. Henry III's patronage of Westminster Abbey initiated its reconstruction from 1245; thereafter, parliaments met regularly in the chapter house of the Abbey and from the 16th century in St Stephen's Chapel at the palace. From the 13th century growth was constant here and the link between the royal court and ecclesiastical centre brought many visitors and officials for public and ceremonial occasions. Many alterations and embellishments have been made since, including Edwards III's Jewel Tower and Richard II's rebuilding of the Great Hall with a new and elaborate roof (Fig. 7.2).

William I had a wooden castle hastily built at the Watergate at the south-east corner of the city, with the fortified nobleman's residence of Baynard's Castle and the Montfitchet Tower built similarly at the south-west corner. The wooden castle was replaced as soon as practical by the present White Tower, a solid keep

Fig. 7.2 View of Westminster from the River (Civitas Westmonasteriensis pars), by Wenceslaus Hollar, 1647. *The etching shows St Stephen's Chapel ('Parliament House') to the left, Westminster Hall and the Abbey.*

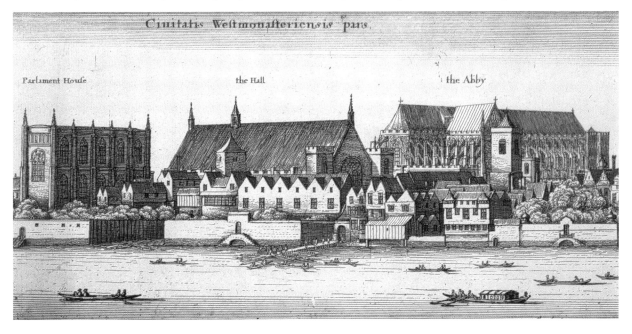

built of stone robbed from the Roman walls together with imported Caen stone from Normandy, which was completed in 1097. In the 13th century Henry III and Edward I expanded the Tower of London beyond the Roman walls. It remains impressive to this day and is unparalleled in size and completeness in any other European capital; its status was reflected in its designation as a World Heritage Site in 1988.

London formally became a capital city with the withdrawal of the Crown from Winchester to London under Henry II, and especially under Edward I. Processions and pageantry added to the splendour, and civic displays of wealth – such as the Corpus Christi processions, for which Cheapside was particularly favoured, or the Lord Mayor's procession to Westminster – were emblematic of the negotiation between City and royal power. There were also more than 100 parish churches, dominated by Westminster and the Gothic St Paul's, together with the religious precincts of monasteries, nunneries, the Dominican Blackfriars and others. By the 12th century London was the country's leading ecclesiastical centre, the home of charities, schools and hospitals as well as churches. These included the large priory and hospital of St Bartholomew at Smithfield (1123), the Norman chancel, transepts and restored Lady chapel of which remain and give it a seniority among City churches despite the loss of its nave to the Dissolution speculators. The Priory of the Holy Trinity within Aldgate is gone, and others such as the nunnery church of St Helen's, Bishopsgate survive as parts of places of worship that still exist on their sites. South of the river was Southwark Cathedral, originally the Priory of St Mary Overy, and Lambeth Palace – the riverside base of the Archbishops of Canterbury from the 1190s. More than 50 parish churches were enlarged or rebuilt in the 15th century, although at the Dissolution their enclaves were much sought after for redevelopment and their landscapes transformed by subdivision.

Although population densities were extremely high within the walls, there were open spaces too, prominent among which were gardens, orchards, areas for cattle markets and spaces for the processing of cloth. Markets were small and specialised, serving different parts of the city. Outside the old Roman walls of the city the Knights Templars established themselves immediately to the west, although the order was later suppressed and its property partly leased to a body of lawyers, thereby originating a legal precinct that became the Inns of Court. Further west again were separate villages such as Chelsea; until the 17th century the Saxon settlement by the church and Thames was the only known area of settlement in the parish. Most of the parish was covered by two large open arable fields, Eastfield and Westfield, which were separated by Church Lane. North of the City, the upper reaches of the Walbrook were still marshy; this was a place for skaters in hard winters and the Moorfields remained an open space until effectively drained in the 17th century. Slaughterhouses and livestock markets were moved from within the walls to Smithfield outside the City, and likewise the tanners were moved from the lower Fleet valley to Bermondsey, south of the Thames. The port was to the east of the walls and attracted migrants and poor housing to an eastern suburb – an incipient East End. And beyond the ruling powers of the City, Southwark grew towards its 16th-century character as a conglomeration of taverns, brothels, bear-gardens and bull-rings, and noxious tanning, soap-making and lime-burning industries. On the south bank were several prisons, including the Clink and the Marshalsea in Southwark, but also the great town houses of churchmen from all over the South East.

During the 13th century London stretched for 5km from Whitechapel to Westminster, through crowded streets. The map of 1572 by Braun and Hogenberg shows London with an extent and density of building that was much the same as it would have been at the end of the 13th century (Fig. 7.3). House, shop and workshop frontages on to important thoroughfares could be very narrow – as little as 3 or 4m – and there was much subdivision, with gardens often containing still

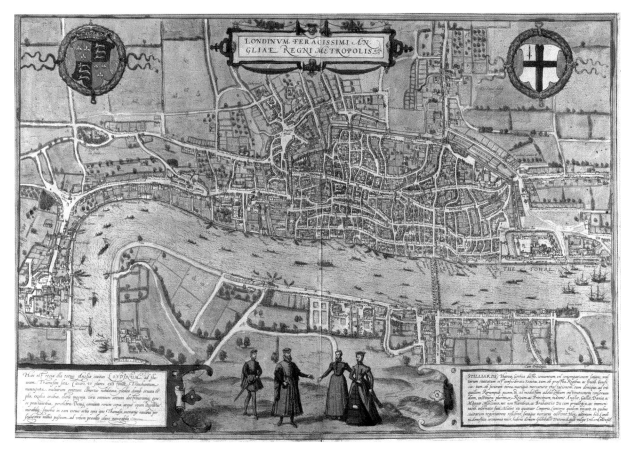

smaller clusters of cottages accessed through alleyways. Three storeys and a cellar gave vertical space but the maze of passages, courtyards and alleys was often tortuous and evil-smelling. The medieval fabric of London was decaying and insanitary, and also easily destroyed – a fire in 1087, for example, had destroyed St Paul's, although it was quickly rebuilt but still making much use of timber. The use of thatch was banned in 1189 in favour of tiles. Human life, too, could be fragile in these crowded conditions; in 1348–50 the Black Death claimed up to half the city's population, with the dead being shovelled into plague pits at Smithfield.

The line of the Roman city wall, much rebuilt and with the Tower of London at its south-east corner, St Paul's cathedral with its spire and London Bridge (constructed by 1209 but demolished in 1832) all remained dominant landscape features. The last of these was seen as a wonderful creation with its 19 arches, drawbridge (which was pulled up at curfew), chapel and fine houses; it also acted as a weir to separate the river traffic from sea-going vessels, moored downstream in what became the Pool of London. This latter was part of the transformation of the waterfront that took place between the 10th and 12th centuries and involved the construction of large new warehouses, mills and fisheries. The wall along the waterfront was retained until it collapsed in the 12th century. Although it was not rebuilt, the reclamation of land on the south side of medieval London through the use of increasingly sophisticated timber or stone revetments and masonry river walls may have added as much as 15 per cent to the area of London, with new narrow lanes now leading down to the Thames as a consequence. Indeed, a combination of dendrochronology, coin and artefact analysis shows that the period 1120–1220 was particularly important.[3] The excavation of the Old Customs House (where Chaucer worked), near the Tower, has in particular heralded a new interest in London's waterfront landscape history.

Fig. 7.3 Map of London, from Civitates Orbis Terrarum *by Braun and Hogenberg, 1572. The map was compiled before 1561, since St Paul's is shown with the spire that was struck by lightning in that year.*

The secular great Guildhall, protruding above the skyline, was built in about 1411 on a site previously used for public meetings, and the new Leadenhall (market, granary and schools) followed it in 1448. Great company halls were also built within the walls in the later medieval period, along with grand houses for wealthy merchants such as Sir John Pulteney and Richard Whittington, which joined those of the earls, bishops and abbots. Some initial extramural growth had also begun to sprawl along the north bank of the Thames to Westminster, and small enclaves of European merchants and Jews added a cosmopolitan element to the scene within the City.

THE EARLY-MODERN LANDSCAPE

Between 1500 and 1800 London's landscape was utterly transformed. Its role as a melting pot for provincial England was fuelled by a rapid rate of inward migration that alarmed the authorities, who tried, unsuccessfully, to restrict house-building and the subdivision of properties ('pestering') in the 16th century. The links between the primary sector of the economy and London were mutually beneficial, stimulating the north-eastern coal industry, food production and communications. Capital was transferred to London and both private commerce and public requirements were responsible for a burst of building, especially after the Dissolution of the Monasteries made the properties of 23 religious houses available for redevelopment. Major changes to the landscape were being generated by expanding commerce, an overseas empire, continental wars, and all the professional, retail, cultural and leisure functions associated with the great behemoth that London had become. Social impulses could also stimulate change, such as the humanitarian movement, which engendered schools, churches and lunatic asylums, or the prison reform movement and legislation, which led to the building of prisons in the 1770s and 1780s.

In 1598 John Stow's great *Survey of London* (his 'discovery of London, my native soyle and countrey') showed the city walls and gates in good repair, but at the end of the 16th century there were already signs of London breaking its bounds and urbanising its rural hinterland. Stow clearly did not approve of the sight, and one of the common fields outside the walls

> is so incroached upon by building of filthy cottages, and with other
> preposterous like inclosures: and Laystalles, (that notwithstanding all
> Proclamations and Acts of Parliament made to the contrary) that in some
> places it scarce remaineth a sufficient highway for the meeting of Carriages
> and droves of Cattel, much lesse is there any faire, pleasant, or wholesome
> way for people to walk on foote.[4]

Events in the 17th century dramatically affected London's evolving landscape including, of course, plague and the Fire. It was in fact not just one but a series of plagues that were inflicted upon London: in 1603 30,000 died, in 1625 a further 40,000 perished and in 1665 the Great Plague claimed a total of 100,000 lives. In the September of the following year the most damaging fire up to that date began in a bakery in Pudding Lane and eventually consumed about 80 per cent of the City. As well as rendering 80,000 people homeless, it destroyed St Paul's Cathedral, 87 parish churches, 44 livery company halls and the Guildhall. The subsequent re-planning of the capital provoked great debate: several abortive schemes were drafted, including those of Sir Christopher Wren and John Evelyn, which incorporated geometric designs according to Renaissance ideals. But London as usual escaped being controlled from above and the reconstruction, under the authority of the 1667 and 1670 Acts for Rebuilding, took place rapidly, informally and along pre-existing property lines. For pragmatic reasons some new wider thoroughfares were added to replace 'eminent and notorious' streets, and regulations were instituted to govern the height of buildings, the thickness of walls, floor and roof timbers and the use of brick and stone. Size also had to relate to location: there were to be no mansions in small alleys. The controls were developed further, so that external embellishments were banned or regulated as fire risks; all the successive guidance was finally wrapped up in the Building Act of 1774. The rebirth of London was symbolised by The Monument (1671–7) but there are some – perhaps not understanding that London was its own creature – who have since commented unfavourably on the failure to introduce a radical, planned townscape at this time. The 'grand design' seemed not to appeal to English tastes. Diversity ruled instead. In 1712 a piece in the *Spectator* commented: 'When I consider this great city in its several Quarters and Divisions I look upon it as an aggregate of various Nations, distinguished from each other by their respective Customs, Manners and Interests.'[5]

Three great residential building booms now consolidated and extended the townscape of London: in the 1720s, 1760s and early decades of the 19th century. More bridges were built and these enabled the city to start its spread southwards: Westminster (1750), Blackfriars (1769), Vauxhall (1816), John Rennie's magnificent Waterloo with its nine arches of Cornish granite (1817, demolished 1934) and his Southwark (1819, demolished 1913). During this period we also witness a renewed interest in church construction; baroque churches joined the townscape, led by the rebuilding of St Paul's between 1675 and 1711, which included Wren's iconic dome. No fewer than 51 City churches, such as St Mary-le-Bow and St Bride, were built between 1670 and 1695; and as a result of the Fifty New Churches Act of 1711 another dozen were built in the suburbs, financed through a tax on London's huge supplies of imported coal. Today these churches, with their white porticoes and steeples, remain well-known landmarks. Nicholas Hawksmoor's contribution included the marvellous Christ Church, Spitalfields (reopened, with its nave restored, in 2004, having been closed for worship since 1956), as well as churches in Stepney, Limehouse, the City and Bloomsbury. James Gibbs's St Mary-le-Strand (1714), inspired by the Italian baroque but with the afterthought of a delicate steeple, still sits uncomfortably on its island in the Strand. Later came his impressive and influential classical design for St Martin-in-the-Fields (1721–6).

Meanwhile to the west and still separate from the City was Westminster. Hemmed in by Tothill Fields, Pimlico marshland and by St James's, Green and Hyde parks, it expanded little although there was some renewal of government buildings. The Tudor palace of St James (1528) was a royal nucleus around which elites gathered; Sir Thomas More, for example, moved to Chelsea in the 1520s to form an estate near to the seat of government. There was now little room left within the City walls and the Strand, fringing the Thames, developed as a link between the City and Westminster, populated with grand houses (for example Somerset House and Northumberland House), coffee houses, with nearby theatres (for example Drury Lane in the 1790s), gentlemen's clubs (for example Decimus Burton's Athenaeum 1828–30) and educational buildings such as King's College. Thus the twin power blocs of the crown at Westminster and commerce in the City were physically joined.

Many magnates, driven out by the plague and fire, now lived more spaciously outside the City, at least for part of the year. It was the Taplow Terrace gravel ledge in central London that saw most development, and upon which the privatisation and segregation of housing reached its most extreme. The fourth Earl of Bedford was the first landowner to capitalise on such demands when he released part of his estate, the former convent garden north of the Strand, for building. The royal surveyor and architect Inigo Jones had already designed the innovative Banqueting House in Whitehall (1622) and now turned to what came to be known as Convent (Covent) Garden (1631). This comprised a central piazza surrounded by arcades and housing, with a church on the western side.

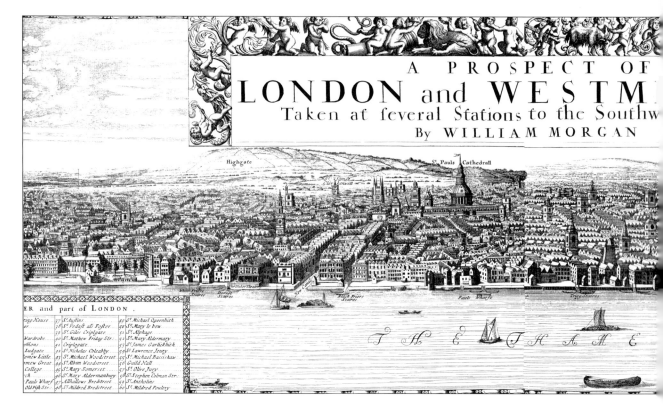

A PROSPECT OF
LONDON and WESTM.
Taken at several Stations to the Southw
By WILLIAM MORGAN

Fig. 7.4 Part of William Morgan's Survey of London, 1682. On the long prospect of London from a southerly vantage point, Morgan, 'His majesty's cosmographer', attempted to show all the Thames-side buildings. To the south of the Strand, riverside palaces stretch down to the Thames and development was proceeding rapidly westwards, although not yet towards the distant hills at Highgate. The New Canal was an attempt, which failed, to turn the polluted River Fleet into a waterway.

OPPOSITE PAGE: *Fig. 7.5 A Prospect of City of London, Westminster and St James's Park by Johannes Kip. This view of 1710 shows the trees of St James's Park with the broad sweep of London's terraced housing to the east. St James's Palace is in the foreground and the Strand curves around the north bank of the Thames.*

Leading courtiers followed, and had the Civil War not intervened, this Renaissance development might have spread across many other parts of the West End. Oliver Cromwell insisted, however, that such activities should be controlled, and only a few schemes were completed before the Restoration, such as Lincoln's Inn Fields in 1657. Many returning Royalist sympathisers then looked to avoid the Puritan-dominated City and chose to locate themselves closer to Court. Ten years later, the fifth Earl of Bedford obtained a licence to hold a market to sell fruit and vegetables and the Covent Garden piazza took on the more commercial role that it maintained until recently. In 1662 Sir William Petty also noted another great benefit of living to the west of the City, namely that:

> … because the winds blow near three-quarters of the year from the west, the dwellings of the west end are so much the more free of fumes, steams and stinks of the whole easterly pile; which, where seacoal is burnt, is a great matter.[6]

By the 1680s the London rebuilding and the developments west of the City along the Strand were well advanced (Fig. 7.4). It was here that the landscape of the speculatively built London square, with its feeling of *rus in urbe*, was developed most fully. Each was to be a peaceful green oasis surrounded by dignified houses, the ensemble completed by secondary streets, a market and often a church; much was also encompassed by railings and gates and only later thrown open to the public. Elements of public design had nevertheless emerged, led by the aristocracy and reinforced by leases and covenants that subsumed the individual building within a wider shared space. The London squares were developed mostly between the 1660s and the 1880s, and for many they represent a particularly British contribution to architecture and urban development (Figs 7.5 and 7.6).[7]

St James's Square was built in about 1668, followed shortly by Golden and Soho Squares; Hanover and Cavendish Squares were completed by about 1717, as a result of which a new aristocratic quarter began to grow up in Mayfair north

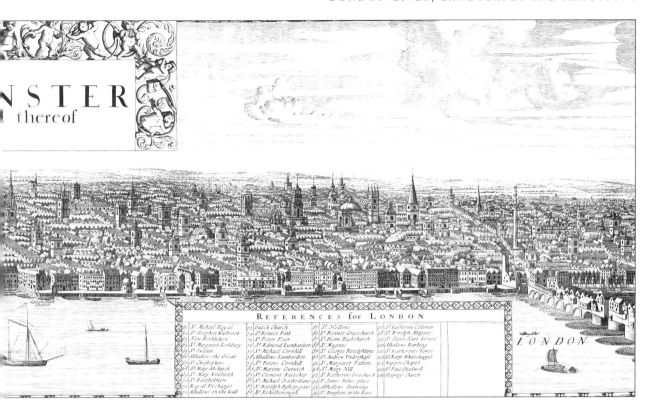

NSTER
thereof

REFERENCES for LONDON

61	St Michael Royal	73	Dutch Church	85	St Mellens	97	St Katherine Coleman
62	St Stephen Walbrook	74	St Bennet Fink	86	St Bennet Gracechurch	98	St Botolph Aldgate
63	New Bethlehem	75	St Peter Poor	87	St Dionis Backchurch	99	St Olave Hart Street
64	St Margaret Lothbury	76	St Edmond Lumbardstr	88	St Magnus	100	Alhallows Barking
65	St Swithin	77	St Michael Cornhill	89	St George Botolphlane	101	St Katherines Tower
66	Alhallows the Great	78	Alhallows Lumbardstr	90	St Andrew Undershaft	102	St Mary Whitechappel
67	St Christophers	79	St Peters Cornhill	91	St Margaret Pattons	103	Wappin Chapel
68	St Mary Abchurch	80	St Martins Outwich	92	St Mary Hill	104	St Paul Shadwell
69	St Mary Woolnoth	81	St Clement Eastchep	93	St Katherine Creechurch	105	Stepney Church
70	St Bartholmew	82	St Michael Crookedlane	94	St James Dukes place		
71	Royal Exchange	83	St Botolph Bishopsgate	95	Alhallows Stainning		
72	Alhallows on the Wall	84	St Ethelborough	96	St Dunstans in the East		

LONDON

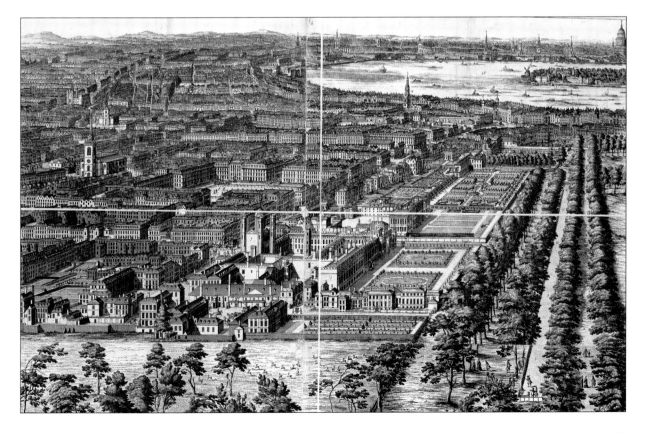

Fig. 7.6 Bloomsbury Square 1787, from an original hand-coloured aquatint.

A semi-rural scene with elegant buildings, street lighting, a paved road and pavement and drainage channels in the gutter rather than in the centre of the street. Note the girl driving cows from door to door for fresh milk.

OPPOSITE PAGE:

TOP: *Fig. 7.7 The great estates of west London in the early 19th century.*

The building contractor Thomas Cubitt developed the Grosvenor estate (14) near Hyde Park as Belgravia in the 1820s before moving south on to the Grosvenor land nearer the Thames to develop Pimlico. For more detail on the differences in 19th-century building developments see Fig. 7.14.

BOTTOM: *Fig. 7.8 Regent's Park. The area remained a royal chase until 1646. John Nash, developing the park for the Prince Regent, created the large space, surrounded by palatial stucco façades for terraces, a lake, a canal, 56 villas and a second home for the prince. The public were allowed limited entry from 1845. From Nash's original conception only St John's Lodge and The Holme now remain. The park is still part of the Crown Estate.*

of St James's. New squares and streets proliferated and their Palladian principles of symmetry were informed by pattern books, as in the exclusive and organic 'little town' of Bloomsbury (from 1661), at Hanover Square or in the Harley-Cavendish estate north of the Oxford Road. Informal town gardens now appeared at the rear of the terraced houses. In 1725 the first English Improvement Commissioners were established for St James's Square, thereby demonstrating a concern for public space that had hitherto been largely unknown. Rather later, in 1762, the innovation was extended to Westminster. Now street lighting and paving were improved and the swinging pictorial signs outside shops were banned as health hazards and replaced by lettering. By the later 18th century most street names were painted at each corner, and houses were numbered or showed their owners' names on a brass plate. The New Road (1757), an early bypass that is now the Euston Road and lined with glass-walled buildings, was built from Paddington to Islington to replace an earlier track and for a few decades became the northern boundary of London.[8]

The pace and scale of change impressed themselves on contemporaries. Christian Goede, a German visiting London in 1802–4, wrote:

> *I resided in Southampton Row, Bloomsbury, near which the Duke of Bedford is engaging in very extensive building, and has some thousands of workmen in constant employment … I remember that on my return to town after an absence of some months I could scarcely believe myself at home. On reviewing the neighbourhood I could have fancied myself transported into a fairy world, where by the power of a magic wand palaces and gardens had suddenly found existence. I … asked myself whether I had not previously seen that new street, new square, new garden; in a word this city; or whether in reality the heaps of stones and rubbish which I had left piled up from the material of old houses, had been metamorphosed into new and elegant buildings … People crowded along the well-lighted*

pavement ... everything bore the appearance of enchantment. The opposite side of Southampton Row, late an open space, was not only built upon but inhabited: a coffee house was open and some very handsome shops exposed their merchandise for sale. Tavistock Square ... and streets intersecting each other, were novelties that raised new wonders in my head.[9]

Although the activities of different speculative builders and their architects sometimes made the development of unified estates difficult, the concept of a centrally planned creation persisted on the great estates to the west of the City (Fig. 7.7). Bedford Square (1778–83) offered a particularly fine example of unity of composition. In time the squares would give way to crescents, as in John Nash's spectacular stuccoed later Georgian work at Regent's Park (formerly Marylebone Park). Around its perimeter great mansions, such as those of Park Crescent or Cumberland Terrace, could look on to a parkland landscape of lawns, trees, lakes and the Regent's Canal (Fig. 7.8). Nash also carried out the largest planning project of this time, the provision of a 'spine' to London's multi-focal West End. This took the form of the sweeping Regent Street (1810–30), which was built to follow the natural division between Soho and Mayfair. Once completed, it linked Regent's Park to the St James's area, where the park had been remodelled and a triumphal new Trafalgar Square laid out on the site of former royal stables. Nash saw his new street as 'a boundary and complete separation between the streets and squares occupied by the nobility and gentry, and the narrow streets and meaner houses occupied by mechanics and the trading part of the community'.[10] Later, the developers of other estates copied the sweeps of Nash with enthusiasm; in Belgravia, and even more so in the late 19th-century buildings at Ladbroke Grove and

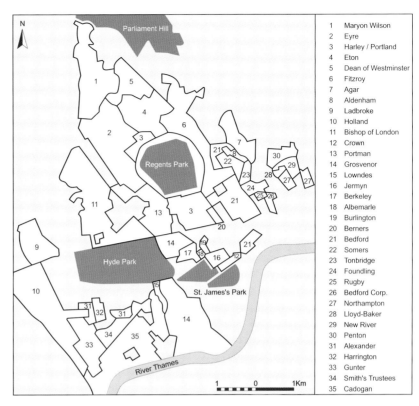

1	Maryon Wilson
2	Eyre
3	Harley / Portland
4	Eton
5	Dean of Westminster
6	Fitzroy
7	Agar
8	Aldenham
9	Ladbroke
10	Holland
11	Bishop of London
12	Crown
13	Portman
14	Grosvenor
15	Lowndes
16	Jermyn
17	Berkeley
18	Albemarle
19	Burlington
20	Berners
21	Bedford
22	Somers
23	Tonbridge
24	Foundling
25	Rugby
26	Bedford Corp.
27	Northampton
28	Lloyd-Baker
29	New River
30	Penton
31	Alexander
32	Harrington
33	Gunter
34	Smith's Trustees
35	Cadogan

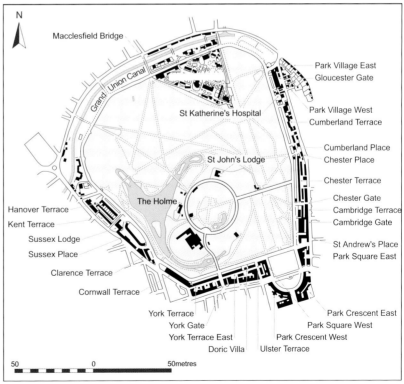

OPPOSITE PAGE: ***Figs 7.9 and 7.10 London in the mid-18th century.*** *Fig. 7.9 (top) shows London in 1766 by John Rocque. Three years after John Rocque completed his great 24-sheet plan of London, he issued this smaller version for general use. Fig. 7.10 (bottom), based on Roque, depicts London's spatial organisation in about 1750 and outlines the main functional and landscape zones.*

Belsize Park, this freer style of planning was adopted in a form that would be copied endlessly throughout the South East after 1918. Along the riverside the largest public building to be opened in the Georgian period was Somerset House (1776–1801), which housed various previously dispersed government departments; others included the Royal Mint (1805–15), the Custom House (1813–29) and Millbank Prison with its 1,200 cells (1812–22).

Within the City, businesses clustered into certain areas: marine insurance around Lloyd's coffee-house; stockbrokers in the Exchange coffee-house in Sweeting's Alley; banking in Lombard Street. The Bank of England was established in Threadneedle Street in 1732. The law courts also attracted large numbers of workers, although the resident population was falling appreciably as offices ousted homes. The Mansion House for the Lord Mayor, with its impressive porticoed Palladian façade, was finished in 1753. Where the natural gravel terrace widens between the rivers Fleet and Lea the Spitalfields were developed as regular streets of small properties, largely inhabited by weavers and especially silk workers. Clerkenwell, on the eastern slopes of the Fleet, along with Shoreditch and Bishopsgate, was an area of artisan lanes and twisting alleys; along the waterside all manner of ropewalks, breweries, foundries and forges, oil and soap works were interspersed with houses and taverns. Much of the sense of the growth of Hanoverian London is caught in the map by John Rocque, published in 1749, three years after the appearance of his extraordinary 24-sheet topographical map of the city (Figs 7.9 and 7.10).

At Southwark a 'third London' of suburban manufacturing complemented the City on the one hand, and the West End, geared to conspicuous consumption, on the other. By the late 16th century the area of the Clink and Paris Gardens was established as a site for 'unchaste interludes and bargains of incontinence'. Inns lined the street leading to London Bridge, and theatres such as The Rose (built in about 1587) and The Globe (1599) brought Shakespeare and others to live here. By 1678 Southwark's population alone had reached 26,000, and was possibly much higher still, much of it crammed into the crowded and subdivided tenements that lined the poorly drained alleys and yards. Leather-working, the docks and boat-building at Rotherhithe and Deptford were important, as were the timber-yards at Lambeth. By the later 17th century some former church properties were much subdivided, and the poverty and squalor in the marshier areas brought disease and death; the area's high population level was only maintained through constant in-migration. Shipping amassed on both banks of the river and a great forest of masts crowded the facilities. Sometimes more than a thousand ships waited to dock, if not laden with coal, then with perishable and exotic cargoes from the West Indies and elsewhere. Acts of Parliament finally allowed the building of docks outside the City's jurisdiction, including the West India Dock on the Isle of Dogs (1806), the London Dock at Wapping (1805), the East India Dock at Blackwall (1806) and the Surrey Commercial Docks (1807). St Katherine's Dock opened in 1828; because it was closest to the City it involved the demolition of 1,250 dwellings and some church buildings, and also rendered 11,000 people homeless. The Millwall Docks came later, in 1868. Shipbuilding, warehouses and commodity exchanges also formed part of this waterfront scene, as did the factories that dealt with the refining and processing of imported materials.

Although London had become Europe's largest city by 1700 and was fully integrated into the European economy, it was still relatively compact and stretched now from Westminster to Wapping. But during the late 17th century the pressure for the capital to expand beyond its old boundaries and into outlying villages meant that the old order of poverty at the periphery and wealth in the urban centre was upset. In pre-industrial days the Thames had constituted a barrier to movement, and London was actually a bi-polar city, split between finance in the City and administration at Westminster. Hanoverian merchants and aldermen were increasingly inclined to purchase retreats and villas on the Thames near Horace

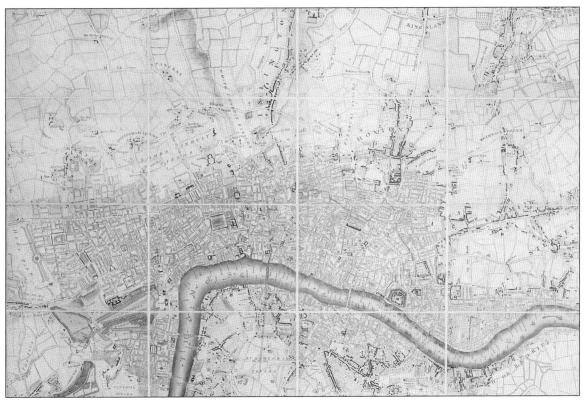

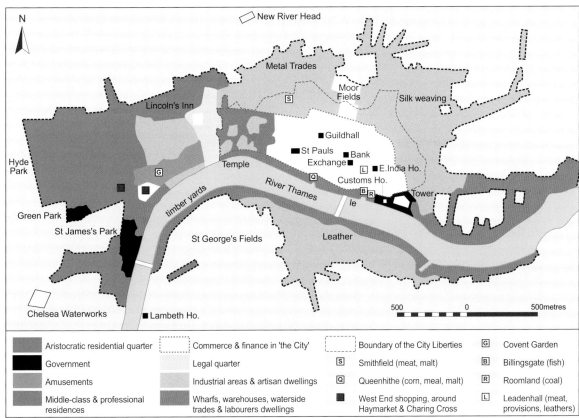

	Aristocratic residential quarter	Commerce & finance in 'the City'	Boundary of the City Liberties	[G] Covent Garden
	Government	Legal quarter	[S] Smithfield (meat, malt)	[B] Billingsgate (fish)
	Amusements	Industrial areas & artisan dwellings	[Q] Queenhithe (corn, meal, malt)	[R] Roomland (coal)
	Middle-class & professional residences	Wharfs, warehouses, waterside trades & labourers dwellings	West End shopping, around Haymarket & Charing Cross	[L] Leadenhall (meat, provisions, leathers)

Walpole's sensational 'little plaything house' in the Gothick style at Strawberry Hill, which was the precursor of many mock-rustic *fermes ornées*, such as the Craven Cottage at Fulham. Helped by turnpiking, villages such as Hackney became popular with London financiers, but the more comfortable middle classes were to be found in greatest numbers in the western and central parts, with fewer to the east and south. Because elite areas generated their own demand for local services, and what John Gwynn referred to as 'habitations of the useful and laborious people', the social segregation could never be complete.[11] Thus the notorious Seven Dials 'rookery' of St Giles in Soho housed criminals and a reserve army of casual labourers while bordering on to a particularly wealthy area. The fashionable West End classical terraces and squares, however, were part of an early centrifugal tendency. By 1800 London had expanded to such an extent that it now stretched from Hyde Park to Limehouse and from Southwark to Hoxton, with further ribbons of development spreading along the main thoroughfares outwards through Kensington, Camden Town (planned in 1791 and growing thereafter towards Kentish Town but with 'miserable fourth-rate building'), Islington, Mile End and Camberwell. Beyond were the Northern Heights, picturesque and still rural in character, which stretched between Kilburn, Hampstead Heath, Highgate, Muswell Hill and Alexandra Palace. Beyond them again were scores of separate hamlets with place-name components including 'end' or 'green', such as Crouch End or Golders Green. This relentless centrifugal process was to be enhanced considerably after 1800 as smoking brick kilns marked the existing peripheries of London with a new 'ring of fire'. As well as signalling the building frenzy that was now taking place, they provided overnight warmth for those tramping to London in search of better lives.

VICTORIAN LONDON

To the Victorian mind London's landscape was hugely contradictory: it was at once the glorious epitome of empire, but also the feared 'abyss' that was almost beyond control. By 1750 the population of the capital had reached about 675,000; by 1801 it was 959,000. London now ranked alongside Edo (Tokyo) and Beijing as one of the world's largest cities and it housed as much as 50 per cent of the urban population of England and Wales. By 1900 there were no fewer than 6.5 million Londoners, about 20 per cent of the total population of England and Wales (*see* Table 7.1). London, 'a province covered by houses', ate up the space around. It was, after all, as the first census of 1801 described it, 'the Metropolis of England, at once the seat of government and the greatest Emporium in the known world'. It was still the chief residence of royalty (at St James's and from the 1760s at Buckingham House, later Palace). It was the head of an expanding empire, symbolised beyond all else, perhaps, by the Great Exhibition of 1851; it was at the same time an international port, the centre of finance, a market for inland trade and a manufacturing base. It was also the cultural centre of England, expressed through the imposing British Museum (1823–48), built to house George IV's Royal Library for the nation, Burlington House with its learned societies, University College (1826–7), the South Kensington museum area (1860s to the early 20th century) and the National Gallery (1832–8).

Grand buildings and monumental architecture were called for. As the Georgian period, with its aristocratic dominance, gave way to a more heterogeneous building regime, 'the battle of the styles' was joined. While most authorities could admire Inigo Jones's Palladian Banqueting House, Augustus Pugin popularised a return to the Gothic style, which was adopted enthusiastically by the leading architect of the mid-19th century, George Gilbert Scott. But many, including Palmerston, saw the Classical and Italianate styles as offering greater imperial gravitas. London's 19th-century landscape was thus shaped by political opinion as well as financial, functional and aesthetic concerns.

The one thing that was agreed upon was the need for an appropriate style to match the importance of the building. At the beginning of the 19th century many buildings were therefore demolished to make way for new works at the Houses of Parliament, including the Speaker's House as well as offices for the expanding civil service in Whitehall. The Foreign Office (1863–8) was an example of Classicism; the New Law Courts in the Strand (1870s) of Gothic, while The Admiralty and War Office (completed in 1906) saw a further return to Classicism. But the greatest outlay on a single building in the 19th century was the £2.4 million spent on the Houses of Parliament between the fire of 1834 (which had destroyed much of the old palace of Westminster apart from Westminster Hall and the Crypt Chapel) and the completion of the new buildings, except for more minor works, by 1860. Following the decision to rebuild in the Gothic style on the same site, Charles Barry and Augustus Pugin created the Palace of Westminster, surely one of the most instantly recognisable and iconic buildings in the World, on the newly embanked river front. Here the Victoria Tower, Central Tower and Clock Tower (the modern Big Ben was installed in 1858) created a symbol of British reassurance. Further rebuilding was needed following bomb damage during the Second World War, again in a (modernised) Gothic style that paid close attention to historical continuity.[12]

The Victorian period also saw the first large-scale rebuilding of the City itself since the Great Fire. By the late 1850s many streets were undergoing transformation and the site at Bank Junction was now a focal point of British Victorian imperialism. The current outline of the Bank of England was achieved by 1828; by 1844 the Royal Exchange had been rebuilt after a second fire, and since the 1750s the Mansion House had offered imposing landscapes of power, emphasised by the ornamentation and scale of its buildings. The surrounding buildings of commerce now dwarfed Hawksmoor's 18th-century church of St Mary Woolnoth. And a further symbolic link between the City and Westminster, each with their many examples of civic monumentalism, was the opening of the majestic Embankment in 1870.

It was the value of interpersonal contact that ensured that the financial services sector remained firmly in the City, although specialist Victorian exchanges (for example the Stock Exchange of 1854 or the Baltic Exchange of 1858) and merchant banks replaced 18th-century coffee houses as the foci for meetings. Classical porticoes, massive frontages and commercial buildings displaced housing as the resident population of the City declined from 127,000 in 1851 to 26,000 in 1901. Social segregation had certainly existed by 1700, but economic specialisation and a strengthening division of labour were now making a more marked impact on the landscape. A zone of small Victorian industrial workshops ran around the north and east sides of inner London in an arc from the western end of the City to Stepney and Southwark; other branches then led off towards Kentish Town and Holloway and towards south Hackney and Stoke Newington. Small-scale workshops, easily missed by the casual observer, served the needs of the clothing, furniture, printing and light engineering industries. Clothing accounted for about one-third of all London's manufacturing workers by 1901, but certain quarters had their own specialisations, such as the Camden Town piano-making area, or the watchmakers of Clerkenwell.

A stark contrast emerged between East End and West End; their separation by the 'depopulated fortress of finance' that was the City was already evident by the 1820s and had become a familiar concept by the 1870s. Grand buildings might characterise the West End and City, but the population displaced in the course of their construction now gathered instead in the narrow alleys and poor courtyards of a zone of transition on the City's fringes. And as that zone expanded outwards, its central and, especially, eastern and south-eastern areas were seen to contain pockets of horror – here was 'the abyss' or 'darkest London' that drew investigators who compared these 'town swamps' with contemporary popular

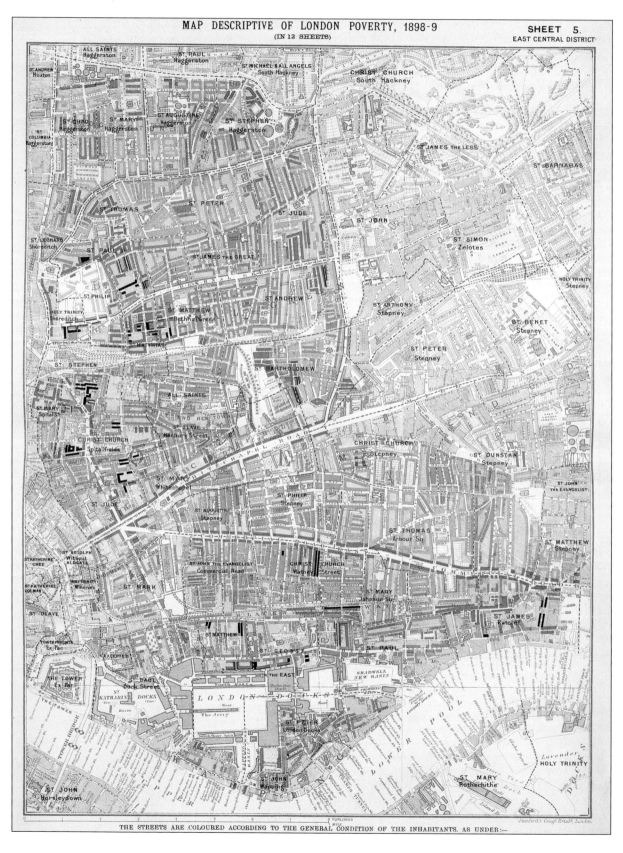

MAP DESCRIPTIVE OF LONDON POVERTY, 1898-9
(IN 12 SHEETS)

SHEET 5.
EAST CENTRAL DISTRICT

THE STREETS ARE COLOURED ACCORDING TO THE GENERAL CONDITION OF THE INHABITANTS. AS UNDER:—

images of the explorers' Africa (Chapter 8). These social explorers used a variety of methods to bring the London poor to wider attention: investigative journalism, participant observation, mapping and statistical analysis. By the 1880s Charles Booth's surveys had created an enduring image of poverty (Fig. 7.11). In Dickens's weekly *Household Words* the incumbent of the parish of St Thomas Charterhouse, near Cripplegate, wrote in 1856 of the 9,500 people living in 1,178 houses, many of them 'mere kennels' where cholera was rife and which should have been condemned long ago.[13]

Other pockets of poverty and dismal landscape occurred throughout the metropolis: the Wandle valley had 'building of a vile character' according to Charles Booth; and railways, canals and gasworks could generate degradation, as in the Kings Cross and St Pancras area. The Church Commissioners, in letting their properties in the Agar Town area of St Pancras on short leases, were also responsible for what had become an unpaved and poorly drained shanty town by the beginning of the Victorian period. Communities in the south-eastern areas of Rotherhithe, Wapping and the Isle of Dogs were virtually cut off from the rest of London since there was no crossing point downstream from London Bridge before the construction of Tower Bridge and the Rotherhithe and Blackwall tunnels in the 1890s. South of the river the descent of Southwark continued; once-genteel mansions in Jacob's Island were sub-let in tenements and their gardens covered in poor housing (Fig. 7.12 and Chapter 8). Here quick access was needed to the uncertain employment on offer in the Surrey Docks, the many riverside trades, the engineering companies in Lambeth or food-processing at Bermondsey. Mayhew, visiting here in 1849, found a 'Venice of Drains' with overcrowding, filth, hunger and disease, but he also found the inhabitants stoical because it was so close to their work.[14]

OPPOSITE PAGE:

Fig. 7.11 Charles Booth's descriptive map of London poverty. This is a section from the original north-east sheet centred on Whitechapel Road. The twelve Maps Descriptive of London Poverty, 1898–9 cover the area from Hammersmith in the west to Greenwich in the east, and from Hampstead in the north to Clapham in the south. The City of London was not included because it lacked significant numbers of residents. Booth's colouring scheme incorporated seven categories, which were, in his words:

BLACK: Lowest class. Vicious, semi-criminal.
DARK BLUE: Very poor, casual. Chronic want.
LIGHT BLUE: Poor. 18s to 21s a week for a moderate family.
PURPLE: Mixed. Some comfortable others poor.
PINK: Fairly comfortable. Good ordinary earnings.
RED: Middle class. Well-to-do.
YELLOW: Upper-middle and Upper classes. Wealthy.

The section of the map shown here therefore shows middle classes fronting onto the Whitechapel Road but with lower class and poor families in the streets behind. Wealthy streets are conspicuously absent.

THIS PAGE:

LEFT: *Fig. 7.12 Jacob's Island at the Butler's Wharf complex, Southwark.* The plaque recalls that this was once indeed an island, and a notorious slum – in which Dickens set Oliver Twist (1837–8).

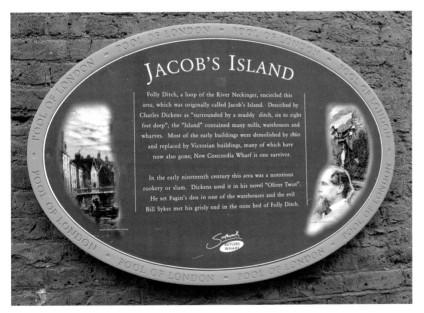

Olsen has perceptively argued that 'What the Victorians desired was privacy for the middle classes, publicity for the working classes, and segregation for both.'[15] In fact quite complex social gradations could exist even within the most tightly controlled developments: Camberwell, for example, could demonstrate moderate wealth and respectability at Peckham Grove, cheek by jowl with the notorious Sultan Street slum. This graphic description of the latter area could serve for many such others:

This tendency towards overcrowding, the intermixture of cowsheds and piggeries with dwelling-houses, and the opening of glue and linoleum factories, a brewery, and the establishment of haddock smoking and tallow-melting yards soon combined to give to the whole area both the odours and the society of the authentic slum. The sickly smell of costermongers' refuse combined with these to make an atmosphere which seemed in the nostrils of one regular visitor to the district to be a concoction of haddocks and oranges, of mortar and soot, of hearthstones and winkles, of rotten rags and herrings. [16]

Poorer areas of the East End, such as Bethnal Green, offered their own landscapes. In his *Ragged London in 1861* John Hollingshead graphically noted:

There are steaming eating houses, half-filled with puddings as large as sofa squabs, and legs of beef to boil down into a cheap and popular soup; birdcage vendors; mouldy, musty dens full of second-hand garments, or gay 'emporiums' in the ready-made clothing line; pawnbrokers with narrow, yellow side entrances, whose walls are well marked with the traces of traffic; faded groceries; small print shops, selling periodicals, sweetstuff and stale fruit; squeezed up barbers, long factories and breweries, with the black arches of the Eastern Counties Railway running through the midst. [17]

Although such townscapes should not be judged from a modern perspective, the worst areas at this time of very rapid urbanisation seem to have been those along the Stepney and Limehouse waterfronts, between the Whitechapel and Bethnal Green roads, and northwards to Shoreditch and Hoxton. Here physical decay and overcrowding was at its most intense, and the daily attempt to procure work at the docks the most desperate – the earlier docks had now been joined by the Royal Victoria Dock (1855), followed by the Royal Albert and Tilbury docks in the 1880s. It was hoped, however, that such destitute landscapes could be transformed. Parliamentary investigations, journalism and optimistic philanthropic attentions were all focused here. But it was private enterprise, rather than any concerted public effort, that pushed through a piecemeal redevelopment of these cheaper properties – piecemeal because the highly complex pattern of landownership in London prevented any wholesale redevelopment on the scale undertaken in contemporary Paris. For example, many tenements were demolished during the building of New Oxford Street (1845–7), Shaftesbury Avenue (1877–86) and Charing Cross Road (1887), and Victoria Street, the Aldwych and Kingsway.

Life and landscape in Victorian London were not totally pleasant for anyone. There had been pollution scares for centuries, but the cholera outbreak of 1848–9 claimed 14,000 lives and led to a ban on drinking-water being drawn from the Thames downstream of Teddington Lock (*see* Fig. 6.9). Inhabitants of Jacob's Island, Mayhew's 'very capital of cholera', had been taking drinking-water from their sewage ditch. Much of this area has now been razed and redeveloped, and modern two-bedroomed units in Scott's Sufferance wharf are now in high demand.

By the 1870s the main drainage system for London was finished, although public street fountains were still used by the poor at the end of the century. Intercepting sewers now ran east–west to capture London's effluent and carry it downstream to Barking and Crossness. The chief engineer was Joseph Bazalgette, also responsible for the Victoria Embankment above the sewer in the 1860s that reclaimed land and put 'chains on the river' (*Flumini vincula posuit*, on his memorial plaque on the Victoria Embankment).[18] The livestock market at Smithfield was moved to Islington in 1852, but animals still lived among crowded human beings, with pigs posing a particular problem. Traffic congestion and noise pollution were intense; 'pea-souper' fogs were well known (that of 1886 was

A THAW IN THE STREETS OF LONDON.—SEE PRECEDING PAGE.

Fig. 7.13 London street scene, 1865.
A thaw. The crossing sweepers were in great demand by polite society! London's horses produced approximately 1,000 tonnes of dung a day in the 19th century, which was collected by dung carts and deposited in huge heaps. Much of the manure was sent to market gardens such as those in the Lea Valley, Essex.

particularly dangerous), and everything could be covered in what Dickens, in *Little Dorrit* (1857), referred to as a 'penitential garb of soot'. Underfoot the going could be unpleasant, and crossing sweepers were in demand to assist the more genteel pedestrian. London's crowded streets offered a variety of hazards (Fig. 7.13).

By contrast the West End was designed for a select group. George IV's Buckingham Palace, extended by John Nash (1825–30) after its purchase from the Duke of Buckingham in 1762, was the London seat of the ruler of the United Kingdom and British Empire. Its setting at the end of The Mall was appropriately stately, although further improved when Nash's Marble Arch was moved from the front of the palace in 1851. In the 1820s the Grosvenor estate was developed as fashionable housing close to the palace. This was Thomas Cubitt's Belgravia (1825–50), the network of residential streets that surrounded the spacious mansions of Belgrave Square; it was followed by his Pimlico (1835–50), also on Grosvenor land. The cachet of 'the right address' also meant movement: as each new development were completed, the wealthy moved ever further west – to Belgravia by the 1850s, to South Kensington following the 1851 Great Exhibition in Hyde Park, and to the mansions of the Cadogan estate in Chelsea. The upper middle class, on the other hand, were attracted to the large new Italianate houses at Notting Hill, Bayswater and south Paddington. To the west, developers began to offer detached villas with private gardens, as at St John's Wood, where, by the late 1820s a fundamental change·in building style could be seen, as Bryanstone and Montagu squares in the south gave way to the detached and semi-detached villas of the Eyre estate adjacent to Nash's Park Villages (Fig. 7.14).

Residential suburbanisation took various forms in the 19th century, but for many the essential Victorian scene was one of slate-roofed semi-detached houses,

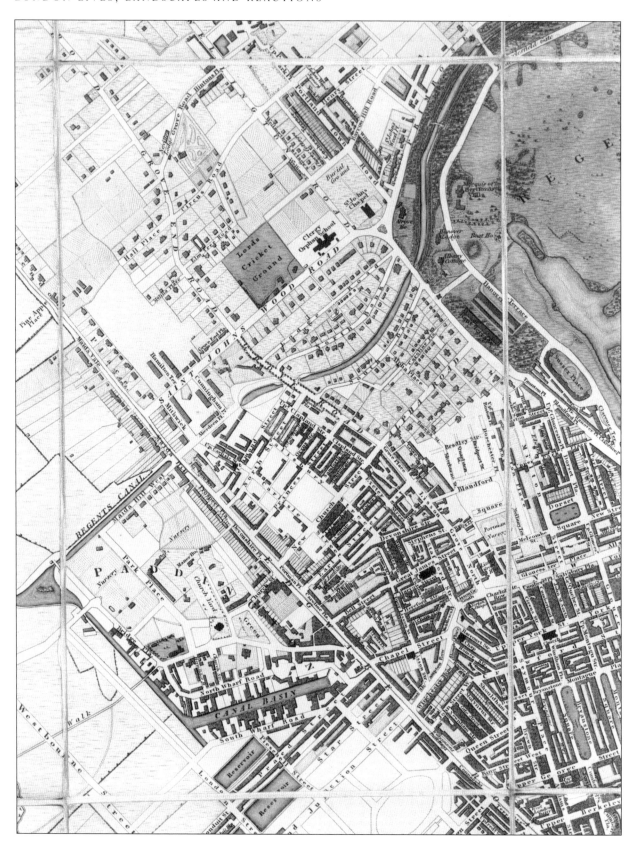

the suburban railway station and solid Victorian churches. However, earlier suburban forms included the graceful crescent of Blackheath Paragon (1794–1805) on the edge of Blackheath, which was then becoming fashionable. Suburban building also concentrated at first on cottages and villas to which 'respectable' working class families might move, for example Clapham Park, begun in 1825, or Battersea Fields and Highbury New Park in the 1860s. But from the 1860s onwards, cheap Victorian and Edwardian terraced housing moved outwards from London to engulf outlying villages, although it provided little more than 'settlement tanks for submerged Londoners'.[19] Areas such as Ilford, Catford and Eltham were developed for respectable service workers and skilled artisans. A little further out were wealthier residents who could afford such places as Wimbledon or Bromley, whence a 7s 6d weekly rail fare allowed commuting to London Bridge station. The provision of cheaper fares to allow working men and women to commute came only with the Cheap Trains Act of 1883. Thereafter the Great Eastern Railway's lines from Liverpool Street into Essex led the way and allowed a greater proportion of London's working-class housing to spring up to the north-east of the capital. In the late 18th century settlements such as Leyton, Leytonstone, West Ham, Plaistow, Barking and Ilford were all distinct from one another, and Barking had been a thriving fishing village, but London's physical presence was now overwhelming. The manager of the Great Eastern told a Royal Commission in the 1880s that:

> Wherever you locate the workmen in large numbers you utterly destroy that neighbourhood for ordinary passenger traffic. Take, for instance, the neighbourhood of Stamford Hill, Tottenham, and Edmonton. That used to be a very nice district indeed, occupied by good families, with houses of from £150 to £250 a year, with coach-houses and stables, and gardens, and a few acres of land. But very soon after this obligation was put upon the Great Eastern Company, and accepted by the Great Eastern Company, of issuing workmen's tickets, speculative builders went down into the neighbourhood, and, as a consequence, each good house was one after another pulled down, and the district is given up entirely I may say now to the working man.[20]

By 1901 more than half of the county of Essex's population lived in West Ham, East Ham and metropolitan Essex. London County Council (LCC) and private housing expanded rapidly, as was noted in Chapter 6. Walthamstow, Edmonton, Leytonstone and Enfield now began to grow, and the White Hart Lane estate in Tottenham (1904) was developed in response to the availability of the 'twopenny trains' to Liverpool Street. By 1905 the limit for such fares was 34km into Essex but only 14km south of the Thames, although cheap LCC tram fares helped here with the cost of commuting. The provision of Local Authority housing began after 1890 and the popular LCC Totterdown cottage estate at Tooting, begun in 1903, reached a population of 4,500 after the First World War. The first LCC 'out county' estate was built at Norbury in Surrey between 1906 and 1910.

MODERN LONDON: POST-1900

Rapid Victorian population growth meant that by 1901 the population of the County of London had reached 4.4 million, and that of Greater London (a term first used in the 1881 census for the area within a 15-mile (24km) radius of Central London) reached 6.6 million (Table 7.1). By 1951 the latter's population had reached 8.1 million, but the population of the original City had fallen from 27,000 to a mere 5,000. In other words, as London continued to grow outwards its centre became less densely inhabited. The theme of the century after 1900 was thus one of centrifugal population movements (though this was slightly reversed for the City by 2001), a demographic trend that is reflected in the landscape.

OPPOSITE PAGE:

Fig. 7.14 The St John's Wood area in 1827. Georgian streets and squares in the south on the Portman estate (see *Fig. 7.7, 13*) give way to incipient villa-dom around Thomas Lord's cricket ground on the Eyre Estate (see *Fig. 7.7, 2*). The Regent's Canal snakes through the centre of the map and skirts the northern edge of the Park to connect with the Grand Junction Canal basin at Paddington.

New government offices and quasi-governmental buildings such as the BBC (in 1926) now began to multiply. By 1930 central London's main streets had been widened and straightened; its low-rise buildings were replaced by ones of five or six storeys; Portland Stone was now used instead of brick and stucco. In Regent Street the imperial parade route designed by Norman Shaw and Reginald Blomfield replaced Nash's earlier stucco Quadrant. In the late Victorian period street-widening schemes had helped such firms as Barkers, Derry and Toms and Pontings in Kensington to erect unified frontages to their shops. Large stores now massed along Regent Street and Oxford Street to join Debenham and Freebody (1906) and Selfridges (1909), while further west the later modernity of Peter Jones's Grade II*-listed building came to dominate Sloane Square. Cutting-edge lighting and horizontal glazing techniques could now be seen in the modernist men's department store at Simpson's Piccadilly (1936, now occupied by Waterstones). Dramatic and novel architecture and fashion combined to make this area one of the world's key landscapes of elite retailing. Such glimpses of modernity should not, however, lead one to forget another quite different London retailing landscape scene: the street market. Most licensed stalls were to be found in the East End and north London; the 1920s were the peak years and the bustle and camaraderie appealed even to those who had moved out but who still came back weekly to such areas as Petticoat Lane. By the mid-1960s there were still an estimated 13,000 people working as street pedlars and hawkers in Greater London, although this figure had shrunk from the 23,600 costers and street sellers recorded by Charles Booth in the LCC area alone in 1891.[21]

The search for more space and cheaper rents and labour, however, drew firms out of London and towards the west. Napiers moved their growing motor-car business to Acton in 1903, and by the First World War the Park Royal show-ground had attracted factories, as had Hayes, Southall, Chiswick, Willesden and Wembley. J B Priestley, in his *English Journey* (1934), travelled out of London on the Great West Road and saw proof that new types of industry had indeed moved to the south of England, though he affected not to take them seriously:

> *… decorative little buildings, all glass and concrete and chromium plate, seem to my barbaric mind to be merely playing at being factories. You could go up to any one of the charming little fellows, I feel, and safely order an ice cream or select a few picture post cards … You notice them decorating all the western borders of London … Potato crisps, scent, tooth pastes, bathing costumes, fire extinguishers; those are the concerns behind these pleasing façades …*[22]

At Slough, outside the London wage area, labour costs were lower and more factory space could be rented, thus saving on large capital outlays. Modern products such as vacuum cleaners (from the art-deco Hoover Building built on the A40 in 1935), radios and washing machines were produced. A modern, efficient and clean landscape emerged in the industrial estates that stretched from Ealing to Perivale and on to Greenford, Uxbridge, Denham and Harefield, and then in an arc through to Welwyn Garden City, where in 1936 'everything is modern, light, bright, cheerful and efficient'. At Ealing one managing director claimed that:

> *The workers can lead a much fuller life in the open surroundings of the district … they can walk to and from work … They don't have to make long journeys through the smog, roar, dust and fumes of the city to a place that is drab and uninteresting.*[23]

The South East now benefited from structural shifts in the economy, and had fuller employment and a cleaner environment at a time when other regions, especially in the North, were struggling as a result of the decline of their basic industries. Between 1932 and 1937 the Greater London area accounted for five-sixths of the net increase in numbers of factories and two-fifths of employment in these new workplaces. As the century progressed the factories along the Great West Road extended along what is now the M4 corridor to become the heartland of British research and development, but not everyone was impressed: in 1937 John Betjeman delivered his condemnation of the sprawl to the west of London in his well-known poem, 'Slough':

> *Come friendly bombs and fall on Slough!*
> *It isn't fit for humans now,*
> *There isn't grass to graze a cow.*
> *Swarm over, Death!*
>
> *Come, bombs and blow to smithereens*
> *Those air-conditioned, bright canteens,*
> *Tinned fruit, tinned meat, tinned milk, tinned beans,*
> *Tinned minds, tinned breath.*[24]

Suburbanisation in the early 20th century became strongly associated with the extensions of the underground system. By 1907 the Underground had tunnelled below the hills at Hampstead to reach such locations as Golders Green, which within seven years was covered with more than 3,600 new houses (Fig. 7.15). After the First World War attention was again turned to this process as the Bakerloo, Northern and Piccadilly lines were each extended. By this time, however, the suburb was being vilified by commentators ranging from Clough Williams-Ellis and Thomas Sharp to Le Corbusier. For some they were quite simply 'a kind of scum churning against the walls of the city'. Here was the disdainful inter-war and post-war critique of sprawl, or 'subtopia' as it was renamed by Ian Nairn, in one of his many critical architectural judgements. In an era that lacked real planning control, new speculatively built semi-detached houses and bungalows, cul-de-sacs, green lawns and mock Tudor design ('Tudorbethan' with fake half-timbering), and even 'ultra-modern' sunspan homes, sprang up in 'Metroland' Buckinghamshire along the Metropolitan Railway and elsewhere, as mortgages were taken out by families secure in white-collar and professional jobs. The suburbanisation of the clay plain of central Middlesex in the inter-war period was characterised by low-density semi-detached housing, parades of shops around the station, an Odeon cinema and arterial roads – in many places a still-familiar scene. Indeed, Orwell's 'invincible green suburbs' now provide an emblematic landscape of Englishness that was heavily drawn upon by John Major, (Prime Minister 1990–7) whose own background was the London suburb of Worcester Park. For him a mix of 'Middle England' homely landscape and comforting social mores meant that: 'Fifty years on from now, Britain will still be the country of long shadows on cricket grounds, warm beer, invincible green suburbs, dog lovers and pools fillers.' In fact the inter-war

Fig. 7.15 A London Transport poster of 1908. Golders Green, 'a place of delightful prospects' reached by Underground. The contrast with the 'dull and smoky city' is made very emphatically.

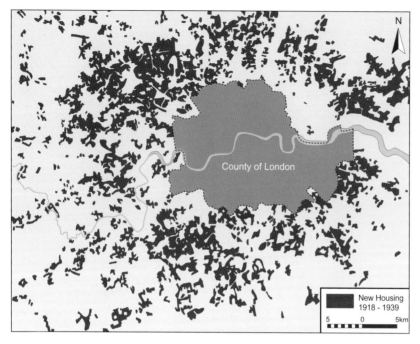

Fig. 7.16 The construction of inter-war housing beyond the County of London's boundaries, 1918–39.

suburbs are now showing their age along the dual-carriageway roads. Small extensions, conservatories and double-glazing too often sit behind two or three cars, mattresses or motorcycles, which spill out on to front gardens or grass verges.[25] Yet recently there have been signs that academics and planners are taking renewed interest in suburban life and landscape, and it may well be that these inter-war suburbs will prove to have been the earlier 20th-century's key contribution to metropolitan townscape.

Between 1918 and 1939 the conurbation of London doubled in area, and between 1921 and 1951 the highest population increases in England were in suburban 'commuterland' Surrey, Middlesex, Buckinghamshire, Bedfordshire and Hertfordshire, further fuelling the demand for homes, amenities and transport. By the 1930s the Greater London area accounted for 20 per cent of the total population of England and Wales, and 25 per cent of its urban population. The number of private homes built in the 1930s has never been matched before or since and involved perhaps 2.5 million people. There was also a surge in the construction of local-authority rented housing in large blocks of flats, especially those built by the LCC. Once admired, they are now being demolished as eyesores and social blackspots. South of the Thames alone, as many as 250,000 people migrated to such development between 1919 and 1939, helped by the electrification of the Southern Railway in the 1920s. The monotony of such housing can be overemphasised: lower-value housing (less than £1,000 to buy) was more prominent at Bexley and Crayford in the south-east; Sutton and Cheam, Merton and Malden and Coombe in the south-west; between Hornchurch and Chingford in the north-east; and in a broad western zone between Wembley and Feltham. Housing costing more than £1,000 was almost absent from west Middlesex and Essex and was to be found instead in the outer south-west, and in the north in Finchley and Hendon and in more scattered patches along the northern fringes of the built-up area (Figs 7.16–18).

In 1937 the Barlow Commission was established to report on the distribution of industry and the industrial population, with the task of recommending the relocation of industry away from London and the curbing of future industrial development in the South East. Following the hiatus of the Second World War (during which 30,000 Londoners died, one-third of the City was destroyed, and more than a million homes were damaged), fears of urban concentration continued. The destruction of many dockland and East End homes and landmarks in the Blitz is vividly caught in wartime film footage. In West Ham alone 14,000 homes were totally destroyed and by 1945 11,000 homes in Stepney were uninhabitable or had been demolished among weed-covered waste ground.

Post-war planning had actually begun during the war: Patrick Abercrombie produced his *County of London Plan* in 1943 and the *Greater London Plan* in 1944 – two documents that envisaged the wholesale redesign of London's fabric. The former advocated residential and industrial zoning and attention to traffic circulation; the latter the strengthening of a Green Belt around the capital and the establishment of the new towns beyond that belt (*see* Fig. 4.19). The latter plans were indeed enacted, but one consequence was that housing, industry and commerce now began to engage in an ever more pronounced struggle for expensive space within the confines of the Green Belt, exacerbated in the 1960s by a boom in demand for office building. Although they were necessarily pragmatic and had to adopt a patchwork approach with regard to the existing historic fabric of the capital, these 1940s' plans were ambitious and pointed the way towards a new holistic conception of London as a region. They also pointed to future struggles between a London landscape dominated (as in the past) by commercial considerations and a utopian London planned for a greater degree of social and environmental justice.[26] Thanks to modern mass consumerism ushered in by 'Swinging London' in the 1960s, Thatcherism in the 1980s and contemporary globalisation, the balance seems permanently tipped one way. Commerce always appears to have the upper hand in the formation of the landscape.

During the 1960s and early 1970s local authorities embarked on a huge slum-clearance programme in the East End: housing had become a poor competitor for space, thousands of homes had been destroyed in the war and much of the remaining stock was very old. In West Ham the council built more than 8,000 homes between 1945 and 1965, of which the largest concentration was on the Keir Hardie estate north of the Royal Victoria Dock in Canning Town. Nevertheless, by the mid-1970s one London household in 12 still had no indoor lavatory, a figure that rose to one in five in the East End. In some areas, such as Churchill Gardens, Pimlico, redevelopment was carried out at high densities. The main instrument at this time, however, was the relocation of communities into Le Corbusier-inspired high-rise blocks. This was not without its problems and planning at this time was frequently censured for its lack of consultation, and for what the sociologists Michael (later Lord) Young and Peter Willmott termed the 'collective madness' of local authorities. From 1950 onwards the newly appointed LCC housing designers and politicians, backed by enthusiasts of modernity, nevertheless pushed through novel conceptions of use and architecture; the result was the high blocks, subsequently copied by authorities throughout the United Kingdom. A new London landscape was brought into being as the height of the towers continued to increase across the capital. By the late 1950s and early 1960s many were pushing beyond the LCC's regulation 11 storeys, as at the Brandon

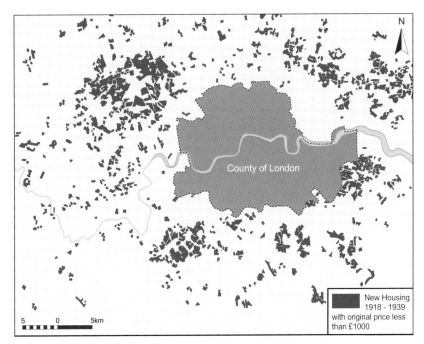

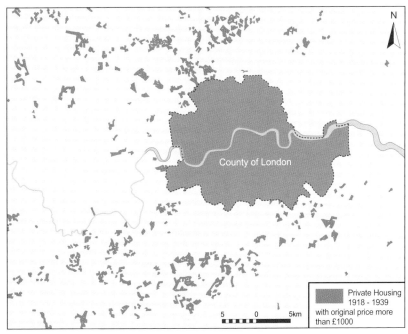

TOP: *Fig. 7.17 Lower-value private enterprise housing, 1918–39.*

ABOVE: *Fig. 7.18 Higher-value private enterprise housing, 1918–39.*

estate in Southwark, with its six blocks of 18 storeys: enthusiasm was (literally) running high. Between 1951 and 1981 the population of Bethnal Green thus fell from 58,000 to 30,000 as neighbourhoods were split asunder. The deeply disliked Ferrier estate at Kidbrooke in north Eltham was of 'grim, grey concrete… an extreme example of the stark geometry produced by industrialised building methods'. Forty per cent of its population were black and ethnic, to which Vietnamese, Eritrean and Somali refugees have now been added; in 2005 it was being redeveloped to the north of Kidbrooke Station on Nelson Mandela Road.[27]

Many working-class communities were thus being relocated to sites on the capital's peripheries, such as the mammoth LCC blocks built in the 1950s on the Alton Estate in Roehampton, the Roundshaw estate on the site of Croydon Aerodrome (1967–71) and Thamesmead. The latter was a large-scale project planned by the GLC for land released by the closure of Woolwich Arsenal and its marshland firing ranges in 1967. It was an unprepossessing site on the Erith and Plumstead marshes, bordered by power stations, industrial plant, including the Ford car plant across the river, and the Crossness sewage works. Linear concrete blocks of flats and low-rise dwellings with interconnecting walkways were built in neighbourhood units with car-free zones, to architectural acclaim but social condemnation, especially after the filming there of Stanley Kubrick's *A Clockwork Orange* (1970). Building stalled for financial reasons but was restarted in the late 1970s, using conventional bricks instead of concrete. The original aspirations for Thamesmead have not so far materialised; instead, social problems have beset the development, as they have so often in such landscapes. Belmarsh Prison became operational here in 1991.

Because the Green Belt was restricting private housing development and lengthening commuter journeys, there were those who began to seek alternative living space within London. This led to the gentrification process in which younger people with capital colonised former artisan terraces on the fringes of fashionable areas and began to upgrade the housing stock, in tune with the revised ideas of planners that rehabilitation and renewal were better than redevelopment. Conservation Areas, underpinned by stringent development control, were promoted in the 1970s to conserve worthwhile urban environments and promote regenerative re-use, and General Improvement Areas and Housing Action Areas have followed, many of them taking advantage of the availability of publicly funded improvement grants. Streets in Islington were being gentrified from the 1950s, those in Hackney or Brixton are now also upgraded, but these are juxtaposed with those that await transformation. Every year thousands of young homeowners move into areas such as Battersea, where they marginalise long-term residents on council estates and displace the less affluent, including pensioners. The implication is that in more recent years the Modern movement, with its preference for concrete and high-rise landscapes, has given way to a post-modern architectural interest that claims diversity and historical interest as more important values.

London has long been a very heterogeneous multi-ethnic city. In recent years, networks of immigrant households have made a significant contribution to the urban scene in suburban locations such as Southall, where a Sikh Gurdwara was opened in 1959, or in more central locations such as Soho's Chinatown. The beautiful Swaminarayan Hindu Mandir at Neasden (1995), the many halal and kosher shops, Irish pubs, Turkish, Chinese and Japanese food shops, and the Green Street shopping area in Newham have all helped to diversify the townscape. London probably has more mosques than any other western European city, with the Regent's Park Mosque a central focus. The complex symbolism and the historical layers of meaning contained within some religious sites is well illustrated by the Bangladeshi Jamia Masjid Mosque in Brick Lane in East London. The mosque is housed in a former synagogue that was itself converted from a Wesleyan Chapel, the congregation of which had in turn had taken over the building from its original Huguenot worshippers. All around are the food shops, clothes and restaurants of the community, although the area has become subject to gentrification as a centre for artistic production and consumption. In this respect it has been part of a new eastward movement of London's artistic centre of gravity, the participants in which subscribe to and celebrate multiracial and multicultural diversity. Perhaps stranger is the case of the Azizia Mosque in Stoke Newington, a Turkish mosque that was originally one of Hackney's historical cinemas. Ironically 'The Moorish Alhambra' had in its own day adopted a quasi-oriental style for its façade and domes in an attempt to replicate its Andalusian namesake. Near by, the Shacklewell Lane Mosque inhabits a former synagogue that was also originally built in Andalusian style. In the City, meanwhile, Bevis Marks (Britain's oldest synagogue, completed in 1701) has an architectural style that reflects its Spanish and Portuguese Jewish origins as well as the contemporary Classical designs of Sir Christopher Wren.[28]

The extent of physical change in London since 1945 has been extraordinary. In 1951 the Festival of Britain transformed the South Bank area to demonstrate a resurgent nation committed to a planned urban environment. Modernity and an integrated, pedestrianised landscape were its dominant themes, expressed in the form of the Royal Festival Hall (Grade I), the Skylon and the riverside walkway. One of the largest and most celebrated developments within the City has been the Barbican; it was built during the late 1960s on a bombed site and was designed to encourage people to live once more within the City (*see* Table 7.1). The population of Cripplegate Ward stood at 14,000 in 1851 but had fallen to just 48 by 1951. Despite the severity of the architecture, more than 4,000 people have returned to live in the 2,000 flats that are housed in the scheme's 40-storey towers. Parts of the Roman wall were incorporated into the design, as was the church of St Giles Cripplegate, which had survived the Great Fire of 1665.

Other ambitious schemes for redevelopment began to run into opposition, however. At Covent Garden, following the closure of the fruit and vegetable market in 1973, years of campaigning against the GLC's plan for office development have resulted instead in the area becoming a highly popular and gentrified leisure and tourism venue, including, from 2000, the redeveloped Royal Opera House. It was cases such as this and the failed opposition to the demolition of the Euston Arch in 1961 that helped to launch the protectionist strand of modern urban conservation. During the 1980s this was followed by battles over aesthetic taste in urban design. In 1984 these were further stoked by the Prince of Wales when, in his famous 'monstrous carbuncle' speech, he advocated 'community' architecture at such publicly visible sites as the National Gallery, the Mansion House and Paternoster Square, rather than the high-tech modernity of Richard Rogers's Lloyds Building. While these debates were going on, London's continued economic growth, further stimulated by the reinvention of a Greater London Authority and the creation of the Mayoralty, was giving an extraordinary boost to further redevelopment throughout the capital. This has indeed been of such huge proportions that the 'post-postwar' period deserves separate analysis.

The largest programme of redevelopment and upgrading, and one that has changed London's landscape perhaps more than any one other since the Fire of London, has been the London Docklands scheme. As the handling of goods was replaced by the handling of information, so the environment of east London had in its own turn to be transformed. The East India Dock had closed in 1967, St Katherine's Dock in Wapping in 1968, London Dock in 1969, Surrey Commercial Docks in 1970, the West India and Millwall Docks on the Isle of Dogs in 1981 and the Royals in 1982. The dockland landscape had lasted for about 160 years, but was now unwanted. Isolation, unemployment, out-migration, poor schools and social services and extreme dereliction had become so serious that in 1971 they even prompted the Isle of Dogs to make a 'unilateral declaration of independence'! Much business was transferred downstream to Tilbury, where container traffic and larger vessels could be handled.

The scale of the closures and loss of jobs defeated the resources of the local boroughs to regenerate the area for a cross-section of the community. Instead the Conservative government created the London Docklands Development Corporation (LDDC) in 1981 to redevelop more than 2,000ha of former dockland. Powers of compulsory purchase and reclamation were given, but there was no overall master plan. Newspapers and offices began to relocate from Fleet Street to Wapping, but the heart of the development has been Canary Wharf. This has been one of the largest construction projects in Europe and is dominated by the obelisk of its 280m-high office tower (in 1991 the tallest building in London) and its two companions, which together offer a huge area of commercial office space and have attracted many companies to move eastwards from the City (Fig. 7.19). The new Enterprise Zone that had been created in the Isle of Dogs was linked to Tower Hill by a specially constructed elevated light railway, and later on it was further served by an extension of the Jubilee Line. Fifty thousand people are now employed here, served by a continuous line of boutiques, tourist attractions, restaurants, bars and luxury apartments, many of them housed in Grade I-listed 19th-century warehouses. The area even has its own (and London's fifth) airport, City Docklands.

By the time the LDDC had been wound up in 1998 it had channelled £1.86 billion in public-sector investment and £7.7 billion of private-sector investment into infrastructure, commercial and industrial floor space and more than 24,000 new homes. The development reclaimed 780ha of derelict land and has allowed London to continue to compete commercially in a global marketplace. More controversially, however, it has made only limited inroads into the area's housing problems. In the mid-1960s the docklands area still had 55,000 residents, and in 1981 it housed more than 40,000 council tenants. The first of the new housing units were, by contrast, 'flagship' upper-income private developments that few local people could afford. In 1981 the population of the Isle of Dogs was 15,472 and by October 1997 it was estimated to have risen to 23,000 – actually in excess of the 1901 level, but now with a very different social mix. The whole scheme won 94 awards for architecture, conservation and landscaping, but only now, prompted by public concern, has attention been turned to the tenants and the

Fig. 7.19 Docklands landscapes. The towers of Canary Wharf have replaced the earlier landscape of docks and housing, and now constitute an important element of international business and commerce at the western end of the planned Thames Gateway regeneration scheme.

lack of communal facilities in what, after working hours, has been termed a 'human desert'.

The redevelopment of the former docklands is a key element in the larger Thames Gateway project (*see* Chapter 3), which will have an enormous further impact on the landscape of east London. It is the largest redevelopment zone in western Europe and incorporates the residential and industrial suburbs of outer London and the settlements of Dartford and Thurrock on its fringes. This estuarine landscape was formerly dominated by extensive extractive industries; today it includes 3,800ha of brownfield land that are the legacy of large-scale industrial dereliction, set amidst a network of relatively depressed local towns and communities. By 2005 development had been completed on 40 of the 212 available sites, including a new university campus and an exhibition centre at Stratford. The aim is to bring new schools, world-class sports facilities, business opportunities, health, arts and training centres, libraries, nature parks, theatres and sustainable transport links to the area, transforming the landscape and in the process providing an additional 120,000 homes. A huge boost was given to the project in 2005 when it was announced that the 2012 Olympic Games are to be held in London. An Olympic village and stadium are to be constructed at Stratford, other sporting venues in the capital are to be upgraded, and the transport infrastructure will be improved. When the games are over the athletes' village will become affordable housing and the new Stratford City project will provide the area with a shopping centre, new homes and commercial premises.

The 1980s and 1990s witnessed many further alterations to the landscape, especially in central and inner London. Not only have changes in transport and communications technology rendered rail goods yards, wharves, canals and docks redundant, but the shift from an industrial to a post-industrial economy since the 1960s has also meant that there is less need for large factories. By contrast, the demand for modern office space appears to be insatiable. As a result, the West End of London now has the most expensive office accommodation anywhere in the world, closely followed by the City of London, Paris and Frankfurt. The decay and dereliction of one type of landscape is now giving way to a modern successor. As the economy is restructured, so is the landscape of the city that supports it: a good example of Schumpeter's principle of capitalism's 'perennial gale of Creative Destruction' that was referred to in Chapter 1. The old Hoover factory on the A40 is now a retail park; Bryant and May's match factory at Bow has been transformed into desirable apartments. The sites of former utilities companies have also changed: the Becton gasworks site east of the old Royal Albert Dock has been renamed Gallions Reach and given over to housing, as have the Rotherhithe Docks (now Surrey Quays). The former gasworks site at the north of the Greenwich peninsula has become the Millennium Dome, the controversial but visible reminder of the many attempts that are still being made to regenerate eastern Thames-side. The Royal Victoria Docks are now home to a giant exhibition centre and the Bankside power station has become Tate Modern. The Harrods Furniture depository at Barnes has been reinvented as 'Harrods Village'. Other impressive landmarks have included the development of 'Albion Riverside' between the Albert and Battersea bridges, the conversion of Chelsea Harbour into a yacht marina and the transformation of the Oxo Tower on the South Bank into a luxury restaurant and apartments.

The list of changes seems endless as obsolescence gains speed in London. Although there seems little left that can still be converted, developers continue to offer new schemes in a 'revalorisation of the riverside'.[29] The older landmarks are now frequently submerged among newer buildings that pay homage to the service sector, and to high-rise office buildings that are the trophy architecture of the contemporary 'landscapes of financial power'. In a return to the thinking of the 1960s, architects are once again building high. Thus we have seen the rise of a new generation of tall buildings, ranging from Tower 42 (The 'NatWest Tower',

Fig. 7.20 The City of London. *General view towards the City showing the dwarfing of St Paul's by high-rise office blocks, and Foster's 'erotic gherkin' at 30 St Mary Axe.*

Fig. 7.21 Renzo Piano's London Bridge Tower. *An impression of a future 'icon-age' landscape of 67 storeys, to be finished by 2009. The 'shard of glass' is scheduled to be 60m taller than Canary Wharf, and the tallest building in Europe at the time of its completion*

completed in 1981) to Lord Foster's Swiss Reinsurance tower (the 'erotic gherkin' or 'towering innuendo' of 2003–4), which rose on the site at 30 St Mary Axe of the old Baltic Exchange, after the latter had been damaged by an IRA bomb. Late in 2003 planning permission was granted at London Bridge (itself replaced after 1968) for a 'shard of glass' tower higher than Canary Wharf, and more are in the offing (Figs 7.20 and 7.21). New electronic technologies demand buildings with large open-plan floors and space for cabling, leading to ever larger corporate buildings which cover every part of their site and leave little open space around them – and another remaking seems inevitable. A new Thames Gateway Bridge, just east of the Woolwich Ferry, will in the future link Thamesmead with the north bank; and in the King's Cross–St Pancras area a huge redevelopment is creating the principal interchange between national and European rail networks via the new QE2 bridge and the Channel Tunnel: evidence again of London's continuing role as the nation's gateway.

The residual landscapes of London are now major tourist attractions. They are at the forefront of Britain's 'heritage'. The metropolis houses no fewer than four World Heritage Sites: Westminster, The Tower of London, Greenwich and Kew Gardens. Among many other internationally famous sites are the South Kensington Victorian museum complex; the City, the National Gallery and Trafalgar Square; the Tate Gallery and Tate Modern; Docklands; Madame Tussaud's, and the British Museum. All generate profits for London's imposing hotels, which are landscape features in their own right. Cultural fashions wax and wane and during the 1960s Carnaby Street became very popular as a tourist attraction and symbol of 'Swinging London'. Since the late 1960s conservation areas have been designated throughout the capital; the impressive surroundings of the Royal Naval College at Greenwich was the first in London (1968), to be followed by areas such as Belgravia, much of the cities of London and Westminster, and Kensington and Chelsea. House and office prices have correspondingly soared: in April 2004 it was reported that more than £70 million had been paid for a property in Kensington Palace Gardens, the most expensive street in England (its 150th birthday in 2004 was celebrated by a party hosted by members of the royal family for their ultra-rich neighbours). Many conservation areas, such as Primrose Hill, are much smaller: the borough of Richmond has 66 such areas, Ealing 26 and Bromley 44.

By contrast, the government's Index of Multiple Deprivation showed that in 2000 London possessed 20 of the most deprived boroughs in the country. The index highlights an area of central and north-east inner wards that stretches from the heart of London to Haringey and Newham (ranked 6th out of 354 English districts). There are then further outliers in inner south London: Southwark is 14th on the national list, while Peckham is particularly problematic – its council estate landscape is the setting of Britain's favourite TV sitcom, *Only Fools and Horses*. There is so much economic potential in this city, yet such a lack of social cohesion; it is both ends of this spectrum that imprint themselves on the landscape.

The spread of this global city within south-east England makes it difficult to gauge where London ends and the rest of the region begins. Daniel Defoe in the 18th century proposed a unitary authority for London, a suggestion that in his day found little favour. But the large numbers of parishes inside and outside the City, and the myriad other local bodies, have always made it difficult to intervene effectively in matters affecting the landscape and environment. There have thus been successive attempts to establish administrative boundaries that would effectively encompass the London boroughs, beginning with the Metropolitan Board of Works (1855) and moving on to the London County Council (1888–1963) and the larger Greater London Council (1963–86). Even when the GLC had been abolished there was still a London Planning Advisory Committee (LPAC), established to work with central government and the 33 borough authorities to formulate *ad hoc* comprehensive plans. By 2005 there is an elected mayor and assembly, a Greater London Authority and a Government Office for

London. The Mayor sets out and co-ordinates strategies aimed at improving the landscape. These include spatial and economic development, the transport system (except the Underground), air quality, biodiversity, energy, noise, waste and culture.

But however the administrative boundaries of successive authorities are defined, London's influence extends far beyond. The city's outward development has meant that there is an intimate chronological and spatial linkage between the centre, the inner suburbs, the outer suburbs and the detached and economically and socially dependent settlements that lie further out still. In landscape terms we find this symbolised by the re-erection of Paxton's extraordinary prefabricated Hyde Park Crystal Palace (1851) at outlying Sydenham, near Paxton's home, where it remained a great attraction from 1854 until its destruction by fire in 1936. There is now a case for regarding the whole of the South East as London's functional 'regional city', and for much of the past 50 years it has been those areas on the fringes of London, or just outside the Green Belt, which have exhibited the greatest dynamism in their landscapes (*see* Chapter 6). As London's inner city core has lost population and gained environmental problems, so the outer fringes seemed to offer space and environmental quality, but sufficiently close to London's metropolitan heart for any access that is required.[30] By 2000, 21 per cent of London's workforce commuted in from outside. And just as the social divides and deteriorating physical quality of the townscape in London require intervention, so too will they become not just a problem for London but one for the whole region.

LONDON'S LANDSCAPE PALIMPSEST

One conclusion to emerge from this brief survey of London's evolution is that urban landscape history is a complex notion. In peeling back the historical layers of such a global city it is difficult to do justice to earlier periods. So much has changed, is changing or is about to change. Another observation is that London at the local level still retains its historical social diversity – monolithic landscapes do not exist. Olsen referred to London as having either 'picturesque variety … or aesthetic anarchy'.[31] There is no large and exclusively middle-class district, no manufacturing belt, no ghetto. Perhaps the nearest to a single-use area is the square mile of the City itself, and even that has seen some repopulation within the last 20 years.

John Summerson, in his elegant way, summed this up:

> London is remarkable for the freedom with which it developed. It is the city raised by private, not by public, wealth; the least authoritarian city in Europe. Whenever attempts have been made to overrule the individual in the public interest, they have failed. Elizabeth and her Stuart successors tried bluntly to stop any expansion whatever. They failed. Charles II and his pet intellectuals tried to impose a plan after the Great Fire. They failed. Nearly every monarch in turn projected a great Royal Palace to dominate at least part of his capital. All failed until George IV conspired with Nash to cheat Parliament into rebuilding Buckingham House, scoring no triumph in the process. The reasons for all this are embedded deep in England's social and political history. London is one of the few capitals where church property and church interests have not been an overriding factor; where Royal prestige and prerogative in building matters have been set at naught; where defence has never, since the Middle Ages, dictated a permanent circumvallation to control the limits of development. London is above all a metropolis of merchandise. The basis of its building history is the trade cycle rather than the changing ambitions and policies of rulers and administrators. The land speculator and the adventuring builder have

*contributed more to the character of the Georgian city than the minister
with a flair for artistic propaganda, or the monarch with a mission for
dynastic assertion.*[32]

London, unlike St Petersburg or Berlin, was not a planned city. Rome had finer
vistas, Vienna more magnificent palaces, Paris a grandeur of scale. London was
instead inchoate.[33] The landscape reflects opportunity, fragmentation, status, and
an inherited symbolism that persists or changes only slowly. But the value of a
site in London guaranteed its successive use and re-use: the early-19th century
St Katherine's Dock, for example, displaced a medieval college and a Georgian
slum next to the Tower of London. A separate large volume could be devoted to
the complex process and outcome of London's redevelopment over 2,000 years.
The Victorians destroyed much of Georgian London as they remade the capital,
but were shocked by the removal of the Doric colonnades of the Regent Street
Quadrant in 1848 and replacement of Westminster Bridge in the 1850s; they
similarly watched in awe as the Embankment was constructed and Whitehall
filled with impressive government offices. The 20th century witnessed many
other such replacements and although these were more frequently challenged,
the cityscape – perhaps more dramatically and self-evidently than any other
landscape – refuses to remain still.

Because social status has always been measured through cultural consumption,
the quality of the landscape and environment has always loomed large in people's
everyday lives. In recent years this has taken on new and important meanings as
older class divisions within London have been transformed or fragmented. This
may not reduce antagonisms or inequalities of power – witness the growth of
NIMBYism (the Not In My Backyard syndrome) in the suburbs and even more
powerfully in the village and countryside beyond – but it does demonstrate the
strength of feeling that is attached to place. As ideas, finance and culture become
increasingly internationalised in world cities such as London, the accompanying
landscapes both promote and reflect the new cultural mix. It remains to be seen
whether those landscapes will in future experience a counterblast of localism in
the face of the march of globalisation.

NOTES

1 Ackroyd 2000, 2–3.
2 Goodall 2000, 50.
3 Schofield 1999, 216–18; Milne 2002; Quiney 2003, 82–3.
4 Wall 1998, 101.
5 Corfield 1982, 67.
6 Petty 1662, vol. I, 41
7 Rasmussen 1982.
8 McKellar 1999, 19; Cruickshank & Burton 1990, 19.
9 Cruickshank & Burton 1990, 133.
10 Harwood & Saint 1991, 99; Prince 1964, 101; Summerson 1988, 162.
11 Corfield 1982, 78.
12 Chalklin 1998, 207.
13 Rogers 1856.
14 Barker & Robbins 1963, 242.x
15 Olsen 1976, 25.
16 Dyos 1977, 111.
17 Davis 2000, 132.
18 Oliver 2002.
19 Dyos 1982, 144.
20 Hall 1964, 65.
21 Shepherd et al. 1974, 74–5.
22 Priestley 1934 (1968 edn), 4–5.
23 Linehan 2003, 136.
24 Betjeman 1970, 20–4.
25 Oliver et al. 1981, 27–53; Nairn 1955.
26 Hardy 2005, 35–49
27 Shepherd et al. 1974, 42–3; Young & Willmott 1986, xix; Ambrose 1986; Glendinning & Muthesius 1994, 53–65; Cherry & Pevsner 1983, 278.
28 Naylor & Ryan 2003, 176; Hamnett 2003, 247.
29 Hamnett 2003, 221, 246.
30 Buck et al. 2002, 17–88.
31 Olsen 1976, 71.
32 Summerson 1988, 14.
33 Port 1995, 1–25.

PART III

The South-east Landscape as Representation and Inspiration

Although people have always lived in landscapes that are tangible outcomes of their work, the worlds in which they lived were not only material creations but also habitations of the mind. Imagined landscapes have a power over our senses, an ability to evoke passion or enquiry, to restore tranquillity, to transport us back to earlier cherished landscapes of our youth. Real or imagined, they help us to make sense of our lives and they anchor our memories. We all carry these lost landscapes around with us, and react strongly – positively or negatively – to the changes we see happening. One category of imagined landscapes involves those that have been self-consciously and formally imagined through the representational arts, whether written, graphic or auditory. The South East has been the scene for many such landscapes of the imagination, created as 'literary landscapes', as poetic ideals, as paintings, as musical inspiration, performance or film settings.

There are very many places in the South East for which some representation exists, and this chapter must therefore necessarily be selective. London has always had a huge influence over the country's creative talents, both as *genius loci* and place of residence, but the region's many rural environments have also inspired, and been the subject of, imaginative creation. Indeed, it could be said that the perceived charm of the 'Home Counties' springs in part from the very contrast with London, and that creative minds, when released from the capital, appreciated all the more fully the landscape and society of the countryside.

This is not to deny that there were many artists and writers who celebrated the civilisation of the city and compared it to an unpleasant countryside, although such a genre remains largely unexplored. This was, of course, the perception of those thousands of migrants who were flocking to urban areas throughout much of the period described in this book. Certainly the 'rural-as-primitive' regional novel, with its clichés and Hodge-like characters, found great favour in the rural depressions that stretched from the late 1870s through to 1939. It is exemplified by the wealden settings that Sheila Kaye-Smith used for her novels, and even found a place in music-hall routines. As mobility increased from the 18th century onwards, many writers, in particular, began to portray the countryside with a mixture of nostalgia, guilt and superiority. The centrality of London metropolitanism was in particular contrasted with the 'provincialism' of the countryside. In the case of Wessex we should remember Hardy's *The Return of the Native* (1878), and perhaps remind ourselves that Stella Gibbons, in her wonderful 1932 parody of the genre, has Flora, the urbane and modern heroine, finally leaving her appalling cousins at Cold Comfort Farm (on the Sussex downland) by aeroplane for London.

This chapter traces the power of the imagination to create landscapes in south-east England. In looking at these invented landscapes, however, we must remember that their purpose was not necessarily one of verisimilitude, and that such creations were not intended to provide material for landscape historians! The use of artistic representations as 'evidence' for past historical landscapes has therefore to be approached with immense caution, and previous attempts to derive 'fact' from this kind of work have too often resulted in crude history. Artistic representations can, however, tell us a very great deal about the attitudes and prejudices of their creators. A writer might use a similar landscape to create many feelings: fear or joy, apprehension or valour, in the context of a narrative. Thus Arthur Conan Doyle's *Valley of Fear* (1915) and A.A.Milne's *Winnie The Pooh* (1926) are both set, at least in part, within close proximity to each other in the High Weald by two resident authors. D H Lawrence in *The Rainbow* (1915) gives the South Downs an erotic charge, but Rudyard Kipling uses them in *Sussex* (1902) as a symbol of patriotic Englishness. Furthermore we, the readers, can interpret the product within our own circumstances and according to our own imaginations, as 'the text floats free' from its creator.

But we may take these questions of interpretation and meaning a stage further. A representation of a landscape, whether visual, musical or written, has a strong relationship with the landscape itself. There is thus an intertextual movement between the actual landscape and its created image. In 'consuming' a landscape representation our perception of the place that is depicted is altered, and we may see elements that we missed before. We also learn to see a thing by having to describe it and to find words or representations for it. We need to remember, too, that the word 'landscape' can mean simultaneously the thing that is portrayed and the portrayal of it. Less importantly, the fact of an artist's association with a place can create a landscape element of its own, such as the house of a famous writer or painter that today becomes the object of heritage preservation. The imagined landscape has thus created its own reality.

Of course, in a post-modern world we must recognise that *all* representations of landscape are partial and to varying extents subjective. This would include the 'mere antiquarian' (Dr Johnson's phrase) writers of the classic town and county histories such as John Leland, John Stow, William Stukeley or Edward Hasted. Although there is insufficient space to treat their work properly here, their early interest in the preservation of ancient ruins, and the idea of a national heritage, gives them an importance to the later campaigns and interest groups who have fought for landscape preservation.[1] Therefore, this chapter also seeks to analyse the impact of these and the many other imagined/created landscapes because of the influence that they had on the realities of conservation and planning, especially from the 19th century to the present. We will be dealing here with ideas of 'moral landscapes', of planning for a preconceived 'correct' alignment of town and country within which people will live, and of giving landscapes such symbolic importance that in order to protect them, British people might fight and die.

THE PAINTER AND VISUAL ARTIST IN THE SOUTH EAST

English landscapes, and scenes of ordinary life, will never confer a very high character on a school. (Review in the Magazine of Fine Arts *1821)*[2]

Let us say again that representations of the region's landscape are just that: what the creators experience and what they wish to display. No visual representation, whether painting, photograph or film, can be taken 'at face value' for that reason: images may be distorted or emphasised; they may omit the 'dark side of the landscape' or they can create a pure fantasy interwoven with sufficient reality to make it plausible.[3] With Emile Zola we can say that 'A work of art is a corner of nature seen through a temperament'. From the report of the libel action, *Whistler vs Ruskin*, we have, concerning Whistler's *Battersea Bridge*:

BARON HUDDLESTON: Which part of the picture is the bridge? (Laughter) … Do you say this is a correct representation of Battersea Bridge?

WHISTLER: I did not intend it to be a 'correct' portrait of the bridge. It is only a moonlight scene, and the pier in the centre of the picture may not be like the piers of Battersea Bridge as you know them in broad daylight. As to what the picture represents, that depends upon who looks at it. To some persons it may represent all that is intended; to others it may represent nothing.

HUDDLESTON: The prevailing colour is blue?

WHISTLER: Perhaps.[4]

In recent years computerised image-making has given the possibility for the enhancement of all kinds to both still and moving images, to the extent that we now accept that the depiction we see may be a lie, or may only partially exist. Both pictures and words intervene in landscape history to deflect or enhance our enjoyment and studies. With this in mind we can begin by tracing visual portraits of the south-east landscape chronologically – but necessarily selectively because the South East has been the subject of a myriad representations.

   The medieval period has left few images of real landscapes, as opposed to buildings, and arguably none pretended to be 'landscape' paintings. The Bayeux Tapestry shows King Edward the Confessor in his hall in Winchester Palace and on his deathbed in Westminster Palace, and Earl Harold's manorial hall and adjacent church at Bosham in Sussex, although the depictions of Harold were probably intended as a recognisable symbol of lordship rather than a literal representation of landscape. We really have to await the Dissolution of the Monasteries and the awakening of interest in estates and topography during the Tudor and Stuart periods for real illustration of the landscape. Even then, however, we are seeing depictions of 'land' rather than landscape, presented in the form of purely functional estate or manorial maps and plans. Nevertheless, very decorative maps would include bird's-eye and elevation views of mansions and depictions of farmland and animals. County maps also became more fashionable after the publication in 1579 of Christopher Saxton's *Atlas*, and the work of the contemporary cartographer, John Norden, included many elevation views near the cartouches of his work. His *View of London Bridge from East to West* (1597) showed the bridge as a 'contynuall street' with its many weather-boarded buildings, while his stunning masterpiece, *Civitas Londini* (1600), shows a bird's-eye panoramic view of the entire city, and was copied many times in later years. Norden's 1607 survey of the Honour of Windsor contained an elevation of Windsor Castle. The bird's-eye view offers us detail of elevations but often obscures the streets and alleys and leaves little room for labels or place-names, important when dealing with crowded parts of London or other large towns. Increased 17th-century interest in topography was kindled by Dutch artists, whose specific views of houses with their gardens and surroundings built on the landscape painting genre of later 16th-century Flanders. The Dutch *landschap* is adopted as the English 'landskip' or 'Landscape' as a painterly object from about this time, although much of this work began as a celebration of individuals and their political or social power within an idealised landscape. Sir Anthony Van Dyck and Jacob Esselens included views of Rye within their work and Wenceslaus Hollar, from Prague, is credited with panoramic views of 17th-century London and many etchings of Sussex, although he may have based his work on the prior etchings of the local John Dunstall.[5]

   The 18th and 19th centuries, particularly after Richard Wilson's return from Italy to England in the 1760s, ushered in the great age of watercolour painting and topographical art. It was stimulated by the fashion for elite tours as a civilised leisure activity and by the spread of the print trade, which offered landscape depictions to the rising commercial middle classes. Celia Fiennes, writing in about 1703 of Epsom during her tour of England, notes that: 'The commons all about Epsham is very good aire and shews the country like a landskip, woods, plains, inclosures, and great ponds.' When political upheavals in Europe deterred travellers from the customary Grand Tour to Italy and Greece, they turned their attentions closer to London, where improved roads offered safer travel. The Arcadian visions of Poussin and Claude now gave way to the British settings of Gainsborough and Stubbs. A fashion for drawing as a recreation and the sale of topographical views for subscribers encouraged artists to specialise, as for example, in the work of Samuel Buck whose sketches of medieval buildings in Sussex, Surrey, Middlesex and Hertfordshire, among other counties, run into many hundreds, and were well known through the work of his engraver brother, Nathaniel. Francis Grose's well-known *Antiquities of England and Wales* (1772–87) comprised plates and brief descriptive text, and included many south-eastern views – there were 50 for Sussex alone. As a commissioned officer in a Surrey regiment in the 1760s he was marched across the region from Portchester to Maidstone, but sketched as he travelled. He conceived of the great project while at home in Wandsworth in about 1770.[6]

A greater concern for place and specific English landscapes, rather than generalised idyllic scenes, now also appeared, despite the fulminations of commentators such as Fuseli who criticised the 'mere topography' and 'tame delineation of a given spot'. Landscapes, especially churches, medieval monuments and ruins, were meticulously recorded, and offer valuable historical evidence for buildings and landscapes now destroyed or irretrievably altered. Thus Plaistow church, a half-timbered wealden building and probably the last-surviving church in that style, was painted in watercolour by Henry Petrie in 1805 but demolished before 1851 to be replaced by a stone chapel. In the same year, the small cottage-like churches of the Berkshire Downs were portrayed in *Views of Reading Abbey and the Principal Churches Connected Therewith* (1805). On the Sussex downland, West Blatchington and Hove churches were recorded in ruins by James Lambert Sr, the latter before its 19th-century rebuilding (Figs 8.1 and 8.2). Newly surveyed county maps also became more popular, with elaborate depictions of well-known local views. Chichester Cathedral is represented on many such Sussex county maps, for example. The magnificent collection of antiquarian topographical works belonging to William Burrell, of which 42 volumes were bequeathed to the British Museum, with watercolours by the Lamberts (uncle and nephew) and the prolific Swiss artist Samuel Hieronymous Grimm, is testimony to the enthusiasm of many wealthy men at this time.[7] Grimm painted watercolours of ordinary scenes in his extensive travels through the region, as well as providing illustrations for Gilbert White's *Natural History and Antiquities of Selborne* (1789). He finished nearly 900 watercolours of Sussex alone for William Burrell. On a grander scale, Peter Tilleman provided a view of the Twickenham waterside in about 1717 that showed the first glimpses of elegant Georgian houses being constructed. More prosaically, mundane rural scenes might also be depicted, as with J M W Turner's *Ploughing up Turnips Near Slough ('Windsor')* (c. 1809), although the precise meanings of this painting have been debated between those who see it as a celebration of English progressive agricultural achievement (with the agricultural enthusiast George III's Windsor Castle in the misty background), those who see the innovatory portrayal of the labourers as real workers, rather than as rustic clowns, those who perceive a more subtle threat to the socio-economic order through enclosure, and even those who read the turnip as a symbol to mock the Hanoverians.[8]

By the end of the 18th century the picturesque movement, with its taste for the rugged and broken landscape, favoured regions such as the Lake District rather

HOVE

Figs 8.1 and 8.2 Church recording in Sussex. *Fig. 8.1 (above) shows Plaistow Church, recorded by Henry Petrie in 1805 before its destruction by fire and eventual demolition and replacement. The vernacular style echoed that used in the buildings around it, and the steeply pitched roof was originally thatched. In Fig. 8.2 (left), Hove Church is shown by James Lambert Sr in 1776 in a ruinous state. By the 18th century the village of Hove to the south of the church was also ruinous, and there were no funds to effect repairs. The church was finally rebuilt in 1836.*

than the subtler charms and gentler slopes of the South East. Nevertheless, there were parts of the region that were more favoured by the artist than others. Certainly where spectacular scenes presented themselves, artists obliged. Turner and John Constable, for example, offered dramatic renditions of Stonehenge, a favoured tableau for artists for more than 300 years, and the region's main castles, ruins and architectural treasures such as Salisbury Cathedral. Writing about the South Downs, Brandon notes: 'Like any other Eden the Downs have been over-described, over-written, over-painted (and consequently) over-visited … [and the] smooth maternal lines of the Downs became one of the most familiar and mimicked images of the English countryside.' Nevertheless many artists, such as Copley Fielding, were highly influential in their depictions of downland landscape; his work catches the space, colour and flowing lines of the downland, often enveloped in mist or shimmering haze. By contrast the paintings of John Linnell, who came to live at Redhill in around 1851, are imbued with a sentimental pastoralism.[9]

At the beginning of the 20th century the painting of the South Downs reached new heights during the flowering of English rural idyllicism. As many as 36 artists resident in Sussex had exhibited work at the Royal Academy summer exhibition, and, indeed, during the first half of the 20th century the scenery became a visual cliché, particularly that of the eastern Sussex downland. The area around Ditchling, near Brighton, became known for a small colony of artists who were inspired by the ideals of Eric Gill; it included Charles Knight, whose tranquil rendition of *Ditchling Beacon* (1935) became particularly well known. Further east along the downs lived Sir William Nicholson, the self-styled 'painter of the Downs' before the First World War. His woodcut of the Rottingdean windmill became the colophon for Heinemann, the publishers, and he also painted scenes from the Wiltshire downland. East again was Charleston farmhouse, home to the extraordinary household, decamped from Bloomsbury, of Vanessa and Clive Bell, Duncan Grant, Roger Fry and David Garnett, augmented periodically by Leonard and Virginia Woolf from nearby Rodmell, Maynard Keynes, Lytton Strachey and E M Forster. The British post-impressionist movement was nurtured here, represented in Vanessa Bell's downland paintings and the group's murals in neighbouring Berwick church. Vanessa Bell's pointillist version of Alfriston in the Cuckmere valley was used as a Shell poster of 1931. Perhaps better known, though, are the smooth semi-abstract downland watercolour depictions of Eric Ravilious, such as his 1939 series of six watercolours set around the eastern South Downs, Wiltshire and Dorset, which included *The Vale of the White Horse* and *The Westbury Horse*. Ravilious was influenced by Paul Nash's chalkland images, and Nash himself painted at many different south-eastern locations, including the Marlborough Downs, the Chilterns and Savernake Forest. The western downland scarp-foot scenes of Ivon Hitchens are also well known. And finally, the watercolours of Stanley Roy Badmin (d.1990) offer idyllic countryside images of Sussex and Hampshire, devoid of such intrusions as electricity pylons. His gentle depictions are celebrated in greetings cards, calendars and publications such as the Puffin picture book *Village and Town* (1943), the *Shell Guide to Britain* and *Reader's Digest*.

If the picturesque and Romantic movements in aesthetic taste found little to explore in the downland, there was at least the more remote, mysterious, less-tamed Weald. Here were contrasting scenes: the slopes sharper and deep with rocky outcrops, the 'declivities adorned with sylvan riches'. As early as 1717 John Dennis likened the views from Leith Hill to those to be found in Italy – praise indeed:

> *The prospects that in Italy pleas'd me most, were that of the Valdarno from the Appenines, that of Rome and the Mediterranean from the Mountain of Viterbo … But from a hill which I pass'd in my late Journey into Sussex, I had a prospect more extensive than any of these, and which surpass'd them*

at once in Rural Charms, in Pomp and in Magnificence … call'd Lethe Hill.[10]

This Italianate scenery inspired many, including Turner, to depict wealden woodland scenes. By the middle of the 19th century artists were escaping from London and many turned to the Weald. Richard Redgrave forsook his successful career as a genre painter in 1849 to spend 37 successive summers painting *en plein air* at Abinger in Surrey. In North Kensington, Samuel Palmer longed for the ten years he spent at Shoreham in Kent from 1825 to 1835, where his mystical landscapes were suffused with Kentish detail. Reversing the process, John Linnell abandoned portraiture in Bayswater to move to Redstone, near Redhill. The Pre-Raphaelites John Millais and William Holman Hunt used minute detail at Ewell, Hastings and Winchelsea in their

Region	British Institution 1806–67	Royal Academy 1769–1904
London region (within 19km)	14.7	2.6
Weald	18.0	33.2
Lake District and northern England	12.0	13.6
Wales and Welsh Marches	28.1	11.2
West of England	11.1	12.6
Midlands	10.0	4.9
East Anglia	6.4	4.8
Ireland	1.7	0.9
Scotland	–	15.1
TOTALS	102%	98.9%

TABLE 8.1 THE SOUTH EAST IN LANDSCAPE PAINTING 1769–1904: PAINTINGS WITH TOPOGRAPHICAL TITLES (PERCENTAGE OF TOTAL BRITISH ISLES).

Source: Brandon 1984, 73, fn 21. The data and arithmetic are as in the original.

paintings. And a veritable colony of painters joined Redrave at Abinger, including J C Hook, George Vicat Cole, Edmund Warren, G P Boyce and later Benjamin Leader. Clayton Adams had a studio on Coneyhurst Hill, near Ewhurst in Surrey, from where he could paint the Weald. Ruskin applauded his efforts, noting that 'There are no railroads in it … no tunnel or pit mouths … no league-long viaducts … no parks, no gentlemen's seats … no rows of lodging houses … none of these things that the English mind now rages after.' Artists toured the area looking for suitable subject matter for rural genre paintings, with the hop fields in particular catching the attention of Samuel Palmer, Joshua Cristall, Thomas Uwins and others. Because the Weald was less advanced in agricultural progress it was also favoured by artists looking to show traditional and more picturesque farming practices, if possible with biblical or otherwise poetic connotations.[11]

Furthermore, the Weald offered heathland, formerly despised by agricultural improvers such as Arthur Young or Cobbett, but now with its own aesthetic champions. Here was wilderness 'guiltless of boundary or furrow' as described by Mrs Humphrey Ward in 1888, but which was nevertheless friendly and mellow. The large expanses of Surrey heathland particularly attracted the gentle domesticity of Helen Allingham or the idyllicism of Miles Birket Foster at Witley in Surrey; the spread of pine trees among the heather also lured many to live or visit in emulation of royal interest in Scottish landscapes. Witley, conveniently on the London to Portsmouth railway, also became home to an artistic community as Foster and Allingham were joined by Sir Henry Cole, George Eliot and Tennyson.

The Weald had become a vast Victorian open-air studio – an English Barbizon. A veritable wealden landscape school had appeared, highly visible in exhibitions during the 19th century (Table 8.1) and fostering in its later Victorian phase a sentimentalised nostalgia for a lost idyll, rather than the semi-wilderness sought by the earlier generation of artists.[12]

Southern rural scenes such these underpinned the 19th-century social and cultural preferences for rurality as the true repository of the continuing moral character of England. Ruskin's influential campaign against London's 'colourless metropolis … like a landscape in sepia' reinforced a search for aesthetic values in the countryside, as expressed forcefully in his *Fors Clavigera* (1871–84). As the

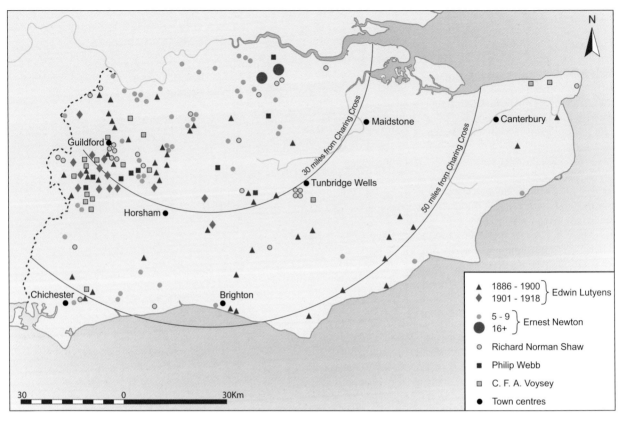

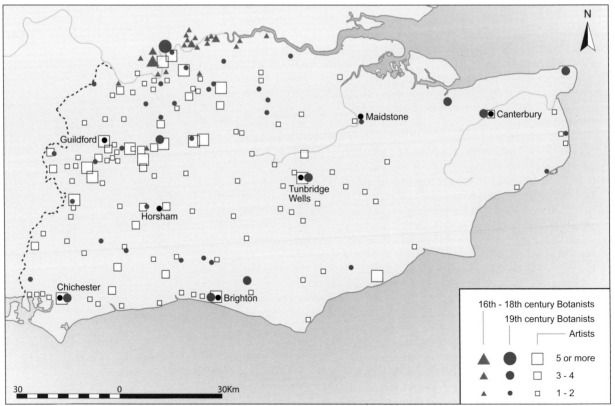

weight of political influence began to move from the older aristocracy towards midland and northern industrial and commercial interests, so the cultural superiority of 'pre-industrial aristocratic and religious values' was reasserted through the landscape iconography of the 'South country'. One result was that industrial profits might be reinvested in cultural consumption, particularly of rural estates or designed country houses, rather than back into commerce.[13] A strong spatial correlation between the location of 19th-century artists in Kent, Surrey and Sussex, and the location of country houses is therefore seen. Houses by Edwin Lutyens, Ernest Newton, Norman Shaw, Aston Webb and C Voysey clustered in wealden Surrey, the Hindhead area, and below the North Downs within 50km of Charing Cross (Figs 8.3 and 8.4).

The old-fashioned woodland wild garden and cottage garden, as designed by Lutyens, William Robinson or Gertrude Jekyll, completed the Victorian landscape of tranquillity, hidden among lush woods and rhododendrons. Gertrude Jekyll was Lutyens's cousin and at 'Munstead Wood' near Godalming he designed a house for her where she created her own 'cosmic wonderland' of a garden, melting imperceptibly into woodland. This movement of capital between sectors, or between town and country, was not new but the alignment of a rural idyll with the southern counties of England at the height of Victorian and Edwardian prosperity was a powerful force in the creation of precisely such idyllic landscapes in the region. Moving easily between London and their country estates, wealthy landowners now wanted their land to resemble the paintings they purchased. Thus, northern industrialists purchased harvest scenes by John Linnell set in Surrey. Such artists therefore had a vested interest in the perpetuation of the myth of the rural idyll, which they managed to sustain despite a later Victorian interest in 'social realism' of the kind offered by George Clausen.

Parallel developments on the coast naturally caught the attention of many artists, some sketching or painting to meet the growing demand for prints of the resorts,

OPPOSITE PAGE:

Figs 8.3 and 8.4 The lure of the 19th-century south-eastern countryside. *Fig. 8.3 (top) shows late 19th- and early 20th-century designed country houses in Kent, Surrey and Sussex. Fig. 8.4 (bottom) marks the location of artists and botanists from the 16th to the 19th century. The relative absence of locations in the eastern half of Kent must reflect the difficulties of communication from London.*

Fig. 8.5 John Constable, **The Beach at Brighton, the Chain Pier in the Distance,** ***of 1826–7.*** *Constable's large-scale composition blends accurate topographical detail and picturesque representation, grounded in a real location.*

or painting while on holiday. W B Cooke's *Picturesque Views on the Southern Coast of England* (1814–26) included engravings based on watercolours by Turner and others. By the 1820s, Brighton was inspiring many artists, including Constable, who called it 'Piccadilly… by the seaside' and who visited because of his wife's health. Among his Brighton pictures was the major piece featuring the new, technologically advanced Chain Pier, 'a place of fashionable and luxurious promenade' (Fig. 8.5). Also active were Turner, commissioned by his patron Lord Egremont to paint *Beach at Brighton* (1828–9); John Wilson Carmichael with his *Kemp Town from the Sea*, and W H Mason, who offered *Panorama of Brighton* (1833). Elsewhere Turner produced oil paintings of Margate in the first decade of the 19th century, as did Joshua Cristall at Margate and Hastings. Richard Horne Lancaster depicted *The Parade at Hastings* (1818), and Abraham Solomon *On the Beach: A Family on Margate Sands* (1867). Most emphasised the gentility or modernity of these relatively new and fast-growing watering places. William Westall's aquatint of *Brighton from the Chain Pier* (1833) therefore emphasises the gentility and novelty of the pier, while also showing the dramatic growth of Brighton in the background. Hastings was similarly treated, with some tension between those images that attempted to show modernity through urban topographical growth and those that opted for the picturesque. Queen Victoria purchased William Powell Frith's panoramic *Ramsgate Sands* (1854) when it was shown at the British Academy. Just along the coast was the setting for William Dyce's well-known landscape painting of *Pegwell Bay – A Recollection of October 5th 1858* (1858–60).[14]

London inspired and horrified in equal measure. And there is no shortage of landscape paintings to choose: two 18th-century contemporaries such as Canaletto and Hogarth saw London very differently. Upon his arrival in London in 1746 the former created grandiose, spacious and sparkling riverside scenes in his topographic art, including the new Westminster Bridge. Hogarth, by contrast, looked to London's darker street life as settings of corruption and venality. In so doing, his prints, frequently pirated, also rendered accurate topographical descriptions of many parts of the city, albeit adjusted for dramatic effect where necessary. His *Gin Lane* (1751) is well known, and *The Four Times of the Day* (1738) take us from a winter's morning in Covent Garden to noon at Hog Lane at St Giles-in-the-Fields, to evening at the leisure resort of Sadler's Wells, and to night in a chaotic, brothel-lined street near Charing Cross. His successors in satirical and savage observation of the London scene included James Gillray, Thomas Rowlandson and George Cruickshank. The latter's *London Going out of Town – Or – the March of Bricks and Mortar* (1829) shows the encroachment of building on to Hampstead Heath. Other contrasting scenes of London in the 18th century included George Morland's *St James's Park* (*c.* 1790) showing an officer with his family being provided with milk from a cow, one of the many kept in Spring Gardens and driven into the park to provide milk at a penny a mug; or Samuel Scott's *A Quay on the Thames at London* (*c.* 1756) with details of shipping and quayside activity. The commercial side of London was not ignored, and large-scale canvases by Callcott of *The Entrance to the Pool of London* (1816), Vincent's *View of Greenwich from Blackwall* (1820), or his *London from the Surrey side of Waterloo Bridge* (1820) demonstrate this theme.

Victorian London's life and environment was also shown in contrasting street, park or river settings. The ambivalence towards London was obvious – the centre of a great empire yet the setting for moral corruption. The work of George Elgar Hicks, Arthur Boyd Houghton or John Ritchie shows Londoners at leisure, at work and all the bustle of the London scene. Although their genre paintings give us insight into urban landscape, the mockery of London life of an earlier age now gave way to the gentler rebukes of *Punch*, until the social realist artists such as Luke Fildes, Frank Holl and Hubert von Herkomer began to depict the horrors of working-class London environments. Even more devastating were the drawings of Gustave Doré, which appeared in his *London: A Pilgrimage* (1872) and *The Street Life of London* (1877). Contrasting the old and the new in London, and the poverty of the East

Fig. 8.6 Gustave Doré, 'Houndsditch', taken from his London: A Pilgrimage of 1872. *Harrow Alley was near the Petticoat Lane district. According to Henry Mayhew in his* London Labour and the London Poor *(1851), it specialised in the sale of second-hand clothes by Jewish families, accounting for the hats and boots to the right of the image.*

ABOVE: *Fig. 8.7 Bishopsgate Street, London.* House of Sir Paul Pindar, *steel engraving by J Wykeham Archer. This was on the site now occupied by 135 Bishopsgate. The house was built in 1598–1600 and a large part of its carved oak façade is now in the Victoria and Albert Museum.*

ABOVE RIGHT: *Fig. 8.8 Sir Paul Pindar's House, as featured in Gustave Doré's 'Bishopsgate Street' from his* London: A Pilgrimage *of 1872. By this time the house had been converted into a tavern in the early 19th century.*

End and Thames-side, the dark haunts of Jack the Ripper, his illustrations still hold a terrible fascination in their revelation of the degrading impact that London's growth could have on the poor (Fig. 8.6). Elsewhere, artists' attention was caught by the destruction of ancient landmarks, as in Birket Foster's depiction of the demolition of Nash's colonnade in Regent Street; the huge upheavals caused by the coming of the railways, as in the work of John Cooke Bourne; or the great ceremonial occasions, such as Holman Hunt's *London Bridge on the Night of the Marriage of the Prince and Princess of Wales* (1863).[15] Detailed depictions exist to show the houses of an older era, such as Sir Paul Pindar's late-Elizabethan suburban house, converted to a tavern, just outside Bishopsgate (Figs 8.7 and 8.8).

Nationally significant paintings, such as Ford Madox Brown's *Work* (1852–65), were set in London, in this case in Heath Street, Hampstead; and the impressionist views of *Thames and the Houses of Parliament* (1871) or *Impression, Sunrise* (1874) by Monet (who loved London's fog) or Pissarro's *Crystal Palace London* (1871) are equally well known. Inspiration was also drawn from London's night-time riverside by Monet's friend Whistler, whose struggles against established conventions in art we met at the beginning of this chapter. Living at Wapping and later at Chelsea, he created his foggy *Nocturnes*. In his 'Ten o'clock' lecture (1885) he sought to conjure up some of the magic that he felt:

> *And when the evening mist clothes the riverside with poetry, as with a veil, and the poor buildings lose themselves in the dim sky, and the tall chimneys become campanili, and the warehouses are palaces in the night, and the whole city hangs in the heavens, and fairy-land is before us – then the wayfarer*

hastens home; the working man and the cultured one, the wise man and the one of pleasure, cease to understand, as they have ceased to see, and Nature, who, for once, has sung in tune, sings her exquisite song to the artist alone, her son and her master – her son in that he loves her, her master in that he knows her.[16]

In a quite different part of London, Walter Sickert, in his Camden Town period, found equal inspiration in the years 1905–14. The power of images was later reinforced by the attention given to Niels Lund's *The Heart of the Empire* (1904) – an iconic image of St Pauls surrounded by the commercial throng of the City of London, embracing both the intimacy of the City townscape and the monumentality of the buildings. More recently in *A Vision of Britain* (1989) the Prince of Wales sought to restore this centrality and to reinforce a national identity through landscape aesthetics, using representations of London by Canaletto and other Old Masters to protest against modernist landscapes.[17]

London's contemporary outer reaches were the subjects of paintings that preserve for us today a sense of the rurality of what were to become London streets. Many were indeed inspired by the contrast of the metropolis with the surviving rural pockets close at hand. Constable's Hampstead Heath scenes are well known, and the Heath was to become his permanent home from 1827. The Bavarian-born George Scharf painted many such scenes, including *Acre Lane, Brixton* (1823), *On Shooter's Hill, London* (1826) showing the 18th-century hotel for wealthy travellers at the top of the hill (Fig. 8.9), *Laying a Water-Main in Tottenham Court Road* (1834) and *Railway Construction at Camden Town* (1836). In similar vein there is W Mulready's *Near the Mall, Kensington Gravel Pits* (1812–13). Later in the century Camille Pissarro visited England, staying with his sister in the suburb of Norwood in 1870–1 and painting Dulwich College and Crystal Palace; he returned to paint many other London scenes in the 1890s, including the newly planned Bedford Park estate.

Fig. 8.9 George Scharf, 'On Shooter's Hill' (1826), showing the 18th-century Bull Hotel. The newer road in the foreground was levelled for easier travel. The proximity of a local gallows and gibbet was a reminder of the possibility of violence in this remote spot. In 1697 Celia Fiennes proceeded out of London along the road to Dover, and wrote in her diary of stopping at 'Shuttershill, on top of which hill you see a vast prospect … some lands clothed with trees, others with grass and flowers, gardens, orchards, with all sorts of herbage and tillage, with severall little towns all by the river, Erith, Leigh, Woolwich etc., quite up to London, Greenwich, Deptford, Black Wall, the Thames twisting and turning it self up and down bearing severall vessells and men of warre on it.'

The Thames itself also attracted much artistic attention; with the Seine, it is probably the most painted river in Europe. Many elite patrons began to move into houses on its banks in the 18th century and a market for views of the river was established, building on the prior work of Dutch artists in the 16th and 17th centuries, and a succession of foreign and English artists. Richard Wilson produced arcadian and patrician images of *The Thames at Twickenham* (1762); picturesque views and gentlemen's houses and parks were depicted, as in the aquatints in Boydell's *History of the River Thames* (1794–6), or W B Cooke's *The Thames: or Graphic Illustrations of Seats, Villas, Public Buildings, and Picturesque Scenery, on the Banks of that Noble River* (1811). A major series of paintings by Turner, who had a house at Twickenham close to that of Sir Joshua Reynolds, focused on the prosperous landscape and commercial success of the Thames. His *Windsor Castle from the Thames* (*c.* 1805) was probably the earliest of these, and more than 20 paintings followed, mostly in the first decade of the 19th century, including classically inspired pastoral scenes such as *View of Pope's Villa at Twickenham during its Dilapidation* (1808). Better known are the Thames settings for masterpieces such as *The Burning of the Houses of Parliament* (1835) and *The Fighting 'Temeraire' Tugged to her Last Berth to be Broken up, 1838* (1839), voted 'Britain's best painting' in 2005, beating Constable's *The Haywain* into second place! Turner's later acclaimed and stylistically contrasting work *Rain, Steam and Speed – the Great Western Railway* (1844) captures a locomotive crossing the Thames at Brunel's Maidenhead Bridge. And when the Clore Gallery opened at the Tate Gallery in 1987 to house Turner's Bequest to the nation, the landscape of London thereby received an additional feature in this addition to the Tate, illustrating the two-way relationship between art and landscape. Art does not merely depict landscape, it changes it both materially, in this case as an extension to an existing building, and in the way we perceive it. Away from London, The Turner Contemporary Centre, to open in Margate in 2007, will also dramatically stamp itself upon the waterfront; as a key element in the regeneration of the town, it will again demonstrate the material influence of art on the landscape to celebrate the artist's many visits to, and depictions of, the resort. Similarly, the landscapes by Stanley Spencer of Cookham in Berkshire, often including the Thames, are shown in the former Methodist chapel in his own village, which is now a gallery devoted to his work.

These examples of 'high art' do not exhaust by any means the representations of south-eastern landscape. The series of popular posters created for Shell in the 1930s, for example, contain many scenes drawn from the region: Vanessa Bell's 1931 image of Alfriston already noted; the graphic designer E McKnight Kauffer's Stonehenge and New Forest (1931) and Bodiam Castle (1932); Graham Sutherland's oast-houses near Leeds in Kent (1932); John Armstrong's Newlands Corner in Surrey (1932); Paul Nash's Rye Marshes (1932) (Fig. 8.10), and R J Kinnear's poster of the sham ruins at Virginia Water (1936). Attitudes of the middle classes towards London's landscape in particular were also caught by illustrated magazines, especially *Punch* and the *Illustrated London News*, although the artistic conventions employed in these precluded any real topographical detail and the darker alleyways of poorer areas were given short shrift.

Photography, too, has provided innumerable images of the region and is frequently cited as going beyond painting in its attempts to offer more realistic representations of people and place. Although we now accept that selectivity, perspective, subjectivity and interpretation are as important in photography as any other art form, and that the human subjects were often posed, photographs nevertheless open up a whole new world of landscape images from the Victorian period onwards. There is a long history of townscape photography in London and elsewhere in the region, such as the photo-journalism of John Thomson, whose *Street Life in London* (1877–8) was originally published in monthly episodes. Here we see fish stalls, markets, street advertising, itinerant workers and street

Fig. 8.10 Paul Nash, **The Rye Marshes** *(1932). Shell employee Jack Beddington created the distinctive posters of the 1930s that incorporated the work of many artists of that period, to convey the message that motoring with Shell gave you the British landscape.*

musicians, public disinfectors and water carts. Archives, libraries and museums hold thousands of historic and contemporary images of both urban and rural life (Figs 8.11 and 8.12). Photography was used increasingly from the late 19th century in the mass production of postcards; these often show local views but favour rural landscapes rather more than the more demanding coastal scenes. The firm of Judges at Hastings from 1902 achieved a firm grip on the production of the cards, which popularised landscape among all classes of society.

Films, too, have featured the South East, and indeed have been made commercially in the region: Brighton is the bleak interwar setting of *Brighton Rock* (1947), the well-known adaptation of the Graham Greene novel, and in *Quadrophenia* (1979) Brighton features again as the backdrop to the Mods and Rockers violence in the 1960s. Other locations for well-known films include Hampton Court for the *Man for All Seasons* (1966) and Bolebrook water-mill in Sussex for *Carrington* (1995); in 1991 Burnham Beeches and the New Forest even doubled up as Sherwood for *Robin Hood, Prince of Thieves*! And again art has created its own landscape: the early film industry came to Shoreham in Sussex, where the shingle beach with its bohemian bungalows was the location for film studios from 1913; the Prospect Film Company even went so far as to claim Shoreham as 'undoubtedly the Los Angeles of English production'. The most extensive and successful studios clustered to the west of London, however, where large amounts of space could be combined with easy access to the capital. The great names of British 20th-century cinema therefore include Ealing (from 1902), Shepperton at Littleton Park (from 1931), Pinewood at Heatherden Hall (from 1935), as well as the studios at Lime Grove, Borehamwood, Denham, Elstree and Twickenham. In quite different vein, Derek Jarman, poet, author,

film-maker, artist, video director, gardener and gay-rights activist, on learning that he was HIV Positive in the mid-1980s, moved to Prospect Cottage under the shadow of the Dungeness nuclear power station, where he created his well-known garden from debris from the beach (Fig. 8.13).

REPRESENTATIONS OF THE SOUTH EAST IN CREATIVE LITERATURE

No City or landscape is truly rich unless it has been given the quality of myth by writer, painter or by association with great events.[18]

Fig. 8.13 Derek Jarman's 'Prospect Cottage' on the shingle of Dungeness, Kent. The garden and cottage have become tourist attractions in this otherwise inhospitable location. Part of the nuclear power station can be seen in the background.

As with visual representations, there is a huge wealth of material awaiting the student of literature for this region. It has been said, for example, that 'Victorian fiction typically lives at low altitudes' and this would certainly encompass the South East.[19] Literary representations cover a variety of texts: maps, poems, architectural guides, plays, topographical writing and novels. Two forms of literature will be separated here, although in practice they might overlap. First, there is writing that may have been based upon reality but which was created as a poem, novel or otherwise as a largely fictional account. Secondly, there is literature that emanated from the travel writings of individuals who recounted the scenes they had witnessed, whether as tourists or as more specialist observers of agriculture, social conditions or landscape. One focuses the detail on the human actors, social conditions or class and uses nature or the city as a backdrop: the other might be precise as to topographical detail. There were authors who spanned the two types, of course, such as Daniel Defoe, Thomas Hardy, Charles Dickens and Richard Jefferies. Hardy and Dickens, internationally renowned, were the literary giants of the region, the first unable to develop empathy with urban surroundings, the second utterly dependent upon them.

As with painting, much early writing purporting to describe landscape has also to be treated with caution. Often it might be generalised and intended to do no more than provide a spatial and ethical contrast between rural idyllicism and urban corruption, with the particulars of a landscape tailored to fit the pastoral or georgic genre. Thus, early 17th-century country-house poems such as Ben Jonson's 'To Penshurst' are more concerned with literary decorum than with topography. Milton, whose father's home was at rural Hammersmith and who had spent some of his earlier years in the 1630s at Horton in Buckinghamshire, had real English flowers around the hearse of his friend Lycidas in his poem of that name, but his landscape details remain strewn with classical references. The myth of an idyllic age dominated literature, and the facts of labour and landscape were muted. Stephen Duck, the autodidact Wiltshire farm worker and poet, did subvert the idyllic canon to some extent, although on being taken into royal favour and given accommodation at Richmond in 1730, his tone softened considerably. One problem that he shared with poets such as Robert Bloomfield and John Clare was that his work was intimately bound up with labour and detail, and the idea of landscape as a distanced picture was alien to him. Perhaps James Thomson, moving to London in 1725, provided the turning point because he did attempt to place real labour within real scenery. But even when we turn to later work, such as Jane Austen's acclaimed novels, there is little specificity of landscape, although much of the narrative is set in the southern counties and there are certainly many references to the picturesque as a modish interest. In *Pride and Prejudice* (1813) Kent and Hertfordshire seem interchangeable. Trollope's fictional Barsetshire, clearly a southern county, is also not described as

OPPOSITE PAGE:

TOP: *Fig. 8.11 City of London. Holborn Viaduct under construction in about 1868, photographed by Henry Dixon. The Holborn Valley Improvement Act of 1864 provided for the building of a viaduct across the Fleet valley. Dixon was commissioned to photograph the works in progress. The viaduct was opened by Queen Victoria in November 1869.*

BOTTOM: *Fig. 8.12 Charcoal-burners in the New Forest. A late 19th-century photograph of a family group, with their hut in the background. The hut enabled the charcoal burner to attend to his slowly burning kiln continuously. There is a reproduction of such a hut at the Weald and Downland Museum, Singleton, Sussex.*

a landscape, except to draw on preconceived notions to demonstrate the importance of wealth, property and comfort. Sleepy Barchester is largely left to the imagination and conjures up images of Salisbury, Winchester or Wells. However, the years from 1780 to 1830 did gradually see place and specific landscape assume a greater importance, and much of what follows is therefore drawn from the late 18th century onwards.[20]

The number of individual locations associated with authors in the South East up to the late 1970s offers interesting material for consideration (Table 8.2). Some authors moved frequently, and an 'association' is here defined as an instance of an author having been born, having lived, been educated, died or buried, or having a memorial to them at a particular place. The concentration in the counties to the south of London is clear and provides an interesting similarity to the concentration of painters depicting wealden scenes (*see* Table 8.1). London is quite exceptional, of course. There are 444 different locations within Greater London mentioned in Daiches' and Flower's *Literary Landscapes of the British Isles* (1979), covering 169 different authors. Some moved more than others, or have monuments to them, the most significant in this respect being Dickens and Lamb (12 locations each in London), Thomas Hood (nine), George Eliot, Leigh Hunt and Virginia Woolf (eight). There are 46 buried or otherwise commemorated in Westminster Abbey and another nine at St Paul's. The complete dominance of London is therefore far greater for literary figures than for painters, for whom other regions of Britain provided important inspiration.

There are parts of the region that are intimately linked with particular authors: most obviously Hardy with Wessex and Dickens with London, and their writings seem almost to take on a factual content. Indeed, for many, their work offers a landscape more 'real' than that which may otherwise be unearthed by the landscape historian. Some of the most powerful landscape writing has indeed been offered by authors whose lives have dislodged them from their original bases, such as John Cowper Powys, whose writing on Dorset matured while he was living in the USA, or H E Bates, whose poignant Kentish *Darling Buds of May* (1958) and four subsequent novels about the Larkin family were only a very limited part of his output, much of which was otherwise set in his native Midlands.

Many authors focus on landscape change, given its experiential importance for people and the sense of dislocation that occurs when the taken-for-granted disappears. In urban-based writing this is one element in a more general tendency to recoil from the massive and threatening changes that urbanisation was bringing. Dickens famously describes the landscape changes wrought by the advent of the railways to Camden

TABLE 8.2 LITERARY ASSOCIATIONS IN SOUTH-EAST ENGLAND.

Area	Number of locations with associations*	Number of separate authors associated with county[+]
East Dorset	9	7 (of which Bournemouth has 5)
Chalkland Wiltshire	10	8
Berkshire	12	8
South Buckinghamshire	7	6
Hertfordshire	8	8
South Essex	7	7
Hampshire and Isle of Wight	24	21 (of which Portsmouth has 5, Winchester 3)
West Sussex	17	12
East Sussex	14	15
Kent	29	19 (of which Canterbury has 5)
Surrey	23	17
London	444	169

* Associations include birthplace, domicile, dying, burial place, a dedicated house or museum, a statue or memorial, or a school.

+ many authors were associated with more than one location and with more than one county. Their names have only been counted once for each county in which they are represented, but are repeated across different counties.

Source: Daiches and Flower 1979 (Gazetteer), 235–79.

Town in *Dombey and Son* (1848). In Chapter 6 he describes the strangely idyllic home of the Toodles in Staggs's Gardens:

> It was a little row of houses, with little squalid patches of ground before them, fenced off with old doors, barrel staves, scraps of tarpaulin, and dead bushes; with bottomless tin kettles and exhausted iron fenders, thrust into the gaps. Here the Staggs's Gardeners trained scarlet beans, kept fowls and rabbits, erected rotten summer houses (one was an old boat), dried clothes, and smoked pipes.

At Camden Town, however, he sees the beginning of the enormous changes of the 1840s, and the scene is worth quoting at length for its damning account:

> The first shock of a great earthquake had, just at that period, rent the whole neighbourhood to its centre. Traces of its course were visible on every side. Houses were knocked down; streets broken through and stopped; deep pits and trenches dug in the ground; enormous heaps of earth and clay thrown up; buildings that were undermined and shaking, propped by great beams of wood. Here, a chaos of carts, overthrown and jumbled together, lay topsy-turvy at the bottom of a steep unnatural hill; there, confused treasures of iron soaked and rusted in something that had accidentally become a pond. Everywhere were bridges that led nowhere; thoroughfares that were wholly impassable; Babel towers of chimneys, wanting half their height; temporary wooden houses and enclosures, in the most unlikely situations; carcases of ragged tenements, and fragments of unfinished walls and arches, and piles of scaffolding, and wildernesses of bricks, and giant forms of cranes, and tripods straddling above nothing. There were a hundred thousand shapes and substances of incompleteness, wildly mingled out of their places, upside down, burrowing in the earth, aspiring in the air, mouldering in the water, and unintelligible as any dream. Hot springs and fiery eruptions, the usual attendants upon earthquakes, lent their contributions of confusion to the scene. Boiling water hissed and heaved within dilapidated walls; whence, also, the glare and roar of flames came issuing forth; and mounds of ashes blocked up rights of way, and wholly changed the law and custom of the neighbourhood.
>
> In short, the yet unfinished and unopened railroad was in progress; and, from the very core of all this dire disaster, trailed smoothly away, upon its mighty course of civilisation and improvement.

A few years later, the whole street had vanished, as Dickens describes in Chapter 15:

> There was no such place as Staggs's Gardens. It had vanished from the earth. Where the old rotten summer houses once had stood, palaces now reared their heads, and granite columns of gigantic girth opened a new vista to the railway world beyond. The miserable waste ground, where the refuse-matter had been heaped of yore, was swallowed up and gone; and in its frowsy stead were tiers of warehouses, crammed with rich goods and costly merchandise. The old by-streets now swarmed with passengers and vehicles of every kind: the new streets that had stopped disheartened in the mud and waggon-ruts, formed towns within themselves, originating wholesome comforts and conveniences belonging to themselves, and never tried nor thought of until they sprung into existence.

But change was ubiquitous, whether urban or rural. Hardy in *The Woodlanders* (1887), for example, describes the demolition of the 'brown-thatched' cottages in Wessex. These were not Edenic habitations, however, but often dark and damp slums, the 'pig-sty cottages' of Dorothea Brooke's uncle in George Eliot's *Middlemarch* (1871). In *Tess of the D'Urbervilles* Hardy refers specifically to landscape change at Talbothays dairy farm:

> *Thus they all worked on, encompassed by the vast flat mead which extended to either slope of the valley – a level landscape compounded of old landscapes long forgotten, and no doubt, differing in character very greatly from the landscape they composed now.*

V S Naipaul in *The Enigma of Arrival* (1987) notes the changes in the Wiltshire chalkland landscape around him, as seen through the eyes of a Trinidadian newcomer.

> *Jack lived among ruins, among superseded things. But that way of looking came to me later, has come to me with greater force now, with the writing. It wasn't the idea that came to me when I first went out walking.*
>
> *That idea of ruin and dereliction, of out-of-placeness, was something I felt about myself, attached to myself: a man from another hemisphere, another background, coming to rest in middle life in the cottage of a half neglected estate, an estate full of reminders of its Edwardian past, with few connections with the present. An oddity among the estates and big houses of the valley, and I a further oddity in its grounds. I felt unanchored and strange. Everything I saw in those early days, as I took my surroundings in, everything I saw on my daily walk, beside the windbreak or along the wide grassy way, made that feeling more acute. I felt that my presence in that old valley was part of something like an upheaval, a change in the course of the history of the country.*
>
> *Jack himself, however, I considered to be part of the view. I saw his life as genuine, rooted, fitting: man fitting the landscape. I saw him as a remnant of the past (the undoing of which my own presence portended). It did not occur to me, when I first went walking and saw only the view, took what I saw as things of that walk, things that one might see in the countryside near Salisbury, immemorial, appropriate things, it did not occur to me that Jack was living in the middle of junk, among the ruins of nearly a century; that the past around his cottage might not have been his past; that he might at some stage have been a newcomer to the valley; …*

Not only landscape changes, however, but there can be change in the authors themselves or their characters: there is a theme of return to an earlier child's landscape, and a sense of loss, as with *Great Expectations* where Pip looks back on his childhood days among the 'marsh country, down by the river'. Fictional Chatham – Dullborough – from chapter 12 of *The Uncommercial Traveller*, written as a series of short stories in the 1860s, is also greatly altered:

> *… the two beautiful hawthorn-trees, the hedge, the turf, and all those buttercups and daisies, have given place to the stoniest of jolting roads; while, beyond the station, an ugly dark monster of a tunnel kept its jaws open, as if it had swallowed them and were ravenous for more destruction.*

The South East can readily be identified as a setting for the pastoral poem or novel, part of that tradition which drew on town–country divisions, simplicity compared with complexity; nostalgia; harmony and what Squires refers to as sympathetic realism (idealisation and realism combined).[21] And landscape was important: in *Elegy Written in a Country Churchyard* (1751) Thomas Gray used a very specific setting that is now commemorated at Stoke Poges in Buckinghamshire. The rural paradise myth, with its selective subtleties of

Fig. 8.14 The statue of Thomas Hardy at Dorchester, *unveiled in September 1931, is by Eric Kennington.*

retrospection and refuge, was dominant during much of the late 18th and the 19th centuries, and indeed remains influential today.

Within this genre, there were rarely explicit descriptions of landscape that are helpful to us now, but in the better quality writings that are often included within this category there was often a correspondence between landscape, character and narrative. Thomas Hardy, whose novels are intensely visual, stands as a supreme example (Fig. 8.14). His characters move between downland, woodland and fertile valley, between heath and country town, between coastal resort and Stonehenge. Always he posits tension as a basic theme: between city and country, between tradition and the modern. The sheep-washing, the sheep-shearing, and the shearing supper in *Far from the Madding Crowd* (1874) are splendid examples of Hardy's attention to the detail of landscape and the rhythm of rural life. The importance of Egdon Heath, with 'a face on which time makes but little impression', to Hardy's *Return of the Native* (1878) is a good example. In *Tess*, the eponymous heroine moves between valley (the luxuriant 'Vale of the Great Dairies'), downland (the dreadful 'Flintcombe Ash') and coastal town (the modernity of 'Sandbourne'), with each location interwoven with her life's path. Hardy's recovery of 'Wessex' ensured an evocative and lasting quality – his Wessex novels were 'of character and environment', and his genius lay in the fact

Fig. 8.15 Hardy's Wessex. From the frontispiece of **The Return of the Native (1912 edn).** *The interweaving of fiction and fact can be seen from the place-names, with those of the larger towns being rendered accurately compared with Hardy's fictitious names, of which the best known is 'Casterbridge' for Dorchester.*

that we see contrasting Wessex landscapes as real yet integral to his narratives (Fig. 8.15).

Nevertheless even Hardy fragmented and reshuffled landscapes for the purposes of his narrative. In the 1895 preface to *The Return of the Native* he wrote:

> Under the general name of 'Egdon Heath', which has been given to the sombre scene of the story, are unified or typified heaths of various real names, to the number of at least a dozen; these being virtually one in character and aspect, though their original unity, or partial unity, is now somewhat disguised by intrusive slips and slices brought under the plough with varying degrees of success, or planted to woodland...

And in a 1912 postscript to this original preface he added:

> To prevent disappointment to searchers for scenery it should be added that though the action of the narrative is supposed to proceed in the central and most secluded part of the heaths united into one whole, as above described, certain topographical features resembling those delineated really lie on the margin of the waste, several miles to the westward of the centre. In some other respects also there has been a bringing together of scattered characteristics.

Such reformulations and fictional re-creations of actual landscapes, urban or rural, may, it can be argued, preclude novelists' work from the armoury of the landscape historian. Virginia Woolf once wrote disapprovingly that 'a writer's country is a territory within his own brain; and we run the risk of disillusionment if we try to turn such phantom cities into tangible brick and mortar'.[22] But there are few other sources which so truly capture the essence of place, the true character of a landscape and its people. Indeed, Hardy created not only the written image of Egdon, but also a map that he used to better locate the scenes of the narrative (Fig. 8.16). And in devouring this literature we ourselves become more aware of our own surroundings. Vivid evocations of landscape can be contained in even the most unlikely tales, such as the wealden landscapes in *Puck of Pook's Hill* (1906) by Rudyard Kipling, who was resident in Burwash and very familiar with the surrounding countryside.

Within the South East perhaps the greatest exponent of Hardy's style of writing was Sheila Kaye-Smith, whose novels were primarily set within the eastern Weald, where her characters were firmly entrenched within their landscapes. Opposition to the enclosure of the fictional Boarzell Common is the theme of an opening passage to her *Sussex Gorse* (1916):

> It was some months since
> Sir John Bardon, Squire
> of the Manor of Flightshot,
> had taken advantage of
> the Inclosure Act and
> manoeuvred a bill for the
> inclosure of Boarzell. Since
> then there had been visits of
> commissioners, roamings of
> surveyors, deliveries of
> schedules, strange talk of
> turbary and estovers, fire-
> bote and house-bote. The
> neighbourhood was troubled,
> perplexed. Then perplexity
> condensed into indignation
> when all that Inclosure stood
> for became known – no more

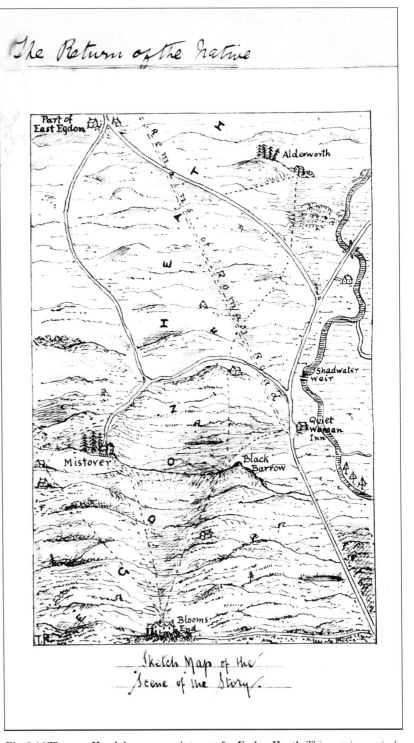

Fig. 8.16 Thomas Hardy's manuscript map for Egdon Heath. *This map, in a revised publishable format, appeared as a frontispiece to the first edition of* The Return of the Native *(1878). This was Hardy's own childhood environment. Mrs Yeobright lived at Bloom's End, presented here as being in a valley running southwards parallel with the Tincleton road (Hardy's Stickleford). Clym and Eustacia after their marriage lived at Alderworth, beyond East Egdon, probably Affpuddle.*

*pasturage for the cow or goat which meant all the difference between
wheaten and oaten bread, no more wood-gleanings for fire or wind-beaten
roof, no more of the tussocky grass for fodder, or of gorse to toughen palings
against escaping fowls.*

The height of such rural writing, roughly between the 1870s and 1939, coincided
with the decline of farm prices and the awakening of interest in folklore and
nostalgia. The genre has merged with that of the regional novel, urban or rural,
and with no necessarily strong emphasis on landscape *per se*. The output of the
latter grew throughout the 20th century and spawned an industry of 'literary
pilgrimages' such as those to 'Hardy Country'.

London, of course, has been a setting for many novels and much poetry, either
in whole or in part. The Restoration period also offers the factual accounts of
John Evelyn and Samuel Pepys, while through to the 1720s Daniel Defoe, John
Dryden, Alexander Pope, John Gay and Jonathan Swift all explore London's
space and assert its identity. The landscape after the Great Fire is caught by
Evelyn in an entry in his diary for 7 September 1666:

> *[T]he vast yron Chaines of the Cittie streets … were many of them
> mealted, & reduc'd to cinders by the vehement heats: nor was I yet able to
> passe through any of the narrower streets, but kept the widest … The
> bielanes & narrower streetes were quite fill'd up with rubbish, nor could
> one have possibly knowne where he was, but by the ruine of some church, or
> hall, that had some remarkable towre or pinacle [sic] remaining.*[23]

The streets and spaces between buildings become well known, listed and
explicitly involved in the narratives, as in Defoe's *The Fortunes and Misfortunes of
the Famous Moll Flanders* (1722). Indeed London at this time 'has come down to
us in a series of literary and artistic images, so detailed and apparently realistic
that one feels one could almost walk in its streets'.[24]

At some point in their lives, many authors lived here. There are far too many to
do them justice in this volume, so if choosing one obvious writer from each
century, we might begin by picking Shakespeare who arrived in London in 1592
and then lived variously in Bishopsgate, Southwark and Cripplegate before
buying a house in Blackfriars in 1613 and eventually retiring to Stratford-upon-
Avon. In the diaries of Samuel Pepys from 1660 we see Restoration London
emerging and are provided with his first-hand account of the Great Fire. Dr
Johnson came in 1737, famously remarking 40 years later that 'When a man is
tired of London he is tired of life; for there is in London all that life can afford.'
He lived on the western edge of the City, and among houses near Fleet Street,
new-built after the Fire. The Dickens family settled in Camden Town in 1822,
and Charles, always a *flâneur*, a walker of London's streets, remained fascinated
by the landscape around him. Although able himself to live in the more
prosperous Marylebone and Tavistock Square, his attention was always caught
by the City and the poorer districts to the east and by the river, as well as by the
expanding suburbs. Virginia Stephen (later Woolf) was born in Hyde Park Gate,
Kensington, and acquired a keen sense of topography and social geography. On
the death of her father in 1904 she famously moved to Bloomsbury and later
lived at Gordon Square and Fitzroy Square, other members of her circle living
near by. She and Leonard Woolf lived at Brunswick Square, then in Richmond
(1914–24), then at Tavistock Square, although from 1911 much of their time was
also spent in Sussex. In her 1927 essay 'Street Haunting' she wrote of 'rambling
the streets of London' as 'the greatest pleasure of town life in winter'. In *Mrs
Dalloway* (1925) Clarissa Dalloway also views London from buses or walks the
streets before returning to her Westminster home. In this novel, dealing with the
psychic space of London, the characters and their landscapes are again integral

to one another, and in *The Years* (1937), interwar London is perhaps best revealed.[25] More recently London has been explored in novels by Iris Murdoch – the setting for about two-thirds of her novels, primarily based in central London – and we also have C P Snow's Whitehall, Anthony Powell's Fitzrovia, Doris Lessing's Bloomsbury and Earl's Court, and Nell Dunn's Catford.

For some, London was the infernal city (Shelley's 'Hell is a city much like London'), a modern Babylon of many voices (Wordsworth's 'babel din'), for others the New Jerusalem. It had what Henry James called 'a great illustrative and suggestive value' but in its huge complexity it was ultimately inexpressible. It could only be seen in fragments. Dickens is, of course, the brilliant interpreter of such landscapes, and the phrase 'Dickens's London' seems to be an unassailable given. There remains some ambiguity as to whether his portraits were products of his creative imagination, were mimetic documentary accounts, or a little of both.[26] The vivid account of Jacob's Island (*see* Fig. 7.12) in *Oliver Twist* (1837–9), where Bill Sikes meets his death, is a case in point:

> *Beyond Dockhead in the Borough of Southwark, stands Jacob's Island, surrounded by a muddy ditch, six or eight feet deep and fifteen or twenty feet wide when the tide is in, once called Mill Pond but known in the days of this story as Folly Ditch. It is a creek or inlet from the Thames, and can always be filled at high water by opening the sluices at the Lead Mills from which it took its old name. At such times, a stranger, looking from one of the wooden bridges thrown across it at Mill Lane, will see the inhabitants of the houses on either side lowering from their back doors and windows, buckets, pails, domestic utensils of all kinds, in which to haul the water up; and when his eye is turned from these operations to the houses themselves, his utmost astonishment will be excited by the scene before him. Crazy wooden galleries common to the backs of half a dozen houses, with holes from which to look upon the slime beneath; windows, broken and patched, with poles thrust out, on which to dry the linen that is never there; rooms so small, so filthy, so confined that the air would seem too tainted even for the dirt and squalor which they shelter; wooden chambers thrusting themselves out above the mud and threatening to fall into it – as some have done; dirt besmeared walls and decaying foundations; every repulsive lineament of poverty, every loathsome indication of filth, rot, and garbage – all these ornament the banks of Folly Ditch.*
>
> *In Jacob's Island the warehouses are roofless and empty, the walls are crumbling down, the windows are windows no more, the doors are falling into the streets, the chimneys are blackened but they yield no smoke. Thirty or forty years ago, before losses and chancery suits came upon it, it was a thriving place; but now it is a desolate island indeed. The houses have no owners; they are broken open, and entered upon by those who have the courage; and there they live, and there they die. They must have powerful motives for a secret residence, or be reduced to a destitute condition indeed, who seek a refuge in Jacob's Island.*

Many similar examples of Dickens's stated 'attraction of repulsion' could be given, such as the grim slum of 'Tom-All-Alone' in *Bleak House* (1853), or the tale in *Household Words* of the surprised visitor in search of a middle-class house in Agar Town who finds that the fine-sounding Salisbury Crescent is made up of 'several wretched hovels, ranged in a slight curve, that formed some excuse for the name. The doors were blocked up with mud, heaps of ashes, oyster-shells, and decayed vegetables.' Here the stench on a rainy morning was enough 'to knock down a bullock' and the roads were deplorable being cut up by the wheels of the carts from the brick-yards.[27] The East End was later described by Arthur Morrison in his *A Child of the Jago* (1896), an influential novel based on the criminal ghetto around Old Nichol Street between Bethnal Green and

Shoreditch. The novel's impact affected the landscape of that area directly by the demolition of the slums in about 1900 by the LCC. Since then, the doss houses, soup kitchens, dark pubs, dingy shops, seedy cafés, hidden and labyrinthine courtyards and the legend of Jack the Ripper at Whitechapel have all made for the stuff of fiction as well as having an unfortunate basis in fact; the number of novels, plays, musicals and other creative entertainments that feature them, is legion. Lionel Bart, Joe Orton and Peter Ackroyd are just a few of the very many 20th-century creative artists who have worked within these environments, many of which possess a rich literary history.

The Thames has held a fascination for poets since at least the 17th century, just as it has for painters. Pope had used the Thames valley, 'Old Father Thames', for his Pastorals, and referred to 'Windsor's blissful plains', while James Thomson, from his Richmond vantage point, invited the reader in 'Summer' from *The Seasons* (1726–46) to see the delights of 'the matchless Vale of Thames' with its wealthy estates and patrons. Thomas Love Peacock's 'The Genius of the Thames' (1810) celebrated the wealth, peace and national freedom symbolised by this chief of rivers. Very different idyllic landscapes on the banks of the river were also conjured up by Kenneth Grahame's visions of his childhood at Cookham Dean in *The Wind in the Willows* (1908). For many later novelists, such as Nicola Barker writing about Canvey and Sheppey, the river with its fog was, by contrast, a literary device – a trope that offered emblematic obscurity and mystery (as also exploited by Conan Doyle for his Sherlock Holmes's Baker Street settings), and in which many authors literally followed Dickens once more. Thus, in the famous opening passage of *Bleak House*:

> Fog everywhere. Fog up the river, where it flows among the green aits and meadows, fog down the river, where it rolls defiled among tiers of shipping, and the waterside pollutions of a great (and Dirty) city. Fog on the Essex Marshes, fog on the Kentish heights …

The Thames features in many other Dickens novels, such as *Our Mutual Friend* (1864–5) and *Little Dorrit* (1855–7), where 'Through the heart of the town a deadly sewer ebbed and flowed, in the place of a fine fresh river'. Despite the stinking pollution, the Thames was also exciting and powerful. The river also appears in the opening of Conrad's *Heart of Darkness* (1902), in J B Priestley's *Angel Pavement* (1930), and many more novels through to the present day.

The spread of suburbia and its consequent impact on social class aspirations has also been a recurrent theme within the region's literature, and given the 19th- and 20th-century spread of London, this would indeed have been difficult to ignore. If Dickens describes earlier Victorian suburbs such as Camden Town, George and Weedon Grossmith's *Diary of a Nobody* (1892) deals gently with middle-class pretensions in Holloway, and George Gissing's *In the Year of the Jubilee* (1894) is set in suburban Camberwell. In *The Whirlpool* (1897) he sets his scene variously at Gunnersbury or Pinner. In a discussion about leaving their suburban home, Harvey and Alma think about the respective advantages of moving to a country town or the countryside:

> But one ought to have an interesting house to live in. Nobody's ancestors ever lived in a semi-detached villa. What I should like would be one of those picturesque old places down in Surrey – quite in the country, yet within easy reach of town; a house with a real garden, and perhaps an orchard. I believe you can get them very cheap sometimes. Not rent the house, but buy it. Then we would have our portraits painted, and …

E M Forster sees the threat of an encroaching suburbia in the early 20th century in *Howards End* (1910):

> *The city herself … rose and fell in continual flux, while her shallows washed*
> *more widely against the hills of Surrey and over the fields of Hertfordshire*
> *… And month by month the roads smelt more strongly of petrol, and were*
> *more difficult to cross, and human beings heard each other speak with*
> *greater difficulty, breathed less of the air, and saw less of the sky. Nature*
> *withdrew: the leaves were falling by midsummer; the sun shone through*
> *dirt with an admired obscurity.*

And with the car adding further ease of movement to that provided by the existing railway network there was, Forster perceived, less and less material reason why anyone should live permanently anywhere; this, in turn, 'tended to turn anywhere into everywhere, or nowhere'.[28] Perhaps most closely associated with outer suburbia is John Betjeman whose concentration on middle-class lives and landscapes in the Home Counties was affectionate rather than critical, as in his poem 'Middlesex':

> *Gaily into Ruislip Gardens*
> *Runs the red electric train,*
> *With a thousand Ta's and Pardon's*
> *Daintily alights Elaine;*
> *Hurries down the concrete station*
> *With a frown of concentration,*
> *Out into the outskirt's edges*
> *Where a few surviving hedges*
> *Keep alive our lost Elysium – rural Middlesex again.*[29]

Other writers living in the outer London suburbs included Enid Blyton at Beckenham and later at Bourne End and Beaconsfield; and Richmal Crompton at Bromley. Both became well known for their prodigious output of children's literature, generally set within idyllic rural or middle-class suburban surroundings.

TRAVEL AND NON-FICTION REPRESENTATIONS

Not all writing was fiction, of course. The region also produced some of the most insightful and lyrical perceptions of rural landscape, by naturalists, travellers, agriculturalists and authors whose lives generally overlapped, such as Daniel Defoe, Gilbert White, William Marshall, Arthur Young, William Cobbett, W H Hudson, Richard Jefferies, the Lambeth-born Edward Thomas or George Sturt alias Bourne. The work of all these men is well known, and the richness of their writings leaves no room here to do them other than scant justice.

   Gilbert White is celebrated as an absorbed artist, countryman and field scientist. His book *The Natural History and Antiquities of Selborne, in the County of Southampton* (1789) is seen by many as the supreme example of localised natural history writing, although the 'Antiquities' section lacked the flair of the collected letters on natural history that were written between 1767 and 1787 and that make up the first and best-known part of the publication. But his ecological observations have made the book one of the most reprinted volumes in the English language. 'All nature is so full', he wrote, 'that that district produces the most variety that is the most examined'. One example must suffice here, being a description of a scene often depicted in art, namely that of cattle standing in a Wolmer Forest pond:

> *A circumstance respecting these ponds, though by no means peculiar to*
> *them, I cannot pass over in silence; and that is, that instinct by which in*

*summer all the kine, whether oxen, cows, calves, or heifers, retire constantly
to the water during the hotter hours; where, being more exempt from flies,
and inhaling the coolness of that element, some belly deep, and some only to
mid-leg, they ruminate and solace themselves from about ten in the
morning till four in the afternoon, and then return to their feeding. During
this great proportion of the day they drop much dung, in which insects
nestle; and so supply food for the fish, which would be poorly subsisted but
from this contingency. Thus nature, who is a great economist, converts the
recreation of one animal to the support of another!* [30]

Moving from his family's farm in Suffolk, Arthur Young farmed at North
Mymms, Hertfordshire from 1768 to 1777, but is perhaps best known for his
work as secretary to the Board of Agriculture from 1793 and for his oversight of
English agriculture through the *General Views* published county by county from
1793 and with revised accounts going through to 1817. These include a great
amount of detail on landscape as well as farming practices, as also do Young's
various tours in which he made detailed observations on the farming practices of
the different regions of England. These included *A Six Weeks Tour Through the
Southern Counties of England and Wales* (1768) and *A Farmer's Tour through the
East of England* (4 vols 1771). In 1784 he began the *Annals of Agriculture*, and 46
volumes were produced through to 1809 to proselytise agricultural innovations.
A typical commentary combining an eye for landscape with practical farming is
to be found in his 'Fortnight's Tour in Kent and Essex' published in 1788. Struck
by the fertility of Foulness, around which he was conducted by 'blind John', a
pedlar and harvestman, he went on:

*It is probably owing to this great fertility that I did not see any thing like a
farm-yard in the whole island; no attention is given to that sort of
confinement of cattle which has manure for its object. They wander in the
winter over the marshes, having access to the barn-door, from which straw
is turned with prodigality in great heaps, without cribs, racks, or any
similar contrivance; and much more trodden to waste than consumed.
They, however, chalk their lands a little; heaps are seen on the sea-bank,
landed out of hoys that bring it from the Kentish coast.* [31]

Cobbett's *Rural Rides* through the southern counties in 1822–6 were written as a
traveller's scornful critique of the establishment and London ('the WEN'), but
with a keen eye to landscape and people. From the Isle of Thanet in September
1823, one of the richest wheat areas in the region, Cobbett writes:

*I got to a little hamlet, where I breakfasted; but could get no corn for my
horse, and no bacon for myself! All was corn around me. Barns, I should
think, two hundred feet long; ricks of enormous size and most numerous;
crops of wheat, five quarters to an acre, on the average, and a public house
without either bacon or corn! The labourers' houses, all along through this
island, beggarly in the extreme. The people dirty, poor-looking; ragged, but
particularly dirty. The men and boys with dirty faces, and dirty-smock-
frocks, and dirty shirts; and good God! what a difference between the wife
of a labouring man here and the wife of a labouring man in the forests and
woodlands of Hampshire and Sussex!*

From this observation he generalises:

*Invariably I have observed that the richer the soil, the more destitute of
woods that is to say, the more purely a corn country, the more miserable the
labourers.*

His preconceived analysis follows:

> The cause is this, the great, the big bull frog grasps all. In this beautiful island every inch of land is appropriated by the rich. No hedges, no ditches, no commons, no grassy lanes; a country divided into great farms; a few trees surround the great farmhouses. All the rest is bare of trees; and the wretched labourer has not a stick of wood, and has no place for a pig or a cow to graze, or even to lie down upon.[32]

Cobbett could also be damning where he perceived waste, as at Windsor Forest 'as bleak, as barren and as villainous a heath as ever man set his eyes on'. Similarly:

> A much more ugly country than that between Egham and Kensington would with great difficulty be found in England. Flat as a pancake, and, until you come to Hammersmith, the soil is a nasty stony dirt upon a bed of gravel. Hounslow Heath, which is only a little worse than the general run, is a sample of all that is bad in soil and villainous in look. Yet this is now enclosed, and what they call 'cultivated'. Here is a fresh robbery of villages, hamlets, and farm and labourers' buildings and abodes![33]

The Wiltshire-born Richard Jefferies was also radical in many ways, though his writings adopted a gentler tone. He urged artists in the 1880s to depict the modern agricultural practices of their time in their landscapes, the steam-plough and reaping machine, rather than more traditional ones. He also invoked a counter-pastoral tradition with his stress on the monotonous, burdened and toilsome nature of working rurality.[34] His autobiographical *The Story of my Heart* (1883) combines nature mysticism with a strong feel for the landscapes of downland Wiltshire, a feeling he took with him when he moved to the South Downs in later life. W H Hudson's *A Shepherd's Life* (1910), based on the countryside on the borders of Wiltshire, Dorset and Hampshire, includes a typical description of Winterbourne Bishop, in reality the village of Martin, which is worth quoting at length for its rich perspective and detail:

> Then, as to the village itself, when you have got down into its one long, rather winding street, or road. This has a green bank, five or six feet high, on either side, on which stand the cottages, mostly facing the road. Real houses there are none – buildings worthy of being called houses in these great days – unless the three small farm-houses are considered better than cottages, and the rather mean-looking rectory – the rector, poor man, is very poor. Just in the middle part, where the church stands in its green churchyard, the shadiest spot in the village, a few of the cottages are close together, almost touching, then farther apart, twenty yards or so, then farther still, forty or fifty yards. They are small, old cottages; a few have seventeenth-century dates cut on stone tablets on their fronts, but the undated ones look equally old; some thatched, others tiled, but none particularly attractive. Certainly they are without the added charm of a green drapery – creeper or ivy rose, clematis, and honeysuckle; and they are also mostly without the cottage-garden flowers, unprofitably gay like the blossoming furze, but dear to the soul; the flowers we find in so many of the villages along the rivers, especially in those of the Wylye valley …
>
> The trees, I have said, are few, though the churchyard is shady, where you can refresh yourself beneath its ancient beeches and its one wide-branching yew, or sit on a tomb in the sun when you wish for warmth and brightness. The trees growing by or near the street are mostly ash or beech, with a pine or two, old but not large; and there are small or dwarf yew-, holly-, and thorn-trees. Very little fruit is grown; two or three to half a dozen apple- and

damson-trees are called an orchard, and one is sorry for the children. But in late summer and autumn they get their fruit from the hedges. These run up towards the downs on either side of the village, at right angles with, its street; long, unkept hedges, beautiful with scarlet haws and travellers-joy, rich in bramble and elder berries and purple sloes and nuts – a thousand times more nuts than the little dormice require for their own modest wants.

Finally, to go back to its disadvantages, the village is waterless; at all events in summer, when water is most wanted ... This unblessed, high and dry village has nothing but the winterbourne which gives it its name; a sort of surname common to a score or two of villages in Wiltshire, Dorset, Somerset, and Hants. Here the bed of the stream lies by the bank on one side of the village street, and when the autumn and early winter rains have fallen abundantly, the hidden reservoirs within the chalk hills are filled to overflowing; then the water finds its way out and fills the dry old channel and sometimes turns the whole street into a rushing river, to the immense joy of the village children. [35]

To conclude this array, we have George Bourne, writing about his area of the Bourne in Surrey, from which he derived his pen-name:

If one were to be very strict, I suppose it would be wrong to give the name of 'village' to the parish dealt with in these chapters ... It clusters round no central green; no squire ever lived in it; until some thirty years ago it was without a resident parson; its church is not half a century old. Nor are there here, in the shape of patriarchal fields, or shady lanes, or venerable homesteads, any of those features that testify to the immemorial antiquity of real villages as the homes of men; and this for a very simple reason. In the days when real villages were growing, our valley could not have supported a quite self-contained community: it was, in fact, nothing but a part of the wide rolling heath-country – the 'common', or 'waste', belonging to the town which lies northwards, in a more fertile valley of its own. Here, there was no fertility. Deep down in the hollow a stream, which runs dry every summer, had prepared a strip of soil just worth reclaiming as coarse meadow or tillage; but the strip was narrow – a man might throw a stone across it at some points – and on either side the heath and gorse and fern held their own on the dry sand. Such a place afforded no room for an English village of the true manorial kind; and I surmise that it lay all but uninhabited until perhaps the middle of the eighteenth century, by which time a few 'squatters' from neighbouring parishes had probably settled here, to make what living they might beside the stream-bed. At no time, therefore, did the people form a group of genuinely agricultural rustics. Up to a period within living memory, they were an almost independent folk, leading a sort of 'crofter', or (as I have preferred to call it) a 'peasant' life ... In appearance, too, it is abnormal. As you look down upon the valley from its high sides, hardly anywhere are there to be seen three cottages in a row, but all about the steep slopes the little mean dwelling-places are scattered in disorder. So it extends east and west for perhaps a mile and a half – a surprisingly populous hollow now, wanting in restfulness to the eyes and much disfigured by shabby detail, as it winds away into homelier and softer country at either end. The high-road out of the town, stretching away for Hindhead and the South Coast, comes slanting down athwart the valley, cutting it into 'Upper' and 'Lower' halves or ends; and just in the bottom, where there is a bridge over the stream, the appearances might deceive a stranger into thinking that he had come to the nucleus of an old village, since a dilapidated farmstead and a number of cottages line the sides of the road at that point. The appearances, however, are deceptive. I doubt if the cottages are more than a century old; and even if any

of them have a greater antiquity, still it is not as the last relics of an earlier
village that they are to be regarded. On the contrary, they indicate the
beginnings of the present village.[36]

Urban social explorers have also left a tradition of social enquiry, particularly for
London, and the work of Henry Mayhew, Friedrich Engels, Charles Booth,
William Booth and others has been highly influential within the development of
social policy (*see* Chapter 7). Although their work was primarily concerned with
the social conditions, rather than urban landscapes, the two were inseparable and
the Victorians, in particular, believed that by demolishing the slums and
providing cleaner environments they could mitigate the worst social evils.
Although Dickens drew great inspiration from the fact that 'repletion and
starvation threw them down together', middle-class fear of the proximity of the
poor to their own homes fuelled attempts to understand the differences. George
Sims, for example, was a successful writer whose newspaper articles *How the*
Poor Live (1883) included the common social explorers' trope of paradox:

> *I propose to record the result of a journey into a region which lies at our*
> *own doors – into a dark continent that is within easy walking distance of*
> *the General Post Office. This continent will, I hope, be found as interesting*
> *as any of those newly explored lands which engage the attention of the*
> *Royal Geographical Society – the wild races who inhabit it will, I trust,*
> *gain public sympathy as easily as those savage tribes for whose benefit the*
> *Missionary Societies never cease to appeal for funds.*[37]

As we saw in Chapter 7, the London landscape of the poor was constantly referred
to in terms of an abyss, whether by personal investigators or by those using later
techniques of social analysis. Thus we have C F G Masterman's *From the Abyss*
(1902), the crusading William Booth's reference to being 'On the verge of the
Abyss' in his *In Darkest England and the Way Out* (1890), or Jack London's *The*
People of the Abyss (1903). Many of the urban landscapes certainly required urgent
intervention, since, left to 19th-century *laissez-faire* they had rapidly deteriorated.
Whether inspired by middle-class fear of the political and moral consequences –
the widening electorate had become 75 per cent working class by the beginning of
the 20th century – or by a genuine preservationist instinct to care for fine landscape
elements in an age of rapid change, intervention certainly did take place.

FROM LANDSCAPE REPRESENTATION TO
PROTECTION IN SOUTH-EAST ENGLAND

The various ways in which these imaginative constructions of the South East
have been consumed by a large audience have been fundamentally important for
the material landscape. A romanticisation of tradition has inspired a love of the
landscape, of threatened traditions and buildings – the stuff of old England. The
landscape aesthetics of the early conservation movement in England were heavily
influenced by literary and artistic readings. Expanding interest in antiquarianism
during the 19th century also fuelled this movement among educated readers. The
copper-plate and early steel engravings gave wider access to the region's better-
known scenery, for example to Turner's *Picturesque Delineation of the Southern*
Coast of England (1814–26), *Views in Sussex* (1816–20), *The Ports of England*
(1826–8) or *Picturesque Views in England and Wales* (1825–38) as did David
Lucas's mezzotint engravings of Constable's *English Landscape Scenery*, including
his view of Old Sarum.[38] And as an alternative world to London the rural South
East received special attention. Thus Martin Tupper wrote his historical romance
Stephen Langton (1858) with the avowed intention of giving Albury near

Guildford some 'special literary lift'. His novel was set in sites all now recognised as 'beauty spots', but then virtually unknown to all but the natives. Here was the landscape for the 'simple lifers', the middle-class intellectuals.

For many wealthy middle-class urban families, the region's countryside proved an irresistible magnet. Newly enriched professional, industrial and business leaders sought a better quality of life in the Weald, the middle Thames and Chilterns woodlands, Surrey hills and the South Downs. Surrey's special attraction ensured a largely gentrified landscape. Amidst the splendid scenery of the neighbouring parishes of Abinger and Holmbury St Mary, for example, new mansions belonged to the heads respectively of the Castle Shipping Line, Doulton's Lambeth and Wedgwood potteries, Stephen's inks, Guinness, Brooke Bond Tea, and accountants Price Waterhouse; together with the then Lord Chief Justice, High Court judges, ex-colonial administrators, doctors, and artists and architects. Ten large country houses were built in the space of 20 years, all with extensive gardens and parks planted with the then popular monkey-puzzles, ginkgos and Himalayan rhododendrons. Cottages were built in villages to house staff not accommodated in the servants' quarters, shopkeepers migrated to set up business, and churches, chapels and schools were erected.

One important impact of the wealth pumped by *nouveaux riches* into the countryside of Victorian and Edwardian Surrey was an enthusiasm for church building and restoration, paid for by the new country-house owners. Typically, Surrey churches had become dilapidated patchworks of varying periods, but many were now completely rebuilt in mass imitation of the greater medieval churches of France or of the 'Stone Belt' of England, as Ruskin had urged. Unfortunately, the loss from the zealous 'restorations' was tremendous, in the form of whitewashed interiors, replacement windows and imported stone.

In this way whole districts were manicured. Wealden Burwash was described by Mark Antony Lower in 1870 as notorious for the lawless 'lower part' of its population, but 'opulent families attracted to the beauty of the situation are choosing this for their homes'. Burwash Down, once dreaded, was now 'a little centre of civilisation'. Similarly, Crowborough was being rescued 'from heathendom to a more Christian condition of things', while Waldron was 'favoured with the presence of several persons of influence and wealth who have completely changed its character'.[39] In respect of Kent alone, Everitt has calculated as many as 9,000 such 'pseudo-gentry' resident by 1870.[40] Whole areas came to be used for inferior landscape parks and game conservation, especially along the main highways between London and the coast, notably around Brighton. Large Victorian houses gentrified their surroundings, and indeed, could overwhelm their neighbourhoods. Thus William James, heir to American logging fortunes, created an enormous mansion at West Dean in West Sussex; it was built originally in the castle style of James Wyatt, but remodelled by Ernest George and Harold Peto in 1891–3 and set in a 500ha downland estate. Even more opulent was William Astor's Hever, built from a fortune in American property and fur. Its 45 guest-rooms were housed as a separate wing to the restored castle and resembled a Tudor village, and construction of the lake and Italian garden occupied 800 men for a period of two years.

For many years prior to the mid-19th century the feeling had grown that suitable landscapes could inspire, teach and nurture improved morals and quality of life. The transformation of the region's urban and rural landscapes through building, enclosure and the reclamation of heathland all had moral undertones connected with improvement, and the social distribution of profit. In line with the more melancholic landscape depictions of the 18th century, a retrospective glimpse of a changing structure of feeling thus has Oliver Goldsmith saying:

> *E'en now, methinks, as pondering here I stand*
> *I see the rural virtues leave the land*

Literary depictions of a lost 'organic' or 'natural' society and landscape were powerful within polite society. By the 19th century, however, many wealthier individuals in the region, having absorbed the representations of painters and writers, replaced reflection with action. Private intervention in the landscape, it was felt, could yield better environments by providing capital for urban, suburban or rural developments such as the 1860s' buildings of the Peabody philanthropic trust in the Victoria Street area of London, or Norman Shaw's planned 1870s' suburban estate of detached houses at Bedford Park (Chiswick). By the early 20th century such views had been taken up by Ebenezer Howard, and the Garden City Pioneer Company Ltd set about building the first garden city at Letchworth in Hertfordshire from 1903. An attractive living environment for all classes was created through the combination of a rural vernacular style, Arts and Crafts details, open space and surrounding farmland. This was closely followed by Henrietta Barnett's determined moral stance to bring human scale and fresh air to the city at Hampstead Garden Suburb. Welwyn Garden City also followed suite.

Elite groups of like-minded individuals, in overlapping circles of affiliation, fostered these sentiments, and the list of organisations that emerged is well known: the Commons, Open Spaces and Footpaths Preservation Society (1865), the Society for the Protection of Ancient Buildings (1877), the Society for Checking the Abuses of Public Advertising (SCAPA) (1893), the National Trust for Places of Historic Interest or Natural Beauty (1894) and the Council for the Preservation of Rural England (1926). State intervention also began to effect landscape change, with the recognition that access to fresh country air and exercise was important for the nation's well-being. Responses from central government included the Ancient Monuments Act 1882 that afforded some protection to Silbury Hill, Stonehenge and Avebury among other listed monuments. Legislation was extended in 1913 to protect scheduled sites by law, and in 1931 to protect their environs also. The latter was particularly important since Stonehenge's immediate surroundings had included a wartime airfield and its buildings, a pig farm and, by 1927, the 'Stonehenge Café'. A public appeal just raised sufficient money for the surrounding land to be purchased and put into the care of the National Trust. The Trust took over Avebury ten years later. The Stonehenge stone circle was itself privately purchased and then gifted into the guardianship of the state, before being administered later by English Heritage. This early protection was all somewhat piecemeal, but there was concomitant growth during the interwar period of legislation to facilitate the control of development by incipient local planning authorities. From the wartime Scott Report (1942) there emerged a commitment to a system of physical planning to control and guide landscape change – a system that has grown in complexity in the last 60 years. Behind all these elements there was the basic human instinct that landscape quality must be preserved and enhanced for a complex of spiritual, aesthetic or practical reasons. The latter certainly included the early Second World War and post-war requirement to preserve good agricultural land for national food sufficiency in the face of pressure for urban and industrial development.[41]

Nowhere in England over the last 150 years has the landscape been under more intense pressure than in the South East. If many early preservationists were inspired by the Lake District, it was the expansion of London, largely by speculative builders, that inspired the creation of the Commons Preservation Society (CPS). Given the concentration of writers, painters and other artists in the region, together with politicians, philanthropists and critical thinkers, it should come as no surprise that the South East nurtured and inspired this landscape protection. Mid-Victorian London was more excavated, rebuilt and extended than ever before, having grown from the 2,200ha on John Rocque's 1746 map, to some 12,950ha in 1851, to more than 31,000ha in 1900 and to over 52,000ha by 1939. Spurred on by such developments, the CPS fought against enclosures of commons and for rights of public access in the South East, as at Knole Park in Kent and Berkhamsted Common in Hertfordshire, or closer to London at Hampstead Heath (1868), Wimbledon (1865–70), Wandsworth (1870–1), Epping Forest (1865–71) and several others. The first National Trust purchase in the region was that of the medieval Old Clergy House at Alfriston in Sussex in 1896. Larger areas of countryside were purchased by 1939 at Box Hill, Leith Hill and Hindhead in Surrey and on the South Downs, while Bodiam Castle was a bequest from the Marquess Curzon of Kedleston. William Morris had been repelled by the growing villa-dom he witnessed on a visit to Hindhead, and from his base at the Red House at Bexleyheath in Kent, which had been built for him by Philip Webb, and later from Kelmscott House in Hammersmith, The Society for the Protection of Ancient Buildings (SPAB) was formed through his energies. Groups more specific to the region were also formed, such as the Society of Sussex Downsmen (1923), which was formed to combat what were seen as threatening changes to the downland, as at the reviled Peacehaven.

But landscape protection by the *cognoscenti* vied with growing demands for outdoor recreation by the many. Popular tourism came with the railway and the paddle steamer. By the late 1850s the various railway companies were furiously competing to offer cheaper fares, with the result that by 1862 bank-holiday crowds at Brighton were lured with the advertisement 'Eight hours at the sea for half-a-crown'. From the beginning, the Brighton railway adjusted its timetables to permit passengers to travel between London and the seaside, or in the reverse direction, and back again, in a single day.

The intervening landscape between London and the south coast, hitherto almost inaccessible by road, was quickly exploited by guidebook writers. As early as 1844 John Thorne's guide, the earliest literary production associated with the London, Brighton and South Coast Railway, led walkers from Balcombe station to 'one of the most fashionable notions of a thoroughly countrified English lane'. The poet and novelist George Meredith was organising rambles to and from Surrey railway stations for London friends as early as the 1860s, and Sir Leslie Stephen's Sunday Tramps, a walking club of London intellectuals founded in 1878, continued this trend. By the 1880s country walking (and even more so the hiking movement of the 1930s) was largely urban in its origin and outlook, and with the rise of the new professional and commercial classes it became a mass recreation. By the late 1920s young workers' organisations and various Church and political bodies became enthusiasts for shared aspects of the 'Simple Life', such as community singing, organised games and camp life. This was helped by the Two Weeks' Holiday Movement and the shorter working hours of the 1930s, and coincided with the similar mass interest in contemporary Germany's *Wandervogel*.

The new sport of 'bicycling', with the invention of the safety cycle in 1894, opened up the countryside for all social classes and especially for working-class Londoners and those from the larger towns. By 1902 London had no fewer than 274 cycling clubs affiliated to the Cycling Association. This mass use of major roads revived many inns to their former glory, including 'The Spread Eagle' at Midhurst, where H G Wells observed ostlers valeting customers' cycles. Cafés and teashops multiplied rapidly, especially after the First World War. Walking has its own literature, as provided by E V Lucas's anthology *The Open Road* (1899) or Hillaire Belloc's *The Four Men* (1904); while the bicycling stories of H G Wells trace how the countryside offered lower-middle and working-class freedom from London. Another recreation growing quickly at this time, and with huge landscape implications, was golf. Most of the few clubs surrounding London by the 1880s were modern, although the Blackheath club (1766) was the oldest organised club in England, and golf has reputedly been played there since 1608. In a short time courses proliferated – on the coastal sandhills of Kent and East Sussex or the Surrey heathlands, where 'a few mad barristers' carved a golf course out of miry and sandy waste near Woking.[42]

For the more affluent, the above activities could be combined with weekend excursions to rural cottages where the 'simple life' could be temporarily experienced. West Surrey was a favoured location for artists and intellectuals: Limpsfield Chart, on its wooded sandstone ridge, housed the best-known colony of 'Simple Lifers', whence came publications that aimed at nothing less than the retrieval of a fast-dissolving rural culture. They include Edward Garnett's *The Imaged World* (1898), Richard Heath's *The English Peasant* (1893), Henry Salt's 1890 biography of Henry Thoreau; and Montague Fordham's *Mother Earth* (1908), which outlined a blueprint for the revival of agriculture, partially incorporated in legislation as the Wheat Act of 1931 and in government planning after the Second World War. The Limpsfield colony was described in Ford Madox Ford's *Simple Life Limited* (1909).

The search for the 'Simple Life' has repeatedly influenced the cultural life and landscape of the South East and has always possessed an element of social nonconformity. From the 1890s up to 1939 this comprised a 'back to the land' movement, a re-affirmation of the rural values of pre-industrial England. Some followed William Cobbett's radicalism, others were organic farming enthusiasts, collectivists, utopian socialists, Fabians, anarchists and pacifists who mingled with occultists, theosophists and spiritualists. But the common thread was the dream of a lost rural idyll, to be seen in the countryside of the South East. The idyll was also inextricably connected with the Arts and Crafts movement in the form of farmer-craftsmen, painters, book-binders, metalworkers, furniture-makers and sculptors. A colony of London craftsmen migrated to Steep near Petersfield in 1900 to found Bedales School on Art and Craft principles. A guild of handicrafts was founded at South Harting by other Londoners working in stained glass, metal, wood and leather. There was a Haslemere colony of weavers, embroiderers and other craftsmen; and similar colonies were founded at Amberley, Storrington and Shere. The most famous, perhaps, was at Ditchling, associated with the sculptor and calligrapher Eric Gill and his followers between 1907 and 1924. Most were relatively short-lived experiences, the philosophical mind finding difficulty in coping with the practical realities inherent in the landscapes of self-sufficiency.

Landscapes were sought which resembled those of the artistic imagination. And if no such landscape existed, then it might be built. Indeed, it could be argued that in its more inspired forms the resurgence of landscaping and domestic building represented one of the most vital forces in English contemporary culture.[43] The alignment of landscape and morality had deep roots: Tory moralists of the 18th century denounced grasping, ambitious and business-like Whigs and reaffirmed the importance of settled, cultivated country estates cared for by old-established families. The landscape was a cultural and political arena for ideological contestation. Alexander Pope argued for landscape gardens that combined utility with a patrician sense of charity, and arguments raged over the social morality on the one hand of isolated houses in landscaped parks, which divorced property from duty, and on the other of a more 'connected' landscape. Pope's

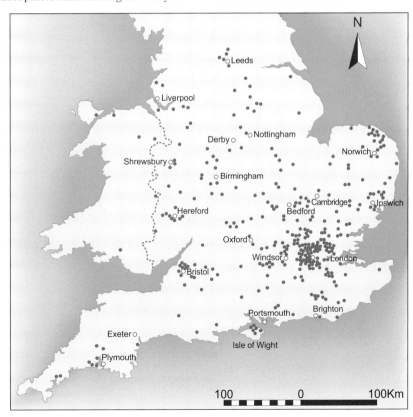

Fig. 8.17 Landscape improvement. The locations of Humphry Repton's consultations in England and Wales. The prestigious areas around London and Windsor feature prominently, in part because of the expanding suburban growth within which Repton designed parks and gardens between the 1790s and 1810s.

miniature landscapes were compared favourably to those of 'pompous tyrants' elsewhere, while the work of Humphrey Repton normally attempted to combine aesthetics with moral purpose, and to dissolve social tensions in landscape beauty. He undertook commissions, consultations and gave advice in all the south-eastern counties but with a pronounced concentration in and around London and Windsor, reflecting the addresses of his prestigious clientele (Fig. 8.17).[44]

Some of the new ideas in gardening and landscape design were anticipated by William Wells of Redleaf, near Penshurst in Kent, whose re-introduced flowers near the house, 'natural' rock gardens, specimen exotic trees, and ferns were widely imitated. George Devey's revival of Kentish vernacular half-timbered houses for Wells was also to prove influential. Subsequently William Robinson and Gertrude Jekyll developed the informal use of hardy plants, shrubs and trees to create their 'wild' or 'woodland' gardens and herbaceous borders; these were intended to be in keeping with the house in its environment, thereby setting out a contrast with modern industrialism. Robinson's ideas on informal, naturalistic plantings were demonstrated in his own landscaping at Gravetye near East Grinstead, where he embellished his estate with woodland plantations. This 'Wild' gardening became popular and traces of Robinson's influence occur all over the South East, especially in the triangle bounded by Horsham, Lewes and Tunbridge Wells, exemplified perhaps by the gardens at Nymans, Leonardslee, Borde Hill and Sheffield Park (Fig. 8.18).

Gertrude Jekyll proved a major force in gardening and her popular *Wood and Garden* (1899) and *Home and Garden* (1900) resonated with suburban gardeners. Inspired by Robinson, she also emulated the Arts and Crafts ideals of Morris, although the most powerful impact on her work was her own local west Surrey landscape with its heaths, woods, fields and cottage gardens, as popularised by the painters Miles Birket Foster, Helen Allingham and Ralph Caldecott. Imbued with the need to preserve traditional landscapes and customs, her *Old West Surrey*

Fig. 8.18 The 'wild garden' influence of Robinson at Sheffield Park, Sussex, together with the work of Repton and Capability Brown. Magnificent autumn foliage in the grounds of the gothicised mansion.

Fig. 8.19 'The Haven' plotland museum, Dunton Hills, Essex. Built in the 1930s, this was a family home for over 40 years and was one of many such sites. The abandoned gardens, orchards and roadside verges of the settlement now constitute a large nature reserve.

(1904) remains a fascinating glimpse into the area around Godalming in the late 19th century, and of a piece with similar attempts to collect and preserve folklore, song and dance by such people as George Butterworth, Percy Grainger and Ralph Vaughan Williams. Jekyll restored the labourer's cottage flowers to favour, but her main achievement was probably the collaboration with her architect-cousin, Edwin Lutyens. Between them they devised 27 gardens between 1890 and 1900 and a further 30 in the following decade for Lutyens's revivalist houses; in all Jekyll undertook more than 300 gardening commissions.

The revival of vernacular building from the 1860s rendered the South East (and especially Surrey) the most accessible and richest source of 'Old English' homes. George Devey's assistant, Charles Voysey, an advocate of the simple outdoor life, built in the traditional vernacular, while the rural buildings near Penshurst sketched by the young Norman Shaw and William Nesfield in the 1860s became the models for the new domestic architecture, which Shaw called the 'Old English' style. Philip Webb's houses such as Coneyhurst and Standen were widely admired for their innovative use of traditional building crafts and his sympathetic relation of new building to its setting. Webb also inspired Lutyens, whose Munstead Wood (for Jekyll herself), Orchards, Goddards and Tigbourne Court captured this 'Old English' feeling. His ideas were promoted by Edward Hudson, whose *Country Life* magazine popularised the Edwardian dream house for country living.

The region's 'Simple Life' movement also gave the impulse to disillusioned urban dwellers to take up smallholdings; after the First World War they were followed by army veterans. The interwar period was the real beginning of the search for 'Arcadia' as a makeshift landscape of single-storey shacks in plotlands, with unmade roads and few services, spread haphazardly across parts of the region. Areas such as Canvey Island and Peacehaven became by-words for rural slums in advance of planning control. South Essex had many such sites: at Dunton Hills, Basildon, the wildlife interest of the abandoned plotland gardens has resulted in the creation of a nature reserve and 'The Haven', now restored to its original condition and furnished in the style of the 1930s and 1940s, houses a plotlands museum (Fig. 8.19). The new town of Basildon replaced many such plotlands; the district for which the Development Corporation had responsibility contained 8,500

Fig. 8.20 Moving to Arcadia in a railway carriage. *The delivery of a new home at Shoreham Beach in about 1910. The carriages were set onto concrete rafts on a shingle spit across the mouth of the River Adur, and initially there was no electricity, gas, or main drainage. Water was brought from the mainland (in the background) in a large zinc cistern and sold at 2d a bucket to supplement stored rainwater.*

dwellings, of which 6,000 were unsewered and 5,500 were chalets, shacks or derelict. Significant amounts of rudimentary development also occurred in the Lea valley, the Thames Estuary, the Isle of Sheppey and parts of the South Coast, including Dungeness, Selsey and the 'Bungalow Town' at Shoreham Beach. Biggin Hill's plots on the North Downs stretched from Walderslade near Chatham to Effingham near Leatherhead – even Surrey, the most prosperous county in England, was not to be spared. The middle Thames between Runnymeade and Thames Ditton was also popular, and the visibility of shacks on the banks of the Thames aroused deep resentment among many of the inhabitants of Eton, Windsor and Henley. Most were on marginal land obtained cheaply or by squatting – steep slopes, shingle, sands, areas liable to flood. Although mostly inhabited by working-class families, some were the haunts of 'bohemians', actors, artists and early film stars. Thus Ivor Novello, in the years around 1914, spent his summers living in a Romany caravan in the garden of his mother's bungalow in Biggin Hill where she had set up an artistic community. For such landscapes, any available material would be incorporated, including surplus army huts and LCC trams, and for £15 one could buy a redundant railway carriage (Fig. 8.20).[45]

For many, this was desecration. Thomas Sharp foresaw that with the use of the car 'all the land in the country can be regarded as building land and consequently all the land in the country is being laid out as a gigantic building estate'. All was becoming greyness and twilight in areas of 'Neither-Town-Nor-Country'.[46] Furthermore 'what hope in the modern world can spring from a chaos of individualism?' Others shared his viewpoint, such as Clough Williams-Ellis and C E M Joad, and although for many this was a time of democratic freedom to build, for others it was clearly a nightmare:

> *All along that south coast road the story is the same. The valley of the Ouse by Newhaven is mean and dirty and bedraggled. Peacehaven is a monstrous blot on the national conscience. The smart, slick little houses which straggle through Saltdean and infest the lovely village of Rottingdean and eat away the beauty of a glorious stretch of downland are monuments to our national stupidity.*
> *How have we allowed the exploiters to filch these downs away from us? What perverted sense of values is it which seeks to turn the coastline of*

England into a concrete promenade, with unlovely suburban colonies stretching away behind it? One by one the quiet places go. Little Bosham will soon be encircled; West Wittering may be developed. Few stretches of southern seaboard will be free from the vulgarities of promenade and bandstand or else of the still more wasteful scatterations of the speculative builder.[47]

Amersham was 'eaten away with shoddiness'; at High Wycombe 'industrial vulgarity is in high command'; Box Hill was floodlit at night; the suburbs of north and east London 'just a sordid, stupid, unnecessary, pathetic mess', while a report on north Middlesex stated that 'the shadow of urbanisation hangs over it like a cloud ready, on the slightest encouragement, to precipitate a rain of bricks and mortar'. The escarpment of the Chilterns near Aston Rowant 'is now honeycombed with hideous shacks thrown haphazard like splodges of mud against a hill-side once covered with trees'. And on the Sussex Coast 'the poison begins at Peacehaven'. The unplanned or haphazard coastal holiday camp, the ribbon development along the new interwar by-passes, with cafés and roadhouses, the suburban sprawl, the advertising hoardings, all gave offence to middle-class tastes.[48]

The protection of open spaces could best be guaranteed by local-authority ownership or statutory control, by the land passing to the National Trust, or by purchase by an enlightened owner. All these avenues were used in the 1920s and 1930s. By 1934, for example, Brighton corporation owned more than 4,000ha of downland of which one-third was outside its own boundaries, including the land at Devil's Dyke. The *ad hoc* arrangements on Salisbury Plain have been noted above. But many examples of the need for a more comprehensive planning approach were also emerging. In 1925 Patrick Abercrombie's report on the requirement for regional planning in east Kent to accommodate the new Kent coalfield pointed to the need to prevent the despoliation of the countryside as well as to generate economic development. In Surrey, Norbury Park and the Fredley Estate, below Box Hill, were purchased by a member of the county council in 1929 when they came on to the market, with the cost and management then passing to the county council. Local-authority action was piecemeal, including attempts to ensure access or restrict development densities at Poole and in the New Forest. Subsequently the Surrey County Council Bill 1931 provided a precedent for landscape protection that was copied in different ways throughout England; it was followed by the Town and Country Planning Act 1932, and the Restriction of Ribbon Development Act 1935. The LCC's Green Belt Act also followed in 1938: an incremental, non-radical approach throughout the 1930s did offer a measure of protection.

The 1932 Act remained the basis of planning until the Second World War. Thereafter, with the advent of the statutory 1947 Town and Country Planning Act, which not only preserved 'beauty spots' but controlled most development, the region's eyesores could now at least be kept in check, if not removed. Landscapes such as the North and South Downs, the Seven Sisters and

Stonehenge were now joined by those of Hertfordshire, south Essex and the Low Weald in receiving protection from unwanted development. But farmland was exempt from this 1947 development-control legislation, and the South East has therefore seen hundreds of kilometres of hedgerows disappear since 1945, prefabricated and large farm buildings erected, and large machinery introduced to drive forward a commercialised agenda within a technologised and restructured landscape that is best exemplified, perhaps, by the Berkshire Downs. Furthermore, the 1949 National Parks and Access to the Countryside Act brought no national park to the South East, as it did elsewhere. The South Downs, originally proposed for designation, were felt to have been too intensively farmed during and after the war for them to be included, despite the original 1947 recommendation of the Hobhouse Committee. Both the South Downs and the New Forest had been nominated to the Addison Committee when it was considering the selection of parks as early as 1929–31, but neither was included in the designations of the 1950s. This omission has at last been corrected, and the New Forest has been declared a National Park, while the final decision on the South Downs is awaited.

The influence of literary and artistic perceptions on the development of landscape protection in the South East cannot be overemphasised. They provided a long-term cultural context within which the evolution of protection took place. In emphasising countryside beauty and urban problems to a growing and mobile middle class, however nuanced the message, they gave impetus to the post-war planning frameworks that sought to protect rural landscape and contain urban expansion. We are currently living with an unprecedented degree of control over our landscape, for better or worse.

NOTES

1   Sweet 2004.
2   Hemingway 1992, 141.
3   Barrell 1980.
4   Whistler 1890, 8.
5   Farrant 2001, 11–12.
6   Chandler 2000, 137; Farrant 2001, 25–6.
7   Smith 1979, no. 260.
8   Farrant 2001, 45–50; Miller 1995.
9   Brandon 1998, 195.
10 Brandon 2003, 220.
11 Brandon & Short 1990, 340; Payne 1993, 21–2.
12 Brandon 1984, 59; 2003, 237–42.
13 Wiener 1981; Howkins 1986.
14 Hemingway 1992, 155–215.
15 Johnson 1973, 449–74.
16 Whistler 1890, 144.
17 Daniels 1993, 11–42.
18 Tindall 1991, 10.
19 Levine 1977, 137.
20 Sale 1986, 4; Drabble 1979, 89–91.
21 Squires 1974, 18.
22 McNeillie 1986, I, 35.
23 Evelyn 1955, III, 461.
24 Earle 1994, 4.
25 Daiches & Flower 1979, 78–9; Hill-Miller 2001, 63–125.
26 Wolfreys 1998, 3, 141–78; Collins 1973, 543–4.
27 Anon 1851, 562–5.
28 Tindall 1991, 69.
29 Betjeman 1970, 204–5.
30 White 1789 (1949 edn), 25.
31 Young 1788, 54–5.
32 Cobbett 1830 (1967 edn), 206.
33 Cobbett 1830 (1967 edn), 67–8.
34 Keith 1975; Jefferies 1884 (1983 edn), 114–25.
35 Hudson 1910 (1979 edn), 30–2.
36 Bourne 1912, 1–2.
37 Sims 1889, 1.
38 Snell 1998, 12–13.
39 Lower 1870, 222–4.
40 Everitt 1979, 79–108.
41 Sheail 1981, 50–3.
42 Brandon & Short 1990, 336–40.
43 Stamp & Goulancourt 1986, 13–43.
44 Daniels 1982, 124–44; 1999, 255–70.
45 Hardy & Ward 1984.
46 Sharp 1932, 11.
47 Marshall 1938, 166.
48 Marshall 1938, 169; Sheail 1981, 9; Mais 1938, 213, 216.

9

The South East: 'Infinite Riches in a Little Room'

The South East has a personality and character that is strongly different in many respects from that of other regions. It shares, of course, some of its basic physiographic characteristics with other regions – free-draining chalk wold landscapes with Lincolnshire or the Cotswolds; flat reclaimed marshlands with the east coast and Somerset Levels; wooded claylands with parts of East Anglia or the West Midlands. Yet these similarities are almost incidental to all the things that we and our predecessors going back many thousands of years have done to the land and to the plants and animals. It is this human interaction with nature and the land – always rooted in place and locality, ultimately in the experience and actions of individual people, and today framed by the perceptions and reactions of us the beholders of landscape – that makes the South East distinctive within England.

The human response to the natural environment also shares features with those of similar *pays* elsewhere: the sheep/corn husbandry of the downland, the wood-pasture of the weald, the grazings of the brooklands and marshes, all bear close resemblance to other English rural economies forged over centuries. This does not, however, detract, especially in the particular combination of these things that we find in the South East, from the *genius loci* of the region, that very special 'south-eastern-ness' that is so celebrated. Indeed, it is perhaps in their very heterogeneity in such a small space that the charm and interest of the landscapes lie. To quote Christopher Marlowe, the region has 'infinite riches in a little room' (*The Jew of Malta c.* 1589, Act I, scene 1). Its very variety has impressed itself upon travellers after their arrival at Dover.

In this book we have encountered these many different sub-regional human landscapes and traced their roots in the past. The importance of external links and the power expressed through the purposeful shaping of landscapes and the use of landscapes as symbols of that power were demonstrated in Chapter 1, and were themes to which we consistently returned. We can now go back to another question posed in Chapter 1, where we noted that while landscapes undoubtedly reflect economic production in the fields, farm buildings and towns of the region, this is not all that they are. They are also essential components of the creation and transmission of cultures, lifestyle and social practices, and they are subject to change; they are not just an inert stage upon which actors play out their important roles but a thing that interacts with those actors just as people interact with nature in the manufacture of landscape.

Landscape is an excellent medium in which to make socio-cultural issues appear 'natural'. As we have seen, physical landscape features were undoubtedly of symbolic importance for prehistoric societies, and within both historical and contemporary times, landscape constitutes our everyday and often taken-for-granted surrounding – and in this lies precisely the latent power that can be tapped for ideological purposes. As the anthropologist Clifford Geertz has it: 'Landscapes are a story … [people] tell about themselves'.[1] Pierre Bourdieu's concept of the 'habitus' is appropriate here: a term which describes the processes of environmental conditioning whereby individuals learn the manners and attitudes appropriate to their social position through their physical environment and personal relationships. Bourdieu defines the habitus as a kind of social unconscious, a 'knowledge without concepts', because it is completely internalised and applied unknowingly.[2] The landscapes of the South East, therefore, replete with symbolic meaning, give us signals about society and culture, which we have unconsciously absorbed for thousands of years.

Buildings, for example, deliberately designed in their setting, make landscapes 'tangible, visible and sensible' and such spaces are therefore both made and in turn help to make us part of our society.[3] The title for this chapter is taken from a Marlowe play and the concept of theatre is also an appropriate one. The idea of performance, carnival or spectacle is frequently employed to enable discussions of the use of public spaces: in the Renaissance the 'theatre' was not only a playhouse but also more broadly a place or region in which phenomena can be unified to aid understanding. Thus we have John Speed's *The Theatre of the Empire of Great Britaine* (1611). In this present volume, the South East has been taken as just such a theatre, within which the scenery and the actors have played out an interactive, ever-changing narrative.

A theme of choreographed public display is very appropriate for the South East, and to take just one centuries-old example drawn from Chapter 7, we may watch the monarch symbolically joining Parliament and Crown in the form of the annual state opening of Parliament – an event in which a procession moves along a route from Buckingham Palace down the Mall through the Admiralty Arch and Trafalgar Square (itself symbolising military victories), down Whitehall to Parliament. Central London here becomes a stage of national importance and symbolism, an historically important space used to demonstrate political order and monarchical power, and one that was created largely, as we have seen, in the 19th century. To this we may add the importance of the landscapes that surround the Trooping of the Colour, royal weddings, state visits, victory parades, or the Order of the Garter parade at Windsor Castle from the state apartments downhill to St George's Chapel. The Great Exhibition of 1851, the Festival of Britain in 1951 and the Coronation of Elizabeth II in 1953 were great open-air theatrical

Fig. 9.1 Landscape of remembrance.
The War Memorial at Lancing, Sussex.
The plain celtic cross on its tapering plinth
is set in a small memorial garden outside
St Michael's church.

displays, where a landscape populated with figures created and reinforced British national heritage and identity. To do this, landscapes need not be so grand: most villages have a landscape for national or locally symbolic occasions, such as a church, church hall, a war memorial, a square or green. Indeed, one of the most familiar yet poignant landscape features is the war memorial with its roll of honour for those killed in service (Fig. 9.1).[4]

Landscapes therefore embody culture and deliver signs and meanings to shape our lives. Landscape is by definition a highly visible thing, but we need to go beyond observation, recording, categorisation and archival study – we need to interpret in order to understand its multiple (and often contested) meanings. An empirical approach, in which landscape objects are seen as largely unproblematic, will not suffice – descriptions are not mirror reflections, and 'the innocent eye is blind'.[5] Thus the attractive village landscapes of the Chilterns at such places as Buckland Common, St Leonards, Hawridge Common or Turville (this last known to millions through its portrayal in the BBC's *Vicar of Dibley*) owe their beauty to a combination of natural and humanised factors, yet behind the beauty one should also see commuter villages with few local amenities or jobs, and house prices in this Area of Outstanding Natural Beauty more than twice the national average.[6] In the 'Cocktail Belt' around London such circumstances are now common. The landscape historian understands the evolution of such villages, but must also surely be prepared to consider the socio-economic and cultural relations, past and present, which surround the landscape and are influenced by it.

These landscapes are regarded as permanent in relation to the human lifespan, in the same way that field boundaries, woodlands and pathways are seen as permanent. But others are not: we should remember that most early domestic buildings will have had a short lifespan, and that medieval houses might be rebuilt on quite different axes, or different sites, leading in extreme instances to entire 'village migrations'. Indeed, the startling speed of change in the London landscape was a *motif* running through the latter part of Chapter 7. But we can go further, and suggest that the character of the landscapes we perceive can be completely ephemeral, depending on the patterns of light or cloud or other weather effects, or the time of day.[7] The influential landscape preservationist Vaughan Cornish, settling in Camberley after 12 years of travel abroad, 'watched the ever-changing lights and shadows upon the everlasting hills, the changing colour of the seasons on the heath, and even the "rhythm of the hours"'.[8] James Barry, in his Lecture on Chiaroscuro, noted the importance of the distribution of light and dark, for on this depended:

> *whether objects shall present themselves with that disgusting confusion and embarrassment which distract our sight, or with that unity and harmony which we can never behold without pleasure. There are times when the scenes about Hyde Park, Richmond, Windsor, and Blackheath, appear very little interesting. The difference between a meridian and evening light, the reposes of extensive shadow, the half lights and catching splendours that these scenes sometimes exhibit, compared with their ordinary appearance do abundantly show how much is gained by seizing upon those transitory moments of fascination, when nature appears with such accumulated advantage.*[9]

Much then depends upon when, and even in what mood, the observer observes: the scene in one of the region's otherwise quiet country towns on market day could be transformed. And the landscape changed and still changes seasonally depending on agricultural land use – the autumnal shift from communal arable to grazings on the stubbles and fallows of the medieval open fields would be one example. The landscape contrast of May blossom compared with the skeletal mid-winter hedgerow may be stark.

Fig. 9.2 The iconic White Cliffs of Dover, here shown at St Margaret's Bay, on the Kentish Foreland. The rates of erosion vary over time but in 1999 a large rock fall took place here, bringing the National Trust's distinctive Victorian South Foreland Lighthouse ever closer to the edge. The photograph shows a large segment of chalk at the foot of the cliffs after a fall in February 2001. In 2005 the White Cliffs were overwhelmingly voted Britain's favourite stretch of coast owned by the National Trust.

Such changes are cyclical; others are simply transient. A good example of a relatively ephemeral but well-known landscape feature, and one whose symbolism has changed comparatively quickly over its short life, was the Greenham Common American airbase in Berkshire and the Greenham Common women's peace camp that was established at its gates. The airbase itself would originally have been perceived in England in its Second World War role as 'moral' or even 'virtuous' in the wartime struggle. Attitudes to this morality changed during the Cold War, and dissatisfaction with the dominant culture was expressed through the peace camp, which ran from 1981 to 2000 to protest against the siting of Cruise missiles at Greenham. And in a post-Cold War political atmosphere, a further twist of landscape change now sees the base as a business park and nature reserve.

There are many other examples of varying rates of change. The speed of London's growth staggered contemporary observers, who watched it moving outwards by the week and month. Only slightly slower was the pace of enclosure in the 18th and 19th centuries, which transformed the chalklands. And over a much longer term there are climatic changes – the Little Ice Age affected the Thames such that in its frozen state the ice might be the site of fairs or ice carnivals, as in 1683. Climate change will continue to affect the region's landscape, particularly the coast, as sea levels rise. And inexorably the cliffs crumble, as at Beachy Head or the White Cliffs of Dover (Fig. 9.2). Sometimes the landscape impact can be dramatic, as after the great storm of 1703 described by Defoe, or the 1987 storm that left so much of the region's woodland flattened – it claimed 20 per cent of all the trees of Sussex, and about 15 million trees overall in the South of England. The well-loved beech trees planted on Chanctonbury Ring in Sussex in 1760 by Charles Goring were decimated. It is estimated that Hampshire lost more than half a million trees in the 1987 storm and another 700,000 in the 1990 storms (Fig. 9.3).

Fig. 9.3 The impact of sudden change on the landscape. *The Great Storm of October 1987 and its aftermath on the Level, Brighton. Many mature elm trees crashed to the ground in hours.*

It is often said that W G Hoskins, doyen of landscape historians, claimed that in landscape, only the last 500 years really mattered. His *Making of the English Landscape* (1955) certainly paid scant attention to landscapes before the Saxon settlement. He also despised modern landscapes with a palpable venom. He might not, therefore, have approved of this book, with its contention that on the one hand much of our landscape can only be understood by the study of prehistoric and Roman impacts, and on the other that the 20th century has seen huge and important changes that are not necessarily for the worse. Indeed the English Heritage 'Change and Creation' programme has been designed to increase awareness of our material surroundings constructed since 1950.[10] In any interpretation one cannot leave out either the beginning or end of the story. Of course, it is possible to criticise 20th-century impacts: writing of the A13 road to Essex and the post-modern scenery currently being assembled, Tom Dyckhoff has said:

> *The old city had richness, texture, diversity, excitement, built in a tight mesh by the small property developer. The new is like prairie planning, vast, monocultural, built by the multinational developer.*[11]

But it is relatively easy to use the past landscape as a stick with which to beat the present. We have seen what one contemporary observer of that rich, textured 'old city' in the 19th century, Dickens, made of it. If he were a resident at that time, would Tom Dyckhoff really have liked the beginning any more than he likes the (gentrified) end? Ultimately we have to recognise that the material remains among which we live today characterise our economy, society and culture in exactly the same way that the relict landscapes of previous generations can be interpreted. Yesterday's landscape destruction or urban sprawl will sooner or later become tomorrow's heritage and is already today's landscape, whether we 'like' it or not.

The theme of landscape change can be taken up elsewhere in the region. The South Downs Area of Outstanding Natural Beauty has nearly 400 nationally designated Scheduled Monuments and several hundred more of local significance recorded in the Sites and Monuments Record. But by 1995, 165 of those recorded monuments had been completely destroyed and there was piecemeal destruction on all but 5 per cent of the monuments. Post-war intensive farming and building has made huge inroads into the archaeological heritage here. In the last 60 years about 8 per cent (3,000ha) of Sussex's ancient woodland has been grubbed out, while replanting with conifers has degraded a further 36 per cent (14,000ha). In both town and countryside, landscape change is ongoing and rapid. On the other hand, aerial archaeologists have recently noted in parts of the South East's chalklands that Bronze Age settlements appear on new air photographs as the overlying Iron Age sites are eroded by ploughing: an interesting but uncomfortable paradox and insight into the meaning of change. We should also recall that we understand better the origins and growth of Roman and Saxon London (and indeed the pre-glacial movements of the Thames) as a result of the redevelopment of London throughout the 1980s and 1990s.

So, this book has attempted to fill in some silences, using multiple methods and sources to interpret, to see the subtext. In Fredric Jameson's words 'confronting the past in a new way and reading its less tangible secrets'.[12] Landscape change, whether slow or fast (together with its instability of meaning, since different people may visualise the landscape in quite different ways) has led some such as David Harvey to distrust tradition, aesthetics and images; in his eyes these stand accused of being unreliable, even duplicitous, compared to texts or narratives, when attempting to understand the deeper processes affecting society.[13] But this book has shown that texts and narratives as well as cultural landscapes are also representations by someone or by a society, and so all are best read with caution and a trained eye.

We have seen that this certainly applies to ways in which the South East's landscape has been lauded in the creative arts. It has been written about exhaustively, and been the inspiration for generations of archaeologists, geologists, botanists, ecologists, topographers and historians, geographers, poets and writers, artists, architects and landscape gardeners. Their interpretations, using the region as an open-air laboratory, have produced classic examples of domestic architecture, gardens, the resurgence of English music, key insights into our prehistoric pasts, landscape painting and country writing.

Such achievements, embodied in and stimulated by the region's multi-faceted landscape, give deep meaning to both town and country. It surely behoves planners and all involved with intervention within these distinctive landscapes to take cognisance of their pasts, to ensure that the individual elements are safeguarded within their contexts and to understand the entirety of the whole. Listed buildings, conservation areas, SSSIs all help in this respect, but are by definition concerned more with the component than the whole landscape. Similarly, while the government's Planning Policy Guidance Note 16 on the relations between archaeological survey and development sites requires developers to carry out archaeological excavations in sensitive areas, the brief seldom encompasses much more than the immediate site. And yet the wider landscapes carry layers of meaning, and the recognition of this fact will surely soon become another element in planning policy:

*Identity is intimately tied to memory: both our personal memory … and
the collective or social memories interconnected with the histories of our
families, neighbours, fellow workers, and ethnic communities. … landscapes
are storehouses for these social memories, because natural features such as
hills or harbours, as well as streets, buildings, and patterns of settlement,
frame the lives of many people and often outlast many lifetimes.*[14]

We need the 'hard-won generalities' as well as the micro-evaluations. Conservation
and regeneration must go together to ensure some quality of life in vibrant cities
and in the living country, and landscape historians therefore must enter into the
hard world of environmental politics, since there are seldom any easy decisions
in an environment as pressurised as that of south-east England. The recent
development of GIS-based Historic Landscape Characterisation, which recognises
the richness of biodiversity and the time-depth of the region's cultural landscapes,
is surely a step forward in this respect, feeding as it will into strategic environmental
decision-making.[15]

At the end of the epilogue to his celebrated study of narrative, *Mimesis: The
Representation of Reality in Western Literature* (1953), Auerbach explains the
difficulties of writing such a book without a good library. He then adds:

*On the other hand it is quite possible that the book owes its existence to just
this lack. … If it had been possible for me to acquaint myself with all the
work that has been done on so many subjects, I might never have reached
the point of writing.*[16]

This is precisely my feeling, confronted with the rich and varied landscapes of a
region which has received much of the wealth, the attention and the political
power of the nation, and that has expressed it through its landscapes. But as well
as we think we know a landscape, there is so much more to explore:

*We shall not cease from exploration
And the end of all our exploring
Will be to arrive where we started
And know the place for the first time.*[17]

And presumptuously, we might even add to Eliot's 'Little Gidding':

*Then we can start again,
And know enough to ask better questions!*

NOTES

1   Geertz 1973, 448.
2   Bourdieu 1980.
3   Tilley 1994, 17.
4   Cosgrove 1989, 130–1; 1997, 101.
5   Duncan 1990, 14.
6   Hepple & Doggett 1994.
7   Brassley 1998.
8   Cornish 1932, 26–7.
9   Barry 1809, vol. I, 487

10 Bradley *et al.* 2004.
11 *The Times* 25 May 2004, T2, 16.
12 Jameson 1991, 364–5.
13 Harvey 1990, 303.
14 Hayden 1995, 9.
15 Fowler 2002, 37; Cherry 2001, 8–11;
    Fairclough 1999; Grenville 1999.
16 Auerbach 1953, 557.
17 Eliot 1943, 143.

Bibliography

Ackroyd, P 2000. *London: The Biography*. London: Chatto & Windus

Ambrose, P 1986. *Whatever Happened to Planning?* London: Methuen

Anon 1851. 'A suburban Connemara' *in* Dickens, C (ed.) *Household Words*, II, 562–5

Applebaum, S 1972. 'Roman Britain' *in* Finberg, H (ed.) *The Agrarian History of England and Wales*, Vol. I, pt 2: *AD 43–1042*. Cambridge: Cambridge University Press, 5–277

Armstrong, J 2000. 'Transport' *in* Waller, P (ed.) *The English Urban Landscape*. Oxford: Oxford University Press, 209–33

Aston, M and Bettey, J 1998. 'The post-medieval rural landscape *c*. 1540–1700: the drive for profit and the desire for status' *in* Everson, P and Williamson, T (eds) *The Archaeology of Landscape: Studies Presented to Christopher Taylor*. Manchester: Manchester University Press, 117–38

Auerbach, E 1953. *Mimesis: The Representation of Reality in Western Literature*. Princeton: Princeton University Press

Baker, A 1973. 'Changes in the later middle ages' *in* Darby, H (ed.) *A New Historical Geography of England*. Cambridge: Cambridge University Press, 186–247

Baker, A and Billinge, M 2004. *Geographies of England: The North–South Divide, Imagined and Material*. Cambridge: Cambridge University Press

Barker, T C and Robbins, M 1963. *A History of London Transport I: The Nineteenth Century*. London: George Allen & Unwin, 242

Barrell, J 1980. *The Dark Side of the Landscape: The Rural Poor in English Painting 1730–1840*. Cambridge: Cambridge University Press

Barry, J 1809. *The works of James Barry esq, historical painter: to which is prefixed some account of the life and writings of the author* (ed. J Fryer, 2 vols). London: T Cadell and W Davies

Bender, B 1993. 'Stonehenge – contested landscapes (medieval to present day)' *in* Bender, B (ed.) *Landscape: Politics and Perspectives*. Oxford: Berg, 245–79

Bender, B 1998. *Stonehenge: Making Space*. Oxford: Berg

Beresford, M 1967. *New Towns of the Middle Ages: Town Plantation in England, Wales and Gascony*. London: Lutterworth

Berry, S 2005. *Georgian Brighton*. Chichester: Phillimore

Betjeman, J 1970. 'Slough' *in John Betjeman's Collected Poems*. London: John Murray, 22–4

Bettey, J 1986. *Wessex from AD 1000*. London: Longman

Blair, J 1991. *Early Medieval Surrey: Landholding, Church and Settlement before 1300*. Stroud: Alan Sutton

Borsay, P 2000. 'Early modern urban landscapes, 1540–1800' *in* Waller, P (ed.) *The English Urban Landscape*. Oxford: Oxford University Press, 99–124

Bourdieu, P 1980. *The Logic of Practice* (trans. R Nice). Cambridge: Cambridge University Press

Bourne, G 1912. *Change in the Village*. London: Duckworth

Bradley, A, Buchli, V, Fairclough, G, Hicks, D, Miller, J and Schofield, J 2004. *Change and Creation: Historic Landscape Character 1950–2000*. London: English Heritage

Brandon, P 1977. *A History of Surrey*. Chichester: Phillimore

Brandon, P 1984. 'Wealden nature and the role of London in nineteenth-century artistic imagination'. *J Hist Geogr* **10**, 53–74

Brandon, P 1998. *The South Downs*. Chichester: Phillimore

Brandon, P 2003. *The Kent and Sussex Weald*. Chichester: Phillimore

Brandon, P and Short, B 1990. *The South East from AD 1000*. London: Longman

Brassley, P 1998. 'On the unrecognised significance of the ephemeral landscape'. *Landscape Res* **23**, 119–32

Bridgland, D R 1994. *Quaternary of the Thames*. London: Chapman & Hall

Brimblecombe, P 1987. *The Big Smoke: A History of Air Pollution in London since Medieval Times*. London: Methuen

Brindle, S 2004. *Paddington Station: Its History and Architecture*. London: English Heritage

Buck, N, Gordon, I, Hall, P, Harloe, M and Kleinman, M 2002. *Working Capital: Life and Labour in Contemporary London*. London: Routledge

Chalklin, C 1974. *The Provincial Towns of Georgian England: A Study of the Building Process 1740–1820*. London: Edward Arnold

Chalklin, C 1998. *English Counties and Public Building, 1650–1830*. London: Hambledon

Chandler, J 1983. *Endless Street: A History of Salisbury*. Salisbury: Hobnob Press

Chandler, J 2000. 'The discovery of landscape' *in* Hooke, D (ed.) *Landscape: The Richest Historical Record*. Amesbury: Society for Landscape Studies, 133–41

Chandler, T 1965. *The Climate of London*. London: Hutchinson

Chapman, J and Seeliger, S 2001. *Enclosure, Environment and Landscape in Southern England*. Stroud: Tempus

Cherry, B and Pevsner, N 1983. *The Buildings of England. London 2: South*. Harmondsworth: Penguin

Cherry, M 2001. 'The historic urban environment: the key to understanding'. *English Heritage Conserv Bull* **41**, 8–11

Clark, P and Slack, P 1976. *English Towns in Transition 1500–1700*. Oxford: Oxford University Press

Cleere, H and Crossley, D. 1985 *The Iron Industry of the Weald*. Leicester: Leicester University Press

Cobbett, W 1830 (1967 edn). *Rural Rides*. Harmondsworth: Penguin

Collins, P 1973. 'Dickens and London' *in* Dyos, H J and Wolff, M (eds) *The Victorian City: Images and Realities*. London: Routledge & Kegan Paul, 537–57

Conzen, M R G 1981. 'Historical townscapes in Britain: a problem in applied geography' *in* Whitehand, J (ed.) *The Urban Landscape: Historical Development and Management*. London: Blackwell, 55–74

Corfield, P 1982. *The Impact of English Towns 1700–1800*. Oxford: Oxford University Press

Cornish, V 1932. *The Scenery of England: A Study of Harmonious Grouping in Town and Country*. London: Council for the Preservation of Rural England

Corporation of London 1993. *The Official Guide to Burnham Beeches*. London: Corporation of London

Cosgrove, D 1989. 'Geography is everywhere: culture and symbolism in human landscapes' *in* Gregory, D and Walford, R (eds) *Horizons in Human Geography*. Totowa: Barnes & Noble, 118–35

Cosgrove, D 1997. 'Spectacle and society: landscape as theatre in premodern and postmodern cities' *in* Groth, P and Bressi, T W (eds) *Understanding Ordinary Landscapes*. New Haven: Yale University Press, 99–110

Countryside Agency 1999. *Countryside Character*, Vol. 7: *South East and London*. Cheltenham: Countryside Agency

Countryside Commission 1993. *The Dorset Downs, Heaths and Coast Landscape*. Cheltenham: Countryside Commission

Crinson, M 2003. *Modern Architecture and the End of Empire*. Aldershot: Ashgate

Crossley, D and Saville, R 1991. *The Fuller Letters: Guns, Slaves and Finance 1728–1755*. Lewes: Sussex Record Society

Cruickshank, D and Burton, N 1990. *Life in the Georgian City*. London: Viking

Cunliffe, B 1974. 'Chalton, Hants: the evolution of a landscape'. *Antiq J* **53**, 173–90

Cunliffe, B 1978. 'Settlement and population in the British Iron Age: some facts, figures and fantasies' *in* Cunliffe, B and Rowley, T (eds) *Lowland Iron Age Communities in Europe*. BAR Supp Ser **48**, 3–24

Cunliffe, B 1993. *Wessex to AD 1000*. London: Longman

Daiches, D and Flower, J 1979. *Literary Landscapes of the British Isles: A Narrative Atlas*. London: Paddington

Daniels, S 1982. 'Humphry Repton and the morality of landscape' *in* Gold, J and Burgess, J (eds) *Valued Environments*. London: George Allen & Unwin

Daniels, S 1993. *Fields of Vision: Landscape Imagery and National Identity in England and the United States*. Cambridge: Polity

Daniels, S 1999. *Humphry Repton: Landscape Gardening and the Geography of Georgian England*. New Haven: Yale University Press

Dark, K and Dark, P 1997. *The Landscape of Roman Britain*. Stroud: Sutton

Darley, G 1978. *Villages of Vision* (2nd edn). London: Paladin/Granada

Davis, J 2000. 'Modern London' *in* Waller, P (ed.) *The English Urban Landscape*. Oxford: Oxford University Press, 125–50

Defoe, D 1971 edn. *A Tour through the Whole Island of Great Britain*. Harmondsworth: Penguin

Department of the Environment 1994. *Biodiversity: The UK Action Plan*. London: DoE

Dickens, P and Gilbert, P 1981. 'Inter-war housing policy: a study of Brighton'. *Southern Hist* **3**, 201–31

Drabble, M 1979. *A Writer's Britain: Landscape in Literature*. London: Thames & Hudson

Drewett, P 2003. 'Taming the wild: the first farming communities in Sussex' *in* Rudling, D (ed.) *The Archaeology of Sussex to AD 2000*. Brighton: University of Sussex, 39–46

Drewett, P and Hamilton, S 2001. 'Caburn: sacred mount or classic hillfort?'. *Curr Archaeol* **174**, 256–62

Drewett, P, Rudling, D and Gardiner, M 1988. *The South East to AD 1000*. London: Longman

Duncan, J S 1990. *The City as Text: The Politics of Landscape Interpretation in the Kandyan Kingdom*. Cambridge: Cambridge University Press

Dyos, H J 1977. *Victorian Suburb: A Study of the Growth of Camberwell*. Leicester: Leicester University Press

Dyos, H J 1982. 'Some social costs of railway building in London' *in* Cannadine, D and Reeder, D (eds) *Exploring the Urban Past*. Cambridge: Cambridge University Press, 119–25

Earle, P 1994. *A City Full of People: Men and Women of London 1650–1750*. London: Methuen

Eddison, J 2000. *Romney Marsh: Survival on a Frontier*. Stroud: Tempus

Eliot, T S 1943. *Four Quartets*. London: Faber & Faber

Ellis, J 2000. 'Regional and county centres 1700–1840' *in* Clark, P (ed.) *The Cambridge Urban History of Britain*, Vol. II: *1540–1840*. Cambridge: Cambridge University Press, 673–704

Environment Agency 2003. *State of the Environment 2003*. London: Environment Agency

Evelyn, J 1955. *The Diary of John Evelyn*. Vol. III *Kalendarium 1650–1672* (ed. E S De Beer, 6 vols). Oxford: Oxford University Press

Everitt, A 1977. 'River and wold: reflections on the historical origins of region and *pays*'. *J Hist Geog* **3**, 1–19

Everitt, A 1979. 'County, country and town'. *Trans Roy Hist Soc* **29**, 79–108

Everitt, A 1986. *Continuity and Colonization: The Evolution of Kentish Settlement*. Leicester: Leicester University Press

Fairclough, G 1999. *Yesterday's World, Tomorrow's Landscape*. London: English Heritage

Farrant, J 2001. *Sussex Depicted: Views and Descriptions 1600–1800*. Lewes: Sussex Record Society

FitzRandolph, H and Hay, M 1926. *The Rural Industries of England and Wales* (3 vols). Oxford: Oxford University Press

Fowler, P 1981. 'Later prehistory' *in* Piggott, S (ed.) *The Agrarian History of England and Wales*, Vol. I: *Prehistory*. Cambridge: Cambridge University Press, 63–298

Fowler, P 2002. *Farming in the First Millennium AD*. Cambridge: Cambridge University Press

Gardiner, M 1998. 'Settlement change on Denge and Walland Marshes, 1400–1550' *in* Eddison, J, Gardiner, M and Long, A (eds) *Romney Marsh: Environmental Change and Human Occupation in a Coastal Lowland*. Oxford: Oxford University Committee for Archaeology, 129–45

Gardiner, M 2003. 'Economy and landscape change in post-Roman and early medieval Sussex, 450–1175' *in* Rudling, D (ed.) *The Archaeology of Sussex to AD 2000*. Brighton: University of Sussex, 151–60

Geertz, C 1973. *The Interpretation of Cultures*. New York: Basic Books

Gilpin, W 1791. Remarks on forest scenery, and other woodland views (relative chiefly to picturesque beauty) illustrated by the scenes of New-Forest in Hampshire. London: R. Blamire (reprinted Richmond Publishing Co 1973)

Glendinning, M and Muthesius, S 1994. *Tower Block: Modern Public Housing in England, Scotland, Wales and Northern Ireland*. New Haven: Yale University Press

Goodall, J 2000. 'The medieval palace of Westminster' *in* Riding, C and Riding, J (eds) *The Houses of Parliament: History, Art, Architecture*. London: Merrell, 49–67

Gray, H L 1915. *English Field Systems*. Cambridge (Mass): Harvard University Press

Grenville, J (ed.) 1999. *Managing the Historic Rural Landscape*. London: English Heritage

Grossmith, G and W 1892. *The Diary of a Nobody*. Bristol: J W Arrowsmith

Hall, A D and Russell, E J 1911. *A Report on the Agriculture and Soils of Kent, Surrey and Sussex*. London: Board of Agriculture and Fisheries

Hall, P 1964 . 'The development of communications' *in* Coppock, J T and Prince, H (eds) *Greater London*. London: Faber & Faber, 52–79

Hallam, H E 1988. 'Rural England and Wales, 1042–1350' *in* Hallam, H E (ed.) *The Agrarian History of England and Wales*, Vol. II: *1042–1350*. Cambridge: Cambridge University Press 966–1008

Hamerow, H 1988. 'Mucking: the Anglo-Saxon settlement'. *Curr Archaeol* **10**, 128–31

Hamerow, H 1993. Excavations at Mucking vol. 2: the Anglo-Saxon settlement. London: English Heritage

Hamerow, H 2002. *Early Medieval Settlements: The Archaeology of Rural Communities in Northwestern Europe, AD 400–900*. Oxford: Oxford University Press

Hamnett, C 2003. *Unequal City: London in the Global Arena*. London: Routledge

Hardy, D 2005. 'Utopian ideas and the planning of London'. *Planning Perspectives* **20**, 35–49

Hardy, D and Ward, C 1984. *Arcadia for All: The Legacy of a Makeshift Landscape*. London: Mansell

Hardy, T 1886 (1965 edn). *The Mayor of Casterbridge*. London: Macmillan

Hardy, T 1891 (1974 edn). *Tess of the d'Urbervilles*. London: Macmillan

Harvey, D 1990. *The Condition of Postmodernity*. Oxford: Blackwell

Harwood, E and Saint, A 1991. *London*. London: HMSO

Hayden, D 1995. *The Power of Place: Urban Landscapes as Public History*. Cambridge (Mass): MIT Press

Hemingway, A 1992. *Landscape Imagery and Urban Culture in Early Nineteenth-century Britain*. Cambridge: Cambridge University Press

Hepple, L and Doggett, A 1994. *The Chilterns* (2nd edn). Chichester: Phillimore

Hepple, L and Doggett, A 2000. 'Stonor: a Chilterns landscape' *in* Thirsk, J (ed) *Rural England: An Illustrated History of the Landscape*. Oxford: Oxford University Press, 265–76

Hill, D 1988. 'Towns as structures and functioning communities through time: the development of central places from 600 to 1066' *in* Hooke, D (ed.) *Anglo-Saxon Settlements*. Oxford: Blackwell, 197–212

Hill-Miller, K C 2001. *From the Lighthouse to Monk's House: A Guide to Virginia Woolf's Literary Landscapes*. London: Duckworth

Hingley, R 1989. *Rural Settlement in Roman Britain*. London: Seaby

Hooke, D 1989. 'Early medieval estate and settlement patterns: the documentary evidence' *in* Aston, M, Austin, D and Dyer, C (eds) *The Rural Settlements of Medieval England*. Oxford: Blackwell

Hoskins, W 1955. *The Making of the English Landscape*. (revised edn 1988, ed. C Taylor). London: Hodder & Stoughton

Howkins, A 1986. 'The discovery of rural England' *in* Colls, R and Dodd, P (eds) *Englishness; Politics and Culture 1880–1920*. London: Routledge, 62–88

Hudson, W H 1910 (1979 edn). *A Shepherd's Life*. London: Futura

Hunt, E H and Pam, S J 1995. 'Essex agriculture in the "Golden Age", 1850–73'. *Agri Hist Rev* **43**, 160–77

Jameson, F 1991. *Postmodernism, or, the Cultural Logic of Late Capitalism*. London: Verso

Jarvis, M G, Allen, R H, Fordham, S J, Hazelden, J, Moffat, A J and Sturdy, R G 1984. *Soils and Their Use in South East England*. Harpenden: Soil Survey of England and Wales

Jefferies, R 1884 (1983 edn). *The Life of the Fields*. Oxford: Oxford Paperbacks

Jenkins, S 2003. 'Historic houses are the nation's greatest glory'. *The Times*, 31 October, 30

Johnson, E D H 1973. 'Victorian artists and the urban milieu' *in* Dyos, H J and Wolff, M (eds) *The Victorian City: Images and Realities*. London: Routledge & Kegan Paul, 449–74

Jones, B and Mattingly, D 1990. *An Atlas of Roman Britain*. Oxford: Blackwell

Jones, David K C 1981. *The Geomorphology of the British Isles: Southeast and Southern England*. London: Methuen

Jones, E L and Falkus, M E 1990. 'Urban improvement and the English economy in the seventeenth and eighteenth centuries' *in* Borsay, P (ed.) *The Eighteenth Century Town: A Reader in English Urban History 1688–1820*. London: Longman, 116–58

Jones, M 2005. *Set for a King: 200 Years of Gardening at the Royal Pavilion*. Brighton: The Royal Pavilion, Museums and Libraries

Kaye-Smith, S 1916. *Sussex Gorse*. London: Nisbet

Keith, W J 1975. *The Rural Tradition: William Cobbett, Gilbert White, and Other Non-fiction Prose Writers of the English Countryside*. Hassocks: Harvester Press

Knoepflmacher, U C 1977. 'Mutations of the Wordsworthian child of nature' *in* Knoepflmacher, U C and Tennyson, G B (eds) *Nature and the Victorian Imagination*. Berkeley: University of California Press 391–425

Levine, G 1977. 'High and low: Ruskin and the novelists' *in* Knoepflmacher, U C and Tennyson, G B (eds) *Nature and the Victorian Imagination*. Berkeley: University of California Press, 137–52

Linehan, D 2003. 'A new England: landscape, exhibition and remaking industrial space in the 1930s' *in* Gilbert, D, Matless, D and Short, B (eds) *Geographies of British Modernity: Space and Society in the Twentieth Century*. Oxford: Blackwell, 132–50

Lowenthal, D 1994. 'European and English landscapes as national symbols' *in* Hooson, D (ed.) *Geography and National Identity*. Oxford: Blackwell, 15–38

Lower, M A 1870. *A Compendious History of Sussex*. Lewes: Geo P Bacon

Mais, S P B 1938. 'The plain man looks at England' *in* Williams-Ellis, C (ed.) *Britain and the Beast*. London: Readers Union, 212–24

Malone, C 1989. *Avebury*. London: Batsford & English Heritage

Manley, J 2002. *AD 43: The Roman Invasion of Britain*. Stroud: Tempus

Marshall, H 1938. 'The Rake's Progress' *in* Williams-Ellis, C (ed.) *Britain and the Beast*. London: Readers Union, 164–75

Martin, D 2003. 'Winchelsea: a royal new town' *in* Rudling, D (ed.) *The Archaeology of Sussex to AD 2000*. Kings Lynn: Heritage Marketing and Publications, 179–90

McKellar, E 1999. *The Birth of Modern London*. Manchester: Manchester University Press

McNeillie, A 1986. 'Literary geography' *in* McNeillie, A (ed.) *The Essays of Virginia Woolf*, Vol. I. London: Hogarth Press

McOmish, D, Field, D and Brown, G 2002. *The Field Archaeology of the Salisbury Plain Training Area*. London: English Heritage

Miller, M L 1995. 'J M W Turner's *Ploughing up Turnips near Slough*: the cultivation of rural dissent'. *Art Bull* **77**, 573–83

Millett, M 1990. *The Romanization of Britain*. Cambridge: Cambridge University Press

Milne, G 2002. 'London's medieval waterfront'. *Brit Archaeol* **68**

Mitchell, B R and Deane, P 1962. *Abstract of British Historical Statistics*. Cambridge: Cambridge University Press

Mitchell, W J T 2002. *Landscape and Power* (2nd edn). Chicago: University of Chicago Press

Naipaul, V S 1987. *The Enigma of Arrival*. London: Viking

Nairn, I 1955. 'Outrage'. *Architect Rev* **117**, 363–460

Naylor, S and Ryan, J 2003. 'Mosques, temples and gurdwaras: new sites of religion in twentieth-century Britain' *in* Gilbert, D, Matless, D and Short, B (eds) *Geographies of British Modernity: Space and Society in the Twentieth Century*. Oxford: Blackwell, 168–83

Needham, S P *et al.* 2000. *The Passage of the Thames: Holocene Environment and Settlement at Runnymede*. Runnymede Bridge Research Excavations, Vol. 1. London: British Museum

Oliver, S 2002. '*Chains on the River': The Thames Embankments and the Construction of Nature*. Hist Geog Res Ser **37**. Historical Geography Research Group

Olsen, D J 1976. *The Growth of Victorian London*. London: Batsford

Oswald, A, Dyer, C and Barber, M 2001. *The Creation of Monuments: Neolithic Causewayed Enclosures in the British Isles*. London: English Heritage

Overton, M 1996. *Agricultural Revolution in England*. Cambridge: Cambridge University Press

Parker Pearson, M and Ramilisoniona 1998. 'Stonehenge for the ancestors: the stones pass on the message'. *Antiquity* **72**, 308–26

Payne, C 1993. *Toil and Plenty: Images of the Agricultural Landscape in England, 1780–1890*. New Haven: Yale University Press

Petty, W 1662 (1963 edn). 'A treatise on taxes and contributions' *in* Hull, C H (ed.) *The Economic Writings of Sir William Petty*. New York: Augustus M Kelly

Pitts, M and Roberts, M B 1998. *Fairweather Eden: Life in Britain Half a Million Years Ago as Revealed by the Excavations at Boxgrove*. London: Century

Port, M H 1995. *Imperial London: Civil Government Building in London 1850–1915*. New Haven: Yale University Press

Porter, S 1990. 'The Great Fire of Gravesend, 1727'. *Southern Hist* **12**, 19–33

Preston, C, Telfer, M, Arnold, H, Carey, P, Cooper, J, Dines, T, Hill, M, Pearman, D, Roy, D and Smart, S 2002. *The Changing Flora of the UK*. London: Defra

Priestley, J B 1934 (1968 edn). *English Journey*. London: Heinemann

Prince, H 1964. 'North-west London 1814–1863' *in* Coppock, J T and Prince, H (eds) *Greater London*. London: Faber & Faber, 80–141

Quiney, A 2003. *Town houses of medieval Britain*. New Haven and London: Yale University Press

Rackham, O 1976. *Trees and Woodland in the British Landscape*. London: Dent

Rackham, O 1986. *The History of the Countryside*. London: Dent

Rasmussen, S E 1982 (rev. edn). *London: The Unique City*. Cambridge (Mass): MIT Press

Rippon, S 2000. 'Landscapes in transition: the later roman and early medieval periods' *in* Hooke, D (ed.) *Landscape: The Richest Historical Record*. Amesbury: Society for Landscape Studies, suppl ser 1, 47–61

Roberts, B and Wrathmell, S 2000. *An Atlas of Rural Settlement in England*. London: English Heritage

Roberts, B and Wrathmell, S 2002. *Region and Place: A Study of English Rural Settlement*. London: English Heritage

Roberts, M and Parfitt, S 1999. *A Middle Pleistocene Hominid Site at Eartham Quarry, Boxgrove, West Sussex*. English Heritage Archaeol Rep **17**. London: English Heritage

Robinson, D and Williams, R 1983. 'The soils and vegetation history of Sussex' *in* Geography Editorial Committee (ed.) *Sussex: Environment, Landscape and Society*. Gloucester: Alan Sutton, 109–26

Robinson, D and Williams, R 1984. *Classic Landforms of the Weald*. Sheffield: Geographical Association

Roden, D 1969. 'Enclosure in the Chiltern Hills' *Geografiska Annaler* **52B**, 115–26

Rogers, Revd W 1856. 'A London parish' *in* Dickens, C (ed.) *Household Words* XIII, 275–6

Rosen, A 1981. 'Winchester in transition, 1580–1700' *in* Clark, P (ed.) *Country Towns in Pre-industrial England*. Leicester: Leicester University Press, 144–95

Rutherford, J 2003. *A Prince's Passion: The Life of the Royal Pavilion*. Brighton: The Royal Pavilion, Museums and Libraries

Sale, R 1986. *Closer to Home: Writers and Places in England, 1780–1830*. Cambridge (Mass): Harvard University Press

Schofield, J 1999. 'Landscapes of the Middle Ages: towns 1050–1500' *in* Hunter, J and Ralston, I (eds) *The Archaeology of Britain*. London: Routledge, 210–27

Schumpeter, J A 1942 (1976 edn). *Capitalism, Socialism and Democracy*. London: George Allen & Unwin

Scott, B 2004. 'Kentish evidence of the Palaeolithic and Mesolithic periods' *in* Lawson, T and Killingray, D (eds) *An Historical Atlas of Kent*. Chichester: Phillimore

Sharp, T 1932. *Town and Countryside*. Oxford: Oxford University Press

Sheail, J 1981. *Rural Conservation in Inter-war Britain*. Oxford: Clarendon Press

Shepherd, J, Westaway, J and Lee, T 1974. *A Social Atlas of London*. Oxford: Clarendon Press

Short, B 1984. 'The South-East: Kent, Surrey and Sussex' *in* Thirsk, J (ed.) *The Agrarian History of England and Wales*, Vol. V: *1640-1750*. Cambridge: Cambridge University Press, 270–313

Short, B 1989. 'The de-industrialisation process: the Weald 1600–1850' *in* Hudson, P (ed.) *Regions and Industries: A Perspective on the Industrial Revolution in Britain*. Cambridge: Cambridge University Press, 156–74

Short, B 2000. 'Forests and wood-pasture in Lowland England' *in* Thirsk, J (ed.) *Rural England: An Illustrated History of the Landscape*. Oxford: Oxford University Press, 122–49

Sidell, J, Cotton, J, Rayner, L and Wheeler, L 2002. *The Prehistory and Topography of Southwark and Lambeth*. MoLAS Monograph 14. London: Museum of London Archaeology Service

Sidell, J, Wilkinson, K, Scaife, R and Cameron, N 2000. *The Holocene Evolution of the London Thames*. MoLAS Monograph 5. London: Museum of London Archaeology Service

Simmons, I 2001. *An Environmental History of Great Britain*. Edinburgh: Edinburgh University Press

Sims, G 1889. *How the Poor Live*. London: Chatto and Windus

Slade, C F 1969. 'Reading' *in* Lobel, M D (ed.) *Historic Towns*, Vol. I. London: Lovell Johns

Smith, V 1979. *Sussex Churches. The Sharpe Collection of Watercolours and Drawings 1797–1809 mainly by Henry Petrie FSA*. Lewes: Sussex Record Society

Snell, K D M 1998. *The Regional Novel in Britain and Ireland, 1800–1990*. Cambridge: Cambridge University Press

Squires, M 1974. *The Pastoral Novel: Studies in George Eliot, Thomas Hardy and D H Lawrence*. Charlottesville: University Press of Virginia

Stamp, G and Goulancourt, A 1986. *The English House, 1860–1914: The Flowering of English Domestic Architecture*. London: Faber & Faber

Steane, J 2001. *The Archaeology of Power: England and Northern Europe AD 800–1600*. Stroud: Tempus

Steer, F W 1962. *The Memoirs of James Spershott* (Chichester Papers 30) Chichester: Chichester City Council

Strong, R 1998. *The Renaissance Garden in England* (reprint of 1979 edn). London: Thames & Hudson

Summerson, J 1988 edn. *Georgian London*. London: Barrie & Jenkins

Sweet, R 2004. *Antiquaries: The Discovery of the Past in Eighteenth-Century Britain*. London: Hambledon

Taylor, C 1983. *Village and Farmstead: A History of Rural Settlement in England*. London: George Philip

Thirsk, J (ed.) 1967. *The Agrarian History of England and Wales*, Vol. IV: *1500–1640*. Cambridge: Cambridge University Press

Thirsk, J (ed.) 1984. *The Agrarian History of England and Wales* Vol. V: *1640–1750*. Cambridge: Cambridge University Press

Tilley, C 1994. *A Phenomenology of Landscape: Places, Paths and Monuments*. Oxford: Berg

Tindall, G 1977. *The Fields Beneath: The History of One London Village*. London: Temple Smith

Tindall, G 1991. *Countries of the Mind: The Meaning of Place to Writers*. London: Hogarth Press

Turner, M 1980. *English Parliamentary Enclosure*. Folkestone: Dawson

UK Biodiversity Steering Group 1995. *Biodiversity: The UK Steering Group Report Meeting the Rio Challenge* (Vol. I). London: HMSO

VCH Middlesex III 1962. *The Victoria History of the County of Middlesex*, Vol. I. Oxford: Oxford University Press for Institute of Historical Research

VCH Wiltshire IV 1959. *The History of Wiltshire*, Vol. IV. Oxford: Oxford University Press for Institute of Historical Research

Vera, F W M 2000. *Grazing, Ecology and Forest History*. Wallingford: CABI Publishing

Wall, C 1998. *The Literary and Cultural Spaces of Restoration London*. Cambridge: Cambridge University Press

Waller, M 1998. 'Wealden vegetational history: the Brede and Pannell valleys' *in* Murton, J, Whiteman, C, Bates, M, Bridgland, D, Long, A, Roberts, M and Waller, M (eds) *The Quaternary of Kent and Sussex: Field Guide*. London: Quaternary Research Association

Walpole, H 1906 edn. *The Letters of Horace Walpole, Fourth Earl of Orford*, Vol. II (ed. P Cunningham). Edinburgh: John Grant

Wenban-Smith, F F and Hosfield, R T (eds) 2001. *Palaeolithic Archaeology of the Solent River*. London: Lithic Studies Society

Whistler, J M 1890. *The Gentle Art of making Enemies*. London: Heinemann

White, G 1789 (1949 edn). *The Natural History and Antiquities of Selborne, in the County of Southampton*. London: Everyman

Whyman, J 1973. 'A Hanoverian watering place: Margate before the railway' *in* Everitt, A (ed.) *Perspectives on English Urban History*. London: Macmillan, 138–60

Wiener, M 1981. *English Culture and the Decline of the Industrial Spirit, 1850–1980*. Cambridge: Cambridge University Press

Williams, R 1973. *The Country and the City*. London: Chatto & Windus

Williamson, T 2002. *The Transformation of Rural England: Farming and the Landscape 1700–1870*. Exeter: University of Exeter Press

Williamson, T and Bellamy, E 1987. *Property and Landscape: A Social History of Land Ownership and the English Countryside*. London: George Philip

Wolfreys, J 1998. *Writing London: The Trace of the Urban Text from Blake to Dickens*. Basingstoke: Macmillan

Woodcock, A 1999. 'Earliest inhabitants' *in* Leslie, K and Short, B (eds) *An Historical Atlas of Sussex*. Chichester: Phillimore, 10–11

Wordie, J R 1984. 'The South: Oxfordshire, Buckinghamshire, Berkshire, Wiltshire and Hampshire' *in* Thirsk, J (ed.) *The Agrarian History of England and Wales*, Vol. V: *1640–1750*. Cambridge: Cambridge University Press, 317–57

Young, A 1788. 'A fortnight's tour in Kent and Essex'. *Annals of Agriculture* **10**, 33–104

Young, M and Willmott, P 1957 (1986 edn). *Family and Kinship in East London*. London: Routledge & Kegan Paul

Zell, M 1994. *Industry in the Countryside: Wealden Society in the Sixteenth Century*. Cambridge: Cambridge University Press

Index

Picture Credits

Aerial survey acknowledgements
New English Heritage aerial photographs were taken by Damian Grady. The Aerial Reconnaissance team would like to thank the following people for their help: a special note of thanks must go to the skills and patience of the pilots Mick Webb and Marten White; the aircraft owner David Sanders; the NMR cataloguing team Rose Ogle, Katy Groves, Catherine Runciman, Cinzia Bacilieri, Philip Daniels, Geoff Hall; Jon Proudman for all the publication scanning; and Sarah Prince for laser copying thousands of aerial photographs to send to the authors.